GLEANINGS FROM THE SCRIPTURES

GLEANINGS FROM THE SCRIPTURES

MAN'S TOTAL DEPRAVITY

By A. W. Pink

❧ ❧ ❧
❧ ❧ ❧

MOODY PRESS

CHICAGO

Copyright © 1969 by
THE MOODY BIBLE INSTITUTE
OF CHICAGO

Library of Congress Catalog Card Number: 73-80942

Moody Paperback Edition, 1981

ISBN 0-8024-3006-6

16 17 18 19 20 Printing/VP/Year 92 91 90 89

Printed in the United States of America

CONTENTS

Part I   THE DOCTRINE OF HUMAN DEPRAVITY

Part II   THE DOCTRINE OF MAN'S IMPOTENCE

Part I

THE DOCTRINE OF HUMAN DEPRAVITY

Chapter 1

INTRODUCTION

THE SUBJECT which this chapter is designed to introduce is likely to meet with a decidedly mixed reception. Some readers will probably be very disappointed when they see the title of this book, considering the subject quite unattractive and unedifying. If so, they are to be pitied; we hope that God will bless the contents to them. Medicine is proverbially unpleasant, but there are times when all of us find it necessary and beneficial. Others will be thankful that, by divine grace, we seek to glorify God rather than please the flesh. And surely that which most glorifies God is to declare *"all* his counsel," to insist on that which puts man in his proper place before Him, and to emphasize those portions and aspects of the truth which our generation is most in need of. As we shall endeavor to show, our theme is one of immense doctrinal importance and of great practical value. Since it is a subject which occupies so prominent a place in God's Word, no apology is needed for our engaging in such a task.

A Vital Contemporary Question

It is our deep conviction that the vital question most requiring to be raised today is this: Is man a totally and thoroughly depraved creature by nature? Does he enter the world completely ruined and helpless, spiritually blind and dead in trespasses and sins? According as is our answer to *that* question, so will be our views on many others. It is on the basis of this dark background that the whole Bible proceeds. Any attempt to modify or abate, repudiate or tone down the teaching of Scripture on the matter is fatal. Put the question in another form: Is man now in such a condition that he cannot be saved without the special and direct intervention of the triune God on his behalf? In other words, is there any hope for him apart from his personal election by the Father, his particular redemption by the Son, and the supernatural operations of the Spirit within him? Or, putting it in still another way: If man is a totally depraved being, can he possibly take the first step in the matter of his return to God?

The Scriptural Answer

The scriptural answer to that question makes evident the utter futility of the schemes of social reformers for "the moral elevation of the masses," the plans of politicians for the peace of the nations, and the ideologies of dreamers to usher in a golden age for this world. It is both pathetic and tragic to see many of our greatest men putting their faith in such chimeras. Divisions and discords, hatred and bloodshed, cannot be banished while human nature is what it is. But during the past century the steady trend of a deteriorating Christendom has been to underrate the evil of sin and overrate the moral capabilities of men. Instead of proclaiming the heinousness of sin, there has been a dwelling more upon its inconveniences, and the abasing portrayal of the lost condition of man as set forth in Holy Writ has been obscured if not obliterated by flattering disquisitions on human advancement. If the popular religion of the churches—including nine-tenths of what is termed "evangelical Christianity"—be tested at this point, it will be found that it clashes directly with man's fallen, ruined and spiritually dead condition.

There is therefore a crying need today for sin to be viewed in the light of God's law and gospel, so that its exceeding sinfulness may be demonstrated, and the dark depths of human depravity exposed by the teaching of Holy Writ, that we may learn what is connoted by those fearful words "dead in trespasses and sins." The grand object of the Bible is to make God known to us, to portray man as he appears in the eyes of his Maker, and to show the relation of one to the other. It is therefore the business of His servants not only to declare the divine character and perfections, but also to delineate the original condition and apostasy of man, as well as the divine remedy for his ruin. Until we really behold the horror of the pit in which by nature we lie, we can never properly appreciate Christ's so-great salvation. In man's fallen condition we have the awful disease for which divine redemption is the only cure, and our estimation and valuation of the provisions of divine grace will necessarily be modified in proportion as we modify the need it was meant to meet.

David Clarkson, one of the Puritans, pointed out this fact in his sermon on Psalm 51:5:

> The end of the ministry of the Gospel is to bring sinners unto Christ. Their way to this end lies through the sense of their misery without Christ. The ingredients of this misery are our sinfulness, original and actual; the wrath of God, whereto sin has exposed us; and our impotency to free ourselves either from sin or wrath. That we may therefore promote this great end, we shall endeavour, as the Lord will assist, to lead you in this way, by the sense of misery, to Him who alone can deliver from it. Now the original of our misery being the corruption of our nature, or original sin, we thought fit to begin here, and therefore have pitched upon these words as very proper for our purpose: "Behold, I was shapen in iniquity; and in sin did my mother conceive me."

Characteristics of the Doctrine

This subject is indeed a most *solemn* one, and none can fitly write or preach on it unless his own heart is deeply awed by it. It is not something from which any man can detach himself and expatiate on it as though he were not directly involved in it; still less as from a higher level looking down on those whom he denounces. Nothing is more incongruous and unbecoming than for a young preacher glibly to rattle off passages of Scripture which portray his own vileness by nature. Rather should they be read or quoted with the utmost gravity. J. C. Philpot stated:

> As no heart can sufficiently conceive, so no tongue can adequately express, the state of wretchedness and ruin into which sin has cast guilty, miserable man. In separating him from God, it severed him from the only source of all happiness and holiness. It has ruined him body and soul: the one it has filled with sickness and disease; in the other it has defaced and destroyed the image of God in which it was created. It has made him love sin and hate God.

The doctrine of total depravity is a very *humbling* one. It is not that man leans to one side and needs propping up, nor that he is merely ignorant and requires instructing, nor that he is run down and calls for a tonic; but rather that he is undone, lost, spiritually dead. Consequently, he is "without strength," thoroughly incapable of bettering himself; he is exposed to the wrath of God, and unable to perform a single work which can find acceptance with Him. Almost every page of the Bible bears witness to this truth. The whole scheme of redemption takes it for granted. The plan of salvation taught in the Scriptures could have no place on any other supposition. The impossibility of any man's gaining the approbation of God by works of his own appears plainly in the case of the rich young ruler who came to Christ. Judged by human standards, he was a model of virtue and religious attainments. Yet, like all others who trust in self-efforts, he was ignorant of the spirituality and strictness of God's law; when Christ put him to the test his fair expectations were blown to the winds and "he went away sorrowful" (Matt. 19:22).

It is therefore a most *unpalatable* doctrine. It cannot be otherwise, for the unregenerate love to hear of the greatness, the dignity, the nobility of man. The natural man thinks highly of himself and appreciates only that which is flattering. Nothing pleases him more than to listen to that which extols human nature and lauds the state of mankind, even though it be in terms which not only repudiate the teaching of God's Word but are flatly contradicted by common observation and universal experience. And there are many who pander to him by their lavish praises of the excellency of civilization and the steady progress of the race. Hence, to have the lie given to the popular theory of evolution is highly displeasing to its deluded votaries. Nevertheless, the duty of God's servants is to stain the pride of all that man glories in, to strip him of his stolen plumes, to lay him low in the dust before God. However repugnant such teaching is, God's emissary must faithfully discharge his duty "whether they will hear, or whether they will forbear" (Ezek. 3:11).

This is no dismal dogma invented by the church in "the dark ages," but a truth of Holy Writ. George Whitefield said, "I look upon it not merely as a doctrine of Scripture—the great Fountain of truth—but a very fundamental one, from which I hope God will suffer none of you to be enticed." It is a subject to which great prominence is given in the Bible. Every part of the Scriptures has much to say on the awful state of degradation and slavery into which the fall has brought man. The corruption, the blindness, the hostility of all Adam's descendants to everything of a spiritual nature are constantly insisted upon. Not only is man's utter ruin fully described, but also his powerlessness to save himself from the same. In the declarations and denunciations of the prophets, of Christ and His apostles, the bondage of all men to Satan and their complete impotence to turn to God for deliverance are repeatedly set forth—not indirectly and vaguely, but emphatically and in great detail. This is one of a hundred proofs that the Bible is not a human invention but a communication from the thrice holy One.

It is a *sadly neglected* subject. Notwithstanding the clear and uniform teaching of Scripture, man's ruined condition and alienation from God are but feebly apprehended and seldom heard in the modern pulpit, and are given little place even in what are regarded as the centers of orthodoxy. Rather the whole trend of present-day thought and teaching is in the opposite direction, and even where the Darwinian hypothesis has not been accepted, its pernicious influences are often seen. In consequence of the guilty silence of the modern pulpit, a generation of churchgoers has arisen which is deplorably ignorant of the basic truths of the Bible, so that perhaps not more than one in a thousand has even a mental knowledge of the chains of hardness and unbelief which bind the natural heart, or of the dungeon of darkness in which they lie. Thousands of preachers, instead of faithfully telling their hearers of their woeful state by nature, are wasting their time by relating the latest news of the Kremlin or of the development of nuclear weapons.

It is therefore a *testing* doctrine, especially of the preacher's soundness in the faith. A man's orthodoxy on this subject determines his viewpoint of many other doctrines of great importance. If his belief here is a scriptural one, then he will clearly perceive how impossible it is for men to improve themselves—that Christ is their only hope. He will know that unless the sinner is born again there can be no entrance for him into the kingdom of God. Nor will he entertain the idea of the fallen creature's free will to attain goodness. He will be preserved from many errors. Andrew Fuller stated, "I never knew a person verge toward the Arminian, the Arian, the Socinian, the Antinomian schemes, without first entertaining diminutive notions of human depravity or blameworthiness." Said the well-equipped theological instructor, J. M. Stifler, "It cannot be said too often that a false theology finds its source in inadequate views of depravity."

It is a doctrine of great *practical* value as well as spiritual importance. The foundation of all true piety lies in a correct view of ourselves and our vileness, and a scriptural belief in God and His grace. There can be no genuine self-abhorrence or repentance, no real appreciation of the saving mercy of God, no faith in Christ, without it. There is nothing like a knowledge of this doctrine so well calculated to undeceive vain man and convict him of the worthlessness and rottenness of his own righteousness. Yet the preacher who is aware of the plague of his own heart knows full well that *he* cannot present this truth in such a way as to make his hearers actually realize and feel the same, to help them stop being in love with themselves and to cause them to forever renounce all hope in themselves. Therefore, instead of relying upon his faithfulness in presenting the truth, he will be cast upon God to apply it graciously in power to those who hear him and bless his feeble efforts.

It is an exceedingly *illuminating* doctrine. It may be a melancholy and humiliating one, nevertheless it throws a flood of light upon mysteries which are otherwise insoluble. It supplies the key to the course of human history, and shows why so much of it has been written in blood and tears. It supplies an explanation of many problems which sorely perplex and puzzle the thoughtful. It reveals why the child is prone to evil and has to be taught and disciplined to anything that is good. It explains why every improvement in man's environment, every attempt to educate him, all the efforts of social reformers, are unavailing to effect any radical betterment in his nature and character. It accounts for the horrible treatment which Christ met with when He worked so graciously in this world, and why He is still despised and rejected by men. It enables the Christian himself to better understand the painful conflict which is ever at work within him, and which causes him so often to cry, "Oh, wretched man that I am!"

It is therefore a most *necessary* doctrine, for the vast majority of our fellowmen are ignorant of it. God's servants are sometimes thought to speak too strongly and dolefully of the dreadful state of man through his apostasy from God. The fact is that it is impossible to exaggerate in human language the darkness and pollution of man's heart or to describe the misery and utter helplessness of a condition such as the Word of truth describes in these solemn passages: "But if our gospel be hid, it is hid to them that are lost: in whom the god of this world hath blinded the minds of them which believe not, lest the light of the glorious gospel of Christ, who is the image of God, should shine unto them" (II Cor. 4:3-4). "Therefore they could not believe, because . . . he hath [judicially] blinded their eyes, and hardened their heart; that they should not see with their eyes, nor understand with their heart, and be converted, and I should heal them" (John 12:39-40). This is yet more evident when we contrast the state of soul of those in whom a miracle of grace is wrought (see Luke 1:78-79).

It is a *salutary* doctrine—one which God often uses to bring men to their senses. While we imagine that our wills have power to do what is pleasing to God, we never abandon dependence on self. Not that a mere intellectual knowledge of man's fall and ruin is sufficient to deliver from pride. Only the Spirit's powerful operations can effect that. Yet He is pleased to use the faithful preaching of the Word to that end. Nothing but a real sense of our lost condition lays us in the dust before God.

Chapter 2

ORIGIN

THAT SOMETHING is radically wrong with the world of mankind requires no labored argument to demonstrate. That such has been the case in all generations is plain from the annals of history. This is only another way of saying that something is radically wrong with man himself, for the world is but the aggregate of all the individual members of our race. Since the whole of anything cannot be superior to the parts comprising it, it necessarily follows that the course of the world will be determined by the characters of those who comprise it. But when we come to inquire exactly *what* is wrong with man, and *how* he came to be in such a condition, unless we turn to God's inspired Word no convincing answers are forthcoming. Apart from that divine revelation no sure and satisfactory reply can be made to such questions as these: What is the source of the unmistakable imperfections of human nature? What will furnish an adequate explanation of all the evils which infest man's present state? Why is it that none is able to keep God's law perfectly or do anything which is acceptable to Him while in a state of nature?

Universal Malady

To ascertain how sin, which involves all men, came into the world is a matter of no little importance. To discover why it is that all men universally and continually are unrighteous and ailing creatures supplies the key to many a problem. Look at human nature as it now is: depraved, wretched, subject to death. Ask philosophy to account for this, and it cannot do so. None can deny the fact that men are what they ought not to be, but *how* they became so human wisdom is unable to tell us. To attribute our troubles to heredity and environment is an evasion, for it leaves unanswered the question How did it come about that our original ancestors and environment were such as to produce what now exists? Look not only at our prisons, hospitals and cemeteries, but also at the antipathy between the righteous and the wicked, between those who fear God and those who do not fear Him. The antagonism between Cain and Abel, Ishmael and Isaac, Esau and Jacob, is repeatedly duplicated in every age and area; but the Bible alone traces that antagonism to its fountainhead.

Judicious ancients recognized and bemoaned the universal tendency of men to be lawbreakers, but were entirely unaware of its real source. They were agreed that the practice of virtue was the chief thing necessary for the promotion of man's good, but they had to lament an irregular bent in the wills and a corruption in the affections of their disciples, which rendered their precepts of little use, and they were completely at a loss to assign any reason why men, who have the noblest faculties of any beings on earth, should yet generally pursue their destruction with as much eagerness as the beasts avoid it. Plato, in the second book of his *Republic,* complained that men by their natures are evil and cannot be brought to good. Tully acknowledged that "man is brought forth into the world, in body and soul, exposed to all miseries and prone to evil, in whom that Divine spark of goodness, and wisdom, and morality, is opposed and extinguished." They realized that all men were poisoned, but *how* the poison came to be in the human constitution they did not know. Some ascribed it to fate; others to the hostile influences of the planets; still others to an evil angel which attends each man.

Most certainly we cannot attribute man's natural inordinance and defectiveness to his Creator. To do so would be the rankest blasphemy, as well as giving the lie to His Word, which declares, "God hath made man upright" (Eccles. 7:29). Even on a much lower ground, such a conclusion is self-evidently false. It is impossible that darkness should issue from the Father of light, or that sin should come from the ineffably holy One. It is infinitely better to confess our ignorance than to be guilty of grossest impiety—to say nothing of manifest absurdity—by placing the onus on God. But there is no excuse for anyone to be ignorant on the matter. The Holy Scriptures supply a definite solution to this mystery, and show that the entire blame for his present wretchedness lies at man's own door. And therefore to say that man is a sinful creature, or even to allow that he is totally depraved, is to acknowledge only half of the truth, and the least humbling half at that. Man is a *fallen* creature. He has departed from his original state and primitive purity. Man, far from having ascended from something inferior to an ape, has descended from the elevated and honorable position in which God first placed him; and it is all-important to contend for this, since it alone satisfactorily explains *why* man is now depraved.

Universal Defection

Man is not now as God made him. He has lost the crown and glory of his creation, and has plunged himself into an awful gulf of sin and misery. By his own perversity he has wrecked himself and placed a consequence of woe on his posterity. He is a ruined creature as the result of his apostasy from God. This requires that we consider, first, man in his original state, that we may perceive his folly in so lightly valuing it and that we may form a better conception of the vastness and vileness of his downward plunge, for that can only be gauged as we learn what he fell *from* as well as *into.* By his wicked defection man brought himself into a state as black and doleful as his original one was glorious and blessed. Second, we need to consider most attentively what it has pleased the Holy Spirit to record about the fall itself, pondering each detail described in Genesis 3, and the amplifications of them supplied by the later scriptures, looking to God to grant us graciously an understanding of the same. Third, we shall be in a better position to view the fearful consequences of the fall and perceive how the punishment was made to fit the crime.

Original Man, God's Masterpiece

Instead of surveying the varied opinions and conflicting conjectures of our fallible and fallen fellow creatures concerning the original condition and estate of our first parents, we shall confine ourselves entirely to the divinely inspired Scriptures, which are the only unerring rule of faith. From them, and them alone, can we ascertain what man was when he first came from the hands of his Creator. First, God's Word makes known His intention to bring man into existence: "And God said, Let us make man in our image, after our likeness" (Gen. 1:26). There are two things exceedingly noteworthy in that brief statement, namely, the repeated use of the pronoun in the plural number, and the fact that its language suggests the idea of a conference between the divine Persons at this point of the "six days' " work. We say "at this point," for there is nothing resembling it in the record of what occurred during the previous days. Thus, the divine conference here conveys the impression that the most important stage of creation had now been reached, that man was to be the masterpiece of the divine workmanship, the crowning glory of the mundane sphere—which is clearly borne out in his being made in the divine image.

It is the usage of the plural number in Genesis 1:26 which in our judgment intimates the first signification of the term "image." God is a trinity in unity, and so also is the man He made, consisting, in his entirety, of "spirit and soul and body" (I Thess. 5:23). While in some passages "spirit" and "soul" are used as synonyms, in Hebrews 4:12 they are distinguished. The fact that the plural pronoun occurs three times in the brief declaration of the Deity in Genesis 1:26 supplies confirmation that the one made in Their likeness was also a threefold entity. Some scholars consider that there is an allusion to this feature of man's constitution in the apostle's averment "In him we live, and move, and have our being" (Acts 17:28), pointing out that each of those three verbs has a philological significance: the first to our animal life; the second (from which is derived the Greek word used by ethical writers for the passions such as fear, love, hatred, and the like) not, as our English verb suggests, to man's bodily motions in space, but to his emotional nature—the soul; the third to that which constitutes our essential being (the "spirit")—the intelligence and will of man.

"So God created man in his own image, in the image of God created he him; male and female created he them" (Gen. 1:27). This announces the actual accomplishment of the divine purpose and counsel referred to in the preceding verse. The repetition of the statement with the change of the pronoun from plural to singular number, implies a second meaning for the term "image." Viewing it more generally, it tells of the excellence of man's original nature, though it must be explained consistently with the infinite distance that exists between God and the highest creature. Whatever this glory was which God placed on Adam, it does not infer that he shared the divine perfections. Nor is the nothingness of the best of finite beings any disparagement when compared with God; for whatever likeness there is to Him, either as created, regenerated or glorified, there is at the same time an infinite disproportion. Further, this excellence of man's original nature must be distinguished from that glory which is peculiar to Christ who, far from being said to be "made in the image of God," "is the image of the invisible God" (Col. 1:15), "the express image of his person" (Heb. 1:3). The oneness and equality between the Father and the Son in no way pertain to any likeness between God and the creature.

Examining the term more closely, "the image of God" in which man was made refers to his moral nature. Calvin defined it as being "spiritual," and stated that it "includes all the excellence in which the nature of man surpasses all the other species of animals" and "denotes the integrity Adam possessed." He stated further that it may be more clearly specified "in the restoration which we obtain through Christ." Without an exception, all the Puritans we have consulted say substantially the same thing, regarding this "image of God" as moral rectitude, a nature in perfect accord with the divine law. It could not be otherwise; for the holy One to make a creature after *His* likeness would be to endow him with holiness. The statement that the regenerate has been "renewed in knowledge after the image of him that created him" (Col. 3:10) clearly implies the same image in which man was originally made, and which sin has defaced. Not only did that image consist of knowledge (i.e., of God) but, as Ephesians 4:24 informs us, of "righteousness and true holiness" also. Thus man's original state was far more than one of innocence (sinlessness, harmlessness), which is mainly a negative thing.

That man was created in positive holiness is also taught in Ecclesiastes 7:29. "God hath made [not 'is now making'] man upright," not only without any improper bias but according to rule—straight with the law of God, conformed to His will. As Thomas Boston expressed it, "Original righteousness was con-created with him." The same Hebrew word occurs in "good and upright is the LORD" (Ps. 25:8). We have dwelt long on this point because not only do Romanists and Socinians deny that man was created a spiritual (not merely natural) and holy (not simply innocent) being, but some hyper-Calvinists—who prefer their own principles to the Word of God—do so too. One error inevitably leads to another. To insist that the unregenerate are under no obligation to perform spiritual acts obliges them to infer the same thing of Adam. To conclude that if Adam fell from a holy and spiritual condition, then we must abandon the doctrine of final perseverance is to leave out Christ and lose sight of the superiority of the covenant of grace over the original one of works.

"And the LORD God formed man of the dust of the ground, and breathed into his nostrils the breath of life; and man became a living soul" (Gen. 2:7). This supplies us with additional information on the making of Adam. First, the matter from which his body was formed, to demonstrate the wisdom and power of God in making out of such material so wonderful a thing as the human body, and to teach man his humble origin and dependence upon God. Second, the quickening principle bestowed on Adam, which was immediately from God, namely, an intelligent spirit, of which the fall did not deprive him (Eccles. 12:7). That "the breath of life" included reason, or the faculty of understanding, is clear from "the life was the light of men" (John 1:4). Third, the effect on Adam. His body was now animated and made capable of vital acts. Man's body out of the dust was the workmanship of God, but his soul was an immediate communication from "the Father of spirits" (Heb. 12:9), and thereby earth and heaven were united in him.

"And the LORD God said, It is not good that the man should be alone; I will make him an help meet for him. . . . And the LORD God caused a deep sleep to fall upon Adam, and he slept: and he took one of his ribs, and closed up the flesh thereof; and the rib, which the LORD God had taken from man, made he a woman, and brought her unto the man (Gen. 2:18-22). It seems that God chose this mode of making the woman, instead of forming her also out of the dust, to express the intimate union which was to take place between the sexes, to denote their mutual relation and dependence, and to show the superiority of man. Those two were so made that the whole human race, physically considered, were contained in them and to be produced from them, making them all literally "of one blood" (Acts 17:26).

Man's Endowments

"And God blessed them, and God said unto them, Be fruitful, and multiply, and replenish the earth, and subdue it: and have dominion over the fish of the sea, and over the fowl of the air, and over every living thing that moveth upon the earth" (Gen. 1:28). Those words intimate that there was yet another meaning to "the image of God," for the position of headship and authority which He conferred upon Adam showed the divine sovereignty. Psalm 8:5-6 tells us, "Thou hast made him a little lower than the angels, and hast crowned him with glory and honour. Thou madest him to have dominion over the works of thy hands; thou hast put all things under his feet." Adam was constituted God's viceroy on earth, the government of all inferior creatures being conferred upon him. That was further demonstrated when the Lord brought all before Adam for him to give names to them (Gen. 2:19-20), which not only evinced that he was a rational creature, endowed with the power of choice, but manifested his superiority over all mundane creatures, his proprietorship in them, and his liberty to use them for God's glory and his own good.

But more. God not only endowed Adam with righteousness and holiness, thereby fitting him to fulfill the end of his creation by glorifying the Author of his being. He also bestowed on him the gift of reason, which distinguished him from and elevated him above all the other inhabitants of the earth, conferring on him the charter of dominion over them. Further, He brought him into a pure and beautiful environment. "And the LORD God planted a garden eastward in Eden; and there he put the man whom he had formed. . . . And the LORD God took the man, and put him into the garden of Eden [which the Septuagint renders 'the paradise of joy'] to dress it and to keep it" (Gen. 2:8-15). Genesis 3:24 confirms the fact that the garden of Eden was distinct from the earth. The whole world was given Adam for a possession, but Eden was the special seat of his residence, a place of preeminent delight. It presented to his view the whole earth in miniature, so that without traveling long distances he might behold the lovely landscape which it afforded. It epitomized all the beauties of nature, and was as it were a conservatory of its fairest vegetation and a storehouse of its choicest fruits.

That the garden of Eden was a place of surpassing beauty, excelling all other parts of the earth for fertility, is evident from other scriptures. Ezekiel, when prophesying in a day of wretchedness and barrenness the bountiful spiritual blessings which would attend the gospel era, used this figurative but graphic language: "This land that was desolate is become like the garden of Eden" (36:35). Still plainer was the promise of Isaiah 51:3: "For the LORD shall comfort Zion: he will comfort all her waste places; and he will make her wilderness like Eden, and her desert like the garden of the LORD; joy and gladness shall be found therein, thanksgiving, and the voice of melody." It is clear that nothing was wanting in Eden, in its pristine glory, to give the completest happiness to man. That it was a place of perfect bliss is further evident from the fact that heaven itself, the habitation of the blessed, is called "paradise" in Luke 23:43; II Corinthians 12:4; Revelation 2:7. Some see in that threefold allusion (there are no others) a pledge for the complete satisfaction of the glorified man's spirit, soul and body.

Several things are imported and implied in the statement that the Lord God put the man into the garden of Eden "to dress it and to keep it." First, and most obvious, God takes no pleasure in idleness, but in active industry. That such an appointment was for Adam's good cannot be doubted. Regular employment preserves us from those temptations which so often attend indolence. Second, secular employment is by no means inconsistent with perfect holiness, or with a person's enjoying intimate communion with God and the blessings resulting from it. Of course Adam's work would be performed without any of the fatigue and disappointment which accompany ours today. The holy angels are not inert, but "ministering spirits" (Heb. 1:14). Of the divine Persons Themselves our Lord declared, "My Father worketh hitherto, and I work" (John 5:17). Thus this employment assigned Adam was also a part of his conformity to God. Third, it implied the duty of keeping his own heart—the garden of his soul—with all diligence (Prov. 4:23), tending its faculties and graces so that he might always be in a condition to pray, "Let my beloved come into his garden, and eat his pleasant fruits" (Song of Sol. 4:16).

Further, in the words "dress it" (Hebrew "serve," "till it") we are taught that God's gracious gifts are to be highly treasured and carefully cultivated by us. "Neglect not the gift that is in thee" (I Tim. 4:14). "Stir up the gift of God, which is in thee" (II Tim. 1:6). In the Genesis phrase "and to keep it" we believe there was a tacit warning given by God to Adam. Not only does the English term convey that thought, but the Hebrew word (*shamar*) here used requires it. Nineteen times it is rendered "preserve," twelve times "take heed," four times "watch," and once it is actually translated "beware." Thus the phrase signified a caution against danger, putting Adam on his guard, warning him to be on the lookout against the encroaching enemy. The Dutch Puritan, Herman Witsius, pointed out that the "keeping of paradise virtually engaged him of all things to be anxiously concerned not to do anything against God, lest as a bad gardener he should be thrust out of the garden, and in that discover a melancholy symbol of his own exclusion from heaven." Finally, since paradise is one of the names of heaven, we may conclude that the earthly one in which Adam was placed was a pledge of celestial blessedness. Had he survived his probation and preserved his integrity, he would have enjoyed "heaven" on earth.

In addition to the institution of marriage (Gen. 2:23-25; 1:28), God appointed the weekly Sabbath. "On the seventh day God ended his work which he had made; and he rested on the seventh day from all his work which he had made. And God blessed the seventh day, and sanctified it: because that in it he had rested from all His work which God created and made" (2:2-3). Should any raise the objection that the term "Sabbath" is not found in those verses, we would remind them that in Exodus 20:11 Jehovah Himself expressly terms that first "seventh day" of rest "the sabbath day." The word "blessed" signifies to declare blessedness; thus on the frontispiece of His Word, God would have every reader know that special divine blessing attends the observance of the Sabbath. The word "sanctified" means that it was a day set apart for sacred use. For Adam it would be a means for his more intimate communion with God, in which he would enjoy a recess from his secular employment and have opportunity of expressing his gratitude for all those blessings of which he was the partaker.

Fall of Man

Though Adam had been made in the image of God, taken into communion with Him, fitted to rejoice in all the manifestations of His wisdom and goodness which surrounded him in Eden, nevertheless he was capable of falling. Since it is a point which has sorely puzzled many of the Lord's people, we will endeavor to explain how it was possible for a holy person, devoid of any corruption, to sin. First, Adam's liability to falling lay in the fact that he was just a creature. As such he was entirely dependent on Him "which holdeth our soul in life" (Ps. 66:9). As our natural life continues only so long as God sustains it, so it was with Adam's spiritual life: he stood only so long as he was divinely upheld. Moreover, as a creature he was finite and therefore possessed no invincible power with which to repel opposition. Nor was he endowed with omniscience, which would have made him incapable of being deceived or mistaking an evil for an apparent good. Thus, though man's original condition was one of high moral excellence, with no evil tendency in any part of his nature, with nothing in him which in the least deviated from the moral law, yet, being only a creature, he was capable of falling.

Second, Adam's susceptibility to falling lay in his mutability. Changeableness is the very law or radical characteristic of the creature, to distinguish it from the Creator. God alone is without variableness or shadow of turning (James 1:17). Therefore He "cannot be tempted with evil" (James 1:13), that is, induced to sin. This statement clearly implies that the creature as such has a capacity to be so tempted—not only a depraved creature, but even an unfallen one. Immutability and impeccability (nonliability to sin) are qualities which essentially distinguish the Creator from the creature. The angels possess neither. Further, God alone acts from His own power, whereas the creature acts by a power given to him which is distinct from himself. Goodwin pointed this out: "God's own goodness and happiness is His ultimate end, therefore He can never act but holily, for He acts by Himself and for Himself, and so cannot fail in acting, but is holy in all His ways and works, and cannot be otherwise." But man neither acts immediately by his own power nor is himself the legitimate end of his acting, but rather God. Thus, with all his faculties, man may falter when using them.

Third, Adam's liability to falling lay in the freedom of his will. He was not only a rational creature, but also a moral one. Freedom of will is a property which belongs to man as a rational and responsible being. As we cannot separate understanding from the mind, neither can we part liberty from the will, especially in connection with things within its own sphere, especially when considering that all the faculties of man's soul were in a state of perfection before the fall. With Adam and Eve the freedom of their will consisted in a power of choosing or embracing what appeared agreeable and good to the dictates of their understandings, or in refusing and avoiding what was evil. There was no constraint or force laid upon them to act contrary to the dictates of their own wills. Such freedom also infers a power to act pursuant to what the will chooses, otherwise it could not obtain the good desired or avoid the evil detested; and in such a case its liberty would be little more than a name. Freedom of action is opposed to that which is involuntary or compelled, and the will is both self-inclining and self-determining in the acting, both internally and externally; for then only can it be said to be free.

Our first parents had that freedom of will, or power to retain their integrity. This is evident from the clearly revealed fact that they were under an indispensable obligation to yield perfect obedience to God, and liable to deserved punishment for the least defection. Therefore they must have been given a power to stand, a liberty of will to choose that which was conducive to their happiness. The same thing is also evident from the difference between man's primitive and present state. As fallen, man is now by a necessity of nature inclined to sin, and accordingly he is denominated "the servant of sin" (John 8:34), a slave to it, entirely under its dominion. But it was far otherwise with

Adam, whose nature was holy and provided with everything necessary to his yielding that obedience demanded of him. Nevertheless, his will being free, it was capable of complying with an external temptation to evil, though so long as he made a right use of his faculties he would defend himself and reject the temptation with abhorrence. It pleased God to leave our first parents without any immediate help from without, to the freedom and mutability of their own will. But that neither made Him the author of their sin nor brought them under any natural necessity of falling.

Before considering the probation under which Adam was placed, and the test to which his loyalty and subjection to God were submitted, it should be pointed out that Scripture requires us to regard him as far more than a private person, the consequences of whose action would be confined to himself. As we purpose showing, that is made very plain from the event itself. Adam was more than the father of the human race. By divine constitution he was made the covenant head of all his natural seed, so that what he did was divinely regarded and reckoned as being done by them—just as Christ came into the world as the covenant Head of all His spiritual seed, acting and transacting in their name and on their behalf. This is considered more fully under the next division of our subject, where we treat of the imputation of his offense to all his posterity. Suffice it to point out that in Romans 5:14 Adam is expressly called "the figure of him that was to come." In what was he a type of the Redeemer? The principal respect in which he was distinguished from all other creatures lay in his being the federal head and legal representative of all his offspring. This is confirmed by I Corinthians 15:45-49 where the first Adam and the last Adam are designated "the first man" and "the second man," for they were the only two who sustained that covenant and federal relation to others before God.

"And the LORD God planted a garden eastward in Eden; and there he put the man whom he had formed. And out of the ground made the LORD God to grow every tree that is pleasant to the sight, and good for food; the tree of life also in the midst of the garden, and the tree of knowledge of good and evil" (Gen. 2:8-9). That is the first mention of those two notable trees, and it is to be observed that, like all the others surrounding them, they were both pleasing to the eye and suitable for eating. Thus God provided not only for Adam's profit but for his pleasure also, that he might serve Him with delight. "And the LORD God commanded the man, saying, Of every tree of the garden thou mayest freely eat: but of the tree of the knowledge of good and evil, thou shalt not eat of it: for in the day that thou eatest thereof thou shalt surely die" (2:16-17). This, as the following verses indicate, took place before Eve was created, and thus the covenant of works was made with Adam alone as the head of our race. Far more was implied in those words than is actually expressed, as we show when considering them more closely under our next division. Meanwhile, a few general remarks may be of interest.

Herman Witsius stated:

The tendency of such a Divine precept is to be considered. Man was thereby taught: (1) That God is Lord of all things—that it is unlawful for man even to desire an apple but with His leave. In all things, therefore, from the greatest to the least, the mouth of the Lord is to be consulted as to what He would or would not have done by us. (2) That man's true happiness is placed in God alone, and nothing to be desired but with submission to God, and in order to employ it for Him. So that it is *He* only on whose account all other things appear good and desirable to man. (3) Readily to be satisfied without even the most delightful and desirable things, if God so command: and to think that there is much more good in obedience to the Divine precept than in the enjoyment of the most delightful thing in the world. (4) That man was not yet arrived to the utmost pitch of happiness, but to expect a still greater good after his course of obedience was over. This was hinted by the prohibition of the most delightful tree, whose fruit was, of any other, greatly to be desired; and this argued some degree of imperfection in that state in which man was forbidden the enjoyment of some good.

In forbidding Adam to eat of the tree of knowledge of good and evil his Maker asserted His dominion and enforced His authority. That it was proper for Him to do so cannot be lawfully questioned, and as the sole Proprietor of the garden it was fitting that He should emphasize His rights by this restriction. Moreover, since man was created a rational creature and endowed with freedom of will, he was a fit subject for command, and accordingly was placed under law. Thereby Adam's loyalty and subjection to his Creator and Lord were put to the test. Trial of his obedience was made to discover whether the will of God was sacred to him. It was both fit and just that man should remain in the state of holiness in which God had made him, if he would continue to enjoy His favor. Thus he was placed on probation, made the subject of divine government. Adam was not an independent creature, for he did not create himself. Being made by God, he owed a debt to Him; he was a moral being, and therefore responsible to serve and please God. The commandment given to him was no arbitrary infliction, but a necessary injunction for evidencing and enforcing man's relationship to God.

The particular stipulation laid upon our first parents (Gen. 2:17) has been a favorite subject of ridicule by the opponents of divine revelation. Those who are wise in their own conceits have considered it unworthy of the Almighty to interpose His authority in a matter so trifling, and have insisted it is incredible to believe that He exposed Adam and Eve to the hazard of ruining themselves and all their progeny by eating the food of a particular tree. But a little reflection ought to show us that nothing in that prohibition was unbecoming to God's wisdom and goodness. Since He had been pleased to give Adam dominion over all creatures here below, it was surely fitting that He should require some peculiar instance of homage and fidelity to Him as a token of Adam's dependence and an acknowledgment of his subjection to his Maker—to whom he owed absolute submission and obedience. And what mark of subjection could be more proper than being prohibited from eating one of the fruits of paradise? Full liberty was granted him to eat all the rest. That single abstention was well suited to teach our first parents the salutary lesson of self-denial and of implicit resignation to the good pleasure of the Most High.

In addition to what was noted by Witsius, it may be pointed out that the character of this prohibition taught Adam and Eve to keep their sensitive appetites in subjection to their reasoning faculty. It showed them they must subordinate their bodily inclinations to finding their highest delight in God alone. It intimated that their desire after knowledge must be kept within just bounds, that they must be content with what God knew to be really proper and useful for them, and not presume to pry with unwarrantable curiosity into things which did not belong to them, and which God had not thought well to reveal to them. It was not sinful per se for Adam and Eve to eat of the tree of knowledge of good and evil, but only because the Lord God had expressly forbidden them to do so. Accordingly, solemn warning of the dire consequences that would certainly follow their disobedience was given, for even in Eden man was placed under the holy awe of divine threatening, which was a hedge placed around him for his protection. Man's supreme happiness lies in God Himself and the enjoyment of His favor, and in Eden he was forbidden to seek satisfaction in any other object. His integrity was put to the test in that single restriction on his liberty.

Far from that arrangement being unworthy of the divine majesty, such an enforcing of His will and authority on the creature of His hand was most becoming. The arrangement was necessary in the nature of the case if the responsibility of a free agent was to be enforced, and his subjection to the divine government insisted on. Also the very triviality of the object withheld from our first parents only served to give greater reality to the trial to which they were subjected. As Professor Dick pointed out,

It is manifest that the prohibition did not proceed from malevolence or an intention to impair the happiness of man: because, with this single reservation, he was at liberty to appropriate the rich variety of fruits with which Paradise was stored. It is certain that, situated as he was, no command could be easier, as it properly implied no sacrifice, no painful privation, but simple abstinence from one out of many things; for who would deem it a hardship, while he was sitting at a table covered with all kinds of delicate and substantial foods, to be told that there was one and only one that he was forbidden to taste? It is further evident that no reason could be assigned why Adam should not eat the fruit of the tree of knowledge of good and evil but the Divine prohibition.

The fruit was as good for food as that of any tree, and as pleasant to the eye; and there was nothing sacred in it which would have been profaned by human touch. Hence you will perceive that if God had an intention to make trial of the newly formed subject He could not have chosen a more proper method, as it indicated nothing like a harsh or tyrannical exercise of authority, and was admirably fitted to ascertain whether His simple command would be to him instead of all other reasons for obedience. It is not a proper trial of reverence for a superior when the action which he prescribes is recommended by other considerations. It is when it stands upon the sole foundation of his authority; when, having no intrinsic goodness, it becomes good only by his prohibition; when the sole inducement to perform it is His command. It is in these circumstances it is known whether we duly feel and recognize our moral dependence upon him. The morality of an action does not depend upon its abstract nature, but upon its relation to the law of God. Men seem often to judge of actions as they judge of material substances—by their bulk. What is great in itself, or in its consequences, they will admit to be a sin; but what appears little they pronounce to be a slight fault, or no fault at all.

Had Adam, it has been remarked, been possessed of preternatural power, and wantonly and wickedly exerted it in blasting the beauty of paradise, and turning it into a scene of desolation, men would have granted that he was guilty of a great and daring offence, for which a curse was justly pronounced upon him. But they can see no harm in so trifling a matter as the eating of a little fruit. Nothing, however, is more fallacious than such reasoning: the essence of sin is the transgression of a law, and whether that law forbids you to commit murder or to move your finger, it is equally transgressed when you violate the precept. Whatever the act of disobedience is, it is rebellion against the Lawgiver: it is a renunciation of His authority, it dissolves that moral dependence upon Him which is founded on the nature of things, and is necessary to maintain the order and happiness of the universe. The injunction therefore to abstain from the tree of knowledge of good and evil was a proper trial of our first parent, and the violation of it deserved the dreadful punishment which was denounced and executed. He was put to the test whether the will of God was sacred in his eyes, and he was punished because he gave preference to his own will.

Our reason for making a longer quotation than usual from the writings of others is that the one just given is of particular weight and importance and greatly needed in this day. We hope the reader will give it a second and more careful perusal.

It only remains for us to add that the foundation of Adam's obligation to render such obedience to God lay, first, in his relations to Him. As his Maker, his Governor, his Benefactor, it was fitting for him to render full subjection to His revealed will. Second, in the privileges and favors bestowed on him: these required that he should express his gratitude and thanksgiving by doing those things which were pleasing in His sight. Third, in his endowments, which qualified him to do so: he was created in God's image, with a nature that inclined his will to obedience—ability and obligation then being coextensive. Fourth, in the relation he sustained to the race: as the head and father of all his progeny, their welfare or ruin was bound up in how he conducted himself, thus greatly augmenting his responsibility to abstain from wrongdoing. Fifth, in that the command forbidding Adam to eat of the tree of knowledge was accompanied by a solemn threat of dire punishment in case of disobedience. Not only should that have acted as an effectual deterrent, but the penalty necessarily implied a promise: since death would be the sure result of disobedience, life would be the reward of obedience—not only a continuation of the blessedness and happiness which he then enjoyed in fellowship with his Maker, but an augmentation of them. That also ought to have served as a powerful incentive to continued fidelity. Thus there was every reason why Adam should have preserved his integrity.

Mutability of Man

Though created in the image and likeness of God, man was not endowed with infallibility. In body perfectly sound, in soul completely holy, in circumstances blissfully happy, still man was but a mutable creature. Pronounced by God "very good" (Gen. 1:31) on the day of his creation, man's character was not yet confirmed in righteousness, therefore he was (like the angels) placed on probation and subjected to trial—to show whether or not he would render allegiance to his Lord. Though "made upright," he was not incapable of falling; nor did it devolve upon God to keep him from doing so. This is clear from the event, for had there been any obligation on God, His faithfulness and goodness would have preserved Adam. Nor would He have censured our first parents had their defection been due to any breach of *His* fidelity. As moral agents, Adam and Eve were required to maintain their pristine purity unsullied, to walk before God in unswerving loyalty and loving submission. But a single restriction was put on their liberty, which was necessary for the testing of their loyalty and the discharge of their responsibility.

Regrettably man did not endure honorably. He valued at a low rate the approbation of his Maker and the inestimable privilege of communion with Him. He chafed against the love-lined yoke that had been laid on him. How quickly he supplied tragic evidence of his mutability and disrupted the tranquillity of paradise. The beauty of holiness in which the parents of our race were clothed was soon succeeded by the most revolting depravity. Instead of preserving their integrity, they fell into a state of sin and misery. They were speedily induced to violate that commandment of God's obedience which was the sole condition of their continued bliss. They did not long enjoy their fair heritage. In spite of the ideal conditions in which they were placed, they became dissatisfied with their lot, succumbed to their very first testing, and evoked the holy displeasure of their Benefactor. How early the fine gold became dim! How soon man forfeited the favor of his Maker, and plunged himself into an ocean of wretchedness and woe! How swiftly the sun of human happiness was eclipsed by man's own folly!

It has been generally held among devout students of God's Word that our first parents remained unfallen for only a brief time. Such a view is in full accord with the general Analogy of Faith, for it is a solemn and humbling fact that whenever God has been pleased to place anything in the hands of human responsibility, man has proved unfaithful to his trust. When He has bestowed some special favor on the creature, it has not been long before he has sadly abused the same. Even a considerable part of the angels in heaven "kept not their first estate," though the Scriptures do not disclose how soon they apostatized. Noah, when he came out onto a judgment-swept earth to be the new father of the human race, defiled his escutcheon at a very early date and brought a curse on his son. Within the space of a few days after Israel had solemnly entered into a covenant with Jehovah at Sinai, they were guilty of the horrible sin of idolatry, so that the Lord complained to

Moses, "They have turned aside quickly out of the way which I commanded them: they have made them a molten calf, and have worshipped it" (Exodus 32:8). How tragically that portended the whole of their future national history!

No sooner were the "times of the Gentiles" inaugurated by Nebuchadnezzar's being made "a king of kings" (Dan. 2:37), so that his dominion was "to the end of the earth" (4:22), than pride led to his downfall. While he was boasting, "Is not this great Babylon, that I have built for the house of the kingdom by the might of my power, and for the honour of my majesty?" a voice from heaven announced, "They shall drive thee from men, and thy dwelling shall be with the beasts of the field: they shall make thee to eat grass as oxen, and seven times shall pass over thee, until thou know that the most High ruleth in the kingdom of men, and giveth it to whomsoever he will" (4:30, 32). Man is a sad failure. Even the honor of the primitive Christian church was speedily tarnished by the sin of Ananias and Sapphira. Thus it has been all through the past, and there is no evidence to show that at the commencement of human history Adam and Eve were any exception. Rather are there clear indications to the contrary, so that God had reason to say of them also, "They have turned aside quickly out of the way."

Personally we doubt if our first parents preserved their integrity for fortyeight hours, or even for twenty-four. In the first place, they were told to "be fruitful, and multiply" (Gen. 1:28); and had they complied with that injunction and the blessing of God had been on them, *a sinless child* would have been conceived, which, following the fall of Adam and Eve, would have been part of a depraved family—a terrible anomaly, involving the utmost confusion. Second, if those words concerning Christ are to be taken without qualification, "that in *all* things he might have the preeminence" (Col. 1:18), then He is the only One who kept the Sabbath perfectly on this earth, and consequently Adam fell before the seventh day ended. Third, in Psalm 49:12, the Hebrew word for "man" is *Adam*—the same as in Genesis 2 and 3 and Job 31:33, while that for "abode" signifies "to stay or lodge for a night." Manton rendered it "Adam being in honour abideth not for a night." And Thomas Watson in his *Body of Divinity* said, "Adam, then, it seems, did not take up one night's lodging in Paradise." Fourth, the devil "was a murderer from the beginning" (John 8:44)—not from the beginning of time, for there was no man *to* slay during the first five days, but from the beginning of *human history*. In the morning man was holy; by night he was a sinner!

We now consider the melancholy and disastrous episode of the fall itself. Genesis 3 describes the event, about which George Whitefield rightly said, "Moses unfolds more in that chapter than all mankind would have been capable of finding out of themselves though they had studied it to all eternity." It is indeed one of the most important chapters in all the Bible, and it should be pondered by us frequently with prayerful hearts. Here commences the great drama which is now being enacted on the stage of human history, and which nearly six thousand years have not yet completed. Here is given the divine explanation of the present debased and ruined condition of the world. Here we are shown how sin entered the world, together with its present effects and dire consequences. Here are revealed to us the subtle devices of our great enemy the devil. We are shown how we permit him to gain an advantage over us. On the other hand, it is a most blessed chapter, for it reveals the grace and mercy of God, and assures us that the head of the serpent will yet be crushed by the victorious Seed of the woman (Rom. 16:20), telling us that His redeemed will also participate in Christ's glorious triumph. Thus we see that in wrath our God from the commencement "remembered mercy"!

A careful reading of Genesis 3 indicates that much is compacted into an exceedingly small space. The historical account of this momentous incident is given with the utmost conciseness—so very different from the way an uninspired pen would have dealt with it! Its extreme brevity calls for the careful weighing of every word and clause, and their implications. That there is not a little contained between the lines is plainly intimated in the Lord's words to Adam: "Because thou hast hearkened unto the voice of thy wife" (v. 17), yet the preceding verses nowhere tell us that she even spoke to him! Again, from the judgment pronounced on the serpent, "Upon thy belly shalt thou go" (v. 14), we may infer that previously it had stood erect. Again, from that part of the divine sentence passed on the woman, "Thy desire shall be to thy husband, and he shall rule over thee" (v. 16), it may be concluded that Eve had acted unbecomingly and exerted an undue influence and authority in inducing Adam to eat of the forbidden fruit. If we fail to ponder thoroughly every detail and meditate on it, we are certain to miss points of interest and importance.

Subtlety of the Serpent

"Now the serpent was more subtil [wiser] than any beast of the field which the LORD God had made" (Gen. 3:1). Great care needs to be taken in the interpreting of this sentence. On the one hand, we must not give free rein to our imagination; on the other, this fact is not to be hurriedly and thoughtlessly skimmed over. Other passages should be compared if a fuller understanding is to be obtained. Personally we believe that the statement refers to a *literal* "serpent" as being the instrument of a superior being. We consider that the terms of verse 14 make it clear that an actual serpent is in view, for the Lord's words there are only applicable to that beast itself: "Because thou hast done this, thou art cursed above all cattle; . . . upon thy belly shalt thou go, and dust shalt thou eat all the days of thy life." Nevertheless, what immediately follows in verse 15 makes it equally plain that more than a beast of the field was involved, namely Satan. Putting the two statements together, we gather that Satan made use of a literal serpent as his mouthpiece in the beguiling of Eve—as the Lord later spoke through the mouth of Balaam's ass (Num. 22:30-31).

Confirmation of what has just been said is found in John 8:44, where our Lord declared that the devil is "a murderer [literally manslayer] from the beginning"—designating him as such because by his wiles he brought death on our first parents. Moreover, in Revelation 12:9 and 20:2, Satan is called "that old serpent," in manifest allusion to the transaction of Genesis 3: "And he said unto the woman, Yea, hath God said, Ye shall not eat of every tree of the garden?" The thoughtful reader is at once struck by the abruptness of this remark, and is almost forced to conclude that the serpent was replying to what Eve had said previously; for his opening "yea" plainly implies something going before. Where was Eve when she was thus addressed and assailed? We believe, as do many others, that she was standing before the very tree whose fruit they had been forbidden to eat. It is apparent from the immediate sequel that she was at least within sight of the tree. The serpent, taking advantage of Eve's looking at the tree, spoke about and commended it to her.

We also agree with those who have concluded that Adam was not with Eve when the serpent first engaged her in conversation, though we know that soon afterward he rejoined her. Ridgley, Whitefield, Gill and many others held that Eve was alone when the serpent confronted her. For ourselves, we base that belief upon what we are told in I Timothy 2:13-14, where the Holy Spirit has emphasized the fact that the woman was first in the transgression, and then became the seducer of the man. That could hardly be said had Adam been present from the beginning, for then he would have been partaker of her evildoing—by allowing her to yield to the temptation instead of making every effort to cause her to reject it. Furthermore, it should be carefully noted that when the guilty couple were arraigned before their Maker, Eve passed no blame upon her husband for making no attempt to dissuade her, but instead sought to throw the onus on the serpent. Nor did the Lord Himself charge Adam with any complicity in his wife's crime, as He surely would have done had Adam been a passive spectator. The serpent, then, must have tempted Eve in the absence of her husband.

We consider that Eve's being alone, and more especially her approach to the fatal tree, casts considerable light on what then occurred. Matthew Henry stated, "Had she kept close to the side out of which she was lately taken, she had not been so exposed." And had she kept away from that which threatened certain death, she would have been on safer ground. Satan cannot injure any of us while we are walking with God and treading the paths of righteousness.

We are expressly told that there is no lion in the "way of holiness," that no ravenous beast shall be found there (Isa. 35:8-9). No, we have to step out of that way and trespass on the devil's territory before he can "get an advantage of us" (II Cor. 2:11). That is why we are so emphatically enjoined, "Enter not into the path of the wicked, and go not in the way of evil men. Avoid it, pass not by it, turn from it" (Prov. 4:14-15). We certainly do not regard Eve as being guilty of any sin at this initial stage, but the sequel shows plainly that she incurred great danger and exposed herself to temptation by approaching so near to that tree whose fruit had been divinely prohibited, and we need not be surprised to discover, as she also did, that that ground was already occupied by the serpent. This has been recorded for our learning and warning.

Gullibility of Eve

"And he said unto the woman, Yea, hath God said, Ye shall not eat of every tree of the garden?" The serpent must have looked very different from the repulsive reptile it now is, not only standing erect but—in keeping with his preeminence above all other beasts, and as the Hebrew word intimates— of a striking and beautiful appearance. Apparently he stood before the tree of the knowledge of good and evil, and it seems more than likely that he personally took and ate its fruit in Eve's presence. This no doubt evoked from her an ejaculation of surprise or a look of horror, which explains why he then said what he did. As Samuel Hopkins long ago pointed out,

> It is probable that the serpent told the woman that by eating of the fruit of that tree he had obtained the use of reason and the faculty of speech which she now saw in exercise; and therefore said that, from his own experience, he could assure her that if she would eat of this fruit she would be so far from dying that she would reach to a higher degree of perfection and knowledge.

While such an inference must not be pressed dogmatically, we have long felt it possesses much probability, and that it is an illuminating one.

Recently we discovered what John Brown of Haddington wrote in his family Bible concerning the serpent's words to Eve: "Perhaps he pretended that himself had acquired what knowledge he had above other beasts by eating of this forbidden fruit. It is certain that he attempted to confirm his contradiction of the threatening by a solemn appeal to God." This requires us to examine closely the tempter's words. The margin of some Bibles gives an alternative rendering, "Yea, *because* God hath said," which makes his statement a declaration rather than a query. (Gen. 13:9; Ps. 25:12; Matt. 26:53; Luke 22:35 are other examples where a strong affirmation or appeal is, for the sake of emphasis, put in the form of an interrogation.) Considering it thus here, we may regard the serpent's opening words to Eve as answering her previous expression of surprise: "Is it 'because God hath said' that you are so startled at seeing me eating the fruit?" Thomas Scott pointed out, "Indeed we cannot satisfactorily account for the woman's entering into conversation with the serpent, and showing no marks of surprise or suspicion, unless we admit a supposition of this kind." It is one of the first duties of an expositor to show the connection, explicit or implicit, of each statement of Holy Writ.

In the serpent's statement we perceive the guile and malice of the enemy. His allusion to the divine restriction made it appear much greater and more severe than it actually was. The Lord had in fact made generous provision for them to eat freely of "every tree of the garden" with but a single exception (Gen. 2:16). Satan sought to bring reproach on the divine law by misrepresenting it. It was as though he said, "Can it be that your Maker has given you appetites and also placed before you the means of gratifying them, only to mock you? You surely must have misunderstood His meaning!" We therefore regard this opening utterance of the serpent as an attempt not only to make Eve doubt God's veracity but also to cause her to suspect the divine beneficence. Satan is ever seeking to inject that poison into our hearts: to distrust God's goodness—especially in connection with His prohibitions and precepts. That is really what lies behind all evil lusting and disobedience: a discontent with our position and portion, a craving for something which God has wisely withheld from us. The more clearly we perceive the precise nature of the serpent's poison the better we are enabled to judge its workings within us. Reject any suggestion that God is unduly severe with you. Resist with the utmost abhorrence anything which causes you to doubt God's loving-kindness. Allow nothing to make you question His love.

We have called attention to the brevity of the narrative of Genesis 3 and the need for us to weigh carefully every word in its opening verses and ponder the implication of each clause. While we must refrain from reading into it what is not there, we must be careful not to overlook anything of importance which *is* there. Matthew Henry pertinently pointed out, "Satan tempted Eve that, by her, he might tempt Adam; so he tempted Job by his wife, and Christ by Peter. It is his policy to send temptations by unsuspected hands, and theirs that have most interest in us and influence over us." Eve's suspicions ought to have been aroused when the serpent introduced such a subject for conversation, and she should have turned away immediately. Those who would escape harm must keep out of harm's way. "Go from the presence of a foolish man, when thou perceivest not in him the lips of knowledge" (Prov. 14:7). "Cease, my son, to hear the instruction that causeth to err from the words of knowledge" (Prov. 19:27). The serpent's opening word was designed to produce in Eve a spirit of discontent. It was really a sly insinuation which amounted to this: "If you cannot eat of all the trees, you might as well eat of none." King Ahab took this view. With all his royal possessions, he was dissatisfied while denied Naboth's vineyard. And Haman, though he had found favor with the king, petulantly exclaimed, "All of this availeth me nothing" because Mordecai refused to pay him deference.

If Eve was not already secretly desiring the forbidden fruit, would she have paid any attention to the cunning query made to her? We very much doubt it. Still less can we conceive of her entering into a discussion with the serpent on the subject. Toying with temptation always implies lusting after the object presented. Had Eve been content with God's grant in Genesis 2:1b, and had she been satisfied with the knowledge He had given her by creation, she would have abhorred the false knowledge proposed by the tempter, and that would have precluded all parleying with him! That is more than a supposition of ours, for it is obviously confirmed by what follows. Compare her conduct with Christ's and observe how very differently He acted. He stead-fastly refused to enter into any debate with the devil. He did not dally with temptation, for He had no desire for anything but the will of God. Each time He firmly repulsed the enemy's advances by taking His stand on God's Word, and concluded by thrusting away Satan's propositions with utmost revulsion. A greater contrast cannot be imagined: the woman's Seed met Satan's tempta-tion with holy loathing; the woman was in a condition to respond to the ser-pent's wiles with unholy compliance.

"And the woman said unto the serpent, We may eat of the fruit of the trees of the garden: but of the fruit of the tree which is in the midst of the garden, God hath said, Ye shall not eat of it, neither shall ye touch it, lest ye die" (Gen. 3:2-3). Instead of fleeing in dread from the serpent, Eve con-ferred with him, which was both foolish and fatal, as the outcome showed. Satan is much wiser than we are, and if we attempt to meet him on his own ground and argue with him, the result will be disastrous. His evil influence had already begun to affect Eve injuriously, as appears from a close examina-tion of the first part of her reply. The Lord had said, "Of every tree of the garden thou mayest *freely* eat." Eve's omission of that word "freely" was both significant and ominous—indicating that the generosity of the divine provision was not influencing her heart as it should have. But on the other hand we do not agree with those who charge her with adding to God's word in verse 3. For while the "neither shall ye touch it" was not distinctly ex-pressed in Genesis 2:17, nevertheless it was clearly and necessarily implied. How could Eve eat of the fruit without touching it? The one act requires the other.

There is a very important principle involved in what has just been pointed out. It may be stated thus: When God forbids any act He at the same time forbids everything encouraging or leading up to it. Our Lord made that very plain in His Sermon on the Mount, as He enforced the spirituality and strict-ness of the law when repudiating the errors of the rabbis, who were guilty of modifying its holy requirements. He insisted that "Thou shalt not kill" is by no means restricted to the bare act of murder, but that it also prohibits every evil exercise of the mind and heart preceding the act, such as hatred, ill will, malice. In like manner He declared that "Thou shalt not commit adultery" includes very much more than outlawing intercourse between the sexes— even impure imaginations and desires. That commandment is broken as soon as there is unchaste lusting or even looking. God demands very much more than merely keeping clean the outside of the cup and platter (Matt. 23:25-26). "Thou shalt not steal" includes not even thinking of doing so, nor handling what is not yours—nor borrowing anything when you have no in-tention of returning it.

Eve, then, was quite right in concluding that the divine commandment forbidding them to eat of the tree of the knowledge of good and evil included not touching it, for the act of eating involves not only desire and intention but also touching, handling, plucking, and placing the fruit in the mouth.

But we are not so sure about the exact force of her words "lest ye die." Many have supposed she was toning down the Lord's "thou shalt surely die." They may be right, but we are not at all sure. "Kiss the Son, *lest* he be angry" (Ps. 2:12) is obviously not the language of uncertainty. The Hebrew for "lest" is rendered "that . . . not" in Genesis 24:6. If the reader will compare John 3:20; 12:42; I Corinthians 1:17, he will see that the force of "lest" in these passages is "otherwise." Gill also states that Eve's employment of the "lest" is not at all conclusive that she expressed any doubt, since the word may also be used of the event of anything, as in Psalm 2:12, and hence may be rendered "that ye die not." We therefore prefer to leave it as an open question.

"And the serpent said unto the woman, Ye shall not surely die" (Gen. 3:4). Perceiving his advantage, now that he had gained Eve's ear, the tempter grew bolder and flatly contradicted the divine threatening. He began by seeking to instill a doubt—Is it so or not?—by casting a reflection upon the divine goodness and making Eve dissatisfied with God's liberal provision. Then he denied that there was any danger in eating the fruit. First he had by implication slandered God's character; and now he told a downright lie. If, as we believe was the case, he had himself eaten of the forbidden tree in the woman's presence, then his action would lend color to his falsehood. It was as though he said, "You need not hesitate. God is only trying to frighten you. You can see for yourself the fruit is quite harmless, for I have eaten it without suffering any ill effects." Thus the enemy of souls seeks to persuade man that he may defy God with impunity, inducing him when "he heareth the words of this curse" to "bless himself in his heart, saying, I shall have peace, though I walk in the imagination of mine heart, to add drunkenness to thirst" (Deut. 29:19).

No excuse can be made for Eve now. If she had acted foolishly in approaching so near to the fatal tree, if her suspicions were not at once aroused by the serpent's opening remark, she certainly ought to have been deeply horrified, turning immediately away, when she heard him imply that the Lord her God had lied. Joseph fled from his temptress (Gen. 39:12). Eve had much more reason to run from the serpent with loathing. Instead, she remained to hear him add, "For God doth know that in the day ye eat thereof, then your eyes shall be opened, and ye shall be as gods, knowing good and evil" (3:5). He declared that not only would no harm be suffered, but they would benefit by heeding his suggestion and doing as he had done. A threefold promise or inducement was set before the woman. First, that by eating this fruit their capacity of discernment and perception would be considerably increased. That is the force of "your eyes shall be opened." Their physical eyes were open already, therefore his reference must have been to the eyes of their understanding. Second, their position would be improved and their power enlarged: they should be as "gods" or angels. Third, their wisdom would be much augmented: "knowing good and evil"—as though that were most desirable. And all of this at once—"then"—without any delay.

It will be observed from the above that the serpent directed his attack not at Eve's bodily appetites but at the noblest part of her being, by the inducement of an increase of wisdom that would elevate our first parents above their condition and fit them to be companions for the celestial creatures. There lay the force of his temptation: seeking to fan a desire for forbidden knowledge and self-sufficiency—to act independently of God. From then until now, Satan's object has been to divert men from the only source of wisdom and cause them to seek it from him. Nevertheless, the bait dangled before Eve in no way hid the barb he was using to catch her. Putting together the whole of his statement in verses 4 and 5, we see the serpent not only charged God with making a threat which He had no intention of fulfilling, but also accused Him of being tyrannical in withholding from them what He knew would be for their good. He said, "You need have no fear that God will be as severe and rigorous as His language sounded. He is only trying to intimidate you. He is well aware that if you eat this fruit, your knowledge will be greatly enlarged; but He is unwilling for this to happen, and therefore He wants to prevent it by this unreasonable prohibition."

"And when the woman saw that the tree was good for food, and that it was pleasant to the eyes, and a tree to be desired to make one wise, she took of the fruit thereof, and did eat" (3:6). Before examining the details of this tragic verse, we shall carefully consider two questions, and endeavor to answer them. First, why did not the divine threat in Genesis 2:17 deter Eve from disobeying God? David declared, "Thy word have I hid in mine heart [to be awed thereby, to put it into practice], that I might not sin against thee" (Ps. 119:11). It is clear from Genesis 3:3 that God's word was at least in Eve's thoughts when the serpent accosted her. Then how was it that it did not preserve her from sin? Surely the answer is that she did not make use of it, but instead dallied with temptation, parleyed with God's enemy, and believed his lie. Here is a most solemn warning for us. If we wish God to deliver us from the destroyer, then we must determine to shun every occasion of evil and, as Joseph did, flee from temptation. If we really take to heart the solemn failure and fall of Eve, then we shall pray with ever increasing earnestness, "Lead us not into temptation" and, if the Lord sees fit to test us, "Deliver us from evil."

Second, in II Corinthians 11:3, we are informed that "the serpent beguiled [cheated] Eve through his subtilty," and in I Timothy 2:14 that she was "deceived." How then are we to explain what is recorded of her in Genesis 3, where the historical account seems to make it very plain that she committed the act after due deliberation, with her eyes wide open? How was she deceived if she knowingly disobeyed God? The answer is that as soon as she ceased to be regulated by the light of God's word, her imagination became filled with the false impressions presented to her by Satan, and her mind became darkened. Unholy desires were born within her. Her affections and appetites overrode her judgment, and she was persuaded to disbelieve what was true and believe what was false. Oh, the "deceitfulness of sin" (Heb.

3:13), which calls good evil and bitter sweet. She was beguiled by consenting to listen to another voice than God's, and because she disregarded her allegiance to her husband. The prelude to every fall from grace is the alienation of the heart from Christ, the Christian's spiritual Husband, with the consequent clouding of the judgment. When the truth is rejected, error is welcome. Satan, in his efforts to induce souls to look for their happiness in departing from God, adapts his temptations to the cases and circumstances of the tempted.

Eve saw that the tree was good for food, and that it was "pleasant to the eyes." Let us consider at what point this statement comes in the narrative: not at the commencement, but after all that is recorded in the preceding verses had transpired. Let us also observe the order of those two clauses. We would expect to find the phrase "pleasant to the eyes" mentioned before "good for food." Why then are the two descriptions reversed? Does not this better enable us to understand exactly what is meant by "when the woman saw that the tree was good for food"? The time element must not be ignored, for it cannot be without significance. We suggest that it looks back to the foregoing action of the serpent, which we believe is clearly implied in the context, namely, his personally eating the forbidden fruit in Eve's presence. How else could she perceive the tree was "good for food" before she had tasted it? Does not the third clause of the verse confirm and clinch this interpretation, for how else could Eve possibly know the fruit was "to be desired to *make one wise*" unless she had previously witnessed what appeared to her to be a visual demonstration of the fact?

Is it not evident that the words "when the woman saw that the tree *was good* for food" signify that since she had seen the serpent eating it without dying or even suffering any injury, she need not fear following his example? Could his action not infer that from his so doing he had acquired the faculty of reason and the power of speech, and that she too would be benefited by doing the same? Instead of acting in faith on the word of God, Eve walked by sight, only to discover—as her sons and daughters often do—that appearances are very deceptive. She saw "that it was pleasant to the eyes." There was nothing in the outward appearance of the fruit to denote that it was unfit for eating; on the contrary, it looked attractive. In Genesis 2:9 we read that "out of the ground made the Lord God to grow every tree that is pleasant to the sight, and good for food." As the remainder of that verse shows, the tree of the knowledge of good and evil was no exception. All creation was beautiful and agreeable to the senses. But Eve, by yielding to the serpent's temptation, found *that* tree particularly appealing. She had a secret hankering after its fruit and unlawfully coveted it.

Had there been any uncertainty in Eve's mind, she could have consulted her husband; this is a wife's duty and privilege. Instead, she saw the tree was "to be desired to make one wise." She judged it entirely by what the serpent had told her—and not by what God had said—as the preceding verse shows. She was flattered with the false hope the enemy had held out to her.

She first gave credence to his "ye shall not surely die." Next she was attracted by the prospect of becoming like the "gods" or angels. And then, on
her believing the promise of augmented knowledge, lustful longing consumed
her. The Hebrew word for "desired" in Genesis 3:6 is translated "covet" in
Exodus 20:17. The same word is termed "concupiscence" in Romans 7:8,
and "lust" in James 1:15. Indeed, that latter passage traces for us in detail
the course of Eve's downfall, for her conduct solemnly illustrates James
1:14-15:

> But every man is tempted, when he is drawn away [from the path of
> rectitude] of his own lust [as Eve was in approaching the forbidden tree],
> and enticed. Then when lust hath conceived [in her by the seductive
> promises of the serpent], it bringeth forth sin [externally]: and sin, when
> it is finished [i.e., the outward act is completed], bringeth forth death.

Shedd stated that God's commandment in its full form was essentially this:
"Thou shalt not lust after but abhor the knowledge of good and evil; thou
shalt not choose but refuse it." The Eden statute, as well as the Ten Commandments, involved both the inward desire and the outward act. Note that
the holiness of Christ is described as a refusing of the evil and a choosing of
the good (Isa. 7:15). He who desires the prohibited evil does in effect choose
it, as he who hates another violates the sixth commandment though he does
not actually kill him. Eve was not to desire the fruit, for God had forbidden
her to eat it. Instead of desiring, she should have dreaded it. In lusting after
what God had prohibited, she turned from God as her everlasting portion and
chief end; she preferred the creature to the Creator. This is an unspeakably
solemn warning for us. If we estimate things by our senses or by what others
say of them, instead of accepting God's evaluation, we are certain to err in
our judgment. If we resort to carnal reasoning, we shall quickly persuade
ourselves that wrong is right. Nothing is *good* for us except that which we
receive from God's hand.

"She took of the fruit thereof, and did eat" (Gen. 3:6) without consulting
Adam. So strong was the desire of her heart that she could no longer check
it, and she committed the act which completed "the transgression." Yes, *she*
took of the fruit thereof, and did eat." The serpent did not put it in her
mouth. The devil may tempt, but he cannot force anyone. By Eve's own
free act she took of the fruit; therefore she could rightly blame no one but
herself. By this time Adam had rejoined her, for we are told that she "gave
also unto her husband *with her*"—the first time he is mentioned as being by
her side. This is the progression of sin: one yielding to temptation, and then
becoming the tempter of others—seeking to drag them down to the same
level. "And he did eat," instead of refusing what his God-defying wife proffered him. He "was not deceived" (I Tim. 2:14), which, if possible, made his
guilt the greater. He "hearkened unto the voice of . . . [his] wife" (Gen.
3:17). Probably she repeated to him what the serpent had said to her,
commending the fruit and possibly pointing out that they must have misunderstood the Lord's words, since she had eaten and was still alive.

Thus man apostatized from God. It was a revolt against his Maker, an insurrection from His supremacy, a rebellion against His authority. He deliberately resisted the divine will, rejected God's word, deserted His way. In consequence he forfeited his primitive excellence and all his happiness. Adam cast himself and all his posterity into the deepest gulf of anguish and wretchedness. This was the origin of human depravity. Genesis 3 gives us the divinely inspired account of how sin entered this world, and supplies the only adequate and satisfactory explanation of both its six thousand years' history and of its present-day condition.

Chapter 3

IMPUTATION

WE ARE NOW to consider the bearing which Adam's sin had on his posterity, and its different effects. In Eden Adam acted not simply as a private person, the results of whose conduct affected none but himself, but rather as a public person, so that what he did, directly concerned and judicially involved others. Adam was much more than the father of the human race: he was also their legal agent, standing in their stead. His descendants were not only in him generatively as their natural head, but also morally and legally as their moral and legal head. In other words, by divine constitution and covenant Adam acted as the federal representative of all his children. By an act of His sovereign will, it pleased God to ordain that Adam's relation to his natural seed should be like that which Christ sustained to His spiritual seed—the one acting on the behalf of many.

The whole human race was placed on probation in the person of its legal representative and covenant head. This is a truth of great importance, for it casts light not only on much in Scripture, but upon human history too. While Adam retained the approbation of God and remained in fellowship with Him, the whole of his constituency did likewise. Had he survived the appointed trial, had he faithfully and fitly discharged his responsibility, had he continued in obedience to the Lord God, then *his* obedience would have been reckoned to their account, and they would have entered into and shared his reward. Contrariwise, if the head failed and fell, then all his members fell with him. If he disobeyed, then his disobedience was charged to those whom he represented, and the frightful punishment pronounced on him fell likewise on those on whose behalf he transacted. Justice required that the whole human race should be legally regarded and dealt with as sharing the guilt of its representative, and subjected to the same penalty. In consequence of this arrangement, when Adam sinned we sinned, and therefore "by the offence of one judgment came upon all men to condemnation" (Rom. 5:18).

Instead of placing each member of humanity on probation separately and successively, it pleased God to put the whole race on formal trial once and for all in the person of their head. Probably it will make it easier to grasp the nature of Adam's legal relation to his descendants if we make use of a simple contrast and analogy which have been employed by other writers on this subject. God did not act with mankind as with a field of corn, where each stalk stands on its own individual root. Rather He has dealt with our race as with a tree—all the branches of which have one common root. While the root of a tree remains healthy and unharmed, the whole of it flourishes. But if an ax strikes and severs the root, then the whole of the tree suffers and falls—not only the trunk but all the branches—and even its smallest twigs wither and die. Thus it was with the Eden tragedy. When Adam's communion with his Maker was broken, all his posterity were alienated from His favor. This is no theory of human speculation, but a fact of divine revelation: "Wherefore, as by one man sin entered into the world, and death by sin; and so death passed upon all men, for that all have sinned" (Rom. 5:12).

Adam, then, occupied a unique position. At his creation all his unborn children were germinally created in him. Not only that, but God entered into a solemn covenant with him in their name. The entire human family was represented by him and stood in him before the Lord. The future well-being of his progeny was suspended on his conduct. He was therefore placed on trial, to show whether he would promote the interests of his Creator or refuse to be subject to His government. Some test must be given him in order for the exercise of his moral agency and the discharge of his responsibility. He was made to love and serve God, being richly endowed and fully capacitated to that end. His supreme blessedness and continued happiness consisted in his doing so. Scripture proves that Adam did transact on the behalf of his descendants, and so stood in their stead before the divine law. What *he* did was in effect what *they* did. Or, as Manton expressed it, "We saw the forbidden fruit with his eyes, gathered it with his hands, ate it with his mouth; that is, we were ruined by those things as though we had been there and consented to his acts."

Adam as Head of Mankind

We propose to show, first, that Adam was the federal head of the race; second, that he entered into a covenant with God on their behalf; third, that the guilt of his original sin was divinely imputed to his descendants. Concerning the first we confine ourselves to two proof texts. The first is Romans 5:14:

> Death reigned from Adam to Moses, even over them that had not sinned after the similitude of Adam's transgression, who is the figure of him that was to come.

That is truly an astonishing statement. Occurring in such a setting it is startling and at once arrests our attention. With what accuracy and propriety could it be said that the father of our fallen race foreshadowed the Lord Jesus? Adam, when tempted, yielded and was overcome; Christ, when tempted, resisted and overcame. The former was cursed by God, the latter was owned by Him as the One in whom He was well pleased. The one is the source of sin and corruption to all his posterity, but the other is a fount of holiness to all His people. By Adam came condemnation, by Christ comes salvation. Thus they are as far apart as the poles. Then how was Adam a "figure" of the coming Redeemer?

The Greek word for "figure" in this verse means "type," and in the scriptural sense of that term a type consists of something more than a casual resemblance between two things or an incidental parallel. There is a designed likeness, the one being divinely intended to show forth the other. From all eternity it was foreordained that the first man should prefigure the incarnate Son of God. In what particular respect? Certainly not in his conduct. Nor in his natural constitution, as consisting of spirit, soul and body; for in that respect all who lived before Christ was born, might as properly be called figures of Him. The whole context makes it clear that Adam was a type of the Lord Jesus in the official position which he occupied—as the federal head and legal representative of others. In Romans 5:12-19 prominence is given to the one acting on behalf of the many, the one affecting the destiny of the many. What the one did, is made the legal ground of what befalls the many. As the disobedience and guilt of Adam entailed condemnation for all who were legally one with him, so the obedience and righteousness of Christ secured the justification of all in whose place He served as surety.

The other passage which proves that Adam sustained the relation of federal head to his posterity is I Corinthians 15:45-49:

> And so it is written, The first man Adam was made a living soul; the last Adam was made a quickening spirit. . . . The first man is of the earth, earthy: the second man is the Lord from heaven. . . . And as we have borne the image of the earthy, we shall also bear the image of the heavenly.

Again, despite marked contrasts between the type and the Antitype, they had something in common. The one had a mundane origin; the other's was celestial. The former was but a man; the latter was "the Lord." The first Adam was made "a living soul"; the last Adam is the Quickener of others. In the one "all die"; in the other "shall all be made alive" (v. 22). But that which marked each alike was his *representative character*—he was the head of an appointed seed, communicating his distinctive "image" to them. Adam is designated "the first man" not simply because he was the first in order—like the first day of the week—but because he was the first to act as the legal representative of a race. Christ is called "the second man," though He lived so long afterward, because He was the second to sustain a federal relation to an appointed seed. He was called "the last Adam" because there is to be no further covenant head.

God's Covenant with Adam

A covenant was entered into between the Lord God and Adam: "And the LORD God commanded the man, saying, Of every tree of the garden thou mayest freely eat: but of the tree of knowledge of good and evil, thou shalt not eat of it: for in the day that thou eatest thereof thou shalt surely die" (Gen. 2:16-17). What are the principal elements in a covenant? A covenant is a formal compact and mutual arrangement between two or more parties whereby they stand solemnly bound to each other to perform the conditions contracted for. On the one side there is a stipulation of something to be done;

on the other side a restipulation of something to be done or given in consideration of the former provision. There is also a penalty included in the terms of the agreement—some unpleasant consequence to the party who violates or fails to carry out his commitment. That penalty is added as a security. Where it is not expressly stated, it is implied by the promissory clause, just as the promise is necessarily inferred from a mention of the punishment (cf. Gen. 31:43-53; Matt. 26:14-16).

Let us closely look at Genesis 2:16-17. Here are all the constituent elements of a covenant. First, here are the contracting parties: the Lord God and man. Second, here is the condition defined and accepted. As the Creator and Governor of His creatures, God was obliged to exercise His authority. Adam, owing his being to God, was bound to comply; and as a sinless and holy person he would heartily consent to the stipulation. Third, there was a penalty prescribed, which would be incurred if Adam failed to carry out his part of the compact. Fourth, there was by clear implication a promise made and a reward assured—"Do this, and thou shalt live"—to which Adam was entitled upon his rendering the required obedience. Where there are a stipulation and a restipulation between two parties, and a binding law pertaining to the same, there is a covenant (cf. Gen. 21:22-32).

Adam was placed not only under divine law but under a covenant of works. The distinction is real and radical. A law requires obedience, and punishment is threatened in proportion to the nature of the offense. A subject is bound to obey the law, but he cannot be justly deprived of that to which he has a natural right, except in case of disobedience. On the other hand, obedience to the law gives him a right to impunity, nothing more; whereas a covenant gives a person the right, upon his fulfilling the conditions, to the stipulated reward or privilege. A king is not obliged to advance a loyal subject to great honor; but if, as an act of favor, he has promised to elevate him upon his yielding obedience in some particular instance, then the subject would have a right to it—not as yielding obedience to a law, but as fulfilling the terms of a covenant. Thus Mephibosheth had a natural and legal right to his life and to the estate which had descended to him from his father, because he had lived peaceably and had not rebelled against David. But this did not entitle him to the special favor of sitting at the royal table continually, which the king conferred on him (II Sam. 9:13). *That* was the result of a covenant between David and Jonathan, in which David had promised to show kindness to Jonathan's house after him (I Sam. 20:11-17, 42).

It should be obvious that Adam had the promise of life upon his performing the condition agreed on, for "In the day that thou eatest thereof thou shalt surely die" necessarily implied the converse, "If thou eatest not thereof thou shalt surely live." Just as "Thou shalt not steal" inevitably requires "Thou shalt act honestly and honorably," and as "Rejoice in the Lord" includes "Murmur not against any of His dealings with thee," according to the simplest laws of construction, the threatening of death as the consequence of eating affirmed the promise of life upon obedience. This is an essential feature of a covenant—a reward guaranteed upon the fulfillment of its terms. Certainly the threat in Genesis 2:17 not only signified God's intention to punish sin, but was also designed as a motivation to obedience; therefore it included a promise of life upon man's maintaining his integrity. Had Adam been given no such promise, he would have been without a well-grounded hope for the future, for the hope which "maketh not ashamed" is always grounded on the divine promise (Rom. 4:18-20). Finally, Romans 7:10 expressly states that the commandment was "to life"—adapted to life, and setting before its complier such a prospect.

A few words need to be said here on the nature of that "life" which was promised Adam. In his original state he was already possessed of spiritual life. What then did the reward consist of? Two different answers have been given by the best of theologians. First, that it was the *ratifying* of the life which he then had. Adam was placed on probation, and his response to the test would determine whether or not he remained in the favor of God, in communion with Him, and continuing to enjoy his earthly heritage. Adam's conduct would decide whether these conditions would be confirmed and then become the inalienable portion of both himself and his posterity. The second solution is that the "life" promised Adam connotes a yet higher degree of happiness than he then possessed, even heavenly blessedness. Those benefits which Christ came into the world to procure for His people, and which are assured for them by the covenant of grace, are the same in substance as those which man would have enjoyed had he not fallen. This, we consider, is clear from these prophetic words: "I restored that which I took not away" (Ps. 69:4). "The Son of man is come to seek and to save that which was lost" (Luke 19:10). Christ came to secure "eternal life" (with all that that means), therefore that would have been man's portion had he maintained his integrity.

This fact may also be concluded from the nature of that "death" declared in Genesis 2:17. When God said, "In the day that thou eatest thereof thou shalt surely *die*," something far more dreadful than the loss of physical or even spiritual life was involved, namely, the "second death," eternal punishment and suffering in the lake of fire. Conversely, the promised "life" included more than physical immortality or even the confirmation of spiritual life, namely, everlasting life, or unclouded fellowship with God in heaven forever. We agree with many able expositors that Romans 8:3-4 treats of the same thing. "The law" there looks back to that which was written on man's heart at the beginning, of which the Sinaitic law was merely a transcript. The statement that the law was "weak through the flesh" alludes to Adam's tendency to error. What the law "could not do" with such material was to produce an indestructible righteousness. Therefore God in His sovereign grace sent His own incarnate Son, impeccable and immutable, to make full atonement for the guilt of His people and to bring in an "everlasting righteousness" (Dan. 9:24) for them. Christ performed that perfect obedience which the first man failed to render, and thereby obtained for all His seed the award of the fulfilled law.

This point should remove any misconception that the view propounded detracts in the slightest degree from the glory of the Saviour. Romans 8:3-4 is treating of something far more essential and weighty than whether or not Christ by His infinite merits obtained for us something more than we lost in Adam. Undoubtedly He did: our establishment in righteousness, our glorification, and much more. Rather that passage intimates the highest motive and ultimate end which God had before Him when He foresaw, foreordained and permitted our fall in Adam. Christ is the grand center of all the divine counsels, and the magnifying of Him is their principal design. Had God kept Adam from sinning, all his race would have been eternally happy. But in that case Adam would have been their savior and benefactor, and all his seed would have gloried in *him,* ascribing their everlasting blessedness to his obedience. But such an honor was far too much for any finite creature to bear. Only the Lord from heaven was worthy of it. Accordingly God designedly made the flesh of the first man "weak" or mutable and allowed his defection in order to make way for His laying our help "upon one that is *mighty*" (Ps. 89:19), that we might owe our endless bliss to Him. Moreover, that obedience which Christ rendered to the law magnified it and made it infinitely more honorable than any mere creature's conformity could have made it.

Further scriptural evidence that God entered into a covenant with Adam is found in Hosea 6:7, where God complained of Israel, "But they *like Adam* have transgressed the covenant: there have they dealt treacherously against me." The Hebrew word for "men" there is *Adam,* as in Job 31:33. Adam was placed under a covenant, the requirement or condition of which was his continued subjection to God—whether or not the divine will was sacred in his eyes. But he failed to love God with all his heart, held His high authority in contempt, disbelieved His holy veracity, deliberately and presumptuously defied Him. He "transgressed the covenant" and "dealt treacherously" with his Maker. Centuries later Israel likewise transgressed the covenant which they entered into with the Lord at Sinai, preferring their own will and way, lusting after those false gods which He had forbidden under pain of death. Finally, the fact of Adam's having stood as the covenant head of his race is conclusively demonstrated by the penal evils which came upon his children in consequence of his fall. From the dreadful curse which entailed upon all his descendants, we are compelled to infer the covenant relationship which existed between him and them; for the Judge of all the earth, being righteous, will never punish where there is no crime. "In Adam all die" because in him all sinned.

Having proved from Scripture that God appointed Adam as covenant head and federal representative of his race, we are now to show that the guilt of his original sin was imputed to all his posterity. Even if there were no explicit statements to that effect in the Bible, we would be obliged to infer the fact, for such a conclusion is inevitable from the principles involved. If the one was acting in the name and on the behalf of many, then the latter are legally responsible for what he did and must suffer the consequences of his conduct, good or evil. Had Adam survived the test to which he was subjected, had he remained obedient to his Maker and Lord, then his obedience would have been reckoned to the account of all his seed, and they would have been joint partakers of his reward. But if he revolted from the divine government and preferred his own will and way, then the punishment he incurred must be visited also upon the whole of his constituency. Such a procedure is neither merciful nor unmerciful, but a matter of righteousness. Justice requires that the penalty of a broken law shall be visited upon its transgressors. A precept without penalty is simply advice or, at most, a request; and compliance is merely a species of self-pleasing, not submission to authority. To divest the divine law of its sanction would be to reduce God to a mere supplicant—begging His creatures to behave themselves.

Not only had God the sovereign right to constitute Adam the covenant head of his race; not only was it strictly just and legal that its members should be held accountable for what he did, whether it issued in their well-being or distress; but such an arrangement was fully valid. Since the loyalty and subjection of man to his Maker must be put to the proof, only two alternatives were possible: either the human race must be placed on probation in the person of a suitable representative and responsible head, or each individual member must enter upon probation for himself. G. S. Bishop stated it thus:

> The race must either have stood in full-grown man, with a full-orbed intellect, or stood as babies, each entering his probation in the twilight of self-consciousness, each deciding his destiny before his eyes were half-opened to what it all meant. How much better would that have been? How much more just? But could it not have been some other way? There was no other way. It was either the baby, or it was the perfect, well-equipped, all-calculating man—the man who saw and comprehended everything. That man was Adam.

Fresh from the hands of his Creator, with no sinful heredity behind and no depraved nature within him, but instead endowed with holiness and indwelt by the Spirit of God, Adam was well equipped for the honorable position assigned him. His fitness to serve as our head, and the ideal circumstances under which the decisive test was made, must forever close every honest mouth from objecting against the divine arrangement and the fearful consequences which Adam's failure has brought down upon us. We again quote Bishop:

> Had we been present, had we and all the human race been brought into existence at once, and had God proposed to us that we should choose one who was to be our representative, that He might enter into covenant with him on our behalf—should not we, with one voice, have chosen our first parent for this responsible office? Should we not have said, "He is a perfect man and bears the image and likeness of God—if anyone is to stand for us, let it be this man Adam"? Since the angels which stood for themselves fell, why should we wish to stand for ourselves? And if it be reasonable

that one stands for us, why should we complain when God has chosen the same person for this office that we should have chosen had we been in existence and capable of choosing ourselves?

Before proceeding further, it is essential that we realize that God is in no way to blame for Adam's fall. After a thorough and extensive investigation Solomon declared, "This only have I found, that God hath made man upright; but they have sought out many inventions" (Eccles. 7:29). There the streams of human foolishness and sin are all traced back to their fountainhead of corruption. Man was created without irregularity or blemish; but he departed from his original integrity. And why? Because he vainly supposed he could better himself. Adam and Eve at first, followed by their crazed descendants, "sought out many inventions." Significant and suggestive words! What are inventions but devices to improve things? And what gives rise to such attempts but dissatisfaction with present conditions? Our first parents meant to find a superior way of happiness by kicking off their traces. Instead of being content with what their Maker had given and appointed them, they preferred their own will to God's, their inventions rather than His institutions. They relinquished their rest in the Lord and tried to improve their situation. They promised themselves liberty, only to become the slaves of Satan.

The course taken by our first parents has been followed ever since by all their children, as is intimated in the change from the singular number to the plural in Ecclesiastes 7:29. As indicated above, we do not regard the prime reference in that passage as being to the "aprons of fig leaves" which Adam and Eve sewed together, but rather to their original sin in being dissatisfied with the state in which God had placed them, vainly hoping to improve their lot by leaning to their own understanding, following the desires of their hearts, and responding to the evil solicitation of the serpent. Thus it has been, and still is, with their descendants. They have turned from the Creator to the creature for their comfort. Having forsaken the living fountain, they engage themselves in hewing out "cisterns, that can hold no water" (Jer. 2:13), preferring the "far country" to the Father's house. Their search after wisdom, their mad quest for pleasure, their pursuit of wealth and worldly honors, are but so many "inventions" or attempts to better their lot, and proofs of a restless and dissatisfied heart. Had our first parents been content with the good heritage their Maker assigned them, they would not have coveted that which He had prohibited. Still today the remedy for covetousness is contentment (see Heb. 13:5).

We subscribe unhesitatingly to this assertion of Calvin: "It is clear that the misery of man must be ascribed wholly to himself, since he was favoured with rectitude by the Divine goodness, but has lapsed into vanity through his own folly." God expressly forbade Adam to eat of the tree of knowledge of good and evil. He plainly told him what would be the consequence of disobedience. God made man a mutable creature, yet not evil. Adam had ability to stand as well as to fall. He was fully capable of loving God as his chief good and of moving toward Him as his last end. There was light in his understanding to know the rule he was to conform to. There was perfect harmony between his reason and his affections. It was therefore easier for him to continue in obedience to the precept than to swerve from it. Though man was created as capable of failing, yet he was not determined by God's influencing his will, by any positive act, to apostasy. God did not induce him, but allowed him to act freely. He did not withdraw any grace from him, but left him to that power with which He invested him at his creation. Nor was God under any obligation to sustain him supernaturally or withhold him from sinning. God created Adam in a righteous state, but he deliberately cast himself and his posterity into a dismal state.

Mankind Guilty in Adam

Adam took things into his own hands, revolted from God and trampled His law beneath his feet. It behooves us to study the relation between Adam's action and the universal miseries consequent on it, for it supplies the clue to all the confusion which perplexes us within and without. It tells us why infants are estranged from God from the womb (Ps. 58:3), and why each of us is born into this world with a heart that is deceitful above all things and desperately wicked (Jer. 17:9). It is because Adam forfeited his Maker's approbation and incurred His awful displeasure, with all its terrible effects. In Adam *we* broke the covenant of works; we offended in his offense and transgressed in his transgression; and thereby we departed from God's favor and fell under His righteous curse. Scott said: "Thus man apostatized, God was provoked, the Holy Spirit forsook His polluted temple, the unclean spirit took possession, the Divine image was defaced and Satan's image imposed in its place." Through the sin of its head the race was ruined and fell into a state of most horrible moral leprosy. Ours is a fallen world: averse to God and holiness, iniquity abounding in it, death reigning over it, lust and crime characterizing it, suffering and misery filling it.

Therefore it is written, "Wherefore, as by one man sin entered into the world, and death by sin; and so death passed upon all men, for that all have sinned" (Rom. 5:12). In the light of Genesis 3 that is a strange and startling statement, for that chapter makes it clear that Eve fell before Adam did. Why then is it not said, "by one woman," or at least "by one man and woman sin entered the world"? Because, as Thomas Goodwin long ago pointed out, "Moses tells us the history of Adam's fall, and Paul explains the mystery and the consequences thereof." In other words Romans 5 opens to us the significance and scope of the Eden tragedy. The opening word of verse 12 indicates that a logical proposition is there advanced, which is confirmed by the "as" and "so." The reason why no notice is taken of Eve is that throughout what follows, the apostle is treating of the condemnation of all mankind, not its debasement. That condemnation is due solely to our having revolted from God in the person of our legal representative, and since Adam alone sinned in that capacity, no mention is made of Eve. Headship always pertains to the man and not to the woman.

Before proceeding, let us consider the relation of this most important passage in Romans 5. In the preceding chapters Paul had dealt at length with the depravity and sinfulness of mankind (especially in 1:18-32; 3:10-20) and had declared that even Christians in their unregenerate days were ungodly, without strength, enemies to God (5:6, 10). Here he shows why they were so, Adam's offense being the cause and source. Second, he had refuted the proud but erroneous view of the Jews, who regarded themselves as holy because they were the seed of a holy father (2:17—3:9). Consequently they lacked a true estimate of their desperate condition by nature and practice, nor did they sense their dire need of divine grace. Here the apostle takes them back to a higher ancestor than Abraham—Adam, who was equally the father of Jew and Gentile, both alike sharing his guilt and inheriting his curse. Third, Paul had presented the grand doctrine of justification by faith (3:21-31) and had illustrated it by the cases of Abraham and David. Here he shows Adam was a "figure" of Christ (5:14), that the one sustained an analogous relation to his race as the other did to His seed, that each transacted as the one for the many, and that therefore the gospel principle of imputation (Christ's righteousness reckoned to the account of the believer) is no novelty, but identical with the principle on which God acted from the beginning.

Observe that it is not through but "by one man." But exactly what is meant by "*sin* entered the world"? Three explanations are possible. First, sin as an act of disobedience: rebellion against God began by one man. But Genesis 3 shows otherwise: transgression of God's law was initiated by Eve! Second, sin as a principle of depravity: by one man our sinful nature originated. This is the view generally taken. But it is equally untenable, for the corruption of our nature is as much by the mother as by the father. Moreover, if such were the force of "sin" in the first clause, then the closing one would necessarily read "for that all are sinful." Furthermore, verses 13 and 14 explain and furnish proof of what is asserted in verse 12, and it would be meaningless to say that a sinful nature is not imputed. Finally, all through this passage "sin" and "righteousness" are contrasted; and righteousness here is judicial and not experiential, something reckoned to our account and not infused into us. "Righteousness" in this passage signifies not a holy nature but conformity to the law's demands; therefore "sin" cannot be corruption of nature but rather the cause of our condemnation. Thus, third, by one man guilt entered into the world, exposing the race to God's wrath.

"By one man sin *entered*." Sin is here personified as an intruding enemy, coming as a solemn accuser as well as a hostile oppressor. It entered the world not the universe, for Satan had previously apostatized. "And *death* by sin," which is not to be limited to mere physical dissolution, but must be understood as the penal consequence of Adam's offense. All through this passage death is opposed to life, and life includes very much more than physical existence or even immortality of soul. When God told Adam, "In the day that thou eatest thereof thou shalt surely die," He signified, first, to die *spiritually*, that is, to be alienated from the source of divine life. Second, in due course, to die *physically*: the body shall go to corruption and return to the dust. Third, to die *eternally*, to suffer "the second death" (Rev. 20:14), to be cast into the lake of fire, there to suffer forever.

"And so death *passed upon* all men" because of their complicity in the one man's sin. Not that death as a principle of evil gained admittance and polluted the nature of Adam's offspring, but that the penal sentence of death was pronounced upon them. Having been charged with his transgression they must suffer its consequence. The apostle's design was to show the connection between the one man's sin and the resultant misery of the many. By Adam's disobedience all men were constituted sinners—guilty criminals before God—and therefore sharers of the sentence passed on Adam. "In Adam all die" (I Cor. 15:22). Those words explain the clause "by man came death" of the preceding verse, and show that all die by virtue of their relation to the covenant head of our race—die because of their legal union with him. Even physical death is far more than "nature's debt," or the inevitable outcome of our frail constitution: it is a penal affliction, a part of sin's "wages." We are subject to mortality because we were "in Adam" by federal representation—we share his fallen nature because we share in his guilt and punishment. We are born into this world neither as innocent creatures nor to enter upon our probation. Rather we come into it as culprits condemned to death by the divine law.

Every man, woman and child is judged guilty before God. The ground of our condemnation is something outside ourselves. Inward corruption and alienation from God are the consequence and not the cause of our condemnation. Antecedent to any personal act of ours (as such), we stand accursed by the divine law. Since "death" came as the result of "sin" because it is the penal sentence on it, that sentence cannot be passed on any except those who are guilty. If, then, death was "passed upon *all* men," it must be because all are guilty, all participated legally in Adam's offense. Clear and inevitable as is that inference, we are not left to draw it ourselves. The apostle expressly states it in the next words: "for that all have sinned"—"for that" meaning "because," or "in consequence of." Here then is the divinely given reason why the death penalty is passed on "all men": "all have sinned," or, as the margin and the Revised Version more accurately render it, "in whom all sinned." The apostle is not here saying that all men sinned personally, but representatively. The Greek verb for "sinned" is in the aorist tense, which always looks back to a past action which has terminated. The curse of the law falls on us not because we are sinful, but because we were federally guilty when our covenant head sinned.

In Romans 5:12 the apostle was not referring to the corrupting of mankind. It is true that as a result of our first parents' sin the springs of human nature were polluted; but this is not what Paul was writing of. Instead he went behind that, and dealt with the cause of which moral depravity is just one of the effects. A corrupt tree can indeed produce nothing but corrupt fruit, but why are we born with corrupt hearts? This is more than a terrible calamity: it is a penal infliction visited on us because of our prior criminality. Punishment presupposes guilt, and the punishment is given to all because *all* are guilty; and since God regards all as guilty, then they must be participants in Adam's offense. George Whitefield put it well:

> I beg leave to express my surprise that any person of judgment should maintain human depravity, and not immediately discover its necessary connection with the imputation, and how impossible it is to secure the justice of God without having recourse to it; for certainly the corruption of human nature, so universal and inseparable, is one of the greatest punishments that could be inflicted upon the species. . . . Now if God has inflicted an evident punishment upon a race of men perfectly innocent, which had neither sinned personally nor yet by imputation [He would be unjust]; and thus while we imagine we honour the justice of God by renouncing imputation, we in fact pour the highest dishonour upon that sacred attribute.

Death, penal death, has been passed on all men because all sinned in Adam. That "all have sinned" cannot signify all men's own personal transgressions is clear because the manifest design of Romans 5:12 is to show that *Adam's sin* is the cause of death; because physical death (a part of sin's wages) is far more extensive than personal transgression—as appears from so many dying in infancy; and because such an interpretation would destroy the analogy between Adam and the One of whom he was "the figure," and would lead to this comparison: As men die because they sin personally, so all earn eternal life because they are personally righteous! It is equally evident that "all have sinned" cannot mean that death comes upon men because they are depraved, for this too would clash with the scope of the whole passage. If our subjective sinfulness were the ground of our condemnation, then our subjective holiness (and not Christ's merits) would be the ground of our justification. It would also contradict the emphatic assertion of verse 18: "By the offence of one judgment came upon all men to condemnation." Thus we are obliged to understand the "all have sinned" of verse 12 as meaning all sinned in Adam.

If the federal headship of Adam and the imputation of his sin to all his posterity are repudiated, then what alternative is left us? Only that of the separate testing of each individual. If the race was not placed on probation in the first man, then each of his offspring must stand trial for himself. But the conditions of such a trial make success impossible, for each probationer would enter it in a state of spiritual death! The human family is either suffering for the sin of its head or it is suffering for nothing at all. "Man is born unto trouble," and from it there is no escape. What then is the explanation of the grim tragedy now being enacted on this earth? Every effect must have a previous cause. If we are not born under the condemnation of Adam's offense, then why are we "by nature the children of wrath" (Eph.

2:3)? Either man was tried and fell in Adam, or he has been condemned without trial. He is either under the curse (as it rests on him from the beginning of his existence) for Adam's guilt, or for no guilt at all. Judge which is more honoring to God: a doctrine which, although profoundly mysterious, represents God as giving man an equitable and most favorable probation in his federal head, or one which makes God condemn man untried, even before he exists.

Examine the verses which immediately follow Romans 5:12. They are not only of deep importance in connection with the present aspect of our subject, but their meaning is little apprehended today, for they receive scarcely any notice either in the pulpit or in the religious press. In Romans 5:13-14 the apostle takes no notice of our personal transgressions, but shows the effects of Adam's sin. In these verses Paul intimates that the universality of physical death can only be satisfactorily accounted for on the ground that it is a penal infliction because of the first man's offense. The argument of verse 13 is as follows: The infliction of a penalty presupposes the violation of a law, for death is the wages of sin. The violation of the Mosaic law does not account for the universality of death, because multitudes died before that law was given. Therefore as death implies transgression, and the law of Moses does not explain all of death's victims, it clearly and necessarily follows that the whole human race is subject to the penal consequence of the primordial law being transgressed by their first father.

"For until the law sin was in the world" (v. 13). The opening "for" indicates that the apostle is now about to furnish proof of the assertion made in verse 12. "The law" here has reference to the Mosaic law. "Sin," as all through this passage, signifies guilt on the judicial ground of condemnation, and not the corruption of human nature. "The world" includes the entire race: all were accursed, and are so regarded and treated by the Judge of all the earth. Having stated in verse 12 that all mankind participated in Adam's original sin, and that in consequence all share in its punishment, Paul pauses to vindicate and amplify his assertion that "all sinned in" Adam. The method he follows is by reasoning backward from effect to cause. The argument is somewhat involved and calls for close attention, yet there is no difficulty in following its course if we perceive that it moves back from death to sin, and from sin to law—the one being necessarily implied by the other. Sin was in the world before the law of Moses was given, as was evident from the fact that death held universal sway from Eden to Sinai. Note the oft-repeated "and he died" in Genesis 5. Thus far the argument is simple, but the next point is more difficult.

"But sin is not imputed when there is no law" (Rom. 5:13). The meaning of this clause has been missed by many, through failing to follow the course of the apostle's reasoning. They have imagined it signifies that, though sin was in the world prior to Moses, it was not reckoned to the account of those who were guilty. Such an idea is not only erroneous but absurd. Where sin exists the holy One must deal with it *as* sin. And He did so from earliest times, as the flood demonstrated. "Sin is not imputed when there is no law." Why? Because sin or guilt is the correlative of law. Sin or condemnation implies the law: one cannot be without the other. "Sin is the transgression of the law" (I John 3:4). No one is guilty where no law exists, for criminality presupposes the violation of a statute. Thus, for any to be judged guilty is the same thing as saying he has broken the law. This prepares us for Romans 5:14, proof that a law given previously to Moses had been violated, and consequently God dealt with the violators as sinners long before the time of Moses.

Read the verse. "Nevertheless death reigned from Adam to Moses." Though it is true that there is no sin where there is no law, and that where there is no law transgressed there can be no death, yet it is a divinely certified fact that death reigned during the first twenty-five centuries of human history. The conclusion is so self-evident that Paul leaves his readers to draw it: The human race must have transgressed an earlier law than the Mosaic. Thus verse 14 clinches the interpretation we have given of verses 12 and 13. Since men died prior to the Sinaitic transaction, there must be some other reason and ground for their exposure to death. Note that "death *reigned*"; it held undisputed and rightful sway. If then men were justly subject to its power they must have been guilty. Death is far more than a calamity: it is a punishment, and that indicates the breaking of a law. If men were punished with death from the beginning, it inevitably follows that they were lawbreakers from the beginning. Moreover, death furnished proof that sin was imputed: men were guilty of Adam's offense.

"Even over them that had not sinned after the similitude of Adam's transgression" refers to those who in their own persons and conduct had never violated any law by which their exposure to death could be accounted for. The word "even" here suggests a contrast. Generally speaking, death had reigned from Adam to Moses over all alike; but it did so even over a class who had not (in their own persons) sinned as Adam had. If we bear in mind that in verses 13 and 14 Paul is proving his assertion (at the end of verse 12) that death comes on all because of the first man's sin, then his line of reasoning is easier to follow. The word "even" here implies that there was a particular class who it *appears* ought to have been exempted from the dominion of sin, namely, infants. Thus the death of infants supplied conclusive proof of the doctrine here taught. Physical death is a penal infliction; falling as it does on infants, it must be because of Adam's sin. On no other ground can their dying be accounted for. They furnish the prime demonstration that all sinned in Adam and suffer the consequences of his wrong.

At the close of verse 14 the apostle states that Adam was "the figure of him that was to come." He foreshadowed Christ as the federal Head and legal Representative of His people. In verses 15-17 it is pointed out that there were contrasts as well as resemblances between the first man and Christ. "But not as the offence, so also is the free gift" (15*a*). The fall differed radically from the restoration. Though they are alike in their far-reaching effects they are quite unlike in the nature of those effects. "For if through the offence of one many be dead ['many died,' legally]" (15*b*). The "many" includes infants, and the fact that they die because of the one man's offense proves that they are judged guilty of it, and that God imputed it to them, for He never punishes where there is no sin.

"Much more the grace of God, and the gift by grace, which is by one man, Jesus Christ, hath abounded unto many" (15*c*). Here the first contrast is drawn—between justice and grace. The "much more" does not mean numerically, as Christ cannot restore more than Adam ruined, for he encompassed the downfall of all his posterity. Nor does this "much more" signify that grace is more abundant and efficacious than the sin in its effects; *that* is brought out in verse 20. No, it is used argumentatively, as a logical inference and as a note of certainty. If God willed it that one man should ruin many, much more can we suppose it to be agreeable that His Son should rescue many. If many suffer from the offense of Adam, much more should we expect that many will benefit from the merits of Christ. Thus it is not a "much more" either of quantity or quality, but of assurance and certainty. If it was arranged in the divine government that the principle of representation should operate though it entailed the curse, much more may we look for that principle to operate in producing blessing. If Scripture teaches the imputation of sin, we should not stumble when we find it affirming the imputation of righteousness. If God dealt in inflexible justice with the original sin, then, from all we know of Him, much more may we look for a display of the riches of His grace through Christ.

Christ as Man's Restorer

"And not as it was by one that sinned, so is the gift: for the judgment was by one to condemnation, but the free gift is of many offences unto justification" (v. 16). Here the second contrast is drawn. Though there is a close resemblance between ruin and redemption, in that each was accomplished by one man, yet there is a great difference between the scope of their respective effects. The destroying power of the former did not go beyond the one sin of Adam, whereas the restoring power of the latter covers our countless iniquities. How vastly more extensive then is the reach of the free gift! This verse explains itself, the second clause interpreting the first. The divine sentence of condemnation fell on the entire human family because of the single deviation of their head, but believers are justified by Christ from many infractions: "having forgiven you *all* trespasses" (Col. 2:13). Christ does very much more than remove the guilt which came upon His people for the first man's sin. He has also made full satisfaction or atonement for all their personal sins: "Who gave himself for us, that he might redeem us from all iniquity" (Titus 2:14).

"For the judgment was by one to condemnation." Each term needs to be carefully weighed. The word "judgment" obviously signifies a judicial sentence—pronounced by God—"to condemnation" and *not* to corruption or destruction of nature. The judgment "was by one"—not here by one man, but rather by one sin, for it is set over against the "many offences" which we have personally committed. It is expressly asserted that judgment came by Adam's initial transgression, and if all are condemned for that sin then all must be counted guilty of it, for the righteous Judge will not condemn the innocent. "But the free gift is of many offenses unto justification." Where sin abounded grace abounded much more. The finished work of Christ not only provides for the cancellation of original sin, but acquits from the accumulated guilt of all our sins. Moreover, believers in Christ are not merely pardoned but justified—exonerated, pronounced righteous by the law. They are not only restored to their unfallen state, but given a title to enjoy the full reward of Christ's obedience. As Adam's posterity participate in his guilt, depravity and death, so Christ's seed receive through Him righteousness, holiness and eternal life.

"For if by one man's offence death reigned by one [if by the offense of the one man death reigned]; much more they which receive abundance of grace and of the gift of righteousness shall reign in life by one, Jesus Christ" (v. 17). Here is the third contrast: death and life, issuing from the two heads. Here the central truth of the whole passage is reiterated: Death comes to men not because their natures have been corrupted, nor because of their own personal transgression, but as a judicial sentence passed on account of Adam's crime. It expressly states that death reigned "by [because of] the one man's offence," and therefore everyone over whom death has dominion must be regarded as guilty. The word "reigned" here is very impressive and emphatic. Those who die are looked upon as death's lawful subjects, for it is regarded as their king. In other words, death has a legal claim on all men. The forceful language of Hebrews 2:14-15 contains the same concept: ". . . that through death he [Christ] might destroy him that had the power [authority] of death, that is, the devil; and deliver them [free death's lawful prisoners]." Note how this passage indirectly confirms Romans 5:14 which shows that death could have no dominion over infants unless they were charged with Adam's sin.

"Much more they which receive abundance of grace." The "much more" of this verse emphasizes a different thought from that of verse 15. There it refers to God's dealing with Adam and his posterity consistently with His own perfections. If God could righteously condemn all mankind because of the disobedience of their first parent, much more could He justify the seed of Christ (Isa. 53:10) on the ground of the obedience of their Representative. But here the phrase has reference to the *modus operandi* of condemnation and justification. If death has come upon us as a judicial infliction for an offense in which we did not actively participate, then much more shall we share the reward of Christ's righteousness which we voluntarily receive by faith. There is a double thought conveyed by "the gift of righteousness," which it is important to observe, for most of the commentators have missed the second. First, it signifies that righteousness is entirely gratuitous, neither earned nor merited. Second, it implies that it is imputed, for a gift is something transferred from one person to another. Not only pointless but senseless is the objection that if righteousness were transferred from Christ to us it would leave Him without any. Does God's gift of life to sinners leave Him without any?

"Shall reign in life by one, Jesus Christ." They who by faith receive the gift of His righteousness are not only saved from the consequences of the fall, but are partakers of eternal life and made joint heirs with Christ and sharers of His celestial glory. They who have been wholly under the power of death are not only completely freed from it and spiritually quickened, but as one with the King of kings they are made "kings . . . unto God" (Rev. 1:6). They are not reinstated in the earthly paradise, but shall be brought to honor and glory and immortality in heaven—given title to a state of eternal and supernal blessedness. The careful student observes both a threefold comparison and a threefold contrast between the first and last Adams in verses 15-17. Both are sources of radical influence: "abounded unto many" (15c). Both are conveyers of a judicial sentence: condemnation, justification (16). Both introduce a sovereign regime: "death reigned," "reign in life" (17). But by Adam we lost, whereas in Christ we gain. We were charged with the one offense, but are cleared from many. We were the subjects of death, but are made coheirs with Christ. By Adam we were ruined; by Christ we are more than restored. In Adam we occupied a position a little lower than the angels; in Christ we are established far above all principality and power.

"Therefore as by the offence of one judgment came upon all men to condemnation; even so by the righteousness of one the free gift came upon all men unto justification of life" (18). In verse 12 only the first member of the contrast was given (vv. 13-17 interrupting as a necessary parenthesis), but here the case is stated in full. Throughout the whole passage Paul contrasts the states of divine wrath and divine favor, and not the states of depravity and holiness. He plainly asserts that all are condemned for Adam's sin. Infants are therefore included, for they would not be punished if innocent—if Adam's sin was not legally theirs. In precisely the same way all for whom Christ acted as their covenant Head are justified by His merits being legally reckoned to their account. As something outside ourselves is the judicial ground of our falling under the divine curse, so something outside ourselves is the judicial ground of our being under the blessing of God. The second half of this verse speaks not of something which is provided for all mankind, but of that which God actually imputes to all believers (cf. 4:20-24).

"For as by one man's disobedience many were made sinners, so by the obedience of one shall many be made righteous" (5:19). This goes farther than the preceding verse. There the causes of condemnation and justification were stated; here their actual issue or results are given. From verse 11 on the apostle has shown that God's sentence is grounded upon the legally constituted unity of all men with their covenant heads. By the first Adam's breaking of the divine law all who were federally one with him were made sinners. And all who were federally one with the last Adam are made righteous. The Greek word for "made" (*kathistēmi*) never signifies to effect any change in a person or thing, but means "to ordain, appoint," "to constitute" legally or officially (cf. Matt. 24:45, 47; Luke 12:14; Acts 7:10, 27). Note that Paul does not here state that Adam's disobedience makes us unholy. He goes further back and explains why this should follow, namely, because we are first constituted sinners by imputation.

Romans 5:12-21 is one of the most important passages in the Bible. In it the fundamental doctrine of federal representation is openly stated, and the fact of imputation is emphatically affirmed. Here is revealed the basic principle according to which God deals with men. Here we see the old and the new races receiving from their respective heads. Here are the two central figures and facts of all history: the first Adam and his disobedience, the last Adam and His obedience. Upon those two things the apostle hammered again and again with almost monotonous repetition. Why such unusual reiteration? Because of the great doctrinal importance of what is here dealt with; because the purity of the gospel and the glory of Christ's atonement pivoted on these points; because Paul was insisting on that which is so repulsive to the proud heart of fallen man. Plain as is its language, this passage has been wrested and twisted to mean many things which it does not teach; and Socinians, Universalists and others refuse to accept what is so plainly asserted.

Wherever this passage has been plainly expounded, it has in all generations encountered the fiercest opposition—not the least from men professing to be Christians. The doctrine of imputation is as bitterly hated as those of unconditional election and eternal punishment. Those who teach it are accused of representing God as dealing unjustly. What do the Scriptures say about it? As we have seen, Romans 5 declares that death has come upon all men because all sinned in Adam (v. 12), that "through the offence of one many be dead" (15), that "the judgment was by one to condemnation" (16), that "by one man's offence death reigned" (17), that "by the offence of one judgment came upon all men to condemnation" (18), that "by one man's disobedience many were made sinners" (19). "In Adam all die" (I Cor. 15:22). God deals with men on the principle of imputation. The sins of the fathers implicate the children (Exodus 20:5). The curse of Canaan fell on all his posterity (Gen. 9:25). The Egyptians perished for Pharaoh's obduracy. Achan's whole family died for his crime (Joshua 7:24). All Israel suffered for David's sin (II Sam. 24:15-17). The leprosy visited upon Gehazi passed to all his seed forever (II Kings 5:27). The blood of all the prophets was exacted of the members of Christ's generation (Luke 11:50).

If there is one word which fitly expresses what every man is by nature, it is "sinner." Waiving all theological systems, if we ask the popular meaning of that term, the answer is "One who has sinned," one who makes a practice of sinning. But such a definition comes far short of the scriptural import of the word. "By the disobedience of *one* many were made sinners." They are sinners, made so legally, neither because of what they have done personally nor by what they are in the habit of doing, but rather by the action of their first parent. It is quite true that it is the nature of sinners to sin, but according to the unmistakable testimony of Romans 5 we all are sinners *antecedent to* and independent of any personal transgressing of God's law. By the offense of Adam we were legally constituted sinners. The universal reign of death is proof of the universal power of sin. Yet death must not be represented as the consequence of individual acts of disobedience, for death reigns over infants, who are incapable of acts of disobedience. Human probation ended with the original sin; in consequence, not only was human nature vitiated at its fountainhead, but all of Adam's descendants fell under the curse of God, the guilt of his transgression being imputed to them.

No finite creature—still less a fallen and depraved one—is capable of measuring or even understanding the justice of the infinite God. Yet which appears to be more consonant with human conceptions of justice—that we should suffer through Adam because we were legally connected with him and he transacted in our name; or that we should suffer solely because we derive our nature from him by generation, though we had no part in or connection with his sin? In the former we can perceive the ground on which his guilt is charged to our account; but in the latter we can discover no ground or cause that any share of the fatal effects of Adam's sin should be visited on us. The latter alternative means that we are depraved and wretched without any sufficient reason, and in such an event our present condition is simply a misfortune and in no way criminal. Nor is God to be blamed. He made man upright, but man deliberately apostatized. Nor was God under any obligation to preserve man from falling. Our salvation depends upon the same principle and fact: If we were cursed and ruined by the first Adam's disobedience we are redeemed and blessed by the last Adam's obedience.

Chapter 4

CONSEQUENCES

THE KEY TO THE MYSTERY of human depravity is to be found in a right understanding of the relations which God appointed between the first man and his posterity. As the grand truth of redemption cannot be rightly and intelligently apprehended until we perceive the close connection which God ordained between the Redeemer and the redeemed, neither can the tragedy of man's ruin be contemplated in its proper perspective unless we view it in the light of Adam's apostasy from his Creator. He was the prototype of all humanity. As he stood for the whole human race, in him God dealt with all who should issue from him. Had not Adam been our covenant head and federal representative, the mere circumstance that he was our first parent would not have involved us in the legal consequences of his sin. Nor would it have entitled us to the legal reward of his righteousness had he maintained his integrity and served his probation by giving his Maker and Lord that obedience which was His due and which he was fully capacitated to perform. The divinely constituted tie (connecting principle) and oneness of the first man with all mankind in the sight of the law explains the latter's participation in the penalty visited on the former.

Consequences for Adam

We have dwelt at some length on the origin of human depravity and the divine imputation of the guilt of Adam's transgression to all his descendants. We now consider the consequences entailed by the fall. Abominable indeed is sin, fearful are the wages it earns, dreadful are the effects it has produced. In sin's consequences we are shown the holy One's estimate of sin, the severity of His punishment expressing His hatred of it. Conversely the terrible doom of Adam makes evident the enormity of his offense. That offense is not to be measured by the external act of eating the fruit, but by the awful affront which was made against God's majesty. In his single sin there was a complication of many crimes. There was base ingratitude against the One who had so richly endowed him, and discontent with the good heritage allotted him. There was a disbelief of the holy veracity of God, a doubting of His word and a believing of the serpent's lie. There was a repudiation of the infinite obligations he was under to love and serve his Maker, a preferring of his own will and way. There was a contempt of God's high authority, a breaking of

His covenant, a defiance of His solemn threat. The curse of heaven fell upon him because he deliberately and presumptuously defied the Almighty.

Very much more was included and involved in Adam's transgression than is commonly supposed or recognized. Three hundred years ago that profound theologian James Ussher pointed out that wrapped up in it was "the breach of the whole Law of God." Summarizing in our own language what the Bishop of Armagh developed at length, Adam's violation of all the Ten Commandments of the moral law may be set forth thus: He broke the first commandment by choosing another "god" when he followed the counsel of Satan. The second, in idolizing his palate, making a god of his belly by eating the forbidden fruit. The third, by not believing God's threatening, in that way taking His name in vain. The fourth, by breaking the sinless rest in which he had been placed. The fifth, by thus dishonoring his Father in heaven. The sixth, by bringing death on himself and all his posterity. The seventh, by committing spiritual adultery, and preferring the creature above the Creator. The eighth, by laying hands upon that to which he had no right. The ninth, by accepting the serpent's false witness against God. The tenth, by coveting that which God had not given to him.

We by no means share the popular idea that the Lord *saved Adam* very soon after his fall; rather we take decided exception to that theory. We cannot find anything whatever in Holy Writ on which to base such a belief; in fact, we find much to the contrary. First it is clear that Adam's sin was not one of infirmity, but instead a presumptuous one, pertaining to that class of willful sins and open defiance of God for which no sacrifice was provided (Exodus 21:14; Num. 15:30-31; Deut. 17:12; Heb. 10:26-29), and which was therefore an unpardonable sin. There is not the slightest sign that he ever repented of his sin, nor any record of his confessing it to God. On the contrary, when charged with it, he attempted to excuse and extenuate it. Genesis 3 closes with the awful statement "So he *drove out* the man." Nothing whatever is mentioned to Adam's credit afterward: no offering of sacrifice, no acts of faith or obedience. Instead we are merely told that he knew his wife (4:1, 25), begat a son in his own likeness, and died (5:3-5). If the reader can see in those statements any intimation or indication that Adam was a regenerated man, then he has much better eyes than the writer—or possibly a more lively imagination.

Nor is there a single word in Adam's favor in later scriptures; rather is everything to his condemnation. Job denied that he covered his transgressions or hid his iniquity in his bosom "as Adam" did (31:33). The psalmist declared that those who judged unjustly and accepted the persons of the wicked should die like Adam (82:7), for the Hebrew word there rendered "men" is *Adam*. In the New Testament he is contrasted in considerable detail with Christ (Rom. 5:12, 21; I Cor. 15:22, 45-47); and if he were saved, then the antithesis would fail at its principal point. Moreover, such an anomaly—that the great majority of those whom he represented should eternally perish, while the responsible head should be recovered—is quite out of keeping with what is revealed of God's justice. In I Timothy 2:14 specific mention is made of the fact that "Adam was not deceived," which emphasizes the enormity of his transgression. In Hebrews 11 the Holy Spirit has cited the faith of Old Testament saints, and though He mentions that of Abel, Enoch, Abraham, Isaac, Jacob and others, He says nothing about Adam's! His being omitted from that list is solemnly significant. After his being driven out of Eden, Scripture makes no mention of God having any further dealing with Adam!

Before taking up the consequences of Adam's defection upon his descendants, we will consider those consequences which fell immediately upon him and his guilty partner. These are recorded in Genesis 3. No sooner had Adam revolted from his gracious Maker and Benefactor than the evil effects became apparent. His understanding, originally enlightened with heavenly wisdom, became darkened and overcast with crass ignorance. His heart, formerly fired with holy veneration toward his Creator and warm with love to Him, now became alienated and filled with enmity against Him. His will, which had been in subjection to his rightful Governor, had cast off the yoke of obedience. His whole moral constitution was wrecked, had become unhinged, perverse. In a word, the life of God had departed from his soul. His aversion for the supremely excellent One appeared in his flight from Him as soon as he heard His approach. His crass ignorance and stupidity were evinced by his vain attempt to conceal himself from the eyes of Omniscience. His pride was displayed in refusing to acknowledge his guilt; his ingratitude, when he indirectly upbraided God for giving him a wife. But let us turn to the inspired account of these things.

"And the eyes of them both were opened, and they knew that they were naked" (Gen. 3:7). Very, very striking is this. We do not read of any change taking place when Eve partook of the forbidden fruit, but as soon as Adam did so "the eyes of them *both* were opened." This furnishes definite confirmation of our previous statement that Adam was the covenant head and legal representative of *his wife*, as well as of the future children which were to issue from them. Therefore the penalty for disobedience was not inflicted by God until the one to whom the prohibition had been made, violated the same, and then the consequences began to be immediately felt by both of them. But what is meant by "the eyes of them both were opened"? Certainly not their physical eyes, for those had previously been open. We have here another intimation that we must not slavishly limit ourselves to the literal meaning of all the terms used in this chapter. The answer, then, must be the "eyes" of their understanding; or, more strictly, those of their conscience—which sees or perceives, as well as hears, speaks and chastises. In that expression, "the eyes of them both were opened," is to be found the key to what follows.

The result of eating the forbidden fruit was not the acquisition of supernatural wisdom, as they fondly hoped, but a discovery that they had reduced themselves to a condition of wretchedness. They knew that they were "naked," and that in a sense very different from that mentioned in Genesis

2:25. Though in their original and glorious state they wore no material clothing, yet we do not believe for a moment that they were without any covering at all. Rather we agree with G. H. Bishop that they

> were not without effulgence shining from them and around them, which wrapped them in a radiant and translucent robe—and in a certain lovely way obscured their outlines. It is contrary to nature and it is repugnant to us that anything should be unclothed and absolutely bare. Each bird has its plumage and each animal its coat, and there is no beauty if the covering be removed. Strip the beautiful bird of its feathers, and, though the form remain unchanged, we no longer admire it. We conceive, then, that artists are wholly at fault and grossly offend against purity, when they paint the human form unclothed, and plead as an excuse the case of Adam in Eden. Could the animals in all their splendid covering coats have bowed down as the vice-regents of God (Gen. i, 28) before beings wholly unclothed? Should Adam, the crown and king of creation, be the only living thing without a screen? Impossible. To the spiritual sense there certainly is a hint of something about our first parents that impressed and overawed the animal creation. What was that thing? What, but that shining forth like the sun, which describes the body of the resurrection (Daniel xii, 3)? If the face of Moses so shone by reflection that the children of Israel were afraid to come nigh him, how much more must the [unimpeded] indwelling Spirit of God in Adam and Eve have flung around them a radiance which made all creation do them reverence at their approach—beholding in them the image and likeness of the Lord God Almighty—glorious in brightness—shining like a sun?

Supplementing the above, let it be pointed out that of the Lord God it is said: "Thou art clothed with honour and majesty: who coverest thyself with light as with a garment" (Ps. 104:1-2); and man was made, originally, in His image! God "crowned him with glory and honour," made him "to have dominion over the works of thy hands" (Ps. 8:5-6), and accordingly covered him with bright apparel, as will be the ultimate case of those recovered from the fall and its consequences, for "they are equal unto the angels" (Luke 20:36; cf. "two men stood by them in shining garments" [Luke 24:4]). Further, the implication of Romans 8:3 is irresistible: "God sending his own Son in the likeness of sinful flesh." Note how discriminating is that language: not merely in the likeness of the flesh, but literally "sin's flesh." Robert Haldane explained those words thus:

> If the flesh of Jesus Christ was the likeness of sinful flesh, there must be a difference between the *appearance* of sinful flesh and our nature or flesh in its original condition when Adam was created. Christ, then, was not made in the likeness of the flesh of man before sin entered the world, but in the likeness of his fallen flesh.

And since Christ *restored* that which He took not away (Ps. 69:4), then its resurrected state shows us its primitive glory (Phil. 3:21).

Following the statement "the eyes of them both were opened," we would naturally expect the next clause to read "and they *saw* that they were naked"; but instead it says, "they *knew* that they were naked"—something more than a discovery of their woeful physical plight. The Hebrew verb is rendered "know" in the vast majority of references, yet eighteen times it is translated "perceive" and three times "feel." As the opening of their eyes refers to the eyes of their understanding, so we are informed of what they now discerned, namely the loss of their innocence. There is nakedness of soul which is far worse than an unclothed body, for it unfits it for the presence of the holy One. The nakedness of Adam and Eve was the loss of the image of God, the inherent righteousness and holiness in which He created them. Such is the awful condition in which all of their descendants are born. That is why Christ bids them buy of Him "white raiment, that thou mayest be clothed, and that the shame of thy nakedness do not appear" (Rev. 3:18). The "white raiment" is "the robe of righteousness" (Isa. 61:10), the "wedding garment" of Matthew 22:11-13, without which the soul is eternally lost.

"They knew that they were naked." As Bishop expressed it, "Their halo had vanished, and the Spirit of righteousness who had been to them a covering of light and purity withdrew, and they felt that they were stripped and bare." But more; they realized that their physical condition mirrored their spiritual loss. They were made painfully conscious of sin and its dire consequences. This was the first result of their transgression: a guilty conscience condemned them, and a *sense of shame* possessed their souls. Their hearts smote them for what they had done. Now that the fearful deed of disobedience had been committed, they realized the happiness they had flung away and the misery into which they had plunged themselves. They knew that they were not only stripped of all the bliss and honor of paradise, but were defiled and degraded. Thus a sense of wretchedness possessed them. They knew that they were naked of everything that is holy. They might be rightly termed "Ichabod," for the glory of the Lord had departed from them. This is always the effect of sin; it destroys our peace, robs our joy and brings in its train a consciousness of guilt and a sense of shame.

There is, we believe, a yet deeper meaning in the words "they knew that they were naked," namely, a realization that they were exposed to the wrath of an offended God. They perceived that *their defense* was gone. They were morally naked, without any protection against the broken law! This is very striking and solemn. *Before* the Lord appeared to them, before He said a word or came near to them, Adam and Eve *knew* the dreadful state they were in, and were ashamed. Oh, the power of conscience! Our first parents stood self-accused and self-condemned. Before the Judge appeared on the scene, man became as it were the judge of his own fallen and woeful condition. Yes, they knew of themselves that they were disgraced, that their holiness was defiled, their innocence gone, the image of God in their souls broken, their tranquillity disrupted, their protection against the law removed. Stripped of their original righteousness, they stood defenseless. What a terrible discovery to make! Such is the state into which fallen man has come—one of which he himself is ashamed.

And what did the guilty pair do upon their painful discovery? How did they conduct themselves? Cry to God for mercy? Look to Him for a covering?

No indeed. Not even an awakened conscience moves its tormented possessor to turn to the Lord, though it *must* do its work before the sinner flies to Him for refuge. A lost soul needs something more than an active conscience to draw him to Christ. That is very evident from the case of the scribes and Pharisees in His very presence, for "being convicted by their own conscience, they *went out*" (John 8:9). Instead of a convicted conscience causing them to cast themselves at the feet of the Saviour, it resulted in their leaving Him! Nothing short of the Holy Spirit's quickening, enmity-subduing, heart-melting, faith-bestowing, will-impelling operations brings anyone into saving contact with the Lord Jesus. He does indeed wound before He applies the balm of Gilead, make use of the law to prepare the way for the gospel, break up the hard soil of the heart to make it receptive to the seed. But even a conscience aroused by Him, accusing the soul with a voice which cannot be stilled, will never of itself bring one into "the way of peace."

No, instead of going to God, Adam and Eve attempted by their own puny efforts to repair the damage they had done in themselves. "They sewed fig leaves together, and made themselves aprons." Here we see the second consequence of their sin: a worthless expedient, a futile attempt to *conceal their real character* and hide their shame from themselves and the other creatures. As others have pointed out, our first parents were more anxious to save face before each other than they were to seek the pardon of God. They sought to arm themselves against a feeling of shame and thereby quiet their accusing conscience. And thus it is with their children to this day. They are more afraid of being *detected* in sin than of *committing* it, and more concerned about appearing well before their fellowmen than about obtaining the approbation of God. The chief objective of the fallen sons of men is to quiet their guilty consciences and to stand well with their neighbors. Hence so many of the unregenerate assume the garb of religion.

"And they heard the voice of the LORD God walking in the garden in the cool of the day: and Adam and his wife hid themselves from the presence of the LORD God amongst the trees of the garden" (3:8). Here was the third consequence of their fall: *a dread of God*. Up to this point they had been concerned only with their own selves and their wretchedness, but now they had to reckon with another, their Judge. Apparently they did not see His form at this moment, but only heard His voice. This was to test them. But instead of welcoming such a sound, they were horrified and fled in terror. But where could they flee from His presence? "Can any hide himself in secret places that I shall not see him? saith the LORD" (Jer. 23:24). In the attempt of Adam and Eve to seclude themselves among the trees, we see how sin has turned man into an utter fool; for none but an imbecile would imagine that he could conceal himself from the eyes of Omniscience.

When Adam and Eve, by an act of willful transgression, broke the condition of the covenant under which they had been placed, they incurred the double guilt of disbelieving God's word and defying His will. Thereby they forfeited the promise of life and brought upon themselves the penalty of death. That one act of theirs completely changed their relation to God and, at the same time, reversed their feelings toward Him. They were no longer the objects of His favor, but instead the subjects of His wrath. As the effect of their sinfulness and the result of their spiritual death, the Lord God ceased to be the object of their love and confidence, and had become the object of their aversion and distrust. A sense of degradation and of God's displeasure filled them with fright and caused them to have awful enmity against Him. So swift and drastic was the change which sin produced in their relations and feelings toward their Maker that they were ashamed and afraid to appear before Him. As soon as they heard His voice in the garden, they fled in horror and terror, seeking to hide from Him among the trees. They dreaded to hear Him pronounce formal sentence of condemnation upon them, for they knew in themselves that they deserved it.

Each action of our first parents after the fall was emblematic and prophetic, for it predicted how their descendants too would conduct themselves. First, upon the discovery of their nakedness, or loss of their original purity and glory, they sewed themselves aprons of fig leaves in an attempt to preserve their self-respect and make themselves presentable to one another. Thus it is with the natural man the world over. By a variety of efforts he seeks to conceal his spiritual wretchedness, yet at best his religious exercises and altruistic performances are just things of time, and will not endure the test of eternity. Second, Adam and Eve tried to hide from the One they now feared and hated. So it is with their children. They are fallen and depraved; God is holy and righteous; and despite their self-manufactured coverings of crea- ture-respectability and piety, the very thought of a face-to-face meeting with their Sovereign renders the unregenerate uneasy. That is why the Bible is so much neglected—because in it *God* is heard speaking. That is why the theater is preferred to the prayer meeting. This is proof that all shared in the first sin and died in Adam, for all inherit his nature and perpetuate his conduct.

How clearly the actions of the guilty pair made evident the serpent's lie. The more closely verses 4 and 5 are scrutinized in the light of the immediate sequel, the more their falsity appears. The serpent had assured them, "Ye shall not surely die," yet they had done so spiritually; and now they fled in terror lest they lose their physical lives. He had declared that they would be advanced—for that was the evident force of his "your eyes shall be opened"; instead, they had been abased. He had promised that they would be increased in knowledge, whereas they had become so stupid as to entertain the idea that they could conceal themselves from the omniscient and omni- present One. He had said they should "be as gods," but here we see them as self-accused and trembling criminals. We do well to bear in mind the Lord's pronouncement concerning the devil: "He is a liar, and the father of it" (John 8:44), the perverter and denier of the truth, the promoter and insti- gator of falsehood of every kind throughout the earth, always employing dis- simulation and treachery, subtlety and deception, to further his evil interests.

Consider the terrible consequences of listening to the devil's lies. See the awful ravage which sin works. Not only had Adam and Eve irreparably damaged themselves, but they had become fugitives from their all-glorious Creator. He is ineffably pure; they were polluted, and therefore sought to avoid Him. How unbearable the thought to a guilty conscience that the unpardoned sinner will yet have to stand before the thrice holy One! Yet he *must*. There is no possible way in which any of us can escape that awful meeting. All must appear before Him and render an account of their stewardship. Unless we flee to Christ for refuge, and have our sins blotted out by His atoning blood, we shall hear His sentence of eternal doom. "Seek . . . the Lord while he may be found, call . . . upon him while he is near" in His gracious overtures of the gospel (Isa. 55:6). For "how shall we escape" the lake of fire "if we neglect so great salvation?" Do not assume that you are a Christian, but examine your foundations; beg God to search your heart and show you your real condition. Take the place of a hell-deserving sinner and receive the sinner's Saviour.

In the verses that follow we are given a solemn preview of the day to come: "And the Lord God called unto Adam, and said unto him, Where art thou?" (Gen. 3:9). It was the divine Judge summoning him to an account of what he had done. It was a word designed to impress upon him the distance from God to which sin and guilt had removed him. His offense had severed all communion between them, for "what fellowship hath righteousness with unrighteousness, and what communion hath light with darkness?" Observe that the Lord ignored Eve and confined His address to the responsible head. God had plainly warned him about the forbidden fruit: "In the day that thou eatest thereof, thou shalt surely die." This death is not annihilation but alienation. Spiritual death is the separation of the soul from the holy One: "Your iniquities have separated between you and your God, and your sins have hid his face from you" (Isa. 59:2). This is the terrible plight of us all by nature—"far off" (Eph. 2:13)—and unless divine grace saves us, we shall be "punished with everlasting destruction from the presence of the Lord" (II Thess. 1:9).

"And he said, I heard thy voice in the garden [which suggests that He was now seen in theophanic manifestation], and I was afraid, because I was naked; and I hid myself" (Gen. 3:10). Note how utterly unable sinful man is to meet the divine inquisition. Adam could offer no adequate defense. Hear his sorry admission: "I was afraid." His conscience condemned him. This will be the woeful plight of every lost soul when, brought out from "the refuge of lies" in which he formerly sheltered, he appears before his Maker—destitute of that righteousness and holiness which He inexorably requires, and which we can obtain only in and from Christ. Weigh those words: "I was afraid, because I was naked." Adam's heart was filled with horror and terror. His apron of fig leaves was of no avail! Thus it is when the Holy Spirit convicts a soul. The garb of religion is discovered to be naught but filthy rags when one is given to see light in God's light. The soul is filled with fear and shame as he realizes he has to do with One before whom all things are naked and opened. Have you passed through this experience, seen and felt yourself to be a spiritual bankrupt, a moral leper, a lost sinner? If not, you will in the day to come.

"And he said, Who told thee that thou wast naked?" (v. 11). To this inquiry Adam made no reply. Instead of humbling himself before his aggrieved Benefactor, the culprit failed to answer. Whereupon the Lord said, "Hast thou eaten of the tree, whereof I commanded thee that thou shouldest not eat?" It is striking to notice that God made no reply to the idle and perverse excuses which Adam had at first proffered. They were unworthy of His notice. If the words of Adam in verse 10 are carefully pondered, a solemn and fatal omission from them will be observed: He said nothing about his sin, but mentioned only the painful *effects* which it had produced. As another has said, "This was the language of impenitent misery." God therefore directed him to the *cause* of those effects. Yet observe the manner in which He framed His words. The Lord did not directly charge the offender with his crime, but instead questioned him: "Hast thou eaten?" That opened the way and made it much easier for Adam contritely to acknowledge his transgression. But he failed to avail himself of the opportunity and declined to make brokenhearted confession of his iniquity.

God did not put those questions to Adam because He wanted to be informed, but rather to provide Adam with an occasion to own penitently what he had done. In his refusal to do so we see the fourth consequence of the fall, namely, *the hardening of the heart* by sin. There was no deep sorrow for his flagrant disobedience, and therefore no sincere owning of it. To the second inquiry of God, the man said, "The woman whom thou gavest to be with me, she gave me of the tree, and I did eat" (v. 12). Here was the fifth consequence of the fall: *self-justification* by an attempt to excuse sin. Instead of confessing his wickedness, Adam tried to mitigate and extenuate it by throwing the onus upon another. The entrance of evil into man produced a dishonest and deceitful heart. Rather than take the blame upon himself, Adam sought to place it upon his wife. And thus it is with his descendants. They endeavor to shelve their responsibility and repudiate their culpability by attributing the wrongdoing to anyone or anything rather than themselves, ascribing their sins to the force of circumstances, an evil environment, temptations or the devil.

But in those words of Adam we may discern something still more heinous, a sixth consequence of his fall, namely, a blasphemous *challenging of God Himself*. Adam did not simply say, "My wife gave me of the tree, and I did eat," but "The woman whom *thou* gavest me. . . ." Thus he covertly reproached the Lord. It was as though he said, "Hadst Thou not given me this woman, I had not eaten. Why didst Thou put such a snare upon me?" See here the pride and stoutheartedness which characterize the devil, whose kingdom has now been set up within man. So it is with his children to this day. That is why we are warned, "Let no man say when he is tempted, I am tempted of God: for God cannot be tempted with evil, neither tempteth he any man" (James 1:13). The depraved mind of the fallen creature is so prone to think that very thing and seek shelter in that excuse. "If God had not ordered things that way, I never would have been so strongly tempted. If He had arranged things differently, I would not have been enticed, still less overcome." Thus, in our efforts at self-vindication, we cast reflection on the ways of Him who cannot err.

"The foolishness of man perverteth his way: and his heart fretteth against the Lord" (Prov. 19:3). This is one of the vilest forms in which human depravity manifests itself: that after deliberately playing the fool, and discovering that the way of transgressors is hard, we murmur against God instead of meekly submitting to His rod. When we pervert our way—through self-will, carnal greed, rash conduct, hasty actions—let us not charge God with the bitter fruits of our wrongdoing. Since we are the authors of our misery, it is reasonable that we should fret against *ourselves*. But such is the pride of our hearts, and our unsubdued enmity against God, that we are foolishly apt to fret against Him, as though He were responsible for our troubles. We must not expect to gather grapes from thorns, or figs from thistles! Do not charge the unpleasant reaping to the severity of God, but to your own perversity. Do not say, "God should not have endowed me with such strong passions if I may not indulge them." Do not ask, "Why did He not give grace so that I could have resisted the temptation?" Do not impeach His sovereignty, do not question His dispensations, harbor no doubts about His goodness. If you do, you are repeating the wickedness of your first father.

"And the man said, The woman whom thou gavest to be with me, she gave me of the tree, and I did eat." Adam indeed recited the facts of the case, yet in so doing he made it worse rather than better. He was the woman's head and protector, and therefore should have taken more care to prevent her falling into evil. When she had succumbed to the serpent's wiles, far from following her example, he should have rebuked her and refused her offer. To plead allurement by others is no valid excuse, yet it is commonly offered. When Aaron was charged with making the golden calf, he admitted the fact, but sought to extenuate the fault by blaming the congregation (Exodus 32:22-24). In like manner, disobedient King Saul sought to transfer the onus to "the people" (I Sam. 15:21). So too Pilate gave orders for the crucifixion of Christ, and then charged the crime to the Jews (Matt. 27:24). Here we learn yet another consequence of the fall: It produced a *breach of affection* between man and his neighbor—in this case his wife, whom he now loved so little as to thrust her forth to receive the stroke of divine vengeance.

"And the Lord God said unto the woman, What is this that thou hast done?" (v. 13a). Here we see both the infinite condescension of the Most High and His fairness as Judge. He did not act in high sovereignty, disdaining to parley with the creature; nor did He condemn the transgressors unheard, but gave them opportunity to defend themselves or confess their crime. So it will be at the great hearing. It will be conducted in such a manner as to make it transparently evident that every transgressor receives "the due reward of his iniquities," and that God is clear when He judges (Ps. 51:4).

"And the woman said, The serpent beguiled me, and I did eat" (v. 13*b*). Eve followed the same course and manifested the same evil spirit as her husband. She did not humble herself before the Lord, gave no sign of repentance, made no brokenhearted confession. Instead, she vainly attempted to vindicate herself by casting the blame on the serpent. It was a weak excuse, for God had capacitated her with understanding to perceive his lies, and with rectitude of nature to reject them with horror. It is equally useless for her children to plead, "I had no intention of sinning, but the devil tempted me"; for he can force no one, nor prevail without one's consent.

As Adam and Eve stood before their Judge, self-accused and self-condemned, He proceeded to pronounce sentence upon the guilty pair. But before doing so He dealt with the one who had been instrumental in their fall: "And the Lord God said unto the serpent, because thou hast done this, thou art cursed above all cattle, and above every beast of the field; upon thy belly shalt thou go, and dust shalt thou eat all the days of thy life. And I will put enmity between thee and the woman, and between thy seed and her seed; it shall bruise thy head, and thou shalt bruise his heel" (vv. 14-15). Observe that no question was put to the serpent. Rather the Lord treated him as an avowed enemy. His sentence is to be taken literally in its application to the serpent, mystically in relation to Satan. Scott said:

> The words may imply a visible punishment to be executed on the serpent, as the instrument in this temptation; but the curse was directed against the invisible tempter, whose abject, degraded condition, and base endeavours to find satisfaction in rendering others wicked and miserable, might be figuratively intimated by the serpent's moving on his belly, and feeding on the dust.

The Lord began His denunciations where sin began—with the serpent. Each part of the sentence expresses the fearful degradation which should henceforth be his portion. First, it was "cursed *above all* cattle"; the curse has extended to the whole creation, as Romans 8:20-23 makes clear. Second, thereafter it would crawl in the dust; this infers that originally it stood erect (cf. our remarks on Gen. 3:1). Third, God Himself now put enmity between it and the female, so that where there had been intimate converse there should now be mutual aversion. Fourth, passing from the literal snake to "that old serpent, the devil," God announced that he should ultimately be crushed, not by His hand dealing immediately with him, but by One in human nature, and—what would be yet more humiliating—by the *woman's* seed. Satan had made use of the weaker vessel, and God would defeat him through the same medium! Wrapped up in that pronouncement was a prophecy and a promise. However let it be carefully noted that it was in the form of a sentence of doom on Satan, *not* a gracious declaration made to Adam and Eve—intimating that *they* had no personal interest in it!

The sentences pronounced upon our first parents need not detain us, for the language is so plain and simple that it needs neither explanation nor comment. Since Eve was the first in the transgression, and had tempted Adam, she was the next to receive sentence. "Unto the woman he said, I will greatly multiply thy sorrow and thy conception; in sorrow thou shalt bring forth children; and thy desire shall be to thy husband, and he shall rule over thee" (v. 16). Thus she was condemned to a state of sorrow, suffering and servitude. "And unto Adam he said, Because thou hast hearkened unto the voice of thy wife, and hast eaten of the tree, of which I commanded thee, saying, Thou shalt not eat of it: cursed is the ground for thy sake; in sorrow shalt thou eat of it all the days of thy life; thorns also and thistles shall it bring forth to thee; . . . in the sweat of thy face shalt thou eat bread" (vv. 17-19). Sorrow, toil and sweat were to be the burden falling most heavily upon the male. Here we see the eighth consequence of the fall: *physical suffering and death*—"Unto dust shalt thou return."

"And Adam called his wife's name Eve ['living']; because she was the mother of all living" (v. 20). This is manifestly a detail communicated by God to Moses the historian, for Eve gave birth to no children until after she and her husband had been expelled from Eden. It seems to be introduced here for the purpose of illustrating and exemplifying the concluding portion of the sentence passed upon the woman in verse 16. As Adam had made proof of his dominion over all the lower creatures (1:28) by giving names to them (2:19), so in token of his rule over his wife he conferred a name upon her. "Unto Adam also and to his wife did the Lord God make coats of skins, and clothed them" (v. 21). We are not told the design of the coats; each reader is free to form his own opinion. Many have supposed these words to intimate that God dealt (typically, at least) in mercy with the fallen pair, and that emblematically they were robed in Christ's righteousness and covered with the garments of salvation. To the contrary, the writer sees in this the ninth consequence of the fall: that man had thereby *descended to the level of the animals*. Observe how in Daniel 7 and Revelation 17, where God sets before us the character of the leading kingdoms of the world (as *He* sees them), He employs the symbol of *beasts!*

"And the Lord God said, Behold, the man is become as one of us, to know good and evil" (v. 22), which is obviously the language of sarcasm and irony. See the one who vainly imagined that by defying God he should "be as gods" (v. 5), now degraded to the level of the beasts! "Therefore the Lord God *sent* him forth from the garden of Eden, to till the ground from whence he was taken" (v. 23). God bade him leave the garden. But, as Matthew Henry intimates, such an order did not at all appeal to the apostate rebel. "So he *drove out* the man; and He placed at the east of the garden of Eden Cherubims, and a flaming sword which turned every way, to keep the way of the tree of life" (v. 24), thereby effectually preventing his return. Hence we note the tenth consequence of the fall: man as *an outcast from God*, estranged from His favor and fellowship, banished from the place of delight, sent forth a fugitive into the world. Observe how this closing verse corroborates our interpretation of verse 21. The Lord does not drive from Him any child of His! And this is the *finally recorded* act of God in connection with Adam! As He cast out of heaven the angels that sinned, so He drove Adam and Eve out of the earthly paradise, in proof of their abhorrence to Him and their alienation from Him.

Consequences for Mankind

Having considered those consequences which fell more immediately upon our first parents for their original offense, we shall now look at the consequences they brought upon their descendants. We do not have to go outside of Genesis 3 to find proof that the penal consequences of their transgression are inherited by their posterity. What God said to them was said to all of mankind, for since the sin was common to all, so was the penalty also. "Unto the woman he said, I will greatly multiply thy sorrow and thy conception; in sorrow thou shalt bring forth children" (v. 16). And such has been the lot of all Eve's daughters. "Cursed is the ground for thy sake: in sorrow shalt thou eat of it all the days of thy life; . . . in the sweat of thy face shalt thou eat bread, till thou return unto the ground . . . for dust thou art, and unto dust shalt thou return" (vv. 17-19). And such has been the portion of Adam's sons—in every generation and in all parts of the earth. The calamity of evil which then descended upon the world continues to this hour. All of Adam and Eve's children are equally involved in the sentence of the pain of childbirth, the curse on the ground, the obligation to live by toil and sweat, the decay and death of the body.

But the things just mentioned above, though severe and painful, are trivial in comparison with the divine judgment which has been visited on man's *soul*. They are but the external and visible marks of the moral and spiritual calamity which overtook Adam and his race. By his disobedience he forfeited the favor of his Maker, fell under His holy condemnation and curse, received the awful wages of his sin, came under the sentence of the law, was alienated from the life of God, became totally depraved and, as such an object of abhorrence to the holy One, was driven from His presence. Since the guilt of Adam's offense was imputed or judicially charged to all those he represented, it follows that they participate in all the misery that came upon him. Guilt consists of an obligation or liability to suffer punishment for an offense committed, and that in proportion to the aggravation of the offense. In consequence, every child is born into this world in a state of antenatal disgrace and condemnation, with entire depravity of nature and makeup which inevitably leads to and produces actual transgression, and with complete inability of soul to change his nature or do anything pleasing to God.

"The wicked are estranged from the womb: they go astray as soon as they be born, speaking lies" (Ps. 58:3). First, from the moment of birth every child is morally and spiritually cut off from the Lord—a lost sinner. Matthew Henry described it thus: "estranged from God and all good: alienated from the Divine life, and its principles, powers, and blessings." Adam lost not only the image of God but His favor and fellowship too, being expelled from His presence. And each of his children was born *outside* Eden, born in a state of guilt.

Second, in consequence of this, Adam's children are delinquents, warped from the beginning. Their very being is polluted, for evil is bred in them. Their "nature" is inclined to wickedness only; and if God leaves them to themselves they will never turn from it.

Third, they quickly supply evidence of their separation from God and of the corruption of their hearts—as every godly parent perceives to his sorrow. While in the cradle they evince their opposition to truth, sincerity, integrity. "Foolishness is bound in the heart of a child" (Prov. 22:15), not childishness but foolishness—leaning toward evil, entering upon an ungodly course, forming and following bad habits. It is "bound in the heart"—held firmly there by chains invincible to human power.

But in all ages there have been those who sought to blunt the sharp edge of Psalm 58:3 by narrowing its scope, denying that it has a race-wide application; these are determined at all costs to rid themselves of the unpalatable truth of the total depravity of all mankind. Pelagians and Socinians have insisted that that verse is speaking only of a particularly reprobate class, those who are flagrantly wayward from an early age. Rightly did J. Owen point out:

> It is to no purpose to say that he speaks of wicked men only; that is, such as are habitually and profligately so. For whatever any man may afterwards run into by a course of sin, all men are morally alike from the womb, and it is an aggravation of the wickedness of men that it begins so early and holds on in an uninterrupted course. Children are not able to speak from the womb, as soon as they be born. Yet here are they said to speak lies. It is therefore the perverse acting of depraved nature in infancy that is intended, for everything that is irregular, that answers not the law of our creation and rule of our obedience, is a *lie*.

"And were by nature the children of wrath, even as others" (Eph. 2:3). That statement is, if possible, even more awful and solemn than Psalm 58:3. It signifies much more than that we are born into the world with a defiled constitution, for it speaks of not simply "children of corruption," but "children of wrath"—obnoxious to God, criminals in His sight. Depravity of our natures is no mere misfortune; if it were, it would evoke pity, not anger. The expression "children of wrath" is a Hebraism, a very strong and emphatic one. The original rendering of I Samuel 20:30 and II Samuel 12:5 mentions "the son of death," that is, one deserving death. In Matthew 23:15 Christ used the fearful term "the child of hell"—one whose sure portion is hell; while in John 17:12 He designated Judas "the son of perdition." Thus "children of wrath" connotes those who are deserving of wrath, heirs of wrath, fit for it. They are born to wrath, and under it, as their heritage. They are not only defiled and corrupt creatures, but the objects of God's judicial indignation. Why? Because the sin of Adam is imputed to them, and therefore they are regarded as guilty of having broken God's law.

Equally forcible and explicit are the words *"by nature* the children of wrath," in designed contrast with that which is artificially acquired. Many have insisted (contrary to the facts of common experience and observation) that children are corrupted by external contact with evil, that they *acquire* bad habits by imitation of others. We do not deny that environment has a measure of influence. Yet if any baby could be placed in a perfect setting and surrounded only by sinless beings, it would soon be evident that he was corrupt. We are depraved not by a process of development, but by genesis. It is not "on account of nature" but "by nature," because of our nativity. It is innate, bred in us. As Goodwin solemnly pointed out, "They are children of wrath in the very womb, before they commit any actual sin." The depraved nature itself is a *penal evil*, and that is because of our federal union with Adam, as sharing in his transgression. We are the children of wrath because our federal head fell under the wrath of God. Calvin stated, "There would be no truth in the assertion of Paul that all are by nature the children of wrath if they had not been already under the curse before their birth."

But a greater than Calvin has informed us: "For the children being not yet born, neither having done any good or evil, that the purpose of God according to election might stand, not of works, but of Him that calleth, it was said unto her, The elder shall serve the younger. As it is written, Jacob have I loved, but Esau have I hated" (Rom. 9:11-13). This goes back still further, before birth. Esau was an object of God's hatred before he was born. Obviously a righteous God could not abominate one who was pure and innocent. But how could Esau be guilty prior to doing any good or evil? Because he shared Adam's criminality; and for precisely the same reason, all of us are by nature the children of wrath—obnoxious and subject to divine punishment—not only by virtue of our own personal transgressions, but because of our constitution. Deviation is coexistent with our very being. We are members of a cursed head, branches of a condemned tree, streams of a polluted fountain. In a word, the guilt of Adam's sin lies on us. No other explanation is possible; since our guilt and liability to punishment are not, in the first place, due to our personal sins, they must be because of Adam's sin being imputed to us.

For the same reason infants *die* naturally, for sin is not merely the occasion of physical dissolution but the cause of it. Death is the wages of sin, the sentence of the broken law, the penal infliction of a righteous God. Had Adam never sinned, neither he nor any of his descendants would have become subject to death. Had not the guilt of Adam's offense been charged to his posterity, none would die in infancy. Yet it does not necessarily follow that any who expire in early childhood are eternally lost. That they are born into this world spiritually dead, alienated from the life of God, is clear; but whether they die eternally, or are saved by sovereign grace, is probably one of those secret things which belong to the Lord. If they are saved it must be because they are among the number elected by the Father, redeemed by the Son and regenerated by the Spirit—without which none can enter heaven; but concerning these things Scripture appears to us to be silent. The Judge of all the earth will do right, and there we may submissively yet trustfully leave it. Parenthood is an unspeakably solemn matter.

In the opening verses of Ephesians 2 the Holy Spirit has described our fallen state. First, we are dead in trespasses and sins (v. 1): dead judicially, under sentence of the law; dead experientially, without a spark of spiritual life. Second, our outward course is depicted (vv. 2-3): as completely dominated by "the flesh" or evil principle, inspired to an ungodly walk by Satan, so that our every action is sinful. Third, the resultant punishment is detailed (v. 3): we are obnoxious to the divine Judge, born in such a condition, and remaining so while in this fallen state. Until the sinner believes, "the wrath of God abideth on him" (John 3:36). Though the sentence is not yet executed, it is suspended over him. The word "abideth" here denotes *perpetuity*: as Augustine said, "It hath been upon him from his birth, and remains to this day upon him." "The children of wrath, *even as others*": this is the case of *all* of Adam's descendants, and it is *equally* so. It is a common heritage: by nature no man is either better or worse than his fellows. The very fact that this awful visitation is *universal* can only be accounted for by our relation to the first man, our covenant head and legal representative.

It would hardly be fair not to take some notice of those who attempt to dismiss all which has been pointed out above by dogmatically insisting that "Christ made atonement for original sin" so that the guilt of our first father's transgression does not rest on his sons. But such an arbitrary assertion is manifestly contrary to those facts which confront us on every side. The judgment which God pronounced upon Adam and Eve is as surely visited upon their children *today* as it ever was before the Son of God died on the cross. The curse upon the ground, the ordeal of women in childbirth, the necessity to toil for our daily bread, the universal reign of death, including the demise of so many infants, are all just as evident and prevalent in the New Testament era as they were in the Old.

Obviously such things could not be if the Arminian view were sound, for if the *guilt* of original sin had been removed, the *effects* of it could no longer continue. Such an affirmation is baseless, unconfirmed by a single clear statement in Scripture, though some do make a farfetched attempt to substantiate it by appealing to John 1:29: "The next day John seeth Jesus coming unto him, and saith, Behold the Lamb of God, which taketh away the sin of the world." We wonder how anyone can perceive anything in those words which strikes them as relevant to the point. Our Lord's forerunner was there presenting the Messiah to the people in that sacrificial character which both type and prophecy had prepared them to look for; he was not raising an abstruse question in theology which is nowhere else mentioned in Scripture. Had those words occurred in one of Paul's profound doctrinal discussions, we should be ready to look for a deeper meaning in them, though we would require something very specific in the context obliging us to define "the sin of the world" as the sin of Adam. John was the herald of a new dispensation, one which would be radically different in its scope from the previous one, and one which would be inaugurated by breaking down the "middle wall of partition."

For two thousand years the grace of God had been restricted almost entirely to a single nation; but now it was on the point of flowing out to all. John the Baptist was there announcing Christ as the heaven-appointed sacrifice which was to expiate the sin not of believing Jews only but of Gentiles also. Though "the world" is a general expression, it is not to be regarded as comprehending a universality of individuals, as synonymous with mankind. It is an indefinite expression, as "The glory of the Lord shall be revealed, and *all flesh* shall see it together" (Isa. 40:5) and "all flesh shall know that I the Lord am thy Saviour" (Isa. 49:26). "*The sin* of the world" signifies all the sins of all God's people as a collective whole, as one great and heavy burden—as in Isaiah 53:6: "The Lord hath laid on him *the iniquity* of us all." It was the entire penalty and punishment of sin, which Christ took on Himself, and bore away from the divine Judge. As Hebrews 9:26 tells us, "But now once in the end of the world hath he appeared to put away sin by the sacrifice of himself." And since that sacrifice was a *vicarious* one, it necessarily removed the guilt of all those in whose stead it was made.

Not only is the theory we are here controverting without any scriptural evidence to support it, but it is refuted by every considerable evidence to the contrary. If attention is paid to *the relations* which Christ sustained to those in whose stead He obeyed and suffered, it at once appears that His work was no mere indefinite and general one, but had a particular and restricted design. He transacted as a Shepherd on behalf of His sheep (John 10:11; cf. 10:26). If He died also for the goats and the wolves, then there was no point in saying He laid down His life for the sheep. He served in the relation of a Husband (Eph. 5:25-27), showing singleness of affection, the exclusiveness of conjugal love! He sustained the relation of Head to His beneficiaries, there being a federal and legal *unity* between them (Heb. 2:11). The redemptive work of Christ was like His coat, "without seam," one complete and indivisible whole, so that what He did for one He did for all—not merely taking away the guilt of original sin.

If it were true that Christ atoned for Adam's offense, then it would necessarily follow that the government under which the human race is now placed does not recognize the original curse. But such is far from being the case. From the fall until now, all are born dead in sin, the objects of God's displeasure. That is very evident from the teaching of Romans 3 where, in unequivocal language, the whole world is pronounced under condemnation, "guilty before God" (vv. 10-19)—not merely as possible condemnation, but an actual one; not one which may be incurred, but which has been incurred already, and under which all are now lying; and the only way of deliverance is by faith in Christ. Precisely the same representation is given in the New Testament of the condition of all when first visited by the gospel. They are described as those who are sinners, lost, lying beneath the curse of a broken law, for the dark background of the gospel is that "the wrath of God is re-

vealed from heaven against all ungodliness and unrighteousness" (Rom.
1:18); and until the terms of that gospel are met, men have no hope (Eph.
2:12).

The very scene into which we are born confronts us with innumerable
evidences that the earth is under the curse of its Maker. To quote J. Thornwell:

> The frowning aspect of Providence which so often darkens our world
> and appals our minds, receives the only adequate solution in the fact that
> the Fall has fearfully changed the relations of God and the creature. We
> are manifestly treated as criminals under guard. We are dealt with as
> guilty, faithless, suspected beings that cannot be trusted for a moment.
> Our earth has been turned into a prison, and sentinels are posted around
> us to awe, rebuke, and check us. Still, there are traces of our ancient
> grandeur; there is so much consideration shown to us as to justify the im-
> pression that those prisoners were once kings, and that this dungeon was
> once a palace. To one unacquainted with the history of our race, the deal-
> ings of Providence in regard to us must appear inexplicably mysterious.
> But the whole subject is covered with light when the doctrine of the Fall
> is understood. The gravest theological errors with respect alike to the
> character of God and the character of man have arisen from the monstrous
> hypothesis that our present is our primitive condition, that we are now
> what God originally made us.

Chapter 5

TRANSMISSION

IN INTRODUCING this aspect of our subject we cannot do better than set before the reader what A. A. Hodge pointed out in *Outlines of Theology* as

the self-evident moral principles which must ever be certainly presupposed in every inquiry into the dealings of God with His responsible creatures. (1) God cannot be the Author of sin. (2) We must not believe that He could consistently with His own perfections create a creature *de novo* (anew, originally) with a sinful nature. (3) The perfection of righteousness, not bare sovereignty, is the grand distinction of all God's dealings. (4) It is a heathen notion that the "order of nature" or "the nature of things" or "natural law" is a real agent independent of God, limiting His freedom or acting with Him as an independent concause in producing effects. (5) We cannot believe that God would inflict either moral or physical evil upon any creature whose natural rights had not been previously forfeited.

State the two distinct questions thence arising, which, though frequently confused, it is essential to keep separate. First, *how* does an innate sinful nature originate in each human being at the commencement of his existence, so that the Maker of the man is not the cause of his sin? If this corruption of nature originated in Adam, how is it transmitted to us? Second, *why*, on what ground of injustice, does God inflict this terrible evil, the root ground of all other evils, at the very commencement of personal existence? What fair probation have infants born in sin enjoyed? When, and why, were their rights as new created beings forfeited? It is self-evident that these questions are distinct and should be treated as such. The first may possibly be answered on physical grounds. The second question, however, concerns the moral government of God and inquires concerning the justice of His dispensations. In the history of theology, of all ages and in all schools, very much confusion has resulted from the failure to emphasize and preserve prominent this distinction.

Guilt of Adam's Posterity

The why has been discussed by us at some length: the guilt of Adam's offense was imputed to all his posterity because he served as their covenant head and federal representative. Since they were legally one with him, the punishment passed upon him falls on them too, involving them in all the dire consequences of his crime. One of the most terrible of those consequences is the receiving of a sinful nature, which brings us to consider the how of the great human tragedy. We do not propose to make any attempt to enter into a philosophical or metaphysical inquiry as to how God can be the Creator and Maker of our beings (Job 31:15), the "Father of spirits" (Heb. 12:9), and yet *not* be the Author of the sin now inhering in our natures. Rather we shall confine ourselves to an examination of the bare facts which Scripture presents on the subject. Nowhere in the Word of God is the pollution of fallen man ascribed to the holy One; it is uniformly attributed to human propagation: by natural generation a corrupt offspring is begotten and conceived by corrupt parents.

It was a divinely instituted law of the original creation that like should produce like, which plainly appears in that clause "whose seed is in itself" (Gen. 1:11-12), and in that oft repeated expression "after his kind" (vv. 21, 24, 25). That law has never been revoked—as the biology of every department of nature demonstrates. Hence it follows that since the whole human race sinned in its covenant head, and since every member of it receives its nature from him, when the fountain itself became polluted, all the streams issuing from it were polluted too. A corrupt tree can bring forth nothing but corrupt fruit. Since the root became unholy, its branches must also be unholy. All of Adam's offspring simply perpetuate what began in him; from the first moment of their existence they become participants of his impurity. Though our immediate parents are the occasion of conveying a depraved nature to their children, that nature is derived originally from the first man. In other words, the present relation of father and son is not that of cause and effect, but that of an instrument or channel in transmitting the sinfulness of Adam and Eve.

In Genesis 5:3 we are told, "Adam lived an hundred and thirty years, and begat a son in his own likeness, after his image." That occurred after his fearful defection, and the statement is in designed and direct contrast with the declaration of verse 1: "In the day that God created man, in the likeness of God made he him." Adam did not communicate to his descendants the pure nature which he had originally by creation, but the polluted one which he acquired by the fall. It is very striking to note the precise *place* where this statement is made in the sacred narrative: not at the beginning of Genesis 4 in connection with the begetting of Cain and Abel, but here, introducing a lengthy *obituary list*—showing that dying Adam could only beget mortals. The image of God included both holiness and immortality, but since Adam had lost them and become sinful and mortal, he could propagate none but those in his own fallen likeness, which had in it corruption and death (I Cor. 15:49-50; cf. v. 22). The copy answered to the original. Adam could not beget in any other way than in his own image, for a clean thing will not issue from an unclean. A depraved parent could produce nothing but a depraved child.

Born in Adam's fallen likeness, not only in substance but in qualities also, all of his posterity are but a continuous repetition of himself. This is remarkably intimated in the opening verse of Psalm 14 which has for its theme the awful depravity of the human race. John Owen pointed out:

There is a peculiar distinguishing mark put upon this Psalm, in that it is found twice in the book of Psalms. The fourteenth and fifty-third Psalms are the same, with the alteration of one or two expressions at most. And there is another mark put upon its deep importance in that the apostle transcribed a great part of it in Romans iii.

Psalm 14 opens with the statement "The fool hath said in his heart, There is no God." The careful reader will notice that the words "there is" have been supplied by the translators—unnecessarily, we feel. The fool does not say in his head, "There is no God"; rather he says in his *heart*, "No God for me. I decline allegiance to Him." It is not intellectual unbelief denying the existence of Deity, but the enmity of a rebel who refuses to practically own or be in subjection to God.

"The fool hath said in his heart, No God. They are corrupt, they have done abominable works" (Ps. 14:1). Most significant and noticeable is that change of number in the pronouns, though for some strange reason it appears to have escaped the notice of the commentators—at any rate none whom we have consulted makes any reference to it. As stated above, the verses which follow give a full description of the deplorable condition of all mankind, and that is prefaced with a statement about "the fool." Nor is there the slightest difficulty in identifying him. Who is the fool of all fools? Adam was the arch-fool. His heart had become devoid of wisdom. Thus was the father of our race. What could his children be like? Our verse answers, "They are corrupt," and prove themselves to be so by doing abominable works.

"Behold, I was shapen in iniquity; and in sin did my mother conceive me" (Ps. 51:5). This is the sad confession which every one of us makes. Born in the likeness of Adam as a fallen creature, all of his descendants are but replicas of himself. And since moral corruption is transmitted by him to them according to a fixed law of heredity, that corruption dates from the very beginning of their existence. Because by being Adam's children they are depraved, it necessarily follows that they must be so as soon as they *are* his children. David was the son of lawful and honorable marriage, yet from his parents he received Adam's vitiated nature with all its evil dispositions. Note that he was careful to intimate that it was not by divine infusion, but by natural generation and human propagation. He mentioned it, not to excuse his fearful fall but to concede it. Matthew Henry states that David said in effect, "Had I duly considered this before I should not have made so bold with the temptation, nor have ventured among the sparks with such tinder in my heart." The realization that our whole being is horribly degenerated from its pristine purity and rectitude should make us thoroughly distrustful of self and cause us to walk most warily.

Because our very nature is contaminated, we enter the world a mass of potential wickedness, which is one reason why Job declared, "I have said to corruption, Thou art my father: to the worm, Thou art my mother, and my sister" (17:14). Hervey tells us the Hebrew word there for worm signifies a grub, which is bred by and feeds upon putrefaction. I commenced my existence with all sorts of impurity in my nature, with every cursed propensity to evil, with everything earthly, sensual, devilish in my mind. That depraved nature is the source of all other miseries, the root from which proceed all evil actions. This solemn and sad fact is demonstrated by antithesis. Why was it necessary for Christ to be incarnated supernaturally by the miracle of the virgin birth? So that what was born of Mary should be "that *holy* thing" (Luke 1:35), which would not have been the case if He had been begotten by natural generation from a man. Though this doctrine of original sin, of antenatal defilement, is purely a matter of divine revelation, it explains what nothing else does, namely, that "the imagination of man's heart is evil from his youth" (Gen. 8:21)—in every instance, Christ alone excepted.

"The wicked are estranged from the womb: they go astray as soon as they be born, speaking lies. Their poison is like the poison of a serpent" (Ps. 58:3-4). There are three indictments here made against fallen human nature. First, that from the beginning of his existence man is alienated from God, divorced from His favor, cut off from fellowship with Him. Second, that he evidences his deplorable state as soon as he enters this world, manifesting his sinfulness in the cradle. Third, that he turns to his own way, and the very first steps he takes are in that broad road which leads to destruction. Why? Because his very being is poisoned and poisonous, malicious; he is at odds with God and goodness and his fellowmen—"hateful, and hating one another" (Titus 3:3). This poison "is like the poison of a serpent." The serpent does not acquire his venom, but is *generated* a poisonous creature. Poison, deadly poison, is its very nature from the outset, and when it bites it only acts out that with which it was born. Though its poison is hidden, it is lurking there, ready for use as soon as it is provoked.

B. W. Newton stated:

> Antecedent to all trespasses and acts of sin, before any apprehension of good or evil has dawned upon our hearts, before any notion respecting God has been formed in our souls, before we have uttered a word or conceived a thought, sin—essential sin—is found to dwell within us. Bound up with our being, it enters into every sensation, lives in every thought, sways every faculty. If the senses, by means of which we communicate with the external world, had never acted: if our eye had never seen, and our ear had never heard; if our throat had never proved itself to be an open sepulchre, breathing forth corruption; if our tongue had never shown itself to be set on fire of hell; still sin would have been the secret mistress of that world of thought and feeling which is found within us, and every hidden impulse there would have been enmity against God.

When therefore Scripture speaks of men as sinners, it refers not only to their practice but chiefly to their evil nature—a nature which is conveyed by Adam and transmitted from parent to child in successive generations.

"Foolishness is bound in the heart of a child; but the rod of correction shall drive it far from him" (Prov. 22:15). This foolishness is not merely intellectual ignorance but a positive principle of evil, for in the book of Proverbs the "fool" is not the idiot but the sinner. This corruption is deep-rooted. It does not lie on the surface, like some of the child's habits, which may easily be corrected. That moral madness, as Matthew Henry pointed out, "is not only *found* there, but *bound* there; it is annexed to the heart." It is rooted and riveted in him from the first breath he draws. This is the birthright of all Adam's progeny. "The little innocent" is a misnomer of fondness and fancy. John Bunyan said:

> I do confess it is my opinion that children come polluted with sin into the world, and that oft-times the sins of youth, especially while they are very young, are rather by virtue of indwelling sin than by examples that are set before them by others; not but they may learn to sin by example, too, but example is not the root, but rather the temptation to sin.

The rod of correction (not of caprice or passion) is the means prescribed by God, and under His blessing it will prevent many an outburst of the flesh. "The rod and reproof give wisdom: but a child left to himself bringeth his mother to shame" (Prov. 29:15). C. Bridges agreed: "Discipline is the order of God's government. Parents are His dispensers of it to their children. The child must be broken in, to 'bear the yoke in his youth' (Lam. 3, 27). Let reproof be tried first; and if it succeed, let the rod be spared (Prov. 17, 10). If not, let it do its work." If parents fail to do their duty, there will be sad consequences. The "mother" only is mentioned as being brought to shame, because she is usually the most indulgent, and because she normally feels most keenly the affliction brought upon herself by her own neglect. But fathers too are disgraced. Eli gave reproof but spared the rod (I Sam. 2:22-25; 3:13), and paid dearly for his folly. What dishonor was brought upon David's name and what poignant grief must have filled him because his perverted fondness brought his sons to their ruin—one excused while in the most aggravated sin (II Sam. 14:28-33; 15:6; 18:33), another not corrected by even a word (I Kings 1:5-9). As E. Hopkins said, "Take this for certain, that as many deserved stripes as you spare from your children, you do but lay up for your own backs."

A child does not have to be taught to sin. Remove all inhibitions and prohibitions and he will bring his parents to the grave in sorrow. If the child is humored and no real efforts are made to counteract its evil propensities, it will assuredly grow more self-willed and intractable. How far the Scriptures are from flattering us! A "transgressor from the womb" (Isa. 48:8) is one of the hereditary titles of everyone entering this world. We are transgressors by internal disposition before we are so in external acts. Every parent is the channel of moral contagion to his offspring, who are by nature "children of disobedience" (Eph. 2:2). Original sin is transmitted as leprosy is conveyed to the children of lepers. That is one reason why the corruption of nature is designated our "old man": it is coeval with our beings. Our very "heart," the center of our moral being, from which are "the issues [outgoings] of life," is deceitful above all things and desperately wicked from the very first moment of its existence.

Some argue that if corruption is passed to all men from their first parents, then why are not all equally corrupt? They contend that some people are not subject to inordinate affections, but are respectable and law-abiding citizens. There are two answers to that objection. First, although, everything else being equal, such a conclusion is logical, it will not necessarily follow that all men will manifest the corruption in the same manner, or even to the same extent. When we say "everything else being equal," we include such things as the watchful care of pious parents, the discipline of a good education, the demands and effects of a refined environment, the positions and circumstances in which one and another may be placed. For while none of these things, nor all of them combined, can produce any change in a person's nature, they are factors which exert an influence on his outward conduct. Nevertheless, though one man may have less dissolute manners than another, still his imaginations are not pure; and though his bodily lusts may be under better control, he may yield more to the lusts of the mind. There are diversities in men's *lives*, but original sin has the same defiling effects upon all *hearts*.

Second, though all men are made in the likeness of fallen Adam, *God restrains*, in different ways and in varying degrees, the outbreakings of the corruption which has been transmitted to them. Nowhere is the sovereignty of God more evident than in His disposing of the lot of one and another: denying to some the opportunity to satisfy their evil desires, hedging up their way by poverty or ill health, or putting them in isolated places; others are given up to their hearts' lusts and God so orders His providences that they fatten themselves as beasts for the slaughter. Some men's callings draw out their sins more than do those of their fellowmen, so that they are subject to frequent and fierce temptations. Various dispositions are excited to action by the conditions in which they are placed, as Jacob was induced to trick his father by an unscrupulous mother, or as a sight of the spoils of Jericho stirred up the cupidity of Achan. It was for this reason that Agur was moved to pray, "Remove far from me vanity and lies: give me neither poverty nor riches; feed me with food convenient for me: lest I be full, and deny thee, and say, Who is the LORD? Or lest I be poor, and steal, and take the name of my God in vain" (Prov. 30:8-9).

Chapter 6

NATURE

IN THE PRECEDING chapter we showed how Scripture casts light on the great moral problem of how an inherently corrupt nature originates in each child from the beginning of its existence *without* its Creator being the Author of sin. David declared, "Behold, I was shapen in iniquity; and in sin did my mother conceive me" (Ps. 51:5). He described his depravity as innate and not created, as derived from his mother and not his Maker, showing that defilement is transmitted directly from Adam through the channel of human propagation. The same fact was expressed by our Lord when He said, "That which is born of the flesh is flesh" (John 3:6). In the Old Testament the word "flesh" is used as a general term for human nature or mankind: "Let all flesh bless his holy name" (Ps. 145:21)—that is, all men; "All flesh is grass" (Isa. 40:6)—the life of every member of our race is frail and fickle. The term occurs in the New Testament in the same sense: "Except those days should be shortened, there should no flesh be saved" (Matt. 24:22); "By the deeds of the law there shall no flesh be justified in his sight" (Rom. 3:20)—by his own obedience no man can merit acceptance with God.

Corruption of the Flesh

But since mankind is fallen and human nature is depraved, the term "flesh" becomes the expression of that fact; and every time it is used in Scripture in a moral sense it refers to *the corruption* of our entire beings, without any distinction between our visible and invisible parts—body and mind. This is evident from those passages where "the flesh" is contrasted with "the spirit" or the new nature (Rom. 8:5-6; I Cor. 2:11; Gal. 5:17). When the apostle declared, "For I know that in me (that is, in my flesh), dwelleth no good thing" (Rom. 7:18), he had reference to far more than his body with its appetites, namely, his entire natural man, with all its faculties, powers and propensities. The whole was polluted, and therefore nothing good could issue from him until divine grace was imparted. Again, when we find "hatred, emulations, wrath, and envyings" included in that incomplete list of the horrible "works of the flesh" supplied by Galatians 5, it is quite plain that the word takes in far more than the corporeal parts of our persons; even more so when we find that these works are set over against "the fruit of the spirit," each of which consists of the exercise of some inward quality or grace.

Thus it is clear that when Christ declared, "That which is born of the flesh is flesh" He signified that that which is propagated by fallen man is depraved, that whatever comes into this world by ordinary generation is carnal and corrupt, causing the heart itself to be deceitful above all things and desperately wicked. It is evident also from the immediate context (John 3:3-5), for what He affirmed in verse 6 was in order to demonstrate the absolute need of regeneration. Our Lord was contrasting the first birth with the new birth, and showing how imperative is the latter because we are radically tainted from the outset. All by nature are essentially evil, nothing but "flesh"; everything in us is contrary to holiness. Our very nature is vitiated, and by no process of education or culture can it be refined and made fit for the kingdom of God. The faculties which men receive at birth have a carnal bias, an earthly trend, a distaste for the heavenly and divine, and are inclined only to selfish aims and groveling pursuits. In the most polished or religious society, equally with the vulgar and profane, "that which is born of the flesh is flesh" and can never be anything better. Prune and trim a corrupt tree as much as you will, it can never be made to yield good fruit. Every man must be born again before he can be acceptable to a holy God.

We shall now attempt to answer the still more difficult question, In what does the vitiation of man by the fall consist? Precisely what is the nature of human depravity? That is far more than a question of academical interest which concerns none but teachers of theology. It is one of deep doctrinal and practical importance. All of us, especially preachers, should be quite clear on this point, for a mistake here is liable to lead to erroneous conclusions and serious consequences. This has indeed proved to be the case, for not a few who were sound and orthodox in many other respects have answered this question in a way that inevitably led them seriously to weaken, if not altogether to repudiate, the full responsibility of fallen man, and caused them to become hyper-Calvinists and Antinomians. We shall endeavor carefully to define and describe the present condition of the natural man, beginning with the negative side and pointing out a number of things in which human depravity does not consist.

First, the fall does not result in the extinguishment of that *spirit* which was a part of man's complex being when created by God. It did not either in the case of our first parents or in any of their descendants. It has, however, been argued from the divine threat made to Adam, "In the day that thou eatest thereof thou shalt surely die," that such was the case, that since Adam did not immediately die physically he must have done so spiritually. That is certainly a fact, yet it requires to be interpreted by Scripture. It is quite wrong to suppose that because Adam's body did not die, his spirit did. It was not something in Adam which died, but Adam himself— in his relation to God. The same is true of his offspring. They are indeed "dead *in* trespasses and sins" toward God, from the beginning of their existence, but nothing *within them* is positively dead in the ordinary meaning of that word. In the scriptural sense of the term, "death" never signifies annihilation, but separation. At physical death the soul is not extinguished but separated from the body; and the spiritual death of Adam was not the extinction of any part of his being but the severance of his fellowship with a holy God.

The same is true of all his children. The exact force of the solemn statement that they are "dead in trespasses and sins" is divinely defined for us as "being *alienated from* the life of God through the ignorance that is in them, because of the blindness of their heart" (Eph. 4:18). When Christ represented the father as saying, "This my son was dead, and is alive again" (Luke 15:24), He most certainly did not mean that the prodigal had ceased to exist, but that while he remained "in the far country" he was cut off from his father, and that he had now returned to him. The lake of fire into which the wicked shall be cast is designated "the second death" (Rev. 20:14), not signifying that they shall then cease to be, but that they are "punished with everlasting destruction *from* the presence of the Lord, and from the glory of his power" (II Thess. 1:9). That fallen man *is* possessed of a spirit is clear: "The LORD . . . formeth the spirit of man within him" (Zech. 12:1); "What man knoweth the things of a man, save the spirit of man which is in him?" (I Cor. 2:11); "The spirit shall return unto God who gave it" (Eccles. 12:7). Man was created a tripartite being, consisting of spirit and soul and body (I Thess. 5:23), and no part of him ceased to exist when he fell.

Second, the fall did not issue in the loss of any man's *faculties*. It did not divest man of reason, conscience or moral taste, for that would have converted him into another species of being. As reason remained, he still had the power of distinguishing between truth and falsehood; conscience still enabled him to distinguish between what was right and wrong, between what was a duty and a crime; and moral taste capacitated him to perceive the contrasts in the sphere of the excellent and beautiful. It is most important to be clear on this point: The fall has not touched the substance of the soul—that remains entire with all its original endowments of intellect, conscience and will. These are the characteristic elements of humanity, and to deprive man of them would be to unman him. They exist in the criminal as well as in the saint. They all have an essential unity in the wholeness of the human person. That is to say, they are coordinate faculties, though each has a sphere that is peculiar to itself. Collectively, they constitute the rational, moral, accountable being. It is not the mere possession of them which makes men evil or good; the manner and motive of their use makes their actions sinful or holy.

Corruption of Man's Spirit

No, the fall deprived man of no mental or moral faculty, but it took from him the power to use them right. These faculties were all brought under the malignant influence of sin, so that man was no longer capable of doing anything pleasing to God. Depravity is all-pervading, extending to the whole man. It was not, as different theorists have supposed, confined to one department of his being—to the will as contradistinguished from the understanding, or to the understanding as contradistinguished from the will. It was not restricted to the lower appetites, as contrasted with our higher principles of

action. Nor did it affect the heart alone, considered as the seat of the affections. On the contrary, it was a disease from which every organ has suffered.
As found in the understanding, it consists of spiritual ignorance, blindness,
darkness, foolishness. As found in the will, it is rebellion, perverseness, a
spirit of disobedience. As found in the affections, it is hardness of heart, a
total insensibility to and distaste for spiritual and divine things. The entrance
of sin into the human constitution has not only affected all the faculties, so as
to produce a complete disqualification for any spiritual exercise in any form,
but it has crippled and enervated them in their exercise within the sphere of
truth and holiness. They were vitiated in respect to everything wearing the
image of God, the image of goodness and excellence.

Third, the fall has not resulted in the loss of man's *freedom of will,* his
power of volition as a moral faculty. Admittedly this is a much harder point
to cover than either of the above. Not because Scripture is ambiguous in its
teaching, nor even because it contains any seeming contradictions, but because of the philosophical and metaphysical difficulties it raises in the minds
of those who give it careful thought. The fall certainly did not reduce man to
the condition of a stock or stone, or even to an irrational animal. He retained
that rational power of volition which was a part of his original constitution, so
that he was still able to choose spontaneously. It is equally certain that man
is not free to do as he pleases in any absolute sense, for then he would be a god,
omnipotent. In his unfallen state Adam was made subservient to and dependent on the Lord. So it is with his children. Their wills are required to be
fully subordinated to that of their Maker and Governor. Moreover, their
freedom is strictly circumscribed by the supreme rule of divine providence, as
it opens doors for them or shuts doors against them.

As pointed out, though each distinct faculty of the soul has a sphere that
is peculiar to itself, yet they are coordinate; therefore the will is not to be
thought of as an independent, self-determining entity, standing apart from
the other faculties and superior to them, capable of reversing the judgments
of the mind or acting contrary to the desires of the heart. Rather the will is
influenced and determined by them. As G. S. Bishop most helpfully pointed
out, "The true philosophy of moral action and its process is that of Genesis
3:6. 'And when the woman saw that the tree was good for food [sense-percep-
tion, intelligence], and a tree to be desired [affections], she took and ate
thereof [the will].'" Thus the freedom of the will is also limited by the
bounds of human capabilities. It cannot, for example, go beyond the extent
of knowledge possessed by the mind. It is impossible for me to observe, love
and choose any object I am totally unacquainted with. Thus it is the *understanding,* rather than the will, which is the dominant faculty and factor.
Hence, when Scripture delineates the condition of fallen men it attributes
their alienation from God to "the ignorance that is in them" (Eph. 4:18),
and speaks of regenerated men as being "renewed in knowledge" (Col. 3:10).

The limitations of human freedom pointed out above pertain alike to man
unfallen or fallen, but the entrance of sin into the human constitution has

imposed much greater limitations. While it is true that man is as *truly* free now as Adam was before his apostasy, yet he is not as *morally* free as he was. Fallen man is free in the sense that he is at liberty to act according to his own choice, without compulsion from without; yet, since his nature has been defiled and corrupted, he is no longer free to do that which is good and holy. Great care needs to be taken lest our definition of the freedom of fallen man clashes with such scriptures as Psalm 110:3; John 6:44; Romans 9:16; for he only wills now according to the desires and dictates of his evil heart. It has been well said that the will of the sinner is like a manacled, fettered prisoner in a cell. His movements are hampered by his chains, and he is hindered by the walls that confine him. He is free to walk, but in such a constrained way and within such a limited space that his freedom is bondage—bondage to sin.

Whether we understand "the will" to be simply the faculty of volition by which the soul chooses or refuses, or whether we regard it as the faculty of volition together with all else within us which affects the choice—reason, imagination, longing—still fallen man is quite free in *exercising volition* according to his prevailing disposition and desire at the moment. Internal freedom is here used in contrast with external restraint or compulsion. Where the latter is absent the individual is at liberty to decide according to his pleasure. Where the Arminian errs on this point is to confound *power* with "will," insisting that the sinner is equally able to choose good as evil. That is a repudiation of his total depravity or complete vassalage to evil. By the fall man came under bondage to sin, and became the captive of the devil. Even so, he first yields *voluntarily* to the enticements of his own lusts before he commits any act of sin, nor can Satan lead him into any wrongdoing without his own consent.

The natural man does as he pleases, but he pleases himself only in one direction—selfward and downward, never Godward and upward. As Romans 6:20 says of the saints while in their unregenerate state, "For when ye were the servants of sin, ye were free *from* righteousness." In all his sinning man acts as a free agent, for he is forced neither by God nor by Satan. When he breaks the law he does so by his own option, and not by coercion from another. In so doing he is freely acting out his own fallen nature. Thus it is a mistake to say that a bias of the mind or a propensity of heart is destructive of his volition. Both must be self-moved in order for there to be responsibility and guilt, and both *are* self-moved. The murderer is not compelled to hate his victim. Though he cannot prevent his inward hatred by any mere exercise of will, yet he can refrain from the outward act of murder by his own volition; therefore he is blameworthy when he fails to do so. These are indisputable facts of our own consciousness.

Fourth, the fall has not resulted in any reduction, still less the destruction, of *man's responsibility*. If all of the above is carefully pondered this should be quite evident. Human responsibility is the necessary corollary of divine sovereignty. Since God is the Creator, since He is supreme Ruler over all, and since man is just a creature and a subject, there is no escape from his accountability to his Maker and rightful Lord. For what is man responsible? Man is obligated to answer to the relationship which exists between him and his Creator. Man occupies the place of creaturehood, subordination, utter dependency for every breath he draws, and therefore must acknowledge God's dominion, submit to His authority, and love Him with all his strength and heart. Human responsibility is discharged by recognizing God's rights and acting accordingly, by rendering Him His due. It is the practical acknowledgment of His ownership and government. We are justly required to be in constant subjection to His will, to exercise in His service the faculties He has given us, to use the means He has appointed, to improve the opportunities and advantages He has granted us. Our whole duty is to glorify God.

From the above definition it should be crystal clear that the fall did not, and could not to the slightest degree, cancel or impair human responsibility. The fall did not change the fundamental relationship between the Creator and the creature. God is the Owner of sinful man as truly and as fully as He was of sinless man. God is still our Sovereign, and we His subjects. Furthermore, as pointed out above, fallen man is still in possession of all those faculties which qualify for discharging his responsibility. Admittedly, the baby in arms and the poor idiot are not morally accountable for their actions. But it is reasonable that those who have reached the age when they are capable of distinguishing between right and wrong *are* morally accountable for their deeds. Fallen man, though his understanding is spiritually darkened, still possesses rationality. Fallen man, though under the dominion of sin, has his power of volition, and is under binding obligation to make a right and good choice every time, to resist temptations and refrain from evildoing, as any human court of justice insists.

Whatever difficulties may be theoretically involved in the fact that man's nature is now totally depraved and that he is in bondage to sin, still God has not lost His right to command because man has lost his power to obey. While the fall has cast us out of God's favor, it has not released us from His authority. It was not God who took from man his spiritual strength and deprived him of his ability to do that which is well pleasing in His sight. Man was originally endowed with power to meet the requirements of his Maker. It was by his own madness and wickedness that he threw away his power. As a human monarch does not forfeit his rights to allegiance from his subjects when they become rebels, but rather maintains his prerogative by demanding that they cease their insurrection and return to their fealty, so the King of kings has an infinite right to demand that lawless rebels shall become loyal subjects. If God could justly require of us no more than we are now able to render Him, it would follow that the more we enslaved ourselves by evil habits, the less would be our liability—a palpable absurdity!

Not only is man's responsibility insisted on throughout the Scriptures from Genesis to Revelation, but it is also asserted by man's own conscience. Whatever quibbles the individual raises from depravity, and however he argues from his moral impotence that his deeds are not criminal, he repudiates such reasoning where his fellow sinners are concerned. When others wrong him, he neither denies their accountability nor offers excuse for them. If he is cruelly slandered, robbed of his possessions or maltreated in his body, instead of saying of the culprit, "Poor fellow, he could not help himself; Adam is to blame," he promptly appeals to the police and seeks redress in the law courts. Moreover, when the sinner is quickened and awakened by the Holy Spirit, far from complaining against God's righteous demands, he freely owns himself as deserving to be eternally damned for his vile rebellion. He acknowledges that he was fully responsible and that he is "without excuse." He feels the burden of his guilt, and humbles himself before God in sincere repentance.

Under this aspect of our subject we are endeavoring to supply an answer to the question What is connoted by the term "total depravity"? Wherein lies the essential difference or differences between man as unfallen and fallen? Precisely what is the nature of that awful malady which afflicts us? We have considered what it does not consist of, showing that man has not ceased to be a complete and tripartite being, that he is in possession of that spirit which is a necessary part of his constitution; that the fall has not resulted in the loss of any faculties of his soul; that he has not been deprived of the freedom of his will or power of volition; and that there has been no lessening of his responsibility as a creature accountable to God. Turning now to what *has* resulted from the fall, we find that there are a negative and a positive side, that there were certain good things of which we were deprived, and that there were some evils things which we derived. Only as both of these are taken into consideration can we obtain a full answer to our question.

First, by the fall man lost *the moral image of God*. As briefly pointed out earlier, the "image of God," in which man was originally created, refers to his moral nature. It was that which made him a spiritual being. As Calvin expressed it, "It includes all the excellencies in which the nature of man surpasses all the other species of animals." What that "image" consisted of is intimated in Ephesians 4:24 and Colossians 3:10, where a detailed summary of that image is supplied. Our being "renewed" in the image (at regeneration) clearly implies it to be the *same* divine image in which man was made at the beginning. In those two passages it is described as consisting of "righteousness and true holiness" and the "knowledge of God." Let us now enlarge upon each of those component parts.

By "righteousness" we are to understand, as everywhere in Scripture, conformity to the divine law. Before the fall there was entire harmony between the whole moral nature of man and all the requirements of that law which is "holy, and just, and good" (Rom. 7:12). This was much more than a merely negative innocence or freedom from everything sinful (or even bias or tendency toward it, which is all that Socinians allow), namely, something nobler, higher and more spiritual. There was perfect agreement between the constitution of our first parents and the rule of conduct set before them, not only in their external actions but also in the very springs of those actions, in the innermost parts of their beings—in their desires and motives, in all the tendencies and inclinations of their hearts and minds. As Ecclesiastes 7:29 declares, God "made man *upright*," which does not refer to the carriage of his body, except so far as that shadowed forth his moral excellence. That righteousness was lost at the fall, but is in principle restored at regeneration, when God writes His laws in our hearts and puts them in our minds, when He imparts to us a love and a taste for them, and makes us willingly subject to their authority.

By "holiness" we are to understand chastity and undefilement of being. As righteousness was that which gave Adam rapport with the divine law, so holiness was that which made him fit for fellowship with his Maker. There was in him that spotless purity of nature which fitted him for communion with the holy One, for holiness is not only a relationship, but a moral quality too—not only a separation from all that is evil, but the endowment and possession of that which is good. Jehovah is "glorious in holiness" (Exodus 15:11), therefore those with whom He converses must be personally suited to Himself. None but the pure in heart shall see God (Matt. 5:8). It is inconceivable that God by an immediate act would have created any other kind of rational and responsible being than one that was pure and perfect, especially since he was to be the archetype of mankind. As Thornwell so aptly expressed it, "Holiness was the inheritance of his [man's] nature—the birthright of his being. It was the state in which all his faculties received their form." That holiness was lost when man fell, but by regeneration and sanctification it is restored to the elect who are made "partakers of his holiness" (Heb. 12:10). This principle of holiness, communicated to them at the new birth, develops as they grow in grace and in the knowledge of the Lord.

By "knowledge" we are to understand the cognizance of God Himself. As Adam's holiness or purity of heart capacitated him to "see God" in the spiritual sense of the word, he also was enabled to know God by the Holy Spirit's indwelling of him. As Goodwin pointed out, "Where holiness was, we may be sure the Spirit was too. . . . The same Spirit (as in the regenerate) was in Adam's heart to assist his graces and to cause them to flow and bring forth, and to move him to live according to those principles of life given to him." It is clear that since Adam was created in maturity of body he must have been created in maturity of mind, and that there was then in him what we acquire only by slow experience. Adam was able to apprehend and appreciate God for what He is in Himself. He had a true and intuitive knowledge of the perfections of the Deity, the heartfelt realization of Their excellence. That knowledge of God was lost at the fall, by Adam and to his offspring, but it is restored to the elect at regeneration, when He shines "in our hearts to give the light of the knowledge of the glory of God in the face of Jesus Christ" (II Cor. 4:6).

Second, by the fall man lost the life of God. The soul was not only made by God but for God, fitted to know, enjoy and commune with Him; and its life is in Him. But evil necessarily severs from the holy One. Then instead of being alive in God the soul is dead in sin. Not that the soul has ceased to be, for Scripture distinguishes sharply between life and existence: "She that liveth in pleasure is dead while she liveth" (I Tim. 5:6). This is moral or spiritual death, not of being, but of *well-being.* "He that hath the Son hath life; and he that hath not the Son of God hath not life" (I John 5:12). To have the Son of God for my very own is to have everything that is really worth having; to be without Him, no matter what temporal things I may momentarily possess, is to be an utter pauper. "Life"—spiritual and eternal life—is a comprehensive expression to include all the blessedness which man is capable of enjoying here and hereafter. He that has "life" is eternally saved, accepted in the Beloved, admitted into the divine favor, made partaker of the divine nature, made righteous and holy in the sight of God. He that is without "life" is destitute of all these things.

To be separated from God is necessarily to be deprived of everything which makes life worth living, for He is "the fountain of life" (Ps. 36:9), and therefore of light, of glory, of blessedness. No finite mind can conceive—still less can any human pen express—the fullness of those words "the fountain of life." We can only compare other passages of the Scripture which make known something of their meaning. As we do so, we learn that there is at least a threefold life which God's people receive from Him. First, His benign approbation: "in his *favour* is life" (Ps. 30:5). In Leviticus 1:4 the word is rendered "accepted" and in Deuteronomy 33:16, "good will." But the verse which best enables us to understand its force is "O Naphtali, *satisfied with favour,* and full with the blessing of the LORD" (Deut. 33:23). Those who are favorably regarded by God need nothing more, can desire nothing better. To have the goodwill of the triune Jehovah is life indeed, the acme of blessedness. To be out of His favor is to be dead to all that is worthwhile.

Second, *joy and blessedness of soul.* "O God, thou art my God; early will I seek thee . . . to see thy power and thy glory . . . because thy lovingkindness is better than life" (Ps. 63:1-3). God's life in His people capacitates them to delight themselves in Him. Thus it was here. David was in rapt adoration of the divine attributes. His soul longed to have further communion with God, and he resolved to seek Him diligently, to have enlarged views of the divine perfections and experiential discoveries of His excellence, in anticipation of the blessedness of heaven. He prized that more than anything else. The natural man values his life above all else. Not so the spiritual man. To him God's loving-kindness is better than all the comforts and luxuries of temporal life, better than the longest and most prosperous natural life. The loving-kindness of God is itself the present spiritual life of the saint, as it is also both an earnest and a foretaste of the life everlasting. It refreshes his heart, strengthens his soul and sends him on his way rejoicing.

Thousands of people are weary of life, but no Christian is ever weary of God's loving-kindness. The latter is infinitely better than the "life" of a king or a millionaire, for it has no sorrow added to it, no inconvenience in it, no evils accompanying it. Physical death will put the final period to the earthly existence of the most privileged, but it will not end God's loving-kindness, for that is from everlasting to everlasting. It is esteemed by the believer beyond everything else, for it is the spring from which every blessing proceeds. In God's loving-kindness the covenant of grace originated. His loving-kindness gave Christ to His people and them to Him. By His loving-kindness they are drawn to Him (Jer. 31:3), are given a saving knowledge of Him, are brought to know personally the love which He has for them. Without God's loving-kindness life is but death. Well may each believer exclaim, "Because thy lovingkindness is better than life, my lips shall *praise thee.*" In other words: "I will revel in Thy perfections and exult in Thee. I will seek to render something of the homage which is Thy due."

That life which God gives His children consists not only in their being the objects of His benign approbation, in the experiential enjoyment of His loving kindness, but also in the reception of a principle of righteousness and holiness by which they are fitted to appreciate Him, and for want of which the unregenerate cannot enjoy Him, for they are "alienated from the life of God" (Eph. 4:18). It is clear, both from the immediate context and from the remainder of the verse, that the "life of God" there has a particular reference to holiness, for the opposite appears in verse 17: "Henceforth walk not as other Gentiles walk, in *the vanity* of their mind." The contrast is further pointed up in verse 18: "Having the understanding darkened, being alienated from the life of God through the ignorance that is in them, because of the blindness of their heart." The unconverted are wholly dominated by their depraved nature. Their minds are in a state of moral poverty, engaged only with vain things; their understandings are devoid of spiritual intelligence, lacking any power to apprehend truth or appreciate the beauties of virtue; their souls are estranged from God, with an inveterate aversion of Him; their hearts are calloused, steeled against Him. Thus the corruption and depravity of the natural man are set over against the grace and holiness communicated at the new birth, here termed "the life of God."

Third, by the fall man lost *his love for God.* There are two cardinal emotions that influence to action: love and hatred. The one cannot be without the other, for that which is contrary to what is desired will be repellent: "Ye that love the LORD, hate evil" (Ps. 97:10). Of the perfect Man the Father said, "Thou lovest righteousness, and hatest wickedness: therefore God, thy God, hath anointed thee with the oil of gladness above thy fellows" (Ps. 45:7). The Lord said, "Jacob have I loved, but Esau have I hated" (Rom. 9:13). It is the great work of grace in the redeemed to direct and fasten those affections on their proper objects. When we put right our love and hatred, we prosper in the spiritual life. Fallen man differs from unfallen man in this: They both have the same affections, but they are *misplaced* in us, so that we now love what we should hate, and hate what we should love. Our affections are like bodily members out of joint—as if the arms should hang down backward. To direct our love and hatred right is the very essence of true spirituality: to love all that is good and pure, to hate all that is evil and vile; for love moves us to seek union with what is good and to make it our own, as hatred repels and makes us leave alone what is loathsome.

Now love was made *for God*, for He alone is its adequate and suited Object as well as its Source. Love is inherent in His attributes, His law, His ordinances, His dealings with us. But hatred was made for the serpent and sin. God is infinitely lovely in Himself, and if things are to be valued according to the greatness and excellence of them, then God is to be supremely valued, for every perfection centers and is found fully in Him. To love Him above everything else is an act of homage due to Him for who and what He is. There is everything in God to excite esteem, adoration and affection. Goodness is not an object of dread, but of attraction and delight.

God freely supplied Adam with all that He required from him. Since Adam was created with perfect moral rectitude of heart and with a holy state of mind, he was fully competent to love God with all his being. He saw the divine perfections shining forth. The heavens declared God's glory, the firmament showed His handiwork, and His excellence was mirrored in everything around Adam. He realized what God deserved from him, and he was impressed with His blessedness. Adam's heart was filled with a sense of the Lord's ineffable beauty, and admiring and adoring thoughts of Him filled his mind, moving him to give Him the worship and submission to which He is infinitely entitled.

Love for God gave unity of action to all the faculties of Adam's soul; for since this love was the dominant principle in him, it made all the functions of those faculties express his devotion to God. Hence, when love for God died within Adam, his faculties lost not only their original unity and orderliness but *the power* to use them right. All his faculties came under an evil and hostile influence, and were debased in their action. The natural man is without a single spark of true affection for God. "But I know you," said the omniscient Searcher of hearts to the religious Jews, "that ye have not the love of God in you" (John 5:42). Being without any love to God, all the outward acts of the natural man are worthless in His sight: "They that are in the flesh *cannot* please God" (Rom. 8:8), for they lack the root from which they must proceed in order for any fruit to be desirable to Him. Love is that which animates the obedience which is agreeable to God: "If a man love me, he will keep my words" (John 14:23). Love is the very life and substance of everything which is gratifying to God.

As the principle of obedience, love takes the precedence, for faith works by love (Gal. 5:6). Note the order in the injunction "Let us consider one another to provoke [1] unto love and [2] to good works" (Heb. 10:24). Stir up the affections and good works will follow, as a stirring up of the coals causes the flames to rise. It is love which makes all the divine commandments "not grievous" (I John 5:3). We heartily agree with Charnock: "In that one word *love* God hath wrapped up all the devotion He requires of us." Certainly our souls ought to be ravished with Him, for He is infinitely worthy of our choicest affections and strongest desires. Love is a thing acceptable in itself, but nothing can be acceptable to God without it. "They that worsihp him must worship him in spirit and in truth" (John 4:24). The most decorous and punctilious forms of devotion are worthless if they lack vitality and sincerity. True worship proceeds from love, for it is the exercise of heavenly affections, the pouring out of its homage to Him who is "altogether lovely." Love is the best thing we can render God, and it is His right in every service. Without it we are an abomination to Him: "If any man love not the Lord Jesus Christ, let him be Anathema Maran-atha" (I Cor. 16:22).

Fourth, by the fall our first parents and all mankind lost communion with God. This was enjoyed at the beginning, for God made man with faculties capable of this privilege, and designed him to have holy converse with Him. Indeed this was the paramount blessing of that covenant under which Adam was placed, and it was a foretaste of that more intimate communion which would have been his eternal portion had he survived his probation. But the apostasy of Adam and Eve deprived first them, and then their posterity, of this inestimable privilege. This was the immediate and inevitable result of their revolt, whether we contemplate it from either the divine or the human side, "for what fellowship hath righteousness with unrighteousness? And what communion hath light with darkness?" (II Cor. 6:14). Two cannot walk together except they be agreed (Amos 3:3). The holy One will not favorably manifest Himself to rebels or admit them into His presence as friends. After their fall our first parents no longer had the desire that He should do so. Having lost all love for God, they had no desire for Him, but hated and dreaded Him.

Here, then, is the terrible nature of human depravity. From the negative side it consists of man's loss of the moral image of God—consciously felt by our first parents in the shameful sense they had of their nakedness. They also lost the life of God, so that they became alienated from His favor, devoid of joy, emptied of holiness—faintly perceived by them, as was evident from their attempt to make themselves more presentable by manufacturing aprons of fig leaves. Their love to God was lost, so that they no longer revered and adored Him, but were repelled by His perfections—manifested by them in fleeing from Him as soon as they were conscious of His approach. They lost communion with God, so that they were utterly unfit for His presence—finalized by His driving them from Eden. None but the regenerate can estimate how irreparable was man's forfeiture by the fall, and how dreadful is the condition of the natural man.

We have already pointed out a number of things in which the depravity of human nature does not consist, and some of the inestimable blessings of which man *was deprived* by the fall. We now turn to the affirmative side, or a consideration of those evils which *have come* upon human nature as the result of our first parents' apostasy from God. We do not agree with those who teach that a merely negative thing—the absence of good—is transmitted from Adam and Eve to their descendants, via the channel of natural generation and propagation. Rather we are fully persuaded that something positive—an active principle of evil—is communicated from parents to their children. While we do not consider that sin is a substance or a material thing, we are sure that it is very much more than a mere abstraction and nonentity. Man's very nature is corrupted; the virus of evil is in his blood. While there is privation in sin—a nonconformity to God's law—there is also a real positive potency in it to mischief. Sin is a power, as holiness is a power, but a power working to disorder and death.

It has been said by some that "men's natures are not now become sinful by putting anything in them to defile them, but by taking something from them which should have preserved them holy." But we much prefer the statement of the *Westminster Catechism*:

> The sinfulness of that estate into which man fell consisteth in the guilt of Adam's first sin, the want of the righteousness wherein he was created, *and* the corruption of his nature, whereby he is utterly indisposed and disabled, and made opposite unto all that is spiritually good, and wholly inclined to all evil, and that continually, which is commonly called original sin, and from which sin proceed all actual transgressions.

That fallen human nature is not only devoid of all godliness, but also thoroughly impregnated with everything that is devilish, may surely be argued from the two different kinds of sin of which every man is guilty: those of omission, in which there is failure to perform good works, and those of commission, or contempt of the law of God. Something answerable to *both* of those must exist in our sinful nature, otherwise we declare the cause inadequate to produce the effect. While the absence of holiness explains the former, only the presence of positive evil accounts for the latter.

Chapter 7

IMPACT

THERE ARE MANY SCRIPTURAL NAMES for original sin, or the depravity of human nature, which serve to cast light upon it. The following list probably contains the most significant ones. Sin is called the plague of the heart (I Kings 8:38), foolishness bound up in the heart (Prov. 22:15), "the stony heart" (Ezek. 11:19), "the evil treasure" of the heart (Matt. 12:35). It is designated "the poison of asps" (Rom. 3:13), "the old man," because it is derived from the first man and is part and parcel of us since the beginning of our own existence, and "the body of sin" (Rom. 6:6), for it is an assortment of evils, the "sin that dwelleth in me" (Rom. 7:17). It is labeled "another law in my members" (Rom. 7:23) because of its unvarying nature and power, "the law of sin and death" (Rom. 8:2), "the carnal mind" which is "enmity against God" (Rom. 8:7). It is frequently spoken of as "the flesh" (Gal. 5:17) because conveyed by natural generation, "the old man, which is corrupt" (Eph. 4:22), "the sin which doth so easily beset us" (Heb. 12:1), man's "own lust" (James 1:14), which inclines him to evil deeds.

It should be quite plain from our definitions and descriptions of congenital sin that the human constitution is not merely negatively defective, but positively depraved. There are in man's heart not only the lack of conformity to the divine law but a deformity. Not only is the natural man without any desire for holiness; he is born with a disposition which is now radically opposed to it. Therefore he not only has no love for God, but is full of enmity against Him. Sin is also likened to "leaven" (I Cor. 5:6-7). Sin is not only the absence of beauty, but the presence of horrid ugliness; not simply the unlovely, but the hateful; not only the want of order, but real disorder. As "righteousness" expresses objectively the qualities which constitute what is good, and "holiness" the subjective state which is the root of righteousness, so sin includes not only outward acts of transgression, but the evil and rotten state of the whole inner man which inclines to and animates those external iniquities. Very far from being only an "infirmity," indwelling sin is a loathsome disease.

Subjection to Spiritual Death

In seeking to define and describe the nature of depravity from the positive side, we would say, first, that the fall has brought man's soul *into subjection to death*. For the soul to be under the dominion of death is a very different

94

thing from the body being so. When the body dies it becomes as inactive and insensible as a stone. Not so in the case of the soul, for it still retains its vitality and all its powers. Fallen man is a rational, moral, responsible agent; but his internal being is thoroughly deranged. Alienated from the life of God, he can neither think nor will, love nor hate, in conformity to the divine rule. All the faculties of the soul are in full operation, but they are all unholy. Consequently man can no more fulfill the design of his being than does a physical corpse. The analogies between the two are dreadful and solemn. As a dead body is devoid of the principle which formerly vitalized it, so the soul has been abandoned by the Holy Spirit who once inhabited it. A physical corpse rapidly becomes a mass of corruption and repulsion. Thus is the depraved soul of man to the thrice holy God. As a lifeless body is incapable of renewing itself, so is the spiritually dead soul completely powerless to better itself.

"And you hath he quickened, who were dead in trespasses and sins" (Eph. 2:1). As John Gill said, "The design of the apostle in this and some following verses, is to show the exceeding sinfulness of sin, and to set forth the sad estate and condemnation of man by nature, and to magnify the riches of the grace of God, and represent the exceeding greatness of His power by conversion." In Ephesians 1:19 Paul prayed that saints might duly apprehend and appreciate the greatness of that power which had been exercised by God in their salvation, and that they might understand that it was precisely the same divine might as that put forth for the resurrection and exaltation of His Son. That same power had now worked a like change in them; the mighty power which had quickened Christ had also quickened them. The blessed scope and purpose of the Holy Spirit here was to bring out *the answerable* parallel or show the similar change which God had so wonderfully wrought in them. What had been effected for Christ their Head had been accomplished also in them His members, the one work being a glorious pattern of the other.

In connection with Christ's exaltation three things were conspicuous. First, the condition of humiliation and death from which He was delivered and raised. Second, the sublime state of life and honor to which He was exalted. Third, the Author, God, whose almighty power was eminently manifested by the vast difference between those two states. There is a vast difference between the glorious miracles described in the closing verses of Ephesians 1 and what is so graphically portrayed in the opening verses of chapter 2. There we see the dreadful state in which God's elect were by nature, namely, that of death in sin. This death brought its subjects under complete bondage to sin and Satan, so that they did not walk in conformity to the divine law, but according to the corrupt maxims and customs of the world. They were not guided by the Holy Spirit, but energized and directed by the evil spirit, here named "the prince of the power of the air." Without any regard for God's will or concern for His glory, they gave free reign to the lusts of the flesh and the desires of their carnal minds. But notwithstanding their horrible condition, God, who is rich in mercy, raised them from the grave of sin and made them one with Christ in the heavenlies, by a vital and indissoluble union. This marvel had been effected solely by the invincible power and amazing grace of God, without any cooperation of theirs.

That death which has come upon man's soul is at least a threefold one. First, he is dead in law, like a murderer in the condemned cell awaiting execution. Second, he is dead vitally, without a single spark of spiritual life. Thus he is totally dead to God and holiness, cast out of His favor, without any power to recover it. He is dead in opposition to justification, and also dead in opposition to being regenerated and sanctified. Third, he is dead to all that is excellent. As "life" is not simply existence but well-being, so "death" is not the negation of existence, but the absence of all the real pleasures of existence. In its scriptural sense life signifies happiness and blessedness; death means wretchedness and woe. As the utmost natural misery which can befall man is for him to die—for "a living dog is better than a dead lion" (Eccles. 9:4)—so spiritual death is the strongest expression to describe our moral wretchedness. Natural death divests man of all those characteristics which are proper to him as man; but spiritual death makes him worse, without any comeliness in the sight of God, and a stench in His nostrils.

In Ephesians 2:1-3, Goodwin stated, "there is an exact description of the state of man by nature, so complete and compendious a one as is nowhere together, that I know, in the whole Book of God." The Holy Spirit has placed special emphasis on the words "dead in sin," for in verse 5 He repeats them. Three things are outstanding in sin: its guilt, its pollution and its power; and in each of those respects man is in his natural state "dead in sin." "Thou art but a dead man," said God to Abimelech (Gen. 20:3); that is, "You are guilty of death by reason of this act of yours." It is said of Ephraim that "when he offended in Baal, he *died*"; sentence of condemnation came upon him (Hosea 13:1). So it is of sin's pollution, for in Hebrews 6:1 we read of "repentance from *dead* works," because every deed the natural man performs issues from a principle of corruption. So too of sin's power, for every sin man commits disables him more from doing good. His very activity in sin *is* his death, and the more lively he is in sin the more dead will he become toward God.

That there *is* such a threefold death of which fallen man is the subject is further evident from the nature of the work of grace in the elect, for their spiritual death must correspond to their spiritual quickening, which is clearly threefold. There is, first, a life of justification from the guilt of sin and from the condemnation and curse of the law—termed by Christ as passing from death to life (John 5:24), and by the apostle as "justification of life" (Rom. 5:18). This is entirely objective, having respect to our status or standing before God, and is a greater relative change than for a condemned murderer to receive pardon. Second, there is a life of regeneration from the power and dominion of sin, called by Christ being "born again" (John 3:3), when a new nature or principle of holiness is communicated. This is wholly subjective, having respect to the change wrought in the soul when it is divinely quickened. Third, there is a life of sanctification from the pollution of sin, promised by God through the prophet: "Then will I sprinkle clean water upon you, and ye shall be clean: from all your filthiness, and from all your idols, will I cleanse you" (Ezek. 36:25). This is something experiential, consisting of the purifying of the heart from the love of sin. It is referred to as "the washing of regeneration" (Titus 3:5). The first is judicial, the second spiritual, and the third moral; the three comprise the principal parts of God's so-great salvation, the glorification of the saint being yet future.

Bondage to Sin

Second, the fall has brought man *into hopeless bondage to sin.* When the Holy Spirit assures the saints, "For sin shall not have dominion over you: for ye are not under the law, but under grace" (Rom. 6:14), He necessarily means that all those still under the covenant of works are beneath sin's dominion, that it holds full sway over them. As the Lord Jesus declared, "Whosoever committeth sin is the servant of sin" (John 8:34); that is to say, sin is his *master.* Nevertheless, he yields voluntary and ready submission to sin's orders: "Know ye not, that to whom ye yield yourselves servants to obey, his servants ye are to whom ye obey; whether of sin unto death, or of obedience unto righteousness?" (Rom. 6:16). No one coerces and compels them. The dominion of sin is not even an indwelling force against the will of those who are under it, but it is natural and congenial to them. Even though, occasionally, conscience feebly protests, its voice is silenced by the clamorings of lust, to which the will freely complies. The dominion of sin over the natural man is entire, for it pervades the spirit with all its powers, the soul with all its faculties, the body with all its members, at all times and under all circumstances.

Sin is likened to a monarch ruling over his subjects: "as sin hath *reigned* unto death" (Rom. 5:21). Its kingdom is worldwide, for all the children of Adam are its subjects. Sin occupies the throne of the human heart until almighty grace deposes it. Sin has taken possession of the complete person, which constantly acts under its direction and influence. The mind is in subjection to evil as a governing principle which determines all its volitions and acts, for sin's lustings are so many imperial and imperious edicts. Yet this rule of sin is not a force upon the mind to which it makes opposition, for the soul is a *subject*—as a king continues to occupy the throne only by the consent and free allegiance of his subjects. While the soul cannot help but will evil because of the reign of sin, still its volitions are spontaneous. The dominion of sin consists in its determining influence upon the will, and it retains this sway to the end, unless victorious grace makes a conquest of the soul by the implantation of a contrary principle, which opposes the influence of indwelling sin and disposes the will to contrary acts. Though conscience may remonstrate sharply against the fatal choice, sin still regulates the decisions and deeds of the natural man.

Brine stated that this dominion of sin

> is not a propensity to some particular evil, but an inclination to deviate
> from the rule of our duty taken in its *full compass*. Yet, as the mind is
> incapable of exerting itself in all manner of ways and about all sorts of
> objects at once and in one instant, it is sometimes acting in one manner
> and sometimes in another as it is variously affected by the different objects
> about which it is conversant; but all its actions are evil. And those who
> study their hearts most will best understand the surprising variety of ways
> wherein evil concupiscence acts its part in the soul. In the several stages
> of human life this sway of sin discovers itself. In childhood, by folly proper
> to that age. In youth it exerts itself in various ways: by a low ambition,
> pride, and a strange fondness for sinful pleasures. In the state of manhood,
> by a pursuit of the transitory things of this world, and this is often under
> specious pretences of more extensive usefulness: but, in fact, men are acted
> upon by a spirit of covetousness. In an advanced age, by impatience. . . .

The dominion of sin is made to appear more plainly and openly in some
than in others, by their following a course of gross and corrupt evil, though
it is just as real and great in those whose wickedness is more confined to the
mind and heart. Scripture speaks not only of the "filthiness of the flesh," but
also of "the spirit" (II Cor. 7:1), that is, vile imaginations, envy, hatred of
others, inward rebellion, and ragings against God when His will crosses ours.
The sovereign God permits and controls the direction and form this dominion
takes in each one. Today the power and reign of sin are more manifest in the
world than they have ever been. Not because human nature has undergone
any deterioration, for that is impossible—it has been rotten to the core since
the time of Cain and Abel. No, rather because God is increasingly removing
His restraining hand, thereby allowing the horrid corruption of men's hearts
to become more visible and obvious. There are indeed degrees of wickedness,
but not in the root from which it proceeds. Every man's nature is equally
depraved, and everyone in an unregenerate state is wholly dominated by sin.

So mighty is the power of sin that it has made all the sons of men its slaves.
Few indeed realize that they are held fast by the cords of their sin (Prov.
5:22), and still fewer realize where its strength lies. Carnality, stemming
from sin, is a powerful thing in itself, for it has a will of its own (John 1:13),
a mind of its own (Rom. 8:6-7), passions (Rom. 1:24; 7:5). First Corinthians
15:56 informs us, "The sting of death is sin; and the strength of sin is the
law." The first part of that statement is obvious, but the second calls for some
explanation. Sin is manifestly what puts venom into the dart of death and
gives it its power to hurt and kill. Sin brought death into the world; had there
been no sin, there would have been no death. It is sin, unpardoned sin, which
makes death so dreadful, for not only does it put a final end to all its pleasures, but it conducts its subjects to certain judgment. But wherein is the law
of God "the strength of sin"? The law is "holy, and just, and good" (Rom.
7:12); how then can it be the strength of that which is corrupt, evil and
abominable?

Most assuredly the law does not give the slightest encouragement to sin;

rather it sternly forbids it. The law is not the essential but the accidental strength of sin, because of sin's inherent depravity, as the pure rays of the sun result in the horrid steam and noxious stench rising from decaying flesh. As the presence of an enemy calls into exercise the malice which lies dormant in the heart, so the holy requirements of the law presenting themselves before man's corrupt heart stir it to active opposition. Thus the exceeding sinfulness of sin is all the more demonstrated, for its potency to evil is drawn forth by any restraint being laid upon it. Though fire and water are opposite elements, that fact is not so evident while there is distance between them; but let them meet together, and there will be great spluttering and striving between them. If the heart of man were pure, the law would be acceptable; but since it is depraved, there is fierce resentment against the spiritual precepts of the law.

As the law makes no provision for pardon, the natural effect of guilt is to widen the breach between the sinner and God. Aware (as in some measure the most degraded are) of divine displeasure, the sinner is prone to withdraw farther and farther from the divine presence. Every augmentation of guilt is an augmentation of estrangement. The more the sinner sins, the wider becomes the gulf between himself and God. This gives strength to sin. It provokes the malignity of the heart against the law, against all holy order, against the Judge. It incites the spirit of rebellion to unwonted fierceness, and makes the sinner desperate in his sin. It causes its subjects to become increasingly reckless and, as they realize the brevity of life, to plunge more eagerly into profligacy. As frosty weather causes a fire to burn more fiercely, so the law increases man's enmity against God. Saul of Tarsus found it so in his experience. The divine prohibition "Thou shalt not covet" was applied in power to his heart, and he tells us, "Sin, taking occasion by the commandment, wrought in me all manner of concupiscence" (Rom. 7:7-8).

Blindness of Heart

Third, the fall has brought man's mind into darkness. As physical blindness is one of the greatest natural calamities, spiritual blindness is much more so. It consists not in universal ignorance, but in total incapacity to take in a real knowledge of divine things. As it is said of the Jews, "Blindness *in part* is happened to Israel" (Rom. 11:25). Men may become very learned in many things, and by focusing their minds upon the Scriptures they may acquire considerable literal knowledge of its contents; but they are quite unable to obtain a vital and effectual knowledge of them. "The natural man receiveth not the things of the Spirit of God: for they are foolishness unto him: neither can he know them, because they are spiritually discerned" (I Cor. 2:14); and he has no spiritual perception. This darkness which is upon the mind makes the natural man incapable of perceiving the excellence of God, the perfection of His law, the real nature of sin, or his dire need of a Saviour. Should the Lord draw near and ask him, "What wilt thou that I should do unto thee?" his answer ought to be "Lord, that I might receive my sight" (Mark 10:51).

This darkness is upon the noblest part of man's being, his soul; and upon the highest faculty of it, the mind, which performs the same office for it as does the eye for the body. By means of our visual organ we observe material objects, distinguish between them, recognize their beauty or repulsiveness. By the mind we think, reason, understand, weigh and discern between the true and the false. Since the mind occupies so high a place in the scale of our beings, and since it is the most active of our inward faculties, ever working, then what a fearful state for the soul to be blind! John Flavel said it is "like a fiery, high-mettled horse whose eyes cannot see, furiously carrying his rider upon rocks, pits and dangerous precipices." Or, as the Son of God declared, "The light of the body is the eye: if therefore thine eye be single, thy whole body shall be full of light. But if thine eye be evil, thy whole body shall be full of darkness. If therefore the light that is in thee be darkness, how great is that darkness!" (Matt. 6:22-23).

Much is said in the Scriptures about this terrible affliction. Men are represented as groping at noonday (Deut. 28:29). "They meet with darkness in the daytime, and grope in the noonday as in the night" (Job 5:14). "They know not, neither will they understand." And why? "They walk on in darkness" (Ps. 82:5). It cannot be otherwise. Alienated from Him who is light, they must be in total spiritual darkness. "The way of the wicked is as darkness: they know not at what they stumble" (Prov. 4:19). They are insensible of the very things which are leading to everlasting woe. Moral depravity inevitably results in moral darkness. As a physically blind eye shuts out all natural light, so the blinded eye of the soul excludes all spiritual light. It renders the Scriptures profitless. In this respect the case of the Gentiles is identical with that of the Jews: "But their minds were blinded: for until this day remaineth the same vail untaken away in the reading of the old testament" (II Cor. 3:14). Consequently the highest wisdom they call foolish, and objects which are the most glorious and attractive are despised and rejected by them.

It is a great mistake to suppose that depravity is confined to the heart or to any one faculty which is closely connected with the distinction between right and wrong. As a grave disease extends its influence to all the functions of the body, so depravity extends to all the powers of the soul. Sin is as really blindness to the mind as it is hardness to the heart; therefore the heart has departed from its original tendencies. Its actions, however intense, are only in the wrong direction. This explains the mental aberrations of men and the immoral conceptions they have formed of Deity. As we attempt to contemplate the manifold forms of ancient and modern religious error, the various superstitions, the disgusting rites of worship, the monstrous and hideous symbols of the Godhead, the cruel flagellations and obscenities which prevail in heathen lands; when we consider all the abominations which have been committed in the name of divine worship, we ask *how* such delusions originated and have been propagated. It is not sufficient to trace them to sin in general; they must be attributed to a deranged mind. Only a debased and darkened understanding adequately accounts for the horrible lies which have taken the name of truth, and the fearful blasphemies which have been styled worship.

This moral darkness which is upon the mind appears in the speculations about Deity by philosophers and metaphysicians, for they are erroneous, defective and degrading, when not corrected by divine revelation. All such speculations are necessarily vain when they attempt to deal with things which transcend the scope of our faculties—things which undertake to carry knowledge beyond its first principles—and try to comprehend the incomprehensible. The creature being dependent and finite can never hope to compass an absolute knowledge of anything. J. H. Thornwell said:

> Intelligence begins with principles that must be accepted and not explained; and in applying those principles to the phenomena of existence, apparent contradictions constantly emerge that require patience and further knowledge to resolve them. But the mind, anxious to know all and restless under doubts and uncertainty, is tempted to renounce the first principles of reason and to contradict the facts which it daily observes. It seeks consistency of thought, and rather than any gaps should be left unfilled it plunges everything into hopeless confusion. Instead of accepting the laws of intelligence and patiently following the light of reason, and submitting to ignorance where ignorance is the lot of his nature as limited and finite, and joyfully receiving the partial knowledge which is his earthly inheritance, man under the impulse of curiosity, had rather make a world that he does understand than admit one which he cannot comprehend. When he cannot stretch himself to the infinite dimensions of truth, he contracts truth to his own little measure. This is what the apostle means by *vanity of mind.*

The only way of escape for fallen man from such vanity of mind is for him to reject the serpent's poison, "Ye shall be as gods, knowing good and evil," and submit unreservedly to divine revelation, according to our Lord's word in Matthew 11:25: "I thank thee, O Father, Lord of heaven and earth, because thou hast hid these things from the wise and prudent, and hast revealed them unto babes." Man must renounce all self-acquired knowledge, forsake all his own erroneous conclusions and fancies, and take the place of a little child before Him. But that is just what the pride of the depraved creature refuses to do. Sin has not only counteracted the normal development of reason; it has so deranged the mind that men *love darkness* rather than light (John 3:19). They are so infatuated with their delusions that they prefer error to the truth. That which may be known about God is clearly manifested on every hand, yet men refuse to see. But the light still shines all around them, though they are carried away with the darkness of their corruption. As created, all men may and ought to know God; as fallen, practical atheism is their sad heritage.

The highest intellects of men, in their fallen and degenerate condition, could not of themselves form any accurate or just speculative knowledge of God and His government. Yet there is a profounder ignorance which requires notice, namely, that theoretical knowledge of God which is common in those countries that have been favored with the gospel. By the light of the Christian revelation many a humble, uneducated person has been made familiar with truths of which Plato and Aristotle knew nothing. Thousands of people are sound on questions which perplexed and confounded the understandings of presumptuous sophists. They believe that God is spirit: personal, eternal and independent; that He made the heavens and the earth, and controls all His creatures and all their actions. They are persuaded that He is as infinitely good as He is infinitely great. Yet in spite of this knowledge they do not glorify Him as God. They lack that loving light which warms as well as convinces. They have no communion with Him; they neither love nor adore Him. In order to have a spiritual, vital and transforming knowledge of God their dead hearts must be quickened and their blind eyes opened. And in order for *that* there must be an atonement, a reconciliation with God. The cross is the only place where men can truly find God, and the incarnate Son the only One in whom God can be adequately known.

If man's mind were not enveloped by darkness, he would not be deceived by Satan's lies nor allured by his bait. If man were not in total spiritual darkness, he would never cherish the delusion that the filthy rags of his own righteousness could make him acceptable to the holy One. If he were not blind, he would perceive that his very prayers are an abomination to the Lord (Prov. 15:8). Though this incapability of understanding heavenly things is common to all the unregenerate, it is more heightened in some than in others. All are equally under the dominion of sin, yet some forge themselves additional fetters of evil habits by drinking iniquity like water. Many of the sons of men immerse themselves in greater darkness by the strong prejudices of their own making, through pride and self-will. Others are still further incapacitated to take in spiritual things, even theoretically, by God's judicial act of giving them over wholly to follow the dictates of their own minds. "He hath blinded their eyes, and hardened their heart; that they should not see with their eyes, nor understand with their heart, and be converted" (John 12:40; cf. II Thess. 2:10-12).

Subjugation to Satan

Fourth, the fall has issued in man's becoming *the bondslave of Satan*. That is another mysterious but very real thing, about which we can know nothing except what is revealed in Holy Writ; but its teaching leaves us in no doubt about the fact. It reveals that men are morally the devil's children (Acts 13:10; I John 3:10), that they are his captives (II Tim. 2:26) and under his power (Acts 26:18; Col. 1:13), that they are determined to do what he wants (John 8:44). He is described as the strong man armed, who holds undisputed possession of the sinner's soul, until a stronger than he dispossesses him (Luke 11:21-22). It speaks of men being "oppressed of the devil" (Acts 10:38), and declares, "The god of this world [the inspirer and director of its false religions] hath blinded the minds of them which believe not, lest the light of the glorious gospel of Christ, who is the image [Revealer] of God, should shine unto them" (II Cor. 4:4). The heart of fallen man is the throne on which Satan reigns, and all the sons of Adam are naturally inclined to yield themselves slaves to him. The awful reality of his enslaving men was authenticated beyond the possibility of doubt by the cases of demoniacal possession in Christ's day.

The corrupt nature of men gives Satan the greatest advantage against them, for they are as ready to comply as he is to tempt. No age or condition of life is exempted from his assaults. He adapts his evil solicitations according to their varied temperaments and tempers, and they are easily overcome. The longer he rules over men the more guilt they contract, and the more they come under his dominion. To be his bondslave is to be in a state of abject misery, for he purposes the eternal ruin of his victims, and every step they take in that direction furthers his evil designs and increases their wretchedness. He is as ready to laugh at and mock them for the pangs and pains which their folly brings on them as he was to tempt and solicit their service. Yet he has *no right* to their subjection. Though God permits Satan to rule over the children of disobedience, He has given him no grant or warrant which renders it *lawful* for him to do so. Thus he is a usurper, the declared enemy of God, and though sinners are allowed to yield themselves up to the devil's control, that is far from being by divine approbation.

Ephesians 2:2-3 contains the most clear and concise description of this awful subject: "Wherein [a status and state of being dead in trespasses and sins] in time past ye walked according to the course of this world, according to the prince of the power of the air, the spirit that now worketh in the children of disobedience." The world and the prince of the power of the air are definitely linked together, for the dead in sin are said to "walk according to" the one equally as the other—the only difference being that the second statement is amplified by the clauses which follow, where we are shown *why* they walked thus. The identifying of the world with Satan is easily understood. Three times our Lord called him "the prince of this world," and I John 5:19 declares that "the whole world lieth in wickedness." The world is distinguished from the church of Christ—the children of God. The radical difference between the two opposing companies was intimated at the beginning in the word of Jehovah to the serpent, when He made mention of "thy seed" and "her seed." Those two seeds were referred to by Christ in His parable of the tares, and designated by Him as "the children of the kingdom" and "the children of the wicked one" (Matt. 13:38).

Our Lord also spoke of the "kingdom" of Satan (Matt. 12:26), referring not only to his power and dominion, but to his subjects and officers being an *organized company*—in opposition to "the kingdom of . . . [God's] dear Son" (Col. 1:13). Thus "the world" signifies "the world of the ungodly" (II Peter 2:5), not only the sum total of the children of the devil in contradistinction from the children of God, but all the unregenerate, which augments their strength and malignity. When coals, each on fire, are placed together, the fire is increased. In like manner there is an intensification from this union of all parts of this "world." Its "course" connotes, first, its "age" or time, each generation having a more or less distinct character, but essentially the same "evil world" (Gal. 1:4). Second, the word means the mold or manner of the world, its custom or way of life—its "spirit" (I Cor. 2:12) and "fashion" (I Cor. 7:31). The unregenerate walk according to the same maxims and morals; they do as the majority of their fellowmen do, because each has the same depraved nature.

"According to the prince of the power of the air." The world is what it is because it is under the dominion of Satan. The mass of the unregenerate are likened to the sea (Isa. 57:20); being bound by a common nature they all move together as the waters of the sea follow the tide. Goodwin said:

> If the wind comes and blows upon the sea, how it rageth, how strong are the streams then! There is breath, a spirit, the spirit of the power of the air, namely the Devil sendeth forth an influence whereby, as the wind that bloweth upon the trees, which way it bloweth, so he bloweth and swayeth the hearts of the multitude one way . . . when all the coals lie together, they make a great fire, but if the bellows be used they make the fire more intense.

The Holy Spirit has here given us a double explanation of *why* the unregenerate follow the course they take. As each one enters and grows up in the world, being a social creature, he naturally goes with the drove of his fellows; and possessing the same evil lusts he finds their ways agreeable to him. The world, then, is the *exemplary* cause according to which men shape their lives, but the devil is the *impelling* cause.

Since the fall this malignant spirit has entered into human nature in a manner somewhat analogous to that in which the Holy Spirit dwells in the hearts of believers. He has intimate access to our faculties, and though he cannot, like God's Spirit, work at the roots to change and transform their tendencies, yet he can ply them with representations and delusions which effectually incline them to fulfill his behests. He can cheat the understanding with appearances of truth, fascinate the fancy with pretenses of beauty, and deceive the heart with semblances of good. By a whisper, a touch, a secret suggestion, he can give an impulse to our thoughts and turn them into channels which exactly serve his evil designs. Men not only do what he desires, but he has a *commanding power* over them, as his being termed a prince plainly implies; and therefore they are said to be "taken captive . . . at his will" (II Tim. 2:26), and when converted they are delivered from his power (Col. 1:13). Yet he does not work *immediately* in all hearts, as the Holy Spirit does in the regenerate, for he is not omnipresent, but employs a host of demons as his agents.

One man can influence another only by external means, but Satan can also affect from within. He is able not only to take thoughts out of men's minds (Luke 8:12), but to place thoughts in them, as we are told he "put into the heart of Judas" to betray Christ (John 13:2); he works *indiscernibly* as a spirit. As men yield to and comply with the devil's insinuations, he gains increasing control over them, and God permits him to enter and indwell them, as Matthew 12:29 shows. When Satan would incite anyone to some particularly awful sin he takes possession of him. We read that the devil, after Judas had consented to the vile insinuation which he had put into his heart, "entered into" Judas (Luke 22:3), in order to ensure the carrying out of his design by strengthening the traitor to do his will. The word for "entered" is the same as in Mark 5:13 where the unclean spirits entered into the herd of swine, which brought about their destruction. Satan is able to "fill the heart" (Acts 5:3), giving an additional impulse to evil, as a person filled with wine is abnormally fired. But let it be noted that there is *no* record in Scripture of either the devil or a demon ever taking possession of a *regenerate* person.

Though the devil works thus in men, and works effectually, yet all their sins are their own. The Spirit is careful to add "worketh in the children of disobedience." Man consents first, then the devil strengthens his resolution. That appears again in Peter's reproaching of Ananias for yielding to temptation: "*Why* hath Satan filled thine heart to lie to the Holy Spirit?" Satan does no violence either to the liberty or the faculties of men, disturbing neither the spontaneity of the understanding nor the freedom of the will. As the work of God's Spirit in His elect is by no means inconsistent with their full responsibility and their entire moral agency, so the work of the devil in the reprobate makes it nonetheless *their* work; therefore the dupes of his craft are without excuse for their sins.

Unlike the Holy Spirit, the devil has no creative power. He can impart no new nature, but only avail himself of what is already there for him to work on. He avails himself of the constitution of man's nature, especially of his depravity as a fallen being. He gives impetus and direction to man's free but evil tendencies. Rightly did Goodwin point out that "as no man doth sin because God decrees him to sin, and therefore none can excuse himself with that; so no man can excuse himself with this, that Satan worketh in him."

Here then is the nature of human depravity as seen from the positive side. The fall has brought man into subjection to the power of death, into hopeless bondage to sin, into complete spiritual blindness. Man has become the bond-slave of Satan. In that dreadful state he does not possess a particle of power to deliver himself or even to mitigate his wretchedness. In addition, his heart is filled with enmity against God.

Chapter 8

ENORMITY

THE THEOLOGY of the last century has failed lamentably at two essential points, namely, its teaching concerning God and its teaching concerning fallen man. As one writer expressed it, "On the one hand, they have not ascended high enough . . . on the other hand, they do not descend low enough." God is infinitely greater and His dominion far more absolute and extensive than most theologians admit, and man has sunk much lower and is far more depraved than they will allow. Consequently man's conduct toward his Maker is vastly more evil than is commonly supposed. Its horrible hideousness cannot really be seen except in the light supplied by Holy Writ. Sin is infinitely more vile in its nature than any of us realize. Men may acknowledge that they sin, but it *appears* as sin to very, very few. Sin was the original evil. Before it entered the universe there was no evil: "God saw every thing that he had made, and, behold, it was very good" (Gen. 1:31). Sin is the greatest of all evils. There is nothing in it but evil, nor can it produce anything but evil—now, in the future, forever. As soon as sin was conceived, all other evils followed.

The Nature of Sin

We may take a survey of everything in and on the earth, and we cannot find anything so vile as sin. The basest and most contemptible thing in this world has some degree of worth in it, as being the workmanship of God. But sin and its foul streams have not the least part of worth in them. Sin is wholly evil, without the least mixture of good—vileness in the abstract. Its heinousness appears in its author: "He that committeth sin is of the devil; for the devil sinneth from the beginning" (I John 3:8). Sin is his trade, and he practices it incessantly. Sin's enormity is seen in what it has done to man: it has completely ruined his nature and brought him under the curse of God. Sin is the source of all our miseries; all unrighteousness and wretchedness are its fruits. There is no distress of the mind, no anguish of the heart, no pain of the body, but is due to sin. All the miseries which mankind groans under are to be ascribed to sin. It is the cause of all penalty: "Thy way and thy doings have procured these things unto thee; this is thy wickedness, because it is bitter, because it reacheth unto thine heart" (Jer. 4:18). Had there been no sin, there would have been no wars, no national calamities, no prisons, no hospitals, no insane asylums, no cemeteries! Yet who lays these things to heart?

Sin assumes many garbs, but when it appears in its nakedness it is seen as a black and misshapen monster. How God Himself views it may be learned from the various similitudes used by the Holy Spirit to set forth its ugliness and loathsomeness. He has compared it with the greatest deformities and the most filthy and repulsive objects to be met with in this world. Sin is likened to:

1. the scum of a seething pot in which is a detestable carcass (Ezek. 24:10-12)

2. the blood and pollution of a newborn child, before it is washed and clothed (Ezek. 16:4, 6)

3. a dead and rotting body (Rom. 7:24)

4. the noisome stench and poisonous fumes which issue from the mouth of an open sepulcher (Rom. 3:13)

5. the lusts of the devil (John 8:44)

6. putrefying sores (Isa. 1:5-6)

7. a menstruous cloth (Isa. 3:22; Lam. 1:17)

8. a canker, or gangrene (II Tim. 2:17)

9. the dung of filthy creatures (Phil. 3:8)

10. the vomit of a dog and the wallowing of a sow in the stinking mire (II Peter 2:22)

Such comparisons show us something of the vileness and horribleness of sin, yet in reality it is beyond all comparison. There is a far greater malignity in sin than is commonly supposed even by the majority of church members. Men regard it as an infirmity, and term it a human frailty or hereditary weakness. But Scripture calls it "an evil thing and bitter" (Jer. 2:19), an abominable thing which God hates (Jer. 44:4). Few people think of it thus; rather the majority regard it as a mere trifle, a matter of so little moment that all they have to do is cry in the hour of death, "Lord, pardon me; Lord, bless me," and all will be eternally well with them. They judge sin by the opinion of the world. But what can a world which "lieth in wickedness" (I John 5:19) know about God's hatred of sin? It does not matter what the world thinks, but it matters a great deal what God says about it. Others measure the guilt of sin by what conscience tells them—or fails to! But conscience needs informing by the Bible. Many uncivilized tribes have put their girl babies and old people to death, and conscience did not chide them. A deadened conscience has accompanied multitudes to hell without any voice of warning. Tens of thousands of religionists see so little filth in sin that they imagine a few tears will wash away its stain. They perceive so little criminality in it that they persuade themselves that a few good works will make full reparation for it.

All comparisons fail to set forth the horrible malignity in that abominable thing which God hates. We can say nothing more evil of sin than to term it what it is: "sin, that it might appear *sin*" (Rom. 7:13). "Who is like unto thee, O LORD?" (Exodus 15:11). When we say of God that He is *God* we say all that can be said of Him. "Who is a God like unto thee?" (Micah

7:18). We cannot say more good of Him than to call Him God. We cannot say more evil of sin than to say it is sin. When we have called it that, we have said all that can be said of it. When the apostle wanted a descriptive epithet for sin, he invested it with its own name: "that sin by the commandment might become *exceeding sinful*" (Rom. 7:13). That was the worst he could say of it, the ugliest name he could give it—just as when Hosea denounced the Ephraimites for their idolatry: "So shall Beth-el do unto you because of the evil of your evil" (10:15, literal trans.). The prophet could not paint their wickedness any blacker than to double the expression.

The hideousness of sin can be set forth no more impressively than in the terms used by the apostle in Romans 7:13. "That sin . . . might become exceeding sinful" is a very forcible expression. It reminds us of similar words used by Paul when magnifying that glory which is yet to be revealed in the saints, and with which the sufferings of this present time are not worthy to be compared, namely, "a far more exceeding and eternal weight of glory." No viler name can be found for sin than its own. Andrew Fuller stated:

> If we speak of a treacherous person, we call him a Judas; if of Judas, we call him a *devil;* but if of Satan, we want a comparison, because we can find none that is worse than himself; we must therefore say, as Christ did, "when he speaketh a lie, he speaketh of his own." It was thus with the apostle when speaking of the evil of his own heart: "that sin by the commandment might become"—what? He wanted a name worse than its own: he could find none; he therefore unites a strong epithet to the thing itself, calling it "exceeding sinful."

There are four great evils in sin: the total absence of the moral image of God, the transgression of His just law, obnoxiousness to His holiness, and separation from Him—entailing the presence of positive evil, guilt cannot be measured by any human standard, the most repulsive defilement, and misery inexpressible. Sin contains within it an *infinite evil,* for it is committed against a Being of infinite glory, unto whom we are under infinite obligations. Its odiousness appears in that fearful description, "filthiness and superfluity of naughtiness" (James 1:21), which is an allusion to the brook Kidron, into which the garbage of the temple sacrifices and other vile things were cast (II Chron. 29:16). Sin's hatefulness to God is seen in His awful curse upon the workmanship of His own hands, for He would not anathematize man for a trifle. If He does not afflict willingly, then most certainly He would not curse without great provocation. The virulence and vileness of sin can only be gauged at Calvary, where it rose to the terrible commission of Deicide; at the cross it "abounded" to the greatest possible degree. The demerits of sin are seen in the eternal damnation of sinners in hell, for the indescribable sufferings which divine vengeance will then inflict upon them are sin's rightful wages.

Sin is a species of atheism, for it is the virtual repudiation of God. It seeks to discredit Him, to rebel against Him: "Who is the Lord, that I should obey his voice?" (Exodus 5:2). Sin is a malignant spirit of independence. Whether imperceptibly influencing the mind or consciously present, it lies at the root of all evil and depravity. Man desires to be lord of himself; hence his ready reception, at the beginning, of the devil's lie "Ye shall be as gods." Man's credence of that lie was the dissolution of the tie which bound the creature in willing subjection to the Author of his being. Thus sin is really the denial of our creaturehood and, in consequence, a rejection of the rights of the Creator. Its language is "I am. I am my own, and therefore I have the right to live unto myself." Thornwell pointed this out:

> Considered as the renunciation of dependence upon God, it may be called unbelief; as the exaltation of itself to the place of God, it may be called pride; as the transferring to another object the homage due to the Supreme, it may be called idolatry; but in all these aspects the central principle is one and the same.

Effect of Sin in Man's Soul

An atheist is not only one who denies the existence of God, but also one who fails to render to God the honor and subjection which are His due. Thus there is a *practical* atheism as well as a theoretical atheism. The former obtains wherever there is no genuine respect for God's authority and no concern for His glory. There are many who entertain theoretical notions of the divine existence, yet their hearts are devoid of any affection to Him. And *that* is now the natural condition of all the fallen descendants of Adam. Since "there is none that seeketh after God" (Rom. 3:11), it follows that there is none with any practical sense of His excellence or His claims. The natural man has no desire for communion with God, for he places his happiness in the creature. He prefers everything before Him, and glorifies everything above Him. He loves his own pleasures more than God. His wisdom being "earthly, sensual, devilish" (James 3:15), the celestial and divine are outside his consideration. This appears in man's works, for actions speak louder than words. Our hearts are to be gauged by what we do, not by what we say. Our tongues may be great liars, but our deeds tell the truth, showing what we really are.

How little recognized and realized is the fact that all outward impieties are the manifestations of an inward atheism! Yet this is indeed the case. As bodily sores evidence impurity of the blood, so actions demonstrate the corruption of human nature. Sin is often termed ungodliness: "Behold, the Lord cometh with ten thousands of His saints, to execute judgment upon all, and to convince all that are ungodly among them of all their ungodly deeds which they have ungodly committed, and of all their hard speeches which ungodly sinners have spoken against him" (Jude 14-15). How vain it is to deny atheism in the heart when there is so much of it in the life! Here too the tree is known by its fruits. As an active and operative principle in the soul, sin is the virtual assertion not only of self-sufficiency but also of self-supremacy. Stephen Charnock rightly pointed out, "Those therefore, are more deserving of being termed atheists who acknowledge a God and walk as if there were none, than those (if there can be any such) that deny God, and walk as if there were one."

As all virtuous actions spring from a due acknowledgment of God, so all vicious actions rise from a lurking denial of Him. He who makes no conscience of sin has no regard for the honor of God, and consequently none for His being. If "by the fear of the LORD men depart from evil" (Prov. 16:6), it clearly follows that in the absence of any awe of Him they rush into evil. Every sin is an invading of the rights of God. When we transgress His laws we repudiate His sovereignty. When we lean on our own understanding and set up reason as the guide of our actions, we despise His wisdom. When we seek happiness in gratifying our lusts, we slight His excellence and consider His goodness insufficient to satisfy our hearts. When we commit those sins in secret which we would be ashamed to do in public, we virtually deny both His omniscience and omnipresence. When we lean on the arm of flesh or put our trust in some device, we disbelieve His power. Sin is turning the back upon God (Jer. 32:33), kicking against Him (Deut. 32:15), treating Him with the utmost contempt.

People do not like to regard themselves as practical atheists. They entertain a much better opinion of themselves than that. They pride themselves on possessing far too much intelligence to harbor so degrading an idea that there is no God. Instead they are persuaded that creation clearly evidences a Creator. But no matter what their intellectual beliefs may be, the fact remains that they are secret atheists. He who disowns the authority of God disowns His divinity. It is the unquestionable prerogative of the Most High to have dominion over His creatures, to make His will known to them, and to demand their subjection. But their breaking of His bands and their casting away of His cords (Ps. 2:3) are a practical rejection of His rule over them. Practical atheism consists of utter contempt of God, conducting ourselves as though there were none infinitely above us who has an absolute right to govern us, to whom we must give a full account of all that we have done and left undone, and who will then pronounce sentence of eternal judgment upon us.

The natural man gives himself that homage which is due God alone. When he obtains something which makes him glitter in the eyes of the world, how happy he is, for men "receive honour one of another, and seek not the honour that cometh from God only" (John 5:44). They dote on their own accomplishments and acquisitions, but do not delight in the divine perfections. They think highly of themselves, but contemptuously of others. They compare themselves with those lower than themselves, instead of with those above. He who considers himself worthy of his own supreme affection regards himself as being entitled to the supreme regard of his neighbors. Yet it is self-idolatry to magnify ourselves to the virtual forgetfulness of the Creator. When self-love wholly possesses us, we usurp God's prerogative by making self our chief end. This consuming egotism appears again in man's proneness to attribute his achievements to his own virtue, strength and skill, instead of to Him from whom comes every good and perfect gift. This was Nebuchadnezzar's attitude: "Is not this great Babylon, that I have built?" (Dan. 4:30). God punished Herod for not giving Him the glory when instead of rebuking the people he accepted their impious adulation.

The same profane spirit is shown by man's envying the talents and prosperity of others. Cain was angry with God, and hated and killed Abel, because his brother's offering was received and his own refused. Since God assigns to each his portion, to look with a grudging eye on that enjoyed by our fellowmen has much of practical atheism in it. It is unwillingness for God to be the Proprietor and Distributor of His favors as He pleases. It is assuming the right to direct the Creator in what He shall bestow on His creatures; denying His sovereignty to give more to one than to another. God disposes of His benefits according to the counsel of His own will, but vain man thinks he could make a better distribution of them. This sin imitates that of Satan who was dissatisfied with the station which the Most High had allotted him (Isa. 14:12-14). It is desiring to take to ourselves that right which the devil lyingly asserted was his—to give the kingdoms of this world to whom he would. Thus would man have the Almighty degrade Himself to the satisfying of *his* whims rather than His own mind.

There is in fallen man a disinclination toward God's rule. Man hates instruction and casts God's words behind his back (Ps. 50:17). God has revealed His great law to man, but it is treated as a strange thing (Hosea 8:12). What God counts valuable man despises. The very purity of the divine rule makes it obnoxious to an impure heart. Charnock said, "Water and fire may as well kiss each other, and live together without quarreling and hissing, as the holy will of God and the unregenerate heart of a fallen creature." Not only is man's darkened understanding incapable of perceiving the excellence of God's commandments, but there is a disposition in his will which rises up against it. When any part of God's revealed will is made known to men, they endeavor to banish it from their thoughts. They do not like to retain God in their knowledge (Rom. 1:28), therefore they resist the strivings of the Spirit for obedient compliance (Acts 7:51). How can a fleshly mind relish a spiritual law? Since the palate of man is corrupted, divine things are unsavory to him, and forever remain so until his taste is restored by divine grace.

The same atheistic spirit is seen again in men's denials of divine providence. They will not concede that God presides over this scene, directing all its affairs, shaping the circumstances of each of our lives. Rather they attribute their lot to fortune or fate, to good or bad "luck." Even when intellectually convinced to the contrary, they continually quarrel with God's government of this world, and particularly with His dealings with them. Whenever His will crosses theirs, they rebel and rave. If their plans are thwarted, how fretful they are! Men appraise themselves highly, and are angry if God appears not to value them at the same rate—as if *their* estimation of themselves were more accurate than His. What an evidence of practical atheism this is. Instead of meekly submitting to God's will and adoring His righteousness, men declare Him an unjust Governor, demand that His wisdom be guided by their folly, and malign Him rather than themselves!

What proof this is of the fearful enormity of human depravity.

We have shown that the heart of the natural man is filled with a secret and unsuspected yet real spirit of atheism. Whatever theological notions he may hold, by his attitude and conduct he repudiates the very being of God. Even that fearful aspect of man's state does not fully express the desperate and deplorable condition to which the fall has reduced him. Not only is he living in this world "without God" (Eph. 2:12)—without due acknowledgment of or practical subjection to Him—but he has a disposition which is directly contrary to Him. With no desire for communion with the true God, man devises false gods and is devoted to them—possessions, pleasures, prestige. Fallen man has cast off all allegiance to God and set himself in open, undisguised opposition to Him. Not only has he no love for God, but his very nature is wholly averse to Him. Sin has worked in all of his being a radical antipathy to God and to His will and ways, for divine things are holy and heavenly and therefore bitter to his corrupt taste. He is alienated from God, inveterately opposed to Him.

Sin, as an operative principle in the soul, is virtually the assertion of self-sufficiency and self-supremacy; thus it produces opposition to God. Sin is not only the negation but the contrary of holiness, therefore it breeds antagonism to the holy One. He who affirms and asserts himself must deny and resist God. The divine claims are regarded as those of a rival. God is looked upon as an enemy—the carnal mind is enmity against Him—and enmity is not simply the absence of love, a condition of mere indifference, but a principle of repugnance and virulent resistance. Hence, as John Owen said:

> Sin's proper formal object is *God*. It hath, as it were, that command from Satan which the Assyrians had from their king: "fight neither with small nor great, save only with the king of Israel," that sin sets itself against. There lies the secret, the formal reason of all opposition to good, even because it relates unto God. . . . The law of sin makes not opposition to any duty, but to God in every duty.

Thus sin is nothing less than high treason against the absolute sovereignty of God.

It is terrible beyond words that any creature of the great God should harbor enmity against Him. He is the sum of all excellence, the source of all good, the spiritual and moral sun of the universe. Yet fallen man is not only His enemy, but his very mind is "enmity against God" (Rom. 8:7). Enemies may be reconciled, but *enmity* cannot be; the only way to reconcile enemies is to destroy their enmity. In Romans 5:10 the apostle spoke of enemies being reconciled to God by the death of His Son. But when he makes reference to enmity he speaks of Christ's "having *abolished* in his flesh the enmity" (Eph. 2:15). There is no other way of getting rid of enmity except by its abolition or destruction. Now enmity operates along two lines: aversion and opposition. God is detested and resisted. Sin brings us into God's debt (Matt. 6:12), and this produces aversion of Him. As debtors hate the sight of their creditors and are loath to meet them, so those who are unable to meet the just claims of God fear His confrontation. This was exemplified at the beginning, when fallen Adam fled as soon as he heard the voice of his Maker.

Sin is a disease which has ravaged the whole of man's being, making God obnoxious to him. As an inflamed eye cannot bear the light, the depraved heart of man cannot endure to look upon God; he has a deep-rooted and inveterate detestation of Him and therefore of everything that is of Him. The more spirituality there is in anything, the more it' is disliked by the natural man. That which has most of God in it is the most unpalatable to him. God says, "Ye have set at nought *all* my counsel, and would none of my reproof" (Prov. 1:25). Not simply a part but all of His revealed will was unacceptable to them. This enmity is universal in its manifestations. Not only is the unregenerate heart indisposed to all holy duties, finding them irksome and burdensome, but it hates God's law and rejects His Christ. It abuses His mercies, despises the riches of His goodness and long-suffering. It mocks His messengers, resists His Spirit, flouts His Word, and persecutes those who bear His image. Those at enmity with God serve His adversary the devil, and are heartily in love with that world of which he is prince.

Enmity Against God

Enmity is a principle which expresses itself by opposition against its object. It contends with what it loathes. As in the regenerate the flesh lusts against the spirit, so in the unregenerate it fights against God. Enmity is the energy behind every sinful act. Though the interests of particular sins may be contrary to one another, they all conspire in a league against God Himself. Back in 1665 an able expositor, W. Jenkyn, expressed it thus:

> Sins are in conflict with one another: covetousness, and profligacy, covetousness and intemperance agree not. But they are one in combining against the interest of God. In betraying Christ, Judas was actuated by covetousness; the high priest by envy, Pilate by popularity; but all shook hands together in the murdering of Christ. And those varied iniquities were blended together to make up one lump of enmity.

Though in all sins there may not be an express hatred of God, nevertheless in every sin there is an implicit and virtual hatred against Him. So deeply rooted is man's enmity that neither the most tender pleading nor the direst threatening will abate it. God may entreat, but men will not heed; He may chastise, but as soon as He lifts His rod they, like Pharaoh, are as defiant as ever.

The message of men's hearts and lives to God is "Depart from us; for we desire not the knowledge of thy ways" (Job. 21:14). Man is compared to a wild ass in the wilderness that "snuffeth up the wind at her pleasure" rather than come under the yoke of God (Jer. 2:24). That fact was exemplified all through the long history of Israel, and the conduct of *that* people was a reflection and manifestation of the nature of all mankind, for "as in water face answereth to face, so the heart of man to man" (Prov. 27:19). The exercise of this enmity is continued without interruption from the very beginning of man's days to the end of his unregenerate life (Gen. 6:5). It does not vary at all, being consistent with itself. Sin never calls a truce or lays down the weapons of its rebellion, but persists in its active hostility to God. If divine grace does not work a miracle in subduing such enmity and planting in the heart a contrary principle which opposes it, what must be the doom of such creatures? "Thinkest thou this, O man, . . . that thou shalt escape the judgment of God?" (Rom. 2:3). Vain imagination. Christ will one day say, "Those mine enemies, which would not that I should reign over them, bring hither, and slay them before me" (Luke 19:27).

But far from owning that they hate God, the vast majority of men will not only vehemently deny it, but affirm that they respect and love Him. Yet if their supposed love is analyzed, it is found to cover only their own interests. While a man concludes that God is favorable and lenient with him, he entertains no hard thoughts against Him. So long as he considers God to be prospering him, he carries no grudge against Him. He hates God not as One who confers benefits, but as a Sovereign, Lawgiver, Judge. He will not yield to His government or take His law as the rule of his life; therefore he dreads His tribunal. The only God against whom the natural man is not at enmity is one of his own imagination. The deity whom he professes to worship is not the living God, for He is truth and faithfulness, holiness and justice, as well as being gracious and merciful. The soul of man is a complete stranger to holiness, even when his head is bowed in the house of prayer. But God is not deceived by any verbal acknowledgments or external homage: "This people draweth nigh unto me with their mouth, and honoureth me with their lips; but their heart is far from me" (Matt. 15:8). They believe in a god of their own devising and not the God of Holy Writ. In their awful delusion they imagine they admire God's character while refusing His Son to reign over them.

This enmity against God is seen in man's insubordination to the divine law. That is the particular indictment which is made against him in Romans 8, for in proof of the statement that "to be carnally minded is death" the apostle declared, "The carnal mind is enmity against God," and then added by way of demonstration, "It is not subject to the law of God, neither indeed can be." It is quite evident that the final clause was not brought in by way of excuse (for that would have greatly weakened his argument), but instead to give added force to the awful fact just affirmed. A servant who does not perform his master's order may or may not be guilty of revolt. He cannot be charged with rebellion if the task assigned is altogether beyond his physical powers because of poor eyesight, the loss of a limb or the frailty of old age. But if moral perversity (a spirit of malice and defiance) prevents the discharge of his duty, he is certainly guilty of revolt. We are told that the brothers of Joseph "hated him, and could not speak peaceably unto him"

(Gen. 37:4). Far from excusing their evil conduct, that only intensified it. They harbored so much ill will against him that they were morally incapable of treating him amicably.

Such is the inability of fallen man to be in subjection to God's law. Originally made upright, created in the divine image, given a nature in perfect harmony with God's statutes, endowed with faculties both mental and moral which fully capacitated him to meet their requirements, he is so hostile to his Maker that he is thoroughly averse to His government. Our respect for God is judged by our conformity to His law. As love for God is to be gauged by obedience (John 14:21), so hatred of Him is both measured and manifested by disobedience (Deut. 5:9-10). The natural man knows that God opposes the gratification of his corrupt desires, and he hates God because His law prohibits the indulging of his lusts with that freedom and security which he covets. God commands that which he loathes, and forbids what he longs after. Consequently, man's war against God is a double one: defensive and offensive. Defensively, he slights God's Word, perverts His gifts, resists the overtures of his Spirit (Acts 7:51). Offensively, man employs all his members and faculties as weapons of unrighteousness against God (Rom. 6:13). To slight and resist the divine law is to hold God Himself in contempt, for the law is an expression of His goodness, the transcript of His righteousness, the image of His holiness.

Here, then, is the ground of the enmity of the carnal mind: "It is not subject to the law of God." We quote Winslow:

> The secret is now revealed. God is the moral Governor of the universe. Oh, this is the *casus belli* between Him and the sinner! This constitutes the real secret of his fall, inveterate hostility to the Divine being. The question at issue is: "Who shall govern—God or the sinner?" The non-subjection of the carnal heart to God's Law—its rebellion against the Divine government—clearly indicates the side of this question which the carnal mind takes. You may, my reader, succeed in reasoning yourself into the belief that you admire, adore, and love God as your Creator and Benefactor, and only feel a repugnance, and manifest an opposition, to Him as a Lawgiver. But this is impossible in fact, however specious it may be in theory. . . . God's nature and His office, His person and His throne, are one and inseparable. No individual can possibly be a friend to the being of God, who is not equally friendly to His government. Why is the moral Law offensive to the carnal mind? Because of the holiness of its nature and the strictness of its requirements. It not only takes cognizance of external actions, but it touches the very springs of action, the motives that lie concealed in the human heart and regulate the life. It demands supreme affection and universal obedience. To this the carnal mind demurs.

There are multitudes today, even in so-called Christian countries, who are almost totally ignorant of even the terms of God's law—so intense is the darkness that has now settled upon us. The majority of those who have been brought up under acknowledgment of the law, far from valuing such a privilege, despise it. The language of their hearts against God's faithful servants is that which Israel used of old to His prophet: "As for the word that thou hast spoken unto us in the name of the LORD, we will not hearken unto thee" (Jer. 44:16). They "refused to walk in his law" (Ps. 78:10). They had rather be their own rulers than God's subjects; they guide themselves to destruction rather than be directed by Him to blessedness. They crave unbridled liberty and will not tolerate the restraints of a command which checks them. Whatever compliance there may be—for the sake of respectability—to any divine precept which forbids a gross outward sin, the heart still rises up against that part of the law which requires inward purity. The more man's inward corruptions are curbed and condemned, the more he is enraged. Therefore God charges him not only with despising His judgments but with abhorring His statutes (Lev. 26:43).

The difference there is between man and God appears in man's unwillingness that any should observe God's law. Not satisfied with being a rebel himself, man would have God left without any loyal subjects in the world; therefore he uses both temptations and threats to induce others to follow his evil example. He paints the pleasures of sin in glowing colors, and sneers at and boycotts those who have any scruples. Ordinarily the workers of iniquity consider those who walk with God to be freaks and fools, and take delight in ridiculing them (I Peter 4:4). It is not that the righteous have wronged the wicked in any way, but that they refuse to have fellowship with them in defying God. This is proof of their awful enmity. Not only are they themselves angry at God's laws, but they cannot bear to see anyone else respecting them. The apostle, after enumerating some of the vilest abominations, brought this indictment against the Gentiles, that they "not only do the same, but have pleasure in them that do them" (Rom. 1:32). They delight in accomplishing the downfall of their fellowmen.

Another result of man's enmity is his manufacturing of false gods. Though this act is not so noticeably committed by some, yet no one is entirely clear of setting up something in the place of God, for this sin is common to all mankind, as history clearly shows. From the days of Nimrod until the appearing of Christ, the whole Gentile world was abandoned to this impiety, having "changed the glory of the uncorruptible God into an image made like to corruptible man, and to birds, and fourfooted beasts, and creeping things" (Rom. 1:23). Even Abraham originally, as well as his parents, was guilty of this sin (Joshua 24:2). From the making of the golden calf at Sinai until their captivity in Babylon, the Israelites repeatedly committed this crime. Today hideous idols are found not only in heathendom but throughout the whole so-called civilized world. Yet the awfulness of idolatry is perceived by very few. Satan cannot invent a more absolute degrading and vilifying of the Most High than calling Him by the names of those senseless objects and repulsive creatures which men erect as representations of Him. Giving an image that homage which belongs to God is making it equal to Him, if not above Him. It portrays the glorious One as though He had no more excellence than a block of stone or a piece of carved wood.

Man's enmity against God is a practical repudiation of His *holiness,* for it cherishes what is directly contrary to it. "Thou art of purer eyes than to behold evil, and canst not look on iniquity" (Hab. 1:13). Since God is infinitely good, He has an infinite detestation of evil. But sin is the very element in which man lives; therefore he hates everything opposed to it. Nothing is more distasteful to him than the company of the godly; and the stricter they are in performing the duties of piety, and the more the image of God is seen shining in and through them, the greater is the longing of the unregenerate to be free from their presence. Man loves sin so much that he seeks to justify himself in the very commission of it. He even goes further and charges it to the holy One. It was thus at the beginning. When arraigned by his Maker, instead of confessing the enormity of his offense, Adam tried to excuse himself by blaming it on God: "The woman whom thou gavest to be with me, she gave me of the tree, and I did eat." Some expositors think that when Cain was charged with the murder of Abel, and answered, "Am I my brother's keeper?" he blatantly put the onus on the Lord. David charged the crime he had contrived to divine providence (II Sam. 11:25). Man still blames God by attributing his sins to his constitution or his circumstances.

This fearful hostility is exercised against the very *being of God.* That was clearly demonstrated when He became incarnate. The Son of God was not wanted here, but was despised and rejected of men. They provided no better accommodation than a manger for His cradle. Before He reached the age of two such a determined effort was made to kill Him that Joseph and Mary had to take Him to Egypt. Though constantly going about doing good, both to the souls and bodies of men, He had to declare, "The foxes have holes, and the birds of the air have nests; but the Son of man hath not where to lay his head" (Matt. 8:20). They called Him the vilest names they could think of: a glutton and drunkard, a Samaritan, a devil. Again and again they took up stones to throw at Him. His miracles of mercy did not lessen their enmity: "This is the heir; come, let us kill him" (Matt. 21:38); and no ordinary death would satisfy them. After heaping the worst possible indignities on His sacred person and inflicting the most barbarous suffering, they nailed Him to a convict's gibbet, then mocked and reviled Him while He was fastened hand and foot to the cross. As the Lord Jesus declared, "He that hateth me hateth my Father also" (John 15:23).

Now such an attitude against God inevitably falls back on ourselves. Alienated from the Source of all real good and purity, what can the consequence be but to be polluted in every part of our beings—a mass of putrefaction? Sin has indeed worked havoc in the human constitution. Man's very nature is degraded. No creature is so debased as man, for he alone has erased the image of God from his soul. Man, once the glory of creation, has become the vilest of all creatures. He who was given dominion over the beasts has sunk lower, for *they* are not guilty of mad and wicked intemperance, they are not without natural affection toward their offspring (as so many of the human species are), nor do they commit suicide. Man's apostasy from his

Maker could not result in anything less than the complete mutilation of his soul, depriving it of that perfect harmony and balance of its faculties with which it was originally endowed, robbing them of their primitive excellence and beauty. The whole of our inner man has been attacked by a loathsome disease, so that there is now no soundness in it.

What villainy is in fallen man! No wonder the Scriptures ask, "Who *can* know it?" (Jer. 17:9). None but the very One against whom it lifts its vile head. What an awful spectacle, to witness the finite in deadly opposition to the Infinite! The creature and the Creator are at direct odds, for while a serpentine nature and a devilish disposition remain unsubdued within fallen man, he will no more seek to glorify the Lord than will Satan himself. The unregenerate man detests Him who is light and love. The ox knows its owner, and the ass his master's crib, but the one who has been endowed with rationality and immortality does not recognize the hand that daily ministers in mercy throughout his life. What long-suffering God shows to those who treat Him so basely! What abundant cause the Christian has to abhor himself and hang his head in shame as he contemplates the awfulness of all the sin that still indwells him!

Chapter 9

EXTENT

NEITHER THE SCIENTIST, the philosopher, nor the psychologist can correctly diagnose the fatal malady which has seized all mankind, and still less is any of them able to gauge its full extent. For a right and true knowledge of this we are dependent on what the Holy Spirit has revealed in Holy Writ. There we are shown that man has become not only fallen and corrupt but totally depraved; that he is not only a criminal before the divine law, but a foul and repulsive object in the eyes of his Maker. There are two inseparable effects of sin: pollution and guilt, neither of which can be avoided. Where there is sin there is a stain. Uncleanness, ugliness, filthiness, and similar characteristics, indicate not only a property of sin but also the effect it produces in its subjects. It defiles, leaving the impress of its odious features, making the soul the reflection of its own hideousness. Wherever it touches, it leaves its filthy slime, making its subject hateful and abominable.

Biblical Description of Sin

No representations of sin are more common in the Scriptures than those taken from its defiling effects. Throughout it is portrayed as ugly and revolting, unclean and disgusting. It is pictured by leprosy, the most loathsome disease which can attack the human frame. It is likened to wounds, bruises and putrefying sores. It is compared to a cage of unclean birds. The inseparable connection of the beautiful and good and the ugly and sinful pervades the moral teaching of both Testaments. That connection is ethical and not aesthetic. To reverse the order would be to reduce righteousness to a matter of taste, and to regulate authority according to its appeal to our sentiments. As someone has said, the aesthetic sentiment is a reflection from the moral sphere, a transfer to our senses of those perceptions found in their purity only in the realm of the spiritual and divine. Sin is really and originally all that is ugly; nothing else is ugly except as a result of its connection with sin. The ugliness which it creates is its own blot. It has deranged the whole structure of the soul, and morally ulcerated man from head to foot.

"We are all as an unclean thing" (Isa. 64:6). Thus God's Word describes us: foul and filthy. That pollution is deep and unmistakable, likened to crimson dye (Isa. 1:18), or to the blackness of the Ethiopian (Jer. 13:23), which cannot be washed away by the niter of positive thinking or the soap of reformation (Jer. 2:22). It is an indelible pollution, for it is "written

119

with a pen of iron, and with the point of a diamond: it is graven upon the table of . . . [the] heart" (Jer. 17:1). The great deluge did not wash it from the earth, nor did the fire that came down upon Sodom burn it out. It is ineradicable. Even the fire of hell through eternity will not take away the stain of sin in the souls there. This pollution spreads, like leaven and leprosy. It is universal, and has defiled all the faculties of the inner man, so that there is "*no* soundness in it" (Isa. 1:6). Soul and body alike are contaminated, for we read of the "filthiness of the flesh and spirit" (II Cor. 7:1). It extends to the thoughts and imaginations, as well as to words and deeds. It is malignant and deadly, "the poison of asps" (Rom. 3:13). "I said unto thee when thou wast in thy blood, Live; yea, I said unto thee when thou wast in thy blood, Live" (Ezek. 16:6). The doubling of that expression shows the deadly nature of the pollution.

Sin is as loathsome as it is criminal; it is like a foul stench in the nostrils of the Lord. Thus the day man corrupted himself, his Maker could no longer endure him, but drove him out of the garden (Gen. 3:24). The Scriptures liken man to foxes for their subtlety, to wild bulls for their intractableness, to briers and thorns for their hurtfulness, to pigs for their greediness and filthiness, to bears and lions for their cruelty and bloodthirstiness, to serpents for their hatefulness. However unpleasant and forbidding this subject, it is an integral part of "the counsel of God" which His ministers are not at liberty to withhold. They are not free to pick and choose their themes, still less to tone them down. Rather each one is told by his Master, "Speak unto them *all* that I commanded thee: be not dismayed at their faces" (Jer. 1:17). Asylums, prisons and cemeteries are depressing sights, yet they are painful facts of human history. Refusal to consider fallen man's condition helps no one. Until we are brought to realize this truth we shall never despair of self and look away to Another. This solemn side of the picture is indeed dark, yet it is the necessary background to redemption.

Biblical Description of Sinful Man

The effects of the fall are not only more terrible but much more wide-reaching than are commonly supposed. Yet this would not be the case were our thoughts formed by the teaching of Holy Writ. God's Word is plain enough: "God saw that the wickedness of man was great in the earth, and that every imagination of the thoughts of his heart was only evil continually" (Gen. 6:5). Those words are as impressive as they are solemn. In Genesis 1:31 we read, "And God saw every thing that he had made, and, behold, it was very good." But here the omniscient One is portrayed as taking a universal survey of the condition of mankind, and recording His righteous verdict of their condemnation. They announce His unerring diagnosis of their inward state in terms which fully explain their outward conduct. The spring of all their actions is thoroughly corrupt. The translators of the Authorized Version have given a marginal note informing us that the Hebrew word for "imagination" included the purposes and desires. The very fount of man's being was defiled, and it was a most offensive sight to the holy One.

The heart is the moral center from which all the issues or outgoings of life proceed, and none but God knows *how* evil it is. The thoughts formed within such a heart are vain and sinful. The imagination or formation of them, their very first stirrings, are evil. As we stated, the Hebrew word for "imagination of the heart" signifies a matrix, the frame in which our thoughts are cast. Observe that *every* imagination is evil. No good ideas are intermingled; all are unrelieved badness—not simply the outward acts, but also the first movements of the soul toward an object. There we have the source from which all the wickedness of men proceeds. The corrupt moods within us are in a constant fermentation. Man's heart is such that, left to itself, it will always be producing inordinate affections and emotions. Men are *"only* evil" without exception, wholly so; there is not a single virtuous one among them. Furthermore, they are "evil *continually*," without intermission all the days of their lives, therefore all their works are evil and fruitless.

"The imagination of man's heart is evil from his youth" (Gen. 8:21). Genesis 6:5 described human nature and conduct as it was prior to the flood; this verse shows what man still was after it. The great deluge had swept away all of that corrupt generation to which Enoch had prophesied and Noah had preached in vain, but it had not cleansed man's nature. That remained as vile as before. Man continued to be conceived in iniquity and born in sin, and what is bred in the bone always comes out in the flesh. From the first moment of his existence, every descendant of Adam is a defiled creature, fit only for God's abhorrence. His very instincts while in embryo are essentially evil. The Hebrew word for "youth" is translated "childhood" in I Samuel 12:2; both personal experience and observation sadly verify the solemn fact that, as Charnock said, there is "not a moment of a man's life wherein our hereditary corruption doth not belch its froth."

"Behold, he putteth no trust in his saints [for they are but mutable creatures in themselves]; yea, the heavens are not clean in his sight. How much more abominable and filthy is man, which drinketh iniquity like water?" (Job 15:15-16). What a description of human nature: obnoxious to God, corrupt in itself! Man is thoroughly unclean, as his life bears witness, his very righteousness being "as filthy rags"—so impure that nothing but the blood of Christ can cleanse him. With such a character man is never weary of sinning. Even when worn out by age, his lusts are still active within. As Peter expressed it, "They cannot cease from sin" for it is their very nature to be sinful. Possessing a disposition which greedily craves indulgence, seeking satisfaction as passionately as parched throats in the burning desert long for the quenching of their thirst, man delights in iniquity and, so far as he is left to follow his inordinate propensities, he is continually seeking to take his fill of it.

"Because sentence against an evil work is not executed speedily, therefore the heart of the sons of men is fully set in them to do evil" (Eccles. 8:11).

Such is the perversity of corrupt human nature that it abuses the very patience and forbearance of God. Since divine judgment is not sent at once to evildoers, they set themselves against the Lord and promise themselves immunity. Thus it was with those in the days of Noah. God deferred the flood for one hundred and twenty years, giving them ample "space for repentance"; but instead of availing themselves of the opportunity they regarded His threats as idle, and became increasingly corrupt and violent. It was thus with Pharaoh, who only hardened his heart when respite was granted him. And it is still thus. Though the marks of divine displeasure against our generation are multiplied, men grow more and more daring and desperate in defying God's law, sinning with a high hand and presuming on their security.

"The heart of the sons of men is full of evil, and madness is in their heart while they live, and after that they go to the dead" (Eccles. 9:3). As Christ was and is "full of grace and truth" (John 1:14), the natural man is filled with unrighteousness and wickedness. He is filled with such enmity against God that as his corruptions kindle it, so divine and spiritual things stimulate it to action. That awful enmity comprises the sum of all evil. "Madness is in their heart"; men are so infatuated as to seek their pleasures in the things which God hates. They cast off all the restraints of reason and conscience (cf. Jer. 1:38) as their heady and violent passions press them forward into sin. Who but a madman would set himself against the Almighty and rush into evil heedless of danger and disaster? They are maddened by their lusts, mad against piety. The clause "after that they go to the dead" signifies more than the grave; they are gathered to their own company, the dead in sin, not to "the spirits of just men made perfect."

The teaching of the Lord Jesus was of course in perfect harmony with that of the Old Testament. He never flattered human nature or extolled its excellences. Instead He painted it in the darkest colors, announcing that He had come to "seek and to save that which was *lost*" (Luke 19:10). Fallen man has lost all likeness to God, all communion with God, all love for God, all true knowledge of God, all delight in God, all favor with God, all power toward God, and has thrown off all subjection to God. The Saviour was not deceived by religious pretense or shallow profession. Even when many believed in His name as they saw the miracles which He did, "Jesus did not commit himself unto them . . . for he knew what was in man" (John 2:23-25). By declaring, "I am not come to call the righteous, but sinners to repentance" (Matt. 9:13), He had not only intimated the need for His mission—for there would have been no occasion for His coming among men unless they were perishing—but inferred that there were *none righteous*, for He called upon all to repent (Mark 1:15; Luke 13:5).

When Christ asserted, "Except a man be born again, he cannot enter the kingdom of God," He showed how desperate is man's plight; for the new birth is not a mere correcting of some defect, nor the righting of a single faculty, but an entire renovation of the soul. The same Spirit which formed

Christ in the virgin's womb must form Him in our hearts to fit us for the presence of God. When Christ averred that "men loved darkness rather than light" (John 3:19), He exposed their awful depravity. They were not only *in* the darkness, but *delighted* in it "because their deeds were evil." When He stated that "the wrath of God abideth on" the unbeliever, Christ testified to man's awful condition. When He said, "I know you, that ye have not the love of God in you" (John 5:42), He again revealed man's fearful state, for since all goodness or virtue consists in love to God and our neighbor, then where love is wanting, goodness or virtue has no existence. Christ's statement "No man can come to me, except the Father which hath sent me draw him" (John 6:44) plainly showed the moral impotence of every descendant of Adam. This impotence consists of turpitude and baseness, of inveterate opposition to God due to bitter hatred of Him. No one seeks the company of a person he loathes: before he does so he must be given an entirely new disposition.

"For from within, out of the heart of men, proceed evil thoughts, adulteries, fornications, murders, thefts, covetousness, wickedness, deceit, lasciviousness, an evil eye, blasphemy, pride, foolishness: all these evil things come from within, and defile the man" (Mark 7:21-23). Note that Christ used "heart" in the singular number, referring to the common and uniform heart of all mankind. Here the Lord made known what a loathsome place is the center of man's being, and what horrible crimes issue from its evil. They rise from that fountain which is poisoned by sin.

The Son of God expressed His estimate of fallen mankind thus: "If ye then, *being* evil . . ." (Matt. 7:11). Men not only do that which is evil, but are so in their very nature. As the psalmist said, "Their inward part is very wickedness" (5:9). Christ spoke not to open enemies but to His own disciples, and His language affirmed that by birth they were defiled both root and branch. How His words abase human pride! Those who prattle about the dignity and nobility of human nature meet with Christ's solemn verdict to the contrary.

"The Spirit of truth; whom the world cannot receive, because it seeth him not, neither knoweth him" (John 14:17). What Christ said in His day, "Because I tell you the truth, ye believe me not" (John 8:45), is still true. Men are so infatuated with lies, they cannot receive the Spirit of truth. In those words the Son of God represented the unregenerate as not having the least degree of spiritual discernment and knowledge, as being completely destitute of holiness. Nothing but total depravity can make man so blind to spiritual things as to be thoroughly opposed to them.

Our English word "depraved" is taken from *depravatus*, which means twisted, wrenched from the straight line. The root of this word is *pravus*, "crooked," "bad." Total depravity connotes that this distortion has affected all of man's being to such an extent that he has no inherent power of recovery left to restore himself to harmony with God, and that this is the case with *every* member of the race. Yet total depravity does not imply that sin has reached its highest intensity in a person so that it is incapable of augmentation, for men add to their sins (I Sam. 12:19). No, fallen man does not enter this world as bad as he can be, but he has "no good thing" in him (Rom. 7:18). Instead he is wholly corrupt, entirely vitiated throughout his constitution.

The natural man has not one iota of holiness in him; rather he is born with the seeds of every form of evil, radically inclined to sin. In our nature we are vileness itself, black as hell, and unless a miracle of grace is worked in us we must inevitably be damned for all eternity. It is not a case of man's having a few imperfections; he is altogether polluted, "an unclean thing" with "no soundness" (Isa. 1:6). Not only has man no holiness, but his heart is inveterately averse to it.

The solemn doctrine of total depravity does not mean that there are no parents with genuine love for their children, and no children who respectfully obey their parents; that there are none imbued with a spirit of benevolence to the poor and kind sympathy for the suffering; that there are no conscientious employers or honest employees. But it does mean that, where the unregenerate are concerned, those duties are discharged *without* any love for God, any subjection to His authority, or any concern for His glory. Parents are required to bring up their children in the nurture and admonition of the Lord, and children are to obey their parents in the Lord (Eph. 6:1, 4). Servants are to serve their masters "in singleness of heart, as unto Christ." Do the unconverted comply with those injunctions? No, therefore their performances not only possess no spiritual value, but are polluted. Every act of the natural man is faulty. "The plowing of the wicked is sin" (Prov. 21:4) because it is for selfish ends. Then is it better not to plow at all? Wrong, for slothfulness is equally sinful. There are different degrees of enormity, but *every* act of man is sinful.

The condition of the natural man is such that in the discharge of his first responsibility to his Maker he is utterly unfaithful. His chief obligation is to live for the glory of God and to love Him with all his heart; but while he remains unrenewed he does not have the least spiritual, holy, true love for Him. Whatever there may be in his domestic and social conduct which is admirable in the eyes of others, it is not prompted by any respect for the divine will. So far as man's self-recovery and self-recuperation are concerned, his depravity is total, in the sense of being decisive and final. Spurgeon stated:

> Man is fallen; every part and passion of his nature is perverted: he has gone astray altogether, is sick from the crown of his head to the soles of his feet: yea, is dead in trespasses and sins and corrupt before God. O pride of human nature, we plough right over thee! The hemlock standing in thy field must be cut up by the roots. Thy weeds seem like fair flowers, but the ploughshare must go right through them, till all thy beauty is shown to be a painted Jezebel, and all human glorying a bursting bubble.

What makes this awful view of man's total depravity yet more solemn is the fact that there is no exception to it, for it is *universal*. Corrupt nature is the same in all. The hand that writes these lines is as capable of perpetrating the foulest crime on the calendar, and the heart of the reader could devise the worst deed committed by the vilest wretch who ever lived. The only distinction of character among men is that which the sovereign power and grace of God effects. "We are all as an unclean thing" (Isa. 64:6); our original purity is gone. "There is no difference: for all have sinned, and come short of the glory of God." In his comments on Romans 3:10-18 Calvin said:

> In this terrible manner the apostle inveighs not against particular individuals, but against all the posterity of Adam. He does not declaim against the depraved manners of one or another age, but accedes the perpetual corruption of our nature. For his design in that passage is not simply to rebuke men in order that they may repent, but rather to teach us that all men are overwhelmed with an inevitable calamity, from which they can never emerge unless they are extricated by the mercy of God.

When the Lord Jesus called Paul, He informed him that He was about to send him to the Gentiles "to open their eyes, and to turn them from darkness to light, and from the power of Satan unto God" (Acts 26:18). In those words Christ indicated the character of the whole Gentile world; they were all as ignorant of God, and of the way of acceptance with Him, as blind men are of the true objects of sight. There were then, as now, devout religionists, esteemed poets and boastful philosophers who gloried in their wisdom, professing to teach what was the true happiness of man. There were renowned sages with innumerable disciples, whose schools were run solely for the study of virtue, knowledge and happiness. Nevertheless "the world by wisdom knew not God," and He declared, "I will destroy the wisdom of the wise, and will bring to nothing the understanding of the prudent" (I Cor. 1:19-21), for it deceived and deluded them. The schools themselves were darkness, and the minds of their authors—men like Pythagoras and Plato, Socrates and Aristotle—were "blinded by the god of this world," completely under the control of the devil.

"The LORD looked down from heaven upon the children of men, to see if there were any that did understand, and seek God" (Ps. 14:2). We quote Spurgeon again:

> Behold the eyes of Omniscience ransacking the globe, and prying among every people and nation. He who is looking down knows the good, is quick to discern it, would be delighted to find it; but as He views all the unregenerate children of men His search is fruitless, for of all the race of Adam no unrenewed soul is other than an enemy to God and goodness. "They are all gone out of the way." Without exception, all men have apostatized from the Lord their Maker, from His Laws, and from the eternal principles of right. Like stubborn heifers they have sturdily refused to receive the yoke. The original speaks of the race as a totality, humanity as a whole has become depraved in heart and life. "They have altogether become filthy." As a whole they are spoiled and soured like corrupt leaven,

or, as some put it, they have become putrid and even stinking. The only reason why we do not more clearly see this foulness is because we are accustomed to it, just as those who work daily among offensive odours at last cease to smell them.

Extent of Carnality

That terrible indictment "The carnal mind is enmity against God: for it is not subject to the law of God, neither indeed can be" (Rom. 8:7) is not restricted to particularly reprobate persons, but is an unqualified statement which applies to every individual. It is "*the* carnal mind," whatever mind may properly be designated "carnal," natural, unspiritual. The undeveloped mind of the infant is "enmity against God." Moreover, that description is true at all times, though it is not equally so evident. Though the wolf may sleep, he *is* still a wolf. The snake which lurks among the flowers is just as deadly as when it lies among noxious weeds. Furthermore, that solemn declaration is true of the whole mind, of all its faculties. It is true of the memory: nursery rhymes, silly jokes and foolish songs are retained without effort, whereas passages of Scripture and spiritual sermons are quickly forgotten. It is so with the affections: the creature is idolized and the Creator slighted. So of the judgment: what erroneous conceptions it forms of the Deity and how fearfully it wrests His Word! It is true even of the conscience, for there have been those who, while killing the saints, thought they did God a service (John 16:2), among them Saul of Tarsus.

As might well be expected, fierce opposition has been made against this flesh-withering truth of the total depravity of man, and always will be where it is faithfully preached. When men are informed that they are suffering from something far more serious than a defect in their characters or an unhappy bias of disposition, namely, that their very *nature* is rotten to the core, it is more than human pride can endure. When told that the center of their moral being is corrupt, that their heart—the potent fountain from which issue their desires and thoughts—is desperately wicked, that it is inherently and radically evil from the first moment of their existence, hot resentment is at once aroused. It is indeed awful to contemplate that not only is sin the element in which the natural man lives, but the whole of his life is one unmixed course of evil. It is scarcely surprising that those who are not subject to the Word of truth should revolt at such a concept, especially as it is contrary to what appears in not a few characters who must be respected for many admirable qualities. Nevertheless, since all sin is a coming short of the glory of God, every act of fallen man has in it the nature of sin.

Even in Christendom this doctrine has been strongly and steadily resisted. The great controversy between Augustine and Pelagius in the fifth century turned upon whether that moral corruption which pertains to all mankind is total or partial. If the latter, then of course it follows that man still has within him something which is good, something which is consistent with the divine law, something which enables him to at least partly discharge the obligations on him as a creature of God. Ever since the days of Augustine there have been those posing as Christians who, while acknowledging that man is a fallen and depraved creature, have flatly denied that he is *totally* depraved. Those who repudiate the inward and invincible call of the Spirit do not realize the actual state of man's soul, nor perceive that a miracle of grace is necessary before he is made willing to comply with the demands of the gospel. Arminians acknowledge the *aid* of the Spirit, but at once negate their admission by affirming that He can be successfully resisted after He has put forth all His efforts to woo the sinner to Christ.

It is important to recognize that the principles of faith and love are not produced by mere moral persuasion, by the external presentation of Christ to a person. Rather they are accomplished by a miracle of divine power and grace in the soul. Such a glorious work must be done by an efficient agent. The natural man is blind and dead to spiritual things, and what mere persuasion can make the blind see or the dead act? Persuasion, far from giving a faculty, presupposes one; the use of it is not to confer a power, but to stir and move it to act. God is far more than an Orator beseeching men; He is a mighty Operator quickening men. His word is a commanding power. As He said, "Let light be," and there was light, so He calls for a new heart and brings it into existence. God is no mere Helper, but a Creator. "We are his workmanship," not our own. It is God who makes us new creatures, and not we ourselves. We are "born, not . . . of the will of man, but of God" (John 1:13). To say that we are in part born of our own wills is to blaspheme the Author of our spiritual being and to place the crown on nature instead of grace.

The evolutionist emphatically denies the total depravity of man, for the only fall he believes in is an upward one. He is loud in insisting that there is a divine spark of life in the soul of every human being, burning very feebly in some, yet capable of being fanned into a flame if the right influences are brought to bear on it. Others term it a divine "seed" of goodness, a seed which only needs cultivating for the ultimate development of a noble and virtuous character. This is a point-blank repudiation of the teaching of Christ that the human tree is essentially "corrupt." Since the whole system of redemption rests upon the basic fact of man's total depravity, and since every false system of religion originates in the repudiation of that fact, it is incumbent on us to expose the fallacy of those objections which are commonly made against it.

Some attempt to show that we do not enter this world in a defiled condition. The engaging simplicity, dependence and harmlessness of infants are stressed, and reference is even made to Scripture in support of the contention that they are born in a state of innocence. But this need not detain us very long, for it scarcely presents even an apparent force. Appeal is made to this statement: "And shed *innocent* blood, even the blood of their sons and of their daughters, whom they sacrificed unto the idols of Canaan" (Ps. 106:38), which simply means they sacrificed their little ones, who had *not* been active participants in their idolatry. "For the children being not yet born, neither

having done any good or evil" (Rom. 9:11) is not to the point, for those
words refer not to their nature but to a time before they committed any deeds.
While in contrast with adults infants possess a relative innocence in that
they are guiltless of personal transgressions, yet it is clear that they partake
of original sin (Ps. 51:5; 58:3; Prov. 22:15). Scripture never contradicts
itself.

Others insist that there is some good in the very worst, that even the most
confirmed villains shudder and turn away from certain deeds of wickedness
when first tempted to do them. The conclusion is drawn that, deeply buried
under the ashes of a life of unbridled crime, the sparks of some power of
goodness still remain. But that is to confuse the faint stirrings of man's
moral nature with potential spirituality. Confusion of thought leads people
to infer that because there are degrees of wickedness there must be a modicum
of good. Because one stage of depravity is lower than another, this does not
warrant the denial that the first stage is degraded. The development of
wickedness is one thing; the presence of any measure of holiness or virtue
is another. The absence of certain forms of sins does not imply any innate
purity. It might as well be affirmed that a recent corpse, which is less loathsome, is therefore *less dead* than one which is far gone in decay and putrefaction.

Voice of Conscience

Many have argued that the *strivings of conscience* in the unregenerate
demonstrate that they are not totally depraved. They point out that every
man is possessed of the faculty which bears witness within him in countless
instances of what is right and wrong. They state that this inward monitor
exerts considerable influence even on wicked men, impelling them to perform
actions which are relatively good, and deterring them from actions which are
evil. That is freely admitted, but it does not minimize the truth we are here
contending for. While conscience is necessary to the performance of both
good and evil, it does not enter into either the one or the other. It is that
part of the mind which takes cognizance of the virtue or vice of our actions
but is quite distinct from both. It is that ethical instinct which passes judgment on the lawfulness or unlawfulness of our desires and actions. The
conscience itself needs instructing, for its dictates go no farther than the
knowledge it possesses. It does not *reveal* anything, but simply declares the
character of what is presented to the mind's eye, according to the light it has.

The conscience is not in itself a standard of duty, for that of a heathen
speaks very differently from that of a Christian, who is taught by the Holy
Spirit. The conscience is an ear to hear, and the character of *what* it hears—
whether true or false—is the measure of its intelligence. In proportion to
the tutoring of this inward eye will be the truthfulness of its perceptions. The
term defines itself: *con-science*, "with knowledge"—to know with oneself.
Conscience informs and impresses us with the difference between good and
evil. But since all duty consists of and is contained in love (of God and our

neighbor), good and evil must consist entirely in the *disposition of the heart*. Since the mere dictates of conscience include no such dispositions, neither good nor evil can be predicated on those dictates. Both men and demons will forever possess consciences witnessing to them what is good and evil, even in hell itself where, as all must allow, they will be utterly destitute of any virtue or goodness. We do indeed read in God's Word of a good conscience and an evil one. We also read of "an evil eye," yet there is neither good nor evil in the sight of the eye, except as it is under the influence of a holy or unholy disposition of the soul. So it is with the dictates of the conscience.

The conscience bears solemn witness to the loss of man's purity and the presence of depravity. But to regard the resistance of conscience to each successive stage of sin as an evidence of innate goodness is to ignore the very real distinction between the authority of conscience and a soul's love for God. The conscience certainly remonstrates and enforces the right in the form of an unconditional and absolute imposition; it also threatens man with the destruction of his peace if he persists in his course of wrongdoing. But the remonstrance and threatening come to him as a *restraint*, as a force, as something against which the current of his soul is set. There is no love for God in it, no respect to His will declared by it, no regard for His honor. The struggle is not between good and evil (as is the case in a saint), but between sinful inclination and positive prohibition. To know duty and yet be reluctant to perform it is no evidence of any goodness of heart. Even to find satisfaction in performing a duty at the dictate of conscience proves no reverence whatever for God Himself.

The conflicts which the natural man experiences are most certainly not between any love he has for God and the inordinate desires of his fallen nature, but rather between his conscience and his lusts. Any remorse which he may suffer is not sorrow for having offended his Maker, but vexation at the sense of his degradation and the injury done to his pride. There is no grief before God for having been a reproach to Him. Nor does the wretchedness which dissipation produces in any way dispose its subject to a more favorable reception of the gospel. The groaning under the chains which sinful habits forge and the sighing for deliverance are not longings to be freed from sin, but rather desires to escape from its painful consequences both to the conscience and to the body. Mental tranquillity and physical health are coveted, not the approbation of the Lord. Any misery suffered by the natural man is not from having offended God, but because he cannot defy Him with impunity and immunity. None but the Holy Spirit can produce a hatred of sin *as sin*; that is something the conscience never does.

Though evolutionists and even openly avowed infidels cannot get away from the fact that man is a very imperfect creature, they are far from allowing that he is *totally* depraved—averse to all that is good, prone to all that is evil. Such a declaration is much too humbling and humiliating for any natural heart honestly to accept and be duly affected by it. Plain and insistent as is God's Word on the subject, not a few professing Christians find it so distasteful that, if they do not repudiate it *in toto*, they go to great lengths in order to blunt its sharp edge and remove its most cutting features. The language of Hazael well expresses their resentment against the dark picture which the divine Artist has drawn of them.

When this Syrian saw Elijah weeping, and inquired what was the occasion of his distress, God's servant replied, "Because I know the evil that thou wilt do unto the children of Israel: their strong holds wilt thou set on fire, and their young men wilt thou slay with the sword, and wilt dash their children, and rip up their women with child" (II Kings 8:12). So little was Hazael aware of the vileness of his nature that he became highly indignant, and answered, "But what, is thy servant a dog, that he should do this great thing?" He fondly imagined himself to be incapable of such foul deeds. Nevertheless the sad sequel fully vindicated the prophet, for although Hazael supposed himself to be as gentle as a lamb, when he came into power he proved himself to be as fierce as a savage dog and as cruel as a tiger. He not only murdered his royal master, usurped the throne of Syria, burned the cities of Israel and killed their inhabitants with the sword, but barbarously massacred the women and children. As II Kings 13:7 states, he went on destroying Israel till he "had made them like the dust by threshing."

Unacceptability of Every Carnal Act

Every passage in the Word of truth which declares the impossibility of the natural man doing anything acceptable to God (e.g., Jer. 13:23; Matt. 7:18; Rom. 8:8; Heb. 11:6) demonstrates man's total depravity. If men performed any part of their duty toward God it would be pleasing to Him, for He is not a capricious or hard Master, but delights in righteousness wherever He sees it. But, as the Lord Jesus pointed out, men will gather grapes of thorns and figs of thistles before unrenewed nature will yield any fruit to God. Every passage in the Bible which insists on the necessity of the new birth emphasizes the total depravity of man, for if there were any degree of virtue in the human heart it could be cultivated and increased, and regeneration would be obviated, since the development and improvement of what is already in man would suffice. But our Lord informed a devout religionist, a master in Israel, that unless he were born again he could not enter the kingdom of God. Likewise, every passage which calls on men to repent and believe the gospel presupposes their present sinful and lost condition, for they that are well do not need a physician. "Except ye repent, ye shall all likewise perish" (Luke 13:5) was the decisive verdict of Christ.

This truth is repudiated in varied and numerous ways, for unbelief is very fertile. That is another way of saying that the carnal mind is enmity against God, and at no one point is that enmity more active and evident than in its antipathy to God's Word in general. Its opposition is particularly directed to those aspects of the Word which expose and condemn mankind. When men are told that all the actions of the unregenerate are not only mixed with sin, but are in their own nature sinful, many sneeringly reply that such is a palpable absurdity. They argue that there are many actions performed by men, such as eating and drinking in moderation, which, being merely natural actions, can have in them neither moral good nor moral evil. But that is a bare assertion rather than a logical argument, and is easily refuted.

When we affirm that all the actions of the unregenerate are sinful, we refer only to those which are performed voluntarily, and which are capable of being exercised for a good purpose. Whatever falls in that category is not merely a natural but a moral action. That eating and drinking and all other voluntary exercises *are* moral actions is evident, for Scripture expressly exhorts us, "Whether therefore ye eat, or drink, or whatsoever ye do, do all to the glory of God" (I Cor. 10:31). In an irrational being, such actions would be merely natural, but in a moral agent they are otherwise— the manner in which he attends to them making them good or evil. The motive largely determines the quality of the act. Eating and drinking are virtuous when, from a gracious motive, one thankfully acknowledges God as the Giver, prayerfully asks His blessing on the food, and purposes to use the strength from it to His praise. But the unregenerate lack that gracious principle, eating and drinking out of no respect to God's authority, without any love to Him in their hearts, and with no concern for His glory. They do so merely to satisfy their appetites and to provide fuel for the further gratification of their lusts.

If every act of the unregenerate is sinful, how is it that God regards favorably and even rewards some of the performances of the wicked, such as the case of Ahab and the repentance of the Ninevites at the preaching of Jonah? We must distinguish between God's governmental ways in connection with this world, and what He requires for admittance to heaven. Though the Most High knows the secrets of all hearts, He does not always proceed accordingly in His administration of the affairs of earth. When God approves of any of the deeds of the wicked, it is not because He regards the deeds as *theirs*, but because those deeds tend to further His own wise counsels. Andrew Fuller said:

> God rewarded Nebuchadnezzar for his long siege against Tyre, in giving him the land of Egypt, yet Nebuchadnezzar did nothing in that undertaking which in its own nature could approve itself unto God. The only reason why he was thus rewarded was, that what he had done subserved the Divine purpose in punishing Tyre for her insulting treatment toward His people (Ezek. 26, 1-7; 29, 17-20). God rewarded Cyrus with the treasures of Babylon (Isaiah 14, 3), not because he did anything that was pleasing in His sight, for his motive was the lust of dominion, but because what he did effected the deliverance of Judah, and fulfilled the Divine predictions upon Babylon.

God's Dealings with Man

In God's governmental dealings with men, actions which appear to have no intrinsic goodness in them may well be rewarded without any compromise of holiness and righteousness. God does not always deal with men according to His omniscience. Rather He generally treats them in this life according to what they profess and appear to be. Thus, the Lord's design in punishing wicked Ahab and his house was to show His displeasure of their idolatries. If, when Ahab humbled himself and tore his garments, God had acted toward him on the ground of His omniscience, knowing him to be destitute of godly sorrow, and had made no difference in His treatment of him, that purpose would not have been answered. Whatever Ahab's motives, they were unknown to men. And had no difference appeared in the divine treatment, they would have concluded it was vain to repent and serve God. It therefore seemed good to Jehovah to deal with Ahab in this life as though his reformation were sincere, leaving his insincerity to be called to account in the day to come.

As Fuller pointed out, there is a case much resembling that of Ahab in the history of Abijah the son of Rehoboam. In II Chronicles 13 we read of his wars with Jeroboam, king of Israel, and how he addressed the apostate Israelites previous to the battle. Having reproached them for forsaking the God of their fathers and turning to idolatry, he added, "But as for us, the LORD is our God, and we have not forsaken him; and the priests, which minister unto the LORD, are the sons of Aaron, and the Levites wait upon their business: and they burn unto the LORD every morning and every evening burnt-sacrifices and sweet incense: the shewbread also set they in order upon the pure table; and the candlestick of gold with the lamps thereof, to burn every evening: for we keep the charge of the LORD our God; but ye have forsaken him" (vv. 10-11). To all appearances this prince was very zealous for the Lord, and one might conclude that the signal victory given him over Jeroboam was an expression of divine approbation. But if we consult the account of his reign in I Kings 15 (where he is called Abijam), we learn that he was a wicked king, and that he walked in all the sins of his father. Although God granted success to his army, it was not out of regard for him, but *for David's sake*, and for the establishment of Jerusalem.

Much of what we have said about Ahab holds good of the Ninevites, and of Pharaoh too. There might have been sincere and spiritual penitents among the Ninevites for all we know; but whether godly sorrow or slavish fear actuated them, they professed and appeared to be humbled before God, displaying the external marks of contrition. For God to respond to their apparently sincere repentance was an exemplification of the divine wisdom, for it magnified His righteous and merciful government in the sight of the surrounding nations. In like manner, the acknowledgments of Pharaoh's sins, and his requests for Moses to entreat the Lord on his behalf, were repeatedly followed by the removal of those judgments which so appalled his proud spirit; yet who would insist that there was any good or spirituality in Egypt's king? Not only God but Moses himself perceived Pharaoh's evident insincerity. Nevertheless the Most High removed His rod when that guilty tyrant made confession, even though He knew that Pharaoh, gaining his point, would laugh up his sleeve at Moses.

In their argument against the doctrine of man's total depravity some have appealed to Christ's words in Mark 12:28-34, where He assured the scribe who had discreetly answered Him, "Thou are not far from the kingdom of God." They argue that though he was unsaved, yet our Lord found in his character something which was praiseworthy. But if the passage is read attentively it is found that Christ was not approving of his spirit or his conduct, but was simply commending his confession of faith. When this Jew acknowledged that the love of God and man was of more importance and value than whole burnt offerings—that the moral law was more excellent than the ceremonial, which was soon to be abolished—he gave utterance to sound doctrine, and came so close to the spirit of the gospel dispensation that Christ very properly informed him he was not far from the kingdom of God. In other words, the principles which the scribe had avowed, if truly embraced and duly pursued, would lead him to the very heart of Christianity, for it is by the law that a knowledge of sin is obtained and the need for mercy is discovered. The things to which the scribe assented were the very ones Christ insisted on in His teaching.

Difference Among the Depraved

If all men alike are totally depraved, then how is it that some lead less vicious lives than others? In examining this question it is necessary to revert to our definition of terms, and bear in mind that total depravity does not consist in what a man *does*, but what he *is* in himself. It also consists in a man's relation and attitude *to God*. Because particular persons are not swearers, morally unclean, drunkards or thieves, they are very apt to imagine they are far from being wholly corrupt; in fact, they consider themselves good and respectable people. These are described in Proverbs 30:12: "There is a generation that are pure in their own eyes, and yet is not washed from their filthiness." However irreproachable may be the walk of the natural man, his nature is polluted and his heart thoroughly defiled. And the very fact that he is quite unaware of his vileness is sad proof of the binding power of indwelling sin.

The total depravity of human nature does not mean that it actually breaks forth into open acts of all kinds of evil in any one man. There are marked differences among the unregenerate in the eruption of sin in their conduct. Some are more honest, sober and benevolent than others, running into less "excess of riot"; nevertheless the seeds of all evils are present in every human breast. "As in water face answereth to face, so the heart of man to man" (Prov. 27:19). It has been truly said of all men that if they were in Cain's or Pharaoh's or Judas' circumstances, and God should allow them, they would do the same. If they were in the same circumstances as the fallen angels, they would be as devilish as they.

True, the enmity against God and the hatred against their fellowmen

(Titus 3:3) are less openly displayed by some than by others, yet that is not because they are any better in themselves than those who are flagrantly irreligious and cast off all pretenses of decency. Their moderation in wickedness must be attributed to the greater restraints which the Governor of this world places on them, either by the secret workings of His Spirit upon their hopes and fears or by His external providences, such as a godly home, early education, the subduing influence of pious companions. But none is born into this world with the smallest spark of love to God in him. Instead, "their poison is like the poison of a serpent" (Ps. 58:4). It should be borne in mind—for our humbling—that there is very much evil within each of us that God does not allow to break out into particular acts of sin, sovereignly preventing temptations and opportunities to do them.

All men are equally depraved, but that depravity shows itself in many different forms and ways. It is a fatal delusion to suppose that, because divine power and mercy keep me from certain crimes, I am less corrupt than my fellowmen, and less a criminal in His sight. God does not judge as man does. Capernaum was more obnoxious to Him than Sodom! Many who do not act a brutish part act a diabolical one; there is a filthiness of the spirit as well as of the flesh (II Cor. 7:1). Though some do not give free rein to their sensual lusts, yet they are under the dominion of mental lusts: pride, covetousness, envy, contempt of others, malice, revenge. God restrains both the internal and external workings of sin as best serves the outworking of His eternal purpose, permitting different degrees of iniquity in different individuals, though all are "clay of the same lump." None by nature possesses the slightest degree of holiness. Different measures of wickedness issue from the same individual at different times. The fact that I have been kept from certain sins in the past is no guarantee that I shall not be guilty of them in the future.

Finally, some contend that if man is so totally depraved as to be entirely incapable of doing anything that is pleasing to God, then there can be no ground for a challenging sermon, no motives for exhorting the unregenerate to cease from evil and do good, and certainly no encouragement left for them to comply. We reply that no minister of the gospel is warranted to entertain the slightest degree of hope of success from his endeavors merely on the ground of the pliability of the hearts of his hearers. Their corrupt state excludes any such expectation. Unless the preacher's confidence is based alone on the power and promise of God, his hopes are certain to be disappointed. But if the objector means that in view of men's total depravity it is unreasonable to exhort them to do good, this can by no means be admitted, for it would follow that if total depravity removes all ground for a rational address, then a *partial* one would take it away in part; in other words, in proportion as we perceive men to be disinclined to good, we are to cease warning and dealing with them. This is a self-evident absurdity.

While men are rational creatures they are justly accountable for all they do, whatever the disposition of their hearts. And, so long as they are not yet consigned to a hopeless perdition, their responsibility is to be enforced, and they are to be regarded as fit subjects of a gospel address. Nor can it be truly asserted that there are no motives by which they may properly be exhorted to cease to do evil and learn to do good. The proper motives for these things retain all their original force, independent of the inclination or disinclination of men's hearts to comply. God's rights, His authority, His law, are unchanged no matter what change has taken place in the creature. The example of Christ and His apostles is too plain to be misunderstood. Neither the one nor the other toned down their demands upon fallen sinners. Repentance toward God and faith toward our Lord Jesus Christ were the grand duties on which they insisted; and far from hesitating to exhort their unregenerate hearers to do what was *spiritually good*, it may be safely affirmed that they never exhorted to do anything else. God still requires nothing less than the heart.

The violent antagonism of men against this truth is precisely what might be expected. Instead of causing us doubt it should be a strong confirmation. Indeed it would be surprising if a doctrine so humbling and distasteful were not resisted. Nor need we be dismayed by its widespread repudiation by preachers and professing Christians. When the Lord Jesus averred, "I am come into this world, that they which see not might see; and that they which [pretend to] see might be made blind" (John 9:39), the Pharisees haughtily asked, "Are we blind also?" (v. 40). When He declared that human nature is in love with sin and possessed of enmity against God, and insisted, "No man can come unto me, except it were given unto him of my Father," we are told that "from that time many of his disciples went back, and walked no more with him" (John 6:65-66). The rejection which this doctrine meets with demonstrates how dense is that darkness which is not dispelled by so clear a light, and how great is the power of Satan when the testimony of divine revelation does not carry conviction. Every effort to tone it down verifies the fact that "the heart *is* deceitful above all things, and desperately wicked."

Chapter 10

RAMIFICATIONS

WHILE ENDEAVORING to present a complete picture of fallen man as he is depicted by the divine pen in the Scriptures, it is very difficult to avoid a measure of overlapping as we turn from one aspect or feature to another, or to prevent a certain amount of repetition. Yet, seeing that this is the method which the Holy Spirit has largely taken, an apology is scarcely required from those who seek to follow His plan. We have shown in a more or less general way the terrible havoc sin has worked in the human constitution: now we shall consider it more specifically. Having presented the broad outline, it remains for us to fill in the details. In other words, our immediate task is to ponder and describe *the several parts* of human depravity as it has vitiated the several sections of our inner man. Though the soul, like the body, is a unit, it also has a number of distinct members or faculties, none of which has been exempted from the debasing effects of man's apostasy from his Maker.

Debasing Effects of Apostasy

This was strikingly exemplified in the miracles of Christ. The various bodily disorders which the divine Physician healed during His sojourn on earth were not only so many advance types of the marvels of grace that He performs in the spiritual realm in connection with the redeemed; they were also so many emblematical representations of the moral diseases which affect and afflict the soul of fallen man. The poor leper, covered with nauseous sores, solemnly portrayed the horrible pollutions of the human heart. The man born blind, incapable of seeing the wonders and beauties of God's external works, expressed the sad state of the human mind, which, because of the darkness that is upon it, is unable to discover or receive the things of the Spirit, no matter how simply and plainly they are explained to him. The paralytic's useless limbs showed beforehand the impotence of the will Godward, being totally devoid of any power to turn us to Christ. The woman lying sick of the fever, experiencing unnatural craving, delirium and restlessness, depicted the disordered state of our affections. The demon-possessed man, living in the tombs, incapable of being securely bound, crying and cutting himself, typified the various activities of the conscience in the unregenerate.

Corruption has invaded every part of man's nature, overspreading the whole of his complex being. As physical disorders spare no members of the body, so even man's spirit has not escaped the ravages of depravity. Yet who is capable of comprehending this in its awful breadth and depth, length and height? It is not simply the inferior powers of the soul which the plague of sin has seized; the contagion has ascended into the higher regions of our persons, polluting the sublimest faculties. This is a part of God's punishment. It is a great mistake to suppose that the divine judgment on man's defection is reserved for the next life. Men are heavily penalized in this world, both outwardly and inwardly, and subject to many adverse providences. Outwardly, in their bodies, names, estates, relations and employments; and finally, by physical death and dissolution. Inwardly, by blindness of mind, hardness of heart, turbulent passions, the gnawing of conscience. However little regarded, by reason of their stupidity and insensibility, yet the inward visitations of God's curse are far more dreadful than the outward ones, and are regarded as such by those who truly fear the Lord and see things in His light. Let us consider each in detail.

Blindness of Mind

The mind is that faculty of the soul by which objects and things are first known and apprehended. In distinguishing the understanding from the mind, the latter is that which weighs, discriminates and determines, judging between the concepts formed in the former, being the guide of the soul, the selector and rejecter of those notions the mind has received. Both are deranged by sin, for we are told that "their minds were blinded" (II Cor. 3:14) and their "understanding darkened" (Eph. 4:18). The fall has completely shuttered the windows of man's soul, yet he is not aware of it; in fact, he emphatically denies it. Heathen philosophers and medieval scholars both believed that the affections, in the lower part of the soul, were somewhat defiled, but insisted that the intellectual faculty was pure, saying that reason still directed and advised us to do the best things.

It is not strange that blind reason should think it sees, for while it judges everything else it is least capable of estimating itself because of its very nearness to itself. Though a man's eye can see the deformity of his hands or feet, it cannot see the bloodshot that is in itself, unless it has a mirror in which to discern the same. In like manner, even corrupt nature, by its own light, recognizes the disorders in the sensual part of man; yet it cannot discern the defilement that is in the spirit itself. The mirror of God's Word is required to discover *that*, and even that mirror is not sufficient. The light of divine grace has to shine within, in order to expose and discover the imbecility of the reasoning faculty. Hence Holy Writ throws the main emphasis on the depravity of this highest part of man's being. When the apostle wanted to show how impure unbelievers are, though they profess to know God, he averred, "Even their mind and conscience is defiled" (Titus 1:15). They least of all suspected those parts as being tainted, especially since they were illumined with some rays of the knowledge of God. Thus, in opposition to their conceit, the superior faculties alone are mentioned, and stressed with an "even."

How weighty and full the testimony of Scripture is on this solemn feature: "When they knew God [traditionally], they glorified him not as God, neither were thankful; but became vain in their imaginations, and their foolish heart was darkened. Professing themselves to be wise, they became fools" (Rom. 1:21-22). That reference is to the Gentiles after the flood. One of the fearful curses executed on Israel, because they did not listen to the voice of the Lord their God and refused to do His commandments, was "The Lord shall smite thee with madness, and blindness, and astonishment of heart: and thou shalt grope at noonday, as the blind gropeth in darkness" (Deut. 28:28-29). Of all mankind it is said, "There is none that understandeth. The way of peace have they not known" (Rom. 3:11, 17). "There is a way which seemeth right unto a man, but the end thereof are the ways of death" (Prov. 14:12). "The world by wisdom knew not God" (I Cor. 1:21). Despite all their schools, they were ignorant of Him, "desiring to be teachers of the law; understanding neither what they say, nor whereof they affirm" (I Tim. 1:7), "ever learning, and never able to come to the knowledge of the truth" (II Tim. 3:7).

In the natural there are two factors which prevent men from seeing: nightfall, unless there is the aid of artificial light, and loss of sight. The one is external, the other internal. So it is in the spiritual: there are an objective and a subjective darkness, both *on* men and *in* men. The first consists in a lack of those means by which they may be enlightened in the knowledge of God and heavenly things. What the sun is to natural things on the earth, the Word is to spiritual things (Ps. 19:1-4; cf. Rom. 10:10-11).

Spiritual darkness is on all to whom the gospel is not declared or by whom it is rejected. It is the mission and work of the Holy Spirit to take away this objective darkness, and until it is done no one can see or enter the kingdom of God. This He does by sending the gospel into a country, nation or town. It does not obtain entrance there, nor is it restrained anywhere, by accident or by human effort. It is dispensed according to the sovereign will of the Spirit of God. He it is who endows, calls and sends men forth to preach, determining, either by His secret impulses or by the operations of His providence (Acts 16:6-10), where they shall minister.

But it is the *subjective* darkness on the minds of the unregenerate, with its influences and consequences, which is here considered. It is not simply ignorance but a foul disease. "He is proud, knowing nothing, but . . . [sick] about questions and strifes of words, whereof cometh envy, strife, railings, evil surmisings, perverse disputings of men of corrupt minds, and destitute of the truth" (I Tim. 6:4-5). Their minds are not only rebellious but diseased and corrupt. This distemper of mind could be called an itch after fables (II Tim. 4:3-4). Scripture calls that contentious wisdom of which the learned of this world are so proud "earthly, sensual, devilish" (James 3:15). Both the verse before and the one following show that envy, malice, lying and deception, though in both the affections and the will, are rooted in the understanding. Hence God must give repentance or a change of mind before there can be an acknowledgment of the truth and a recovery from the snare of the devil (II Tim. 2:25-26).

This darkness of the understanding is the cause of the rebellion in the affections and will. Men seek so inordinately the pleasures of sin because their minds do not know God. They are strangers to Him and can have no fellowship with Him, for friendship and fellowship are grounded on knowledge. To have communion with God, knowledge of Him is necessary. Accordingly the principal thing God does when He gives admittance into the covenant of grace is teach men to know Him (Jer. 31:33-34). Otherwise men are estranged from Him through ignorance (Eph. 4:17-19). The darkness of the mind is not only the root of all sin but the cause of most of the corruptions in men's lives. Hence we find that Paul mentions "fleshly wisdom" as the antithesis of the principle of grace (II Cor. 1:12). For the same reason men are said to be "sottish children, and they have none understanding: they are wise to do evil, but to do good they have no knowledge" (Jer. 4:22). That this *is* the cause of the greatest part of the wickedness in the world is clear from Isaiah 47:10: "Thy wisdom and thy knowledge, it hath perverted thee." Corrupt reasoning and false judgment are the prime motivations of all our sinning. Pride has its chief place in the mind, as Colossians 2:18 shows.

This darkness is forceful and influential—yes, dynamic—according to that expression in Colossians 1:13: "delivered us from the *power* of darkness," the word "power" signifying that which rules. It fills the mind with enmity against God and all His ways, and turns the will in a contrary direction so that, instead of the affections being set on things above, they "mind earthly things" (Phil. 3:19). This is the habitual inclination. The will minds the things of the flesh (Rom. 8:5), setting itself to provide sensual objects for the gratification of the body. It fills the mind with strong prejudices against the spiritual things proposed in the gospel. Those prejudices are called strongholds and imaginations (reasonings), and "every high thing that exalteth itself against the knowledge of God" (II Cor. 10:4-5). They are pulled down and destroyed in the day of God's power, when souls are brought into willing subjection to Him. The sins of the mind continue longest, for though the body decays and its lusts wither, those of the mind are as vigorous and active in old age as in youth. As the understanding is the most excellent part of man, so its corruption is worse than that of the other faculties: "If . . . the light that is in thee be darkness, how great is that darkness!" (Matt. 6:23).

The effects of this darkness are fearful indeed. Its subjects are made incapable of discerning or receiving spiritual things, so that there is a total inability with respect to God and the ways of pleasing Him. No matter how well endowed intellectually the unregenerate man may be, what the extent of his education and learning, how skillful in connection with natural things, in spiritual matters he is devoid of intelligence until he is renewed in the spirit of his mind. As a person who has no sight is unaware of the strongest rays of light directed at him, and cannot form any real ideas of the appearance of things, so the natural man, because of his blindness of mind, is unable to discern the nature of heavenly things. Said Christ to the Jews of His day, "If thou hadst known, even thou, at least in this thy day, the things which belong unto thy peace! But now they are *hid* from thine eyes" (Luke 19:42)—concealed from their perception as effectually as things which are purposely hidden from prying eyes. Even though one had the desire to discover them, he would search in vain for all eternity unless God was pleased to reveal them, as He did to Peter (Matt. 16:17).

The spiritual blindness in the mind of the natural man not only disables him to make the first discovery of the things of God; even when they are published and set before his eyes, as in the Word of truth, he cannot discern them. Whatever notions he may form of them are dissonant to their nature, and the thoughts he has of them are the very reverse of what they actually are. They regard the highest wisdom as foolishness, and despise and reject glorious things. "Behold, ye despisers, and wonder, and perish: for I work a work in your days, a work which ye shall in no wise believe, though a man declare it unto you" (Acts 13:41). The preceding verses show that Paul clearly preached Christ and His gospel, and then cautioned his hearers to escape the doom spoken of by the prophet. It is not the bare presentation of the truth which will convince men. Though clearly propounded, it may still be obscure to them: "It is hid to them that are lost: in whom the god of this world hath blinded the minds of them which believe not" (II Cor. 4:3-4). Their understandings need to be divinely opened in order to understand the Scriptures (Luke 24:45).

The subjects of this darkness are spiritually insensible and stupid. This prevents them from making a true inspection of their hearts. They see only the outward man, and do not feel the deadly wound within. There is a sea of corruption, but it is unperceived. The holiness, beauty and rectitude of their nature have departed, but they are quite unconcerned. They are miserable and poor, blind and naked, yet totally unaware of it. Thus the unregenerate go on in a course of rebellion against the Lord, and at the same time conclude that all is well with them. As the goodness of God does not melt them, neither do His severest judgments move them to amend their ways. Far from it, they are like wicked King Ahaz, of whom it is recorded, "And in the time of his distress did he trespass yet more against the LORD" (II Chron. 28:22). The masses are defiant and unrepentant today, when the peace of the whole world is so seriously menaced: "LORD, when thy hand is lifted up, they will not see" (Isa. 26:11).

Space allows us to mention only one other effect of this blindness of the mind; it is termed "the vanity of their mind" in Ephesians 4:17. Scripture says useless and fruitless things are *vain*. In Matthew 15:9 the word means "to no purpose." Hence the idols of the heathen and the rites used in their worship are called vain things (Acts 14:15). In I Samuel 12:21 we read that vain things "cannot profit nor deliver." Vanity is synonymous with foolishness, for Proverbs 12:11 states that vain men are one with persons "void of understanding." In Jeremiah 4:14 vain things are linked with "wickedness," thus they are sinful. Vain men and sons of Belial are synonymous (II Chron. 13:7). This vanity of the mind induces the natural man to pursue shadows and miss the substance, to be engaged with figments instead of realities, to prefer lies to the truth. This vanity leads men to follow the fashions and revel in the pleasures of a vain world. This sinful state of mind is in all sorts of persons, old and young, showing itself in foolish imaginations by which it makes provision for the flesh and its lusts. It appears as a reluctance to think about holy things; when the Word is preached, the mind wanders like a butterfly in a garden. It "feedeth on foolishness" (Prov. 15:14), and has an itching curiosity about the affairs of others.

Blindness of Heart

The heart is the center of our moral being, out of which flow the issues of life (Prov. 4:23; cf. Matt. 12:35). The nature of the heart is at once indicated by its being designated a "*stony* heart" (Ezek. 11:19). The figure is a very apt one. As a stone is a product of the earth, so it has the property of the earth: heaviness, a tendency to fall. Thus it is with the natural mind. Men's affections are wholly set on the world; and though God made man upright with his head erect, yet the soul is bowed down to the ground. The physical curse pronounced on the serpent is also fulfilled in his seed, for the things on which they feed turn to ashes, so that dust is their meat (Isa. 65:25). Sin has so calloused man's heart that, Godward, it is loveless and lifeless, cold and insensible. That is one reason why the moral law was written on tables of stone: to represent emblematically the stupid, unyielding hearts men had, as is clearly implied by the contrast presented in II Corinthians 3:3.

The heart of the regenerate is also likened to "rock" (Jer. 23:29), and to "adamant stone" (Zech. 7:12), which is harder than flint. Those far from righteousness are called "stout-hearted" (Isa. 46:12); and in Isaiah 48:4 God says, "Thou art obstinate, and thy neck is an iron sinew, and thy brow brass." This hardness is often ascribed to the neck ("stiffnecked"), a figure of man's obstinacy taken from refractory oxen which will not accept the yoke. This hardness evidences itself by a complete absence of spiritual sensibility, so that the heart is unmoved by God's goodness, has no awe of His authority and majesty, no fear of His anger and vengeance; a presentation of the joys of heaven or the horrors of hell makes no impression on it. As the prophet of old lamented, they "put far away the evil day" (Amos 6:3), dismissing it from their thoughts as an unwelcome subject. They have no sense of guilt, no consciousness of having offended their Maker, no alarming realization of His impending wrath, but are at ease in their sins. Far from sin being a burden to them, it is their element and delight.

Hardness of heart, which was referred to in the preceding chapter, is the perverseness and obstinacy of fallen man's nature, which makes him resolve to continue in sin no matter what be the consequences thereof. It renders him unwilling to be rebuked for his folly, and makes him refuse to be reclaimed from it, whatever methods are used in order thereunto. The Prophet Ezekiel mentioned this hardness of heart in his day, referring to those who had been forewarned by earlier judgments, and were at that very time under the most solemn rebuke of Providence. God had to say of them, "They will not hearken unto me: for all the house of Israel are impudent and hardhearted" (Ezek. 3:7). The Lord Jesus said of them, "We have piped unto you, and ye have not danced; we have mourned unto you, and ye have not lamented" (Matt. 11:17). The most touching entreaties and winsome reasoning will not move the unregenerate to accept what is absolutely necessary for their present peace and final joy. "They are like the deaf adder that stoppeth her ear; which will not hearken to the voice of charmers, charming never so wisely" (Ps. 58:4-5; cf. Acts 7:57).

The hearts of the regenerate are docile and pliable, easily bent to God's will, but the hearts of the wicked are wedded to their lusts and impervious to all appeal. There is such unyielding disposition against heavenly things that they do not respond to the most alarming threatenings and thunderings. They will neither be convinced by the most cogent arguments nor won by the most tempting inducements. They are so addicted to self-pleasing that they cannot be persuaded to take Christ's yoke on them. Zechariah 7:11-12 states: "But they refused to hearken, and pulled away the shoulder, and stopped their ears, that they should not hear. Yea, they made their hearts as an adamant stone, lest they should hear the law, and the words which the LORD of hosts hath sent." They are less susceptible to receive any impressions of holiness than granite is to be engraved by the tool of the artificer. They scorn control and refuse to be admonished. They are "a stubborn and rebellious generation" (Ps. 78:8), being subject to neither the law nor the gospel. The doctrines of repentance, self-denial, walking with God, can find no entrance into their hearts.

Disordered Affections

Writers disagree as to the scope of the affections. It is a moot point both theologically and psychologically whether the desires are included in the affections. In the broadest meaning, the affections may be said to be the sensitive faculty of the soul. As the understanding discerns and judges things, so the affections allure and dispose the soul to or against the objects contemplated. By the affections the soul becomes pleased or displeased with what is known by the bodily senses or contemplated by the mind, and thus it is moved to approve or reject. As distinguished from both the understanding and the affections, the will executes the final decision of the mind or the strongest desire of the affections, carrying it into action. Since the affections pertain to the sensitive side of the soul, we are more conscious of their stirrings than we are of the actions of our minds or wills. We shall employ the term in its widest latitude, including the desires, for what the appetites are to the body the affections are to the soul.

Goodwin likened the desire nature to the stomach. It is an empty void, fitted to receive from without, longing for a satisfying object. Its universal language is "Who will shew us any good?" (Ps. 4:6). Now God Himself is man's chief good, the only One who can afford him real, lasting and full satisfaction. At the beginning He created him in His own likeness, that as the needle touched by the lodestone ever moves northward, so the soul touched with the divine image should turn the understanding, affections and will to Himself. He also placed the soul in a material body, and in this world, fitting each for the other, providing everything necessary for and suited to each part of man's complex being. The desire nature carries the soul's impressions to the creature, originally intended as a means of enjoying God in and by them. The wonders of God's handiwork were meant to be admired, but chiefly as displaying His wisdom. Food was to be eaten and enjoyed, but in order to deepen gratitude for the goodness of the Giver and to supply strength to serve Him. But when man apostatized, his understanding, affections and will were divorced from God, and the exercise of them became directed only by self-love.

Originally the Lord sustained and directed the action of human affections toward Himself. Then He withheld that power, and left our first parents on their own footing; in consequence their desires wandered after forbidden joys. They sought their happiness not in communion with their Maker, but in fellowship with the creature. Like their children ever since, they loved and served the creature more than the Creator. The result was disastrous: they became separated from the holy One. That was at once evidenced by their attempt to hide from Him. Had their delight been in God as their chief good, the desire for concealment could not have possessed them. As it was with Adam and Eve, so it has been with all their descendants. Many a proverb expresses that general truth. "The stream cannot rise higher than the fountain." "Men do not gather grapes of thorns, nor figs of thistles." "Like begets like." The parent stock of the human family must send forth scions of its own nature. The hearts and lives of all the unregenerate say to the Almighty, "Depart from us; for we desire not the knowledge of thy ways" (Job 21:14).

The natural center of unfallen man's soul for both its rest and delight was the One who gave him being. Therefore David said, "Return unto thy rest, O my soul" (Ps. 116:7). But sin has caused men to "draw back" from Him, "departing from the living God" (Heb. 10:38; 3:12). God was not only to be the delightful portion of the one whom He had made in His image, but also the ultimate end of all man's motives and actions as he aimed to glorify and please Him in all things. But man forsook "the fountain of living waters" (Jer. 2:13), the infinite and perpetual spring of comfort and joy. And now the inclinations and lusts of man's nature are wholly removed from God, anything and everything being more agreeable to him than He who is the sum of all excellence. Man makes the things of time and sense his chief good, and the pleasing of himself his supreme end. That is why his affections are termed "ungodly lusts" (Jude 18)—they turn man away from God. Man has no relish for His holiness, no desire for fellowship with Him, no wish to retain Him in his thoughts.

But what has just been pointed out (the aversion of our affections from God) is only the negative phase. The positive is the conversion of the affections to other things. Thus God charged Israel, "My people have committed two evils; they have forsaken me the fountain of living waters, and hewed them out cisterns, broken cisterns, that can hold no water" nor give them any satisfaction (Jer. 2:13). All the concern of the natural man is how to live at ease, not how to honor and enjoy God. He observes "lying vanities" and forsakes his own mercy (Jonah 2:8). All his expectations are disappointments, empty vanities. Man is deceived by a vain prospect, and the outcome is vexation of spirit, because of frustration. As the love of God shed abroad in the hearts of the redeemed does not seek its own good (I Cor. 13:5), so self-love does nothing but that: "They all look to their own way, every one for his gain" (Isa. 56:11).

Not only are the desires of the unregenerate turned away from God to the creature, but they are greedy, excessive. Thus we read of "inordinate affections" (Col. 3:5), which indicate both excess and irregularity, a spirit of gluttony and unmitigated craving for things contrary to God, a "lust after evil things" (I Cor. 10:6). We see here two sins: intemperance and "pleasure in unrighteousness" (II Thess. 2:12). The body is esteemed above the soul, for all the efforts of the natural man are directed to making provision to fulfill the lusts of the flesh; his immortal spirit is little thought of and still less cared for. When things go well for him, he says, "Soul, thou hast much goods laid up for many years; take thine ease, eat, drink, and be merry" (Luke 12:19). His thoughts do not rise to a higher and future life. He is more concerned with the clothing and adorning of the outward man than with the cultivation of a meek and quiet spirit, which is of great value in the sight of God (I Peter 3:4). Earth is preferred before heaven, things of time before eternity. Though death and the grave may put an end to all he has here much sooner than he imagines, yet his heart is so set on his possessions that he will not be diverted from them.

Thus it is that the affections, which at the beginning were the servants of reason, now occupy the throne. That which is the glory of human nature—elevating it above the beasts of the field—is turned here and there by the rude rabble of our passions. God placed in man an instinct for happiness, so that he could find it in Himself; but now that instinct gropes in the dust and snatches at every vanity. The counsels and contrivances of the mind are engaged in the accomplishment of man's carnal desires. Not only have his affections no relish for spiritual things, but they are strongly prejudiced against them, for they run counter to the gratifying of his corrupt nature. His desires are set on more wealth, more worldly honor and power, more fleshly merriment; and because the gospel contains no promise of such things it is despised. Because it inculcates holiness, mortifying of the flesh, separation from the world, resisting the devil, the gospel is most unwelcome to him. To turn the affections away from those material and temporal things which they have made their chief good, and to turn them to unseen spiritual and eternal things, alienates the carnal mind against the gospel, for it offers nothing attractive to the natural man in place of those idols on which his heart centers. To renounce his own righteousness and be dependent on that of Another is equally distasteful to his pride.

The affections are alienated from and opposed to not only the holy requirements of the gospel, but also its mystery. That mystery is what the Scriptures term the hidden wisdom of God, which the natural man not only fails to admire and adore, but regards with contempt. He looks on all of its declarations as empty and unintelligible notions. This prejudice has prevailed among the wise and learned of this world in all ages. The wisdom of God seems foolishness to all who are puffed up by pride in their own intelligence, and what seems foolishness to them is despised and scorned. That which is related to faith rather than reason is unpalatable. Not to trust in their own understanding but in the Lord is most difficult for those of towering intellect. To set aside their own ideas, forsake their thoughts (Isa. 55:7) and become as "little children," and to be told they shall never enter the kingdom of heaven unless they do all this, is most abhorrent to them. No small part of man's depravity consists in his readiness to embrace anti-God prejudices and to tenaciously adhere to them, with total lack of power to extricate himself from them.

The disordered state of the affections is seen in the fact that the actions of the natural man are regulated far more by his senses than by his reason. His conduct consists principally in responding to the clamoring of his desires rather than to the dictates of reason. The tendencies of children swiftly turn to any corrupting diversion, but are slow to respond to any improving exercise. They can scarcely be restrained from the one; they have to be compelled to do the other. That the affections are turned away from God is made clear every time His will crosses our desires. This disease appears too in the objects on which the different affections are placed. Instead of love being set on God, it is centered on the world, and dotes on idols. Instead of hatred being directed against sin, it is opposed to holiness. Instead of joy finding its delight in spiritual things, it wastes itself on things which soon pall. Instead of fear being actuated by the displeasure of the Lord, it dreads more the frowns of our fellowmen. If there is grief, it is for the thwarting of our pleasures and hopes, rather than over our waywardness. If there is pity, it is exercised on self, rather than on the sufferings of others.

The very first stirring of our lusts is itself *evil*. The passions or lusts are those natural and unrestrained motives of the creature for the advancement of its nature, inclining to those things which promote its good, and avoiding those which are harmful. They are to the soul what wings are to the bird and sails to the ship. Desire, always in pursuit of satisfaction, must be regulated by right reason. But reason has been dethroned and man's passions and inclinations are lawless; therefore their earliest stirrings after forbidden objects are essentially evil. This was, as Matthew 5 shows, denied by the rabbis, who restricted sin to open and outward transgression. But our Lord declared that unwarrantable anger against another was incipient murder, that to look on a woman with lust was a breach of the seventh commandment, that impure thoughts and wanton imaginations were nothing less than adultery. Hence Scripture speaks of "deceitful lusts" (Eph. 4:22), "foolish and hurtful lusts" (I Tim. 6:9), "worldly lusts" (Titus 2:12), "fleshly lusts, which war against the soul" (I Peter 2:11), "ungodly lusts" (Jude 18).

The very first stirring of desire after anything evil, the slightest irregularity in the motives of the soul, is sin. This is clear from the universal command "Thou shalt not covet," that is, hanker after anything which God has prohibited. This irregular and evil longing is called "concupiscence" in Romans 7:8, by which the apostle meant mental as well as sensual desire. The Greek word is usually rendered "lust"; in I Thessalonians 4:5 it is found in an intensified form: "the lust of concupiscence." These lustings of the soul are its initial motions, often unsuspected by ourselves, which precede the consent of the mind, and are designated "evil concupiscence" (Col. 3:5). They are the seeds from which our evil works spring, the original stirrings of our indwelling corruption. They are condemned by the law of God, for the tenth commandment forbids the first outgoings of the affections after what belongs to another. That incipient longing, *before* the approbation of the mind is obtained, is sinful, and needs to be confessed to God. Genesis 6:5 declares of fallen man that "every imagination of the thoughts of his heart" is evil, for sins even in their embryonic stage defile the soul, being contrary to that purity which the holiness of God requires.

The Council of Trent denied that the original movement of the soul tending to evil is in itself sinful, stating that it only becomes so when it is consented or yielded to. Now it is freely confessed by all sound Calvinists that the mind's entertaining of the first evil desire is a further degree of sin, and that the actual assent to the desire is yet more heinous; but they emphatically contend that the *original impulse* is also evil in the sight of God. If the original impulse is innocent per se, how could its gratification be sinful? Motives and excitements do not undergo any change in their essential nature in consequence of their being humored or encouraged. It cannot be wrong to respond to innocent impulses. The Lord Jesus teaches us to judge the tree by its fruit; if the fruit is corrupt, so too is the tree which bears it.

In Romans 7:7 the term is actually rendered sin: "I had not known *sin*, but by the law: for I had not known *lust*, except the law had said, Thou shalt not covet." Here, then, sin and lust are used interchangeably; any inward nonconformity to the law is sinful. Paul was made aware of that fact when the commandment was applied to him in power—as the sun shining on refuse draws forth its stench. Men may deny that the very *desire* for forbidden objects is culpable, but Scripture affirms that even imaginations are the evil buds of wickedness, for they are contrary to that rectitude of heart which the law requires. Note how that terrible list of things which Christ enumerated as issuing from the heart of fallen man is headed with "evil thoughts" (Matt. 15:19). We cannot conceive of any inclination or proneness to sin in an absolutely holy being. Certainly there was none in the Lord Jesus: "The prince of this world cometh, and hath nothing in me" (John 14:30). There was nothing in Christ that was capable of responding to Satan's vile solicitations, no movement of His appetites or affections of which he could take advantage. Christ was inclined only to what is good.

"For when we were in the flesh [*i.e.*, while Christians were in their unregenerate state], the motions of sins [literally, the affections of sin, or the beginnings of our passions], which were [aggravated] by the law, did work in our members [the faculties of the soul as well as of the body] to bring forth fruit unto death" (Rom. 7:5). Those "affections of sin" are the filthy streams which issue from the polluted fountain of our hearts. They are the first stirrings of our fallen nature which precede the overt acts of transgression. They are the unlawful movements of our desire prior to the studied and deliberate thoughts of the mind after sin. "But sin [indwelling corruption], taking occasion by the commandment, wrought in me all manner of concupiscence" or "evil lustings" (Rom. 7:8). Note that word "wrought in me": there was a polluted disposition or evil propensity at work, distinct from the deeds which it produced. Indwelling sin is a powerful principle, constantly exercising a bad influence, stimulating unholy affections, stirring to avarice, enmity, malice and countless other evils.

The popular idea which now prevails is that nothing is sinful except an open and outward transgression. Such a concept falls far short of the searching and humbling teaching of Holy Writ. It affirms that the source of all temptation lies within fallen man himself. The depravity of his own heart induces him to listen to the devil or be influenced by the profligacy of others. If this were not so, no external solicitations to wrongdoing would have any force, for there would be nothing within man for them to excite, nothing to which those solicitations correspond or over which they could exert any power. An evil example would be rejected with abhorrence if we were pure within. There must be an unsatisfied lust to which temptation from without appeals. Where there is no desire for food, a well-spread table does not allure. If there is no love of acquisition, gold cannot attract the heart. In every instance the force of temptation lies in some propensity of our fallen nature.

The uniqueness of the Bible lies in its exalted spirituality, insisting that any inward bias, the least gravitation of the soul from God and His will, is sinful and culpable, whether or not it is carried into action. It reveals that the first stirring of sin itself is to draw away the soul from what it ought to be fixed upon, by an irregular craving for some foreign object which appears delightful. When our native corruptions are invited by something external which promises pleasure or profit, and the passions are attracted by it, then temptation begins, and the heart is drawn out after it. Since fallen man is influenced most by his lusts, they sway both his mind and his will. So powerful are they that they rule his whole soul: "I see another *law* in my members" (Rom. 7:23). It is an imperious law, dominating the entire man. It is because their lusts are so violent that men are so mad upon sinning: "They . . . weary themselves to commit iniquity" (Jer. 9:5).

James 1:14-15 traces the origin of all our sinning: "But every man is tempted, when he is drawn away of his own lust, and enticed. Then when lust hath conceived, it bringeth forth sin: and sin, when it is finished bringeth forth death." Those words show that sin encroaches on the spirit by degrees; they describe the several stages before it is consummated in the outward act. They reveal that the procreating cause of all sin lies in the lusts of every man's soul; he has within himself both the food and fuel for it. Goodwin declared: "You can never come to see how deeply and how abominably corrupt creatures you are, until God opens your eyes to see your lusts." The old man is "corrupt *according to* the deceitful lusts" (Eph. 4:22). Lust is both the womb and the root of all wickedness on earth. The apostle to God's people spoke of "having escaped the corruption that is in the world through lust" (II Peter 1:4). "The corruption": that wasting destroying blight which is on all mankind. "Which is in the world": like poison in the cup, like dry rot in wood, like an epidemic in the air—inherent, ineradicable. It taints every part of man's being, physical, mental and moral; it affects all his relations of life, whether in the family, society or the State.

"Every man is tempted when he is drawn away of his own lust." When men are tempted they usually try to place the onus on God, the devil, or their fellowmen; actually the blame rests entirely on themselves. First, their affections are removed from what is good and they are incited to wrongful conduct by their corrupt inclinations, attracted to the bait which Satan or the world dangles before them. "Lust" here signifies a yearning for, or longing to obtain, something. And it is so strong that it draws the soul after a forbidden object. The Greek word for "drawn away" means forcibly impelled. The impetuous violence of the desire which covets some sensual or worldly thing demands gratification. This is nothing but a species of self-will, a hankering after what God has not granted, rising from discontent with our present condition or position. Even though that longing is a fleeting and involuntary one, perhaps against our best judgment, nevertheless it is sinful and, when allowed, produces yet deeper guilt.

"And enticed": The drawing away is because of the irregularity and vehemence of the craving; the enticement is from the object contemplated. But that very allurement is something for which we are to blame. It is because we fail to resist, hate and reject the first rising of unlawful desire, but instead entertain and encourage it, that the bait appears so attractive. The temptation promises pleasure or profit, which shows "the deceitfulness of sin" (Heb. 3:13). All this beguiles us. Then wickedness is sweet in our mouth, and we hide it under our tongue (Job. 20:12). "Then when lust hath conceived":

Anticipated delight is cherished, and the mind fully consents. The sinful deed is now present in embryo, and the thoughts are busied in contriving ways and means of gratification. "It bringeth forth sin" by a decree of the will: What was previously contemplated is now actually perpetrated. Manton said: "Sin knows no mother but our own heart." "And sin, when it is finished, bringeth forth death": We pay its wages and reap what was planted, damnation being the ultimate outcome. This is the progress of sin within us, and these are its degrees of enormity.

Corrupted Conscience

If there is one faculty of man's soul which might be thought to have retained the original image of God on it, it is surely the conscience. Such a view has indeed been widely held. Not a few of the most renowned philosophers and moralists have contended that conscience is nothing less than the divine voice itself speaking in the innermost part of our being. Without minimizing the great importance and value of this internal monitor, either in its office or in its operations, it must be emphatically declared that such theorists err, that even this faculty has not escaped from the common ruin of our entire beings. This is evident from the plain teaching of God's Word. Scripture speaks of a "weak conscience" (I Cor. 8:12), of men "having their conscience seared with a hot iron" (I Tim. 4:2). It says that their "conscience is defiled" (Titus 1:15), that they have "an evil conscience" (Heb. 10:22). Let us examine the point more closely.

Those who affirm that there is something essentially good in the natural man insist that his conscience is an enemy to evil and a friend to holiness. They stress the fact that the conscience produces an inward conviction against wrongdoing, a conflict in the heart over sin, a reluctance to commit it. They call attention to Pharaoh's acknowledgment of sin (Exodus 10:16), and to Darius' being "sorely displeased with himself" for his unjust act in condemning Daniel to be thrown into the lions' den (6:14). Some have even gone so far as to affirm that the opposition to greater and grosser crimes—which is found at first in all men—differs little or not at all from that conflict between the flesh and the spirit described in Romans 7:21-23. But such a sophistry is easily refuted. In the first place, while it is true that fallen man possesses a general notion of right and wrong, and is able in some instances to distinguish between good and evil, yet while he remains unregenerate that moral instinct never causes him to truly delight in the former or to really abhor the latter. In whatever measure he may approve of good or disapprove of evil, it is from no consideration for God.

Conscience is only able to work according to the light it has; and since the natural man cannot discern spiritual things (I Cor. 2:14), it is useless in respect to them. How feeble is its light! It is more like the glimmer of a candle than the rays of the sun—merely sufficient to make the darkness visible. Owing to the darkened condition of the understanding, the conscience is fearfully ignorant. When it does discover that which is adverse, it indicates it feebly and ineffectually. Instead of directing the senses, it mostly confuses. How true this is in the case of the uncivilized. Conscience gives them a sense of guilt and then puts them to practicing the most abominable and often inhuman rites. It has induced them to invent and propagate the most impious misrepresentations of Deity. As a salve to their conscience, they often make the very objects of their worship the precedents and patrons of their favorite vices. The fact is that conscience is so sadly defective that it is unable to perform its duty until God enlightens, awakens and renews it.

Its *operations* are equally faulty. Not only is conscience defective in vision, but its voice is very weak. How strongly it ought to upbraid us for our shocking ingratitude to our great Benefactor! How loudly it should remonstrate against the stupid neglect of our spiritual interests and eternal welfare. Yet it does neither the one nor the other. Though it offers some checks on outward and gross sins, it makes no resistance to the subtler secret workings of indwelling corruption. If it prompts to the performance of duty, it ignores the most important and spiritual part of that duty. It may be uneasy if we fail to spend the usual amount of time each day in private prayer, but it is little concerned about our reverence, humility, faith and fervor in prayer. Those in Malachi's day were guilty of offering God defective sacrifices, yet conscience never troubled them about it (1:7-8). Conscience may be scrupulous in carrying out the precepts of men or our personal inclinations, yet utterly neglect those things which the Lord has commanded; like the Pharisees who would not eat food while their hands remained ceremonially unwashed, yet disregarded what God had commanded (Mark 7:6-9).

Conscience is woefully *partial,* disregarding favorite sins and excusing those which most besiege us. All such attempts to excuse our faults are founded on ignorance of God, of ourselves, of our duty. Otherwise conscience would bring in the verdict of guilty. Conscience often joins with our lusts to encourage a wicked deed. Saul's conscience told him not to offer sacrifice till Samuel came, yet to please the people and prevent them from deserting him he did so. And when that servant of God reproved him, the king tried to justify his offense by saying that the Philistines were gathered together against Israel, and that he dared not attack them before calling on God: "I forced myself therefore, and offered a burnt-offering" (I Sam. 13:8-12). Conscience will strain to find some consideration with which to appease itself and approve of the evil act. Even when rebuking certain sins, it will find motives and discover inducements to them. Thus, when Herod was about to commit the dastardly murder of John the Baptist, which was against his convictions, his conscience came to his aid and urged him forward by impressing on him that he must not violate the oath which he had taken before others (Mark 6:26).

Conscience often ignores great sins while condoning lesser ones, as Saul was hard upon the Israelites for a breach of the ceremonial law (I Sam. 14:33) but made no scruple of killing eighty-five of the Lord's priests. Conscience will even devise arguments which favor the most outrageous acts; thus it is not only like a corrupt lawyer pleading an evil cause, but like a corrupt judge justifying the wicked. Those who clamored for the crucifixion of Christ did so under the pretext of its being orderly and necessary: "We have a law, and by our law he ought to die, because he made himself the Son of God" (John 19:7). Little wonder that the Lord says of men that they "call evil good, and good evil; . . . put darkness for light, and light for darkness" (Isa. 5:20). Conscience never moves the natural man to perform duties out of gratitude and thankfulness to God. It never convicts him of the heavy guilt of Adam's offense which is lying upon his soul, nor of lack of faith in Christ. It allows sinners to sleep in peace in their awful unbelief. But theirs is not a sound and solid peace, for there is no ground for it; rather it is the false security of ignorance. Says God of them, "They consider not in their hearts that I remember all their wickedness" (Hosea 7:2).

The accusations of conscience are ineffectual, for they produce no good fruit, yielding neither meekness, humility nor genuine repentance, but rather a dread of God as a harsh Judge or hatred of Him as an inexorable enemy. Not only are its accusations ineffectual, but often they are quite erroneous. Because of the darkness upon the understanding, the moral perception of the natural man greatly errs. As Thomas Boston said of the corrupt conscience, "So it is often found like a mad and furious horse, which violently runs down himself, his rider, and all that come in his way." A fearful example of that appears in our Lord's prediction in John 16:2 which received repeated fulfillment in the Acts: "They shall put you out of the synagogues: yea, the time cometh, that whosoever killeth you will think that he doeth God service." In like manner Saul of Tarsus after his conversion acknowledged: "I verily thought with myself, that I ought to do many things contrary to the name of Jesus of Nazareth" (Acts 26:9). The unrenewed conscience is a most unreliable guide.

Even when the conscience of the unregenerate is awakened by the immediate hand of God and is struck with deep and painful conviction of sin, far from its moving the soul to seek the mercy of God through the Mediator, it fills him with futility and dismay. As Job 6:4 declares, when the arrows of the Almighty strike a man, their poison drinks up his spirit as the terrors of God set themselves to war against him. Formerly this man may have gone to great pains to stifle the accusations of his inward judge, but now he cannot. Instead, conscience rages and roars, putting the whole man in dreadful consternation, as he is terrified by a sense of the wrath of a holy God and the fiery indignation which shall devour His adversaries. This fills him with such horror and despair that instead of turning to the Lord he tries to flee from Him. Thus it was in the case of Judas who, when he was made to realize the awful gravity of his vile deed, went out and hanged himself. That the guilt of sin within the natural man causes him to turn from rather than to Christ was demonstrated by the Pharisees in John 8:9. They, "being convicted by their own conscience, went out one by one."

Disabled Will

The will is not the lord but the servant of the other faculties executing the strongest conviction of the mind or the most imperious command of our lusts, for there can be but one dominating influence in the will at one and the same time. Originally the excellence of man's will consisted in following the guidance of right reason and submitting to the influence of proper authority. But in Eden man's will rejected the former and rebelled against the latter, and in consequence of the fall his will has ever since been under the control of an understanding which prefers darkness to light and of affections which crave evil rather than good. Thus the fleeting pleasures of sense and the puny interests of time excite our wishes, while the lasting delights of godliness and the riches of immortality receive little or no attention. The will of the natural man is biased by his corruption, for his inclinations gravitate in the opposite direction from his duty; therefore he is in complete bondage to sin, impelled by his lusts. The unregenerate are not merely unwilling to seek after holiness; they inveterately hate it.

Since the will turned traitor to God and entered the service of Satan, it has been completely paralyzed toward good. Said the Saviour, "No man can come to me, except the Father which hath sent me draw him" (John 6:44). And why is it that man cannot come to Christ by his own natural powers? Because not only has he no inclination to do so, but the Saviour repels him; His yoke is unwelcome, His scepter repulsive. In connection with the spiritual things the condition of the will is like that of the woman in Luke 13:11 who "was bowed together, and could in no wise lift up herself." If such is the case, then how can man be said to act voluntarily? Because he freely chooses the evil, and that because "the soul of the wicked *desireth* evil" (Prov. 21:10), always carrying out that desire except when prevented by divine restraint. Man is the slave of his corruption, like a wild colt; from earliest childhood he is averse to restraint. The will of man is uniformly rebellious against God. When Providence thwarts his desires, instead of bowing in humble resignation, he frets with disquietude and acts like a wild bull in a net. Only the Son can make him "free" (John 8:36), for there is "liberty" only where His Spirit is (II Cor. 3:17).

Here, then, are the ramifications of human depravity. The fall has blinded man's mind, hardened his heart, disordered his affections, corrupted his conscience, disabled his will, so that there is "no soundness" in him (Isa. 1:6), "no good thing" in him (Rom. 7:18).

Chapter 11

EVIDENCES

AFTER THE GROUND we have already covered in the preceding chapters it might be thought there is no need for a separate section to furnish proof that man is a fallen and depraved creature who has departed far from his Maker and rightful Lord. Though the Word of God needs no confirming by anything outside itself, it is not without value or interest to find that the teaching of Genesis 3 is substantiated by the hard facts of history and observation. But since there is no point on which the world is so dark as that concerning its own darkness, we feel it necessary to demonstrate the fact. All natural men, unrenewed in their minds by the saving operation of the Holy Spirit, are in a state of darkness with respect to any vital knowledge of God. No matter how learned and skillful they are in other things, in spiritual matters they are blind and stupid. But when that fact is pressed upon them their ire is aroused. Proud intellectuals, who consider themselves so much wiser than the humble and simple believer, regard it as just the empty conceit of illiterates when told that "the way of peace they have not known." Such souls are quite ignorant of their very ignorance.

Signs of Man's Ruin

Even in Christendom the average churchgoer is fully satisfied if he learns by rote a few of the elementary principles of religion. By so doing he comforts himself that he is not an infidel, and since he believes there is a God (though it may be one which his own imagination has devised) he prides himself that he is far from being an atheist. Yet as to having any living, spiritual, influential and practical knowledge of the Lord and His ways he is a stranger, altogether unenlightened. Nor does he feel the least need of divine illumination. He has no taste or desire for a closer acquaintance with God. Never having realized himself to be a lost sinner, he has never sought the Saviour. Only those who are aware of sickness value a physician, just as none but those who are conscious of soul starvation yearn for the bread of life. Men may proudly boast that this twentieth century is an age of enlightenment, but however true that may be in a material and mechanical sense, it is certainly far from being the case spiritually. It is often averred by those who ought to know better that men today are more eager in their quest for truth than in former days, but hard facts give the lie to such an assertion.

In Job 12:24-25 we are told that "the chief people of the earth . . . grope in the dark without light." How evident that is to those whose eyes have been

153

anointed by the Holy Spirit. Who but those blinded by prejudice and incapable of seeing what is right before them would still believe in "the progress of man" and "the steady advance of the human race"? And yet such postulates are made daily by those who are regarded as being the best educated and the greatest thinkers. The idle dreams of idealists and theorists should have been dispelled by the happenings of the past fifty years, when millions of earth's inhabitants have engaged in life-and-death struggles in which the most barbarous inhumanities have been perpetrated, thousands of peaceful citizens killed in their homes, thousands more maimed for the rest of their days, and incalculable material damage done. But so persistent is error, and so radically is it opposed to that which we are here contending for, that no efforts should be spared in exposing the one and establishing the other. We thus present some of the abundant evidence which testifies clearly to the utterly ruined condition of fallen mankind.

These proofs may be drawn from the teaching of Holy Writ, the records of historians, our own observations and personal experience. Genesis 3 describes the origin of human depravity. In the very next chapter the bitter fruits of the fall quickly begin to be manifested. In chapter 3 we see sin in our first parents; in chapter 4, sin in their firstborn, who very soon supplied proof of his having received an evil nature from them. In Genesis 3 the sin was against God; in Genesis 4 it was both against Him and against a fellowman. That is always the order: Where there is no fear of God, there will be no genuine respect for the rights of our neighbors. Yet even at that early date we discern the sovereign and distinguishing grace of God at work, for it was by God-given faith that Abel presented an acceptable sacrifice to the Lord (Heb. 11:4); whereas in blatant self-will and self-pleasing, Cain brought the fruit of the ground as an offering. Upon the Lord's rejection of the sacrifice, "Cain was very wroth" (Gen. 4:5) because he could not approach and worship God according to the dictates of his own mind, and thereby displayed his native enmity against Him. Jealous of God's approval of Abel, Cain rose up and murdered his brother.

Like leprosy, sin contaminates, spreads, and produces death. Near the close of Genesis 4 we see sin corrupting family life, for Lamech was guilty of polygamy, murder and a spirit of fierce revenge (v. 23). In Genesis 5 "death" is written in capital letters over the inspired record, for no less than eight times we read "and he died." But again we are shown grace superabounding in the midst of abounding sin, for Enoch, the seventh from Adam, did not die, being translated without seeing death. That much of his time was spent in expostulating with and warning the wicked of his day is intimated in Jude 14-15 where we are told that he prophesied, "Behold, the Lord cometh with ten thousands of His saints, to execute judgment upon all, and to convince all that are ungodly among them of all their ungodly deeds which they have ungodly committed, and of all their hard speeches which ungodly sinners have spoken *against him*." Noah too was a "preacher of righteousness" (II Peter 2:5) to the antediluvians, but seemingly with little effect, for we read,

"And GOD saw that the wickedness of man was great in the earth, and that every imagination of the thoughts of his heart was only evil continually," that "all flesh had corrupted his way upon the earth," and that the earth was "filled with violence through them" (Gen. 6:5, 12-13).

But though God sent a flood which swept away the whole of that wicked generation, sin was not eradicated from human nature. Instead, fresh evidence of the depravity of man was soon forthcoming. After such a merciful deliverance from the deluge, after witnessing such a fearful demonstration of God's holy wrath against sin, and after the Lord's making a gracious covenant with Noah, which contained most blessed promises and assurances, one would suppose that the human race would ever after adhere to the ways of virtue. But the very next thing we read is that "Noah began to be an husbandman, and he planted a vineyard: and he drank of the wine, and was drunken; and he was uncovered within his tent" (9:20-21). Scholars tell us that the Hebrew word for "uncovered" clearly indicates a deliberate act, and not a mere unconscious effect of drunkenness. The sins of intemperance and impurity are twin sisters. The sad lapse of Noah gave occasion to his son Ham to sin; for, instead of throwing the mantle of charity over his father's conduct, he dishonored him, manifesting disrespect for him. In consequence Ham brought on his descendants a curse, the effects and results of which are apparent to this very day (v. 25).

Genesis 9 brings the inauguration of a new beginning, causing our minds to turn back to the very beginning of the human race. A careful comparison of the two reveals a series of most remarkable parallels between the histories of Adam and Noah. Adam was placed on an earth which came up out of "the great deep" (Gen. 1:2); Noah came forth onto an earth which had just emerged from the waters of the great deluge. Adam was made lord of creation (1:28); into the hand of Noah God delivered all things (9:2). Adam was "blessed" by God and told to "be fruitful, and multiply, and replenish the earth" (1:28); in like manner Noah was blessed and told to "be fruitful, and multiply, and replenish the earth" (9:1). Adam was placed by God in a garden to "dress and keep it" (2:15); Noah "began to be an husbandman, and he planted a vineyard" (9:20). It was in the garden that Adam transgressed and fell; the product of the vineyard was the occasion of Noah's sad fall. The sin of Adam resulted in the exposure of his nakedness (3:7); likewise Noah "was uncovered within his tent" (9:21). Adam's sin brought a terrible curse on his posterity (Rom. 5:12); so did Noah's (9:24-25). Immediately after Adam's fall a remarkable prophecy was given, containing in outline the history of redemption (3:15); immediately after Noah's fall a remarkable prophecy was uttered, containing in outline the history of the great divisions of our race.

The Carnal World System

Genesis 10-11 takes up the history of the postdiluvian earth. These chapters show us something of the ways of men in this new world—revolting against God, seeking to glorify and deify themselves. They make known the carnal principles by which the world system is now regulated. Since Genesis 10:8-12 and 11:1-9 interrupt the course of the genealogies given there, they should be regarded as an important parenthesis, the former one explaining the latter. The first is concerned with Nimrod: 1. He was a descendant of Ham, through Cush (10:8), therefore of that branch of Noah's family on which the curse rested. 2. His name means "the rebel." 3. "He began to be a mighty one in the earth," which implies that he struggled for preeminence and by force of will obtained it. 4. "In the earth" intimates conquest and subjugation, becoming a leader of and ruler over men. 5. He was a mighty hunter (10:9): three times in Genesis 10 and again in I Chronicles 1:10 is the term "mighty" used of him, the Hebrew word also being rendered "chief" and "chieftain." 6. He was a "mighty hunter before the LORD"; comparing that with "the earth also was corrupt before God" (6:11) we get the impression that this proud rebel pursued his ambitions and impious designs in brazen defiance of the Almighty. 7. Nimrod was a king and had his headquarters in Babylon (10:10).

From the opening verses of Genesis 11 it is clear that Nimrod had an inordinate desire for fame, that he lusted after supreme dominion or the establishment of a world empire (cf. 10:10-11), and that he headed a great confederacy in open rebellion against Jehovah. Babel means "the gate of God," but afterward, because of the divine judgment inflicted on it, it came to mean "confusion." By putting together the different details supplied by the Spirit, there can be little doubt that Nimrod not only organized an imperial government, over which he presided as king, but also instituted a new and idolatrous worship. Though he is not mentioned by name in Genesis 11, it is evident from the foregoing chapter that he was the leader of the movement here described. The topographical reference in 11:2 is just as morally significant as is "going *down* into Egypt" and "*up* to Jerusalem." "They journeyed *from the east*" connotes that they turned their backs on the sunrise. God had commanded Noah to "multiply, and replenish the earth." But we read: "And they said, Go to, let us build us a city and a tower, whose top may reach unto heaven; and let us make us a name, *lest* we be scattered abroad upon the face of the whole earth" (11:4). That was directly contrary to God, and He at once intervened, brought Nimrod's scheme to naught, and scattered them "abroad upon the face of all the earth" (v. 9).

At the Tower of Babel another crisis had arrived in the history of the human race. There mankind was again guilty of apostasy and outright defiance of the Most High. The divine confounding of man's speech was the origin of the different nations of the earth, and after the overthrow of Nimrod's effort we get the formation of the "world" as it has existed ever since. This is confirmed in Romans 1, where the apostle supplies proof of the guilt of the Gentiles. In verse 19 we read of "that which *may be* known of God"— through the display of His perfections in the works of creation. Verses 21-23 go further and state, "When they *knew God* [i.e., in the days of Nimrod], they glorified him not as God, neither were thankful; but became vain in their imaginations, and their foolish heart was darkened. Professing themselves to be wise, they became fools [in connection with the Tower of Babel], and changed the glory of the uncorruptible God into an image made like to corruptible man." It was then that idolatry commenced. In what follows we are told three times that "God gave them up" (vv. 24, 26, 28). It was then that He abandoned them and "suffered all nations to walk in their own ways" (Acts 14:16).

The next thing after the great crisis in human affairs recorded in Genesis 11 was the divine call of Abraham, the father of the nation of Israel. But before turning to that, let us consider some of the effects of the nations going their own evil ways. The first of the Gentile nations about which Scripture has much to say are the Egyptians, who made their depravity clear by mistreating the Hebrews and defying the Lord. The seven nations which inhabited Canaan when Israel entered that land in the days of Joshua were devoted to the most horrible abominations and wickedness (Lev. 18:6-25; Deut. 9:5). The characters of the renowned empires of Babylon, Medo-Persia, Greece and Rome are intimated in Daniel 7:4-7, where they are likened to wild beasts. Outside the narrow bounds of Judaism the whole world was heathen, completely dominated by the devil. Having turned their backs on Him who is light, they were in total spiritual darkness, given up to ignorance, superstition and vice. One and all sought their happiness in the pleasures of earth, according to their various desires and appetites. But whatever "happiness" was enjoyed by them was sensual and fleeting, utterly unworthy of creatures made for eternity. They were quite insensible of their real misery, poverty and blindness.

It is true that the arts were developed to a high degree by some of the ancients and that there were famous sages among them, but the masses of the people were grossly materialistic, and their teachers propagated the wildest absurdities. They all denied a divine creation of the world, holding for the most part that matter is eternal. Some believed there was no survival of the soul after death, others in the theory of transmigration—the souls of men passing into the bodies of animals. In short, "the world by wisdom knew not God" (I Cor. 1:21). Where there is ignorance of Him there is always ignorance of ourselves. They did not realize they were victims of the great deceiver of souls, who blinds the minds of those who do not believe. No ancient nation was as highly educated as the Greeks, yet the private lives of her most eminent men were stained by the most revolting crimes. Those who had the ear of the public and talked most about setting men free from their passions, although held in the highest esteem as the teachers of truth and virtue, were themselves the abject slaves of sin and Satan. Morally speaking, society was rotten to the core.

The whole world festered in its corruption. Sensual indulgence was everywhere carried to its highest pitch, gluttony was an art, fornication was indulged in without restraint. The Prophet Hosea shows (chap. 4) that where there is no knowledge of God there is no mercy or truth. Instead, selfishness, oppression and persecution bear down on all. There is scarcely a page in the annals of the world which does not furnish tragic illustrations of the greed and grind, the injustice and chicanery, the avarice and consciencelessness, the intemperance and immorality to which fallen human nature is so horribly prone. What a sad spectacle history presents of our race. It abundantly bears witness to the divine declaration, "Surely men of low degree are vanity, and men of high degree are a lie: to be laid in the balance, they are altogether lighter than vanity" (Ps. 62:9). Modern infidels may paint a beautiful picture of the virtues of many of the heathen, and out of their hatred of Christianity exalt them to the highest seats of intellectual attainment and moral excellence, but the clear testimony of history definitely refutes them.

The earth has been deluged with blood by its murders and fightings. "The dark places of the earth are full of the habitations of cruelty" (Ps. 74:20). In ancient Greece, parents were at liberty to abandon their children to perish from cold and hunger, or to be eaten up by wild beasts; and though such exposures were frequently practiced they passed without punishment or censure. Wars were prosecuted with the utmost ferocity, and if any of the vanquished escaped death, lifelong slavery of the most abject kind was the only prospect before them. At Rome, which was then the metropolis of the world, the court of Caesar was steeped in licentiousness. To provide amusement for his senators, six hundred gladiators fought hand-to-hand mortal combat in the public theater. Not to be outdone, Pompey turned five hundred lions into the arena to battle an equal number of his braves, and "delicate ladies" sat applauding and gloating over the flow of blood. Aged and infirm citizens were banished to an island in the Tiber. Almost two-thirds of the "civilized" world were slaves, their masters having absolute power over them. Human sacrifices were frequently offered on the temple altars. Destruction and misery were commonplace, and the way of peace was unknown (Rom. 3:16-17).

The Deists of the seventeenth and eighteenth centuries made much of the charming innocence of the tribes which lived in the "sylvan bowers of primeval forests," untainted by the vices of civilization, unpolluted by modern commerce. But when the woods of America were entered by the white man, he found the Indians as ferocious and cruel as wild beasts. As someone expressed it, "The red tomahawk might have been emblazoned as the red man's coat of arms, and his eyes of glaring revenge regarded as the index of his character." When travelers penetrated into the interior of Africa, where they hoped to find human nature in its primitive excellence, they found instead primitive devilry. Take the milder races. To look into the gentle face of the Hindu one would suppose him incapable of brutality and bestiality, but let the facts of the Sepoy Rebellion of the nineteenth century be read, and one will find the mercilessness of the tiger. Look at the placid Chinaman. The Boxer outbreak and atrocities at the beginning of this century produced similar inhumanities. If a new tribe were discovered, we should *know* it too must be depraved and vicious. Simply to be informed that they were *men* would oblige us to conclude that they were "hateful, and hating one another."

Depravity of Jews as Well as Gentiles

The depravity of the Gentiles may not excite surprise, since their religions, instead of restraining vice, furnished a stimulus to the most horrible practices, in the examples of their profligate gods. But were the Jews any better? In considering their case we shall turn from the general to the particular, examining that people designed by God to be a *specimen* of human nature. The divine Being singled out and separated them from all other nations. He showered His benefits upon them, strengthened them with many encouragements, wrought miracles on their behalf, awed them with the most fearful threatenings, chastised them severely and frequently, and inspired His servants to give us an accurate account of their response. And what a wretched response it was. Except for the conduct of a few individuals among them, which, being the effect of divine grace, proves nothing against what we are here demonstrating—in fact only serves to intensify the sad contrast—the entire history of the Jews was nothing but a series of rebellions and continued departures from the living God. No other nation was so highly favored and richly blessed by heaven, and none so wretchedly repaid the divine goodness.

Provided with a law which was drawn up and proclaimed by God Himself, which was enforced by the most winsome and also the most awesome sanctions, the whole nation within a few days of its reception was engaged in obscenely worshiping a golden calf. To them were entrusted the divine oracles and ordinances, which were neither appreciated nor heeded. In the wilderness they greatly provoked the holy One by their murmuring, their lusting after the plenty of Egypt when supplied with "angels' food" (Ps. 78:25), their prolonged idolatry (Acts 7:42-43) and their unbelief (Heb. 3:18). After they received the land of Canaan for an inheritance, they soon evinced their base ingratitude, so that the Lord had to say to His sorrowing servant, "They have not rejected thee, but they have rejected me, that I should not reign over them" (I Sam. 8:7). So averse were they to God and His ways that they hated, persecuted and killed the messengers which He sent to turn them from their wickedness. "They kept not the covenant of God, and *refused* to walk in his law" (Ps. 78:10). They declared, "I have loved strangers, and after them will I go" (Jer. 2:25).

After furnishing proof in Romans 1 of the total depravity of the Gentile world, the apostle turned to the case of privileged Israel, and from their own Scriptures demonstrated that they were equally polluted, equally beneath the curse of God. He asked, "What then? Are we better than they?" Then he answered, "No, in no wise: for we have before proved both Jews and Gentiles, that they are all under sin" (Rom. 3:9). So too in I Corinthians 1, where the utmost scorn is expressed for that which is highly esteemed among men, the Jew is placed on the same level as the Gentile. There we are shown how God views the arrogant pretensions of the worldly wise. When the apostle asks, "Where is the wise?" he is referring to the Grecian philosophers, who dignified themselves with that title. His question indicates contempt of their proud claims. "With all your boasted knowledge, have you discovered the true and living God?" They are challenged to come forth with their schemes of religion. "After all you have taught others, what have you accomplished? Have you found out the way to eternal felicity? Have you learned how guilty sinners may have access to a holy God?" God declares that, far from being wise men, such sages as Pythagoras and Plato were fools.

Then Paul asks, "Where is the scribe?" (I Cor. 1:20). The scribe was the wise man, the esteemed teacher, among the Jews. He was at just as great a distance from and just as ignorant of the true God. Far from possessing any true knowledge of Him, he was a bitter enemy of that knowledge when it was proclaimed by His incarnate Son. Though the scribes enjoyed the inestimable advantage of possessing the Old Testament Scriptures, they were in general as ignorant of God's salvation as were the heathen philosophers. Instead of pointing to the death of the promised Messiah as the grand sacrifice for sin, they taught their disciples to depend on the laws and ceremonies of Moses, and on traditions of human invention. When Christ was manifested before them, far from being the first to receive Him, they were His most bitter persecutors. His appearing before them in the form of a servant did not suit their proud hearts. Though He was "full of grace and truth," they saw no beauty in Him that they should desire Him. Though He announced glad tidings, they refused to listen to them. When Christ performed miracles of mercy before them, they would not believe in Him. Though He sought only their good, they returned Him nothing but evil. Their reaction was "We will not have this man to reign over us" (Luke 19:14).

Contempt for Christ

The general neglect and contempt which the Lord Jesus experienced among the people afford a very humbling view of what our fallen human nature is. But the awful depths of human depravity were most plainly evidenced by the scribes and Pharisees, the priests and elders. Though well acquainted with the prophets, and though professing to wait for the Messiah, with desperate and merciless malignity they sought His destruction. The whole course of their conduct shows that they acted *against* their convictions that Jesus Christ was the Messiah. Certainly they had full knowledge of His innocence of all which they charged against Him. This is evident from the plain intimation of the One who read their hearts, and who knew that they were saying within themselves, "This is the heir; come, let us kill him" (Matt. 21:38). They were as untiring as they were unscrupulous in their malice. They, or their agents, dogged Christ from place to place, hoping that in His more unguarded fellowship with His disciples they might more readily trap Him, or find something in His words or actions which they could distort into a ground of accusation. They seized every opportunity to poison the minds of the public against Him and, not content with ordinary aspersions of His character, inferred that He was ministering under the immediate inspiration of Satan.

What was the source of such wicked treatment of the Son of God? What but their corrupt hearts? "They hated me without a cause" (John 15:25), declared the Lord of glory. There was nothing whatever in either His character or conduct which merited their vile contempt and enmity. They loved the darkness and therefore hated the light. They were infatuated by their evil lusts and delighted to gratify them. So too their deluded followers gave a ready ear to false prophets who said, "Peace, peace" to them, flattered them, and encouraged them in their carnality. Consequently they could not tolerate that which was disagreeable to their depraved tastes and condemned their sinful ways. Therefore "the people" as well as their chief priests and rulers cried out, "Away with this man, and release unto us Barabbas" (Luke 23:18). After they had hounded Him to a criminal's death, their ill will pursued Him to the grave, for they came to Pilate and demanded that he seal His sepulcher. When their effort was proved to be in vain, the high Sanhedrin of Israel bribed the soldiers who had attempted to guard the tomb, and with premeditated deliberation put a lie in their mouths (Matt. 28:11-15).

Nor did the enmity of Christ's enemies abate after He left this scene and returned to heaven. When His ambassadors went forth to preach His gospel, they were arrested and forbidden to teach in the name of Jesus, and then released under threat of punishment (Acts 4). Upon the apostles' refusal to comply, they were beaten (Acts 5:40). Stephen was stoned to death. James was beheaded, and many others were scattered abroad to escape persecution. Except where God was pleased to lay His restraining hand on those in whom He worked a miracle of grace, Jews and Gentiles alike despised the gospel and wilfully opposed its progress. In some cases their hatred of the truth was less openly displayed than in others, yet it was nonetheless real. It has been the same ever since. However earnestly and winsomely the gospel is preached, most of those who hear it reject it. For the most part they are like those of our Lord's day who "made light of it, and went their ways, one to his farm, another to his merchandise" (Matt. 22:5). The great majority are too unconcerned to seek after even a doctrinal knowledge of the truth. Many regard this carelessness of the unsaved as mere indifference, but actually it is something much worse than that, namely, dislike for the things of God, direct antagonism to Him.

The hostility of the unsaved is made evident by the way they treat the people of God. The closer the believer walks with his Lord, the more he will grate on and be mistreated by those who are strangers to Him. But "blessed are they which are persecuted for righteousness' sake" (Matt. 5:10). As one pointed out, "It is a strong proof of human depravity that man's curses and Christ's blessings should meet on the same persons. Who would have thought a man could be persecuted and reviled, and have all manner of evil said of him for righteousness' sake?" But do the ungodly really hate justice and integrity, and love those who defraud and wrong them? No, they do not dislike righteousness as it respects their own interests, only that species of it which own the rights of God. If the saints would be content with doing justly and loving mercy, and would give up walking humbly with God, they might go through the world not only in peace but with the approbation of the unregenerate; but "all that will live godly in Christ Jesus shall suffer persecution" (II Tim. 3:12) because such a life reproves the ungodliness of the wicked. If compassion moves the Christian to warn his sinful neighbors of their danger, he is likely to be insulted for his pains. His best actions will be ascribed to the worst motives. Yet, far from being cast down by such treatment, the disciple should rejoice that he is counted worthy to suffer a little for his Master's sake.

Disowning of God's Law

The depravity of men appears in their disowning of the divine law set over them. It is the right of God to be the acknowledged Ruler of His creatures, yet they are never so pleased as when they invade His prerogative, break His laws, and contradict His revealed will. How little we realize that it is one and the same to repudiate His scepter and to repudiate His being. When we disown His authority we disown His Godhead. There is in natural man an averseness to having any acquaintance with the rule under which their Maker has placed them: "Therefore they say unto God, Depart from us; for we desire not the knowledge of thy ways. What is the Almighty, that we should serve him? And what profit should we have, if we pray unto him?" (Job 21:14-15). That aversion is seen in their unwillingness to use the means for obtaining a knowledge of His will. However eager they are in their quest for all other kinds of knowledge, however diligent in studying the formation, constitution and ways of creatures, they refuse to acquaint themselves with their Creator. When made aware of some part of His will, they attempt to shake it off, as they do not "like to retain God in their knowledge" (Rom. 1:28). If they do not succeed, they avoid considering such knowledge, and do their utmost to dismiss it from their minds.

A class of the unregenerate who are exceptions to the general rule are those who attend church, make a profession of religion, and become "Bible students." Motivated by pride of intellect and reputation, they are ashamed to be regarded as spiritual ignoramuses, and want to have a good standing in religious circles. Thus they secure a cloak of respectability, and often the esteem of God's own people. Nevertheless, they are devoid of God's grace. They "hold the truth in unrighteousness" (Rom. 1:18); *they* hold it, but *it* does not grip, influence and transform them. If they ponder the truth, it is not with delight; if they take pleasure in it, it is only because their store of information is increased and they are better equipped to hold their own in a discussion. Their design is to inform their understanding, not to quicken their affection for God. There is far more hypocrisy than sincerity within the pale of the church. Judas was a follower of Christ because he "had the bag, and bare what was put therein" (John 12:6), not out of love for the Saviour. Some have the faith or truth of God "with respect of persons" (James 2:1);

they do not receive it from the fountain, but from the channel. Often the truth delivered by another is rejected; but that same truth, coming from the mouth of their idol, is regarded as an oracle. They make man and not God their rule, for though they acknowledge the truth, they do not receive it for love of the truth, but rather because they admire the instrument.

The depravity of human nature is seen in the sad and general *reversion to darkness* of a people after being favored with the light. Even where God has been made known and His truth proclaimed, if He leaves men to the working of their evil hearts, they quickly fall back into a state of ignorance. Noah and his sons lived for centuries after the flood to acquaint the world with the perfections of God, yet all knowledge of Him soon disappeared. Abram and his father were idolaters (Joshua 24:2). Even after a man has experienced the new birth and become the subject of immediate divine influence, how much ignorance and error, imperfection and impropriety, still remains—just because he is not completely subject to the Lord. The backslidings and partial apostasies of genuine Christians are an awful demonstration of the corruption of human nature. Our proneness to fall into error after divine enlightenment is solemnly illustrated by the Galatians. They had been instructed by Paul, and through the power of the Spirit had believed in the Saviour he proclaimed. They were so happy that they received him "as an angel of God" (4:14). Yet in the course of a few years many of those converts gave such credence to false teachers, and so far renounced biblical principles, that the apostle had to say of them, "I stand in doubt of you" (4:20). Look at Europe, Asia, Africa, after the preaching of the apostles and those who immediately followed them. Though the light of Christianity illuminated most sections of the Roman Empire, it was speedily quenched, and gave place to the darkness. The greater part of the world fell victim to Rome and Islam.

Nothing more forcibly exhibits the sinfulness of man than his *proneness to idolatry*. No other sin is so strongly denounced or so severely punished by God. Idols are simply the work of men's hands, and therefore inferior to them. How irrational then to *worship* them! Can human madness go further than for men to imagine they can manufacture gods? Those who have sunk so low as to confide in a block of wood or stone have reached the extreme of idiocy. As Psalm 115 points out, "They have mouths, but they speak not: eyes have they, but they see not. . . . They that make them are like unto them"—as stupid, as incapable of hearing and seeing those things which pertain to their salvation.

The corruption of human nature discovers itself *in little children*. As the adage puts it, "That which is bred in the bone comes out in the flesh." And at what an early date it does! If there were any innate goodness in man, it would surely show itself during the days of his infancy, before virtuous principles were corrupted, before evil habits were formed by his contact with the world. But do we find infants inclined to all that is pure and excellent, and disinclined to whatever is wrong? Are they meek, tractable, yielding readily to authority? Are they unselfish, magnanimous when another child seizes their toy? Far from it. The unvarying result of growth in human beings is that as soon as they are old enough to exhibit any moral qualities in human action they display *evil ones*. Long before they are old enough to understand their own wicked tempers, they manifest self-will, greediness, deceitfulness, anger, spite and revenge. They cry and pout for what is not good for them, and are indignant with their elders on being refused, often attempting to strike them. Those born and brought up in the midst of honesty are guilty of petty pilfering before they ever witness an act of theft. These blemishes are not to be ascribed to ignorance, but to their variance with the divine law to which man's nature was originally conformed, to that horrible change which sin has made in the human constitution. Human nature is seen to be tainted from the beginning of its existence.

The universal prevalence of *disease and death* witnesses unmistakably to the fall of man. All the pains and disorders of our bodies, by which our health is impaired and our way through this world made difficult, are the consequences of our apostasy from God. The Saviour plainly intimated that sickness is an effect of sin when He healed the man with the palsy, saying, "Thy sins be forgiven thee" (Matt. 9:2). The psalmist also linked together God's pardoning the iniquities of His people and healing their diseases (103:3). There is one event that happens to all. Yes, but why should it? Why should there be wasting away and then dissolution? Philosophy offers no explanation. Science can furnish no satisfactory answer, for to say that disease results from the decay of nature only pushes the inquiry farther back. Disease and death are *abnormalities*. Man is created by the eternal God, endowed with a never dying soul. Why then should he not continue to live here forever? Because of the fall; death is the wages of sin.

Man's ingratitude to his gracious Benefactor is still another evidence of his sad condition. The Israelites were a woeful sample of all mankind in this respect. Though the Lord delivered them from the house of bondage, miraculously conducted them through the Red Sea, led them safely across the wilderness, they did not appreciate it. Though He screened them with a cloud from the heat of the sun, gave them light by night in a pillar of fire, fed them with bread from heaven, caused streams to flow in the sandy desert, and brought them into the possession of a land flowing with milk and honey, they were continually murmuring and complaining. Men do not acknowledge or even recognize the hand that so bountifully ministers to their needs. No one is satisfied with the place and portion Providence has assigned him; he is forever coveting what he does not have. He is a creature given to changes; he is afflicted with a malady which Solomon termed "the wandering of the desire" (Eccles. 6:9).

Someone has said that every dog that snaps at us, every horse that lifts up its heel against us, proves that we are fallen creatures. The brute creation had no enmity toward man before the fall. Creation gave willing respect to Adam (Gen. 2:19). Eve no more dreaded the serpent than we would a fly. But when man shrugged off allegiance to God, the beasts by divine permission shook off allegiance to man. What a proof of man's degradation that the sluggard is exhorted to "go to the ant" and learn from a creature so much lower in the scale of being! Consider the *necessity* of human laws, fenced with punishments and terrors to restrain men's lusts. Yet in spite of the vast and costly apparatus of police forces, law courts and prisons, how little success follows their efforts to repress human wickedness! Neither education, legislation nor religion is sufficient.

Finally, take the unvarying *experience of the saints*. It is part of the Spirit's work to open blind eyes, to show souls their wretchedness, and to make them aware of their dire need of Christ. And when He thus brings a sinner to realize his ruined condition by an experiential knowledge of sin, that sinner's comeliness is at once turned to corruption, and he cries, "Behold, I am vile." Though grace has entered his heart, his native depravity has not been expelled. Though sin no longer has dominion over him, it rages and often prevails against him. There is ceaseless warfare within between the flesh and the spirit. There is no need for us to enlarge on this, for every Christian, because of the plague of his heart, groans within himself, "O wretched man that I am!" He is wretched because he does not live as he earnestly longs to do, and because he so often does the very things he hates, grieving daily over evil imaginations, wandering thoughts, unbelief, pride, coldness, pretense.

Chapter 12

COROLLARIES

IN THE INTRODUCTORY SECTION we intimated that we would endeavor to show that our present subject is of immense doctrinal importance and of great practical value. In view of all that has been advanced in our subsequent discussion, that fact should be clear. The Scriptures supply us with a divinely accurate diagnosis of man's present condition. They show us, as nothing else can or does, why the entire course of human history has been what it is, and explain why all the remedial methods and measures of man to effect any radical improvement in society are thorough failures. They account for the fact that man in the twentieth century is essentially the same as in the first, that like moral features pertain to white and black, yellow and red faces, that no change of environment or living conditions can transform a sinner into a saint. Removing thistles and nettles from a stony ground and transplanting them into the most fertile soil and lovely surroundings will not cause them to bear fragrant flowers or edible fruit. Human nature is fundamentally the same whether people live in mansions or hovels. Man does what he does because of what he is.

Value of This Doctrine

The importance of this doctrine of man's total depravity also appears in the close bearing it has on other aspects of the truth, and the light it tends to cast on them. Reject what is revealed in Genesis 3 and the remainder of the Bible becomes entirely meaningless; but accept what is recorded there and everything else becomes intelligible and is seen in its proper perspective. The whole scheme of redemption manifestly proceeds in view of our first parents' ruination of their race. Our defection in Adam and our recovery by Christ plainly stand or fall together. Because man is a sinner he needs a Saviour; and being so great a sinner, none but a divine Saviour is sufficient for him. Since sin has corrupted the whole of man's constitution, vitiating and debasing all his faculties, he is utterly incapable of doing anything to raise himself out of the horrible pit into which the fall has plunged him. Sooner will the Ethiopian change his skin or the leopard his spots than those who are at enmity with God evoke any love to Him or do that which is pleasing in His sight. If such a creature is to be made fit to dwell forever with the thrice holy One, obviously a miracle of grace must be worked in him.

Equally real and great is the practical value of this doctrine. Nothing else is so well calculated to humble the proud heart of man and bring him into the dust before his Maker crying, "Behold, I am vile." Nothing else is so well calculated to demonstrate the utter futility of the sinner's attempting to appease God and obtain His approbation by any efforts of his own, or to gain acceptance with Him by his own performance. A murderer standing in the dock might as well seek to win the judge's favor by his smiles and flattery. Nothing is so well calculated to convince us that, since our hearts are rotten to the core, our very righteousnesses are as filthy rags. And nothing else will so deeply impress on the heart of a believer his entire dependence on the Lord as a keen sense of what he is by nature. He must realize that God must work in him to will and to do of His good pleasure if he is ever to perform His bidding, that nothing but daily supplies of grace can preserve him in the narrow way. Let us particularize what has just been summarized.

Since the entire being of the natural man is under the dominion of sin, it follows that *his will is in bondage also*. Anyone who denies that fact evinces that he does not understand or believe in the total depravity of man, for in effect he is asserting that one of the most important of his faculties has not been debased by the fall. But as the whole of man's body is corrupt, so his entire soul is inclined to evil only, and so long as he remains in the sinful state his will is in captivity to sin. The power of the will can extend itself only to things within its own province and cannot act above it. All actions and powers of action are limited by the nature and capacity of their agent. As creatures below man cannot act rationally, neither can those who lack a holy principle act spiritually. Before divine grace works on and in the heart, man's will is enslaved by sin. He is "in the bond of iniquity" (Acts 8:23), the servant of those lusts and pleasures which he chooses and delights in. Christ must make us free (John 8:36) before there is or can be any deliverance from our moral captivity.

The Lord Jesus declared, "Whosoever committeth sin is the servant [bondman] of sin" (John 8:34). Sin is his master, ordering all his actions. Nevertheless, he voluntarily assents to it. That is why it is termed "the will of *the flesh*" (John 1:13), for it is defiled. It is "without strength" (Rom. 5:6) to do that which is good. Since the tree itself is corrupt, no good fruit can be borne by it. Romans 8:7 not only declares that the carnal mind is enmity against God and that it is not subject to the law of God, but adds "neither indeed can be," which would not be the case were the will of fallen man free, or had it power to do good. Even when the understanding is convinced and sees the truth, the will obstinately opposes and rejects it. Rightly did G. H. Bishop of the Dutch Reformed Church say:

> Man can no more turn to God than the dead can sit up in their coffins. He can no more originate a right desire than he can create a universe. God the Holy Spirit alone, by sovereign, special interference, calls dead sinners to life and creates within them "the desires of their hearts"—the first faint fluttering of a breath toward holiness.

Some may reply, "But my own experience refutes what you have said. I am clearly conscious of the fact that my will accepted the offer of the gospel, that I freely came to Christ as a lost sinner and accepted Him as my own Saviour." We fully admit that. But if they go a little *farther back,* they will find that their experience confirms what we have said. Previous to conversion, their will was opposed to God, and they refused to come to Christ. Though the time arrived when that was reversed, *who* produced or caused that change —they or God? In every conscious act he performs, man necessarily wills. In repenting he wills, in believing he wills, in turning from his evil ways to God in Christ he wills. But does the sinner make himself willing, or does God? The question at issue is Does salvation *begin* by self-movement or divine? Scripture is plain on the matter. God alters the bent or bias of the will by communicating a principle of grace and holiness. A supreme will overcomes man's. He who said, "Let there be light: and there was light" (Gen. 1:3) says, "Let rebellion and opposition cease," and they do so. "So then it is not of him that willeth [originally], nor of him that runneth, but of God that sheweth mercy" (Rom. 9:16). As He loved us before we loved Him, so His will precedes ours in conversion.

Moral Insensibility of Natural Man

Because the natural man is dead in trespasses and sins, *he is quite insensible to his wretched plight.* One of the most terrible elements in the fatal malady which has struck him is that he is so morally paralyzed that he is quite unaware of his desperate state. At this juncture it is necessary to point out that there is a difference between being totally ignorant of our condition and being insensible of it. The unregenerate may acquire a theoretical knowledge of man's total depravity, yet they are without any feeling of the same in themselves. They may hold the theological belief that sin is the transgression of the divine law, but they have no inward horror and anguish over their vileness. That deadly insensibility is in all sinners at all times. Their natural emotions may be stirred as they listen to a portrayal of the sufferings of Christ on the cross—just as they shed tears over some particularly touching incident told in the newspapers or enacted on the stage—but they do not weep over their awful enmity against God, nor mourn because of their contrariety to His holiness. They are quite incapable of doing so, for they have stony hearts as far as God is concerned (Ezek. 36:26) and do not realize that His wrath rests on them.

This explains why sinners generally seem secure and happy. It has always appeared strange as well as distressing to the saints to see the ungodly so unconcerned and lighthearted, though under sentence of death. Job did not understand how the wicked could "take the timbrel and harp, and rejoice at the sound of the organ," spending "their days in wealth, and in a moment go down to the grave" (21:12-13). The psalmist was perplexed when he "saw the prosperity of the wicked" and observed that they were "not in [soul] trouble as other men" (73:3-5). Amos was astonished as he saw the sinners in Zion "put far away the evil day," lie "upon beds of ivory, . . . eat the lambs out of the flock, . . . invent to themselves instruments of musick, . . . drink wine in bowls, and anoint themselves with the chief ointments" (6:1-6), utterly unconcerned about their souls. Though natural men differ from one another in so many respects, in this they are very much alike: they generally live as though there is no God to whom they must render an account, and who will pass sentence of eternal damnation upon them. Such ignorance in rational and immortal creatures can be explained only on the ground of their insensibility. They have eyes, but see not; ears, but hear not; hearts, but perceive not. It is not at all strange that they, neither discerning nor feeling their danger, should not fear it.

Those who deny the moral insensibility of sinners are proclaiming their own insensibility, for they repudiate not only what Scripture maintains but what universal observation confirms. Nothing but ignorance can account for the conduct of the great majority of mankind, who are saying peace and safety while exposed to instant and eternal destruction. They are completely unconcerned that their hearts are desperately wicked, their understandings darkened, and their wills in bondage to evil. They are unaware of Satan's malignant dominion over them, and do not know that he is perpetually causing them to sin. The devil employs a multitude of devices to ensnare them. He knows how to take full advantage of their dullness. Yet though they are led captive by him from day to day they do not perceive his wiles and influence. Even though they recognize the objects which he employs to seduce them, they do not realize his seducing power. They are ignorant that they are continually walking in the paths of the destroyer, who is leading them blindfold to hell. They do not know—or if they do, they do not care—that the friendship of the world is enmity with God, and that to follow a multitude to do evil is the direct road to endless woe. Hence they are not aware of their stumblings. They are united in their disaffection toward God and in their love of sin. They join hand in hand; all lead, and are led. Their very numbers inspire them with boldness and resolution, and encourage them to walk together in the path of ruin.

In view of all that has been advanced, it is crystal clear that *fallen man is in a lost and perishing condition.* He is obnoxious to God, alienated from His life (Eph. 4:18), cast out of His favor (Gen. 3:24), cut off from communion with Him (Eph. 2:12). He is given up to the devil, to be led captive by him as he pleases. He is dead in trespasses and sins, and that means (among other things) that he is utterly powerless where spiritual things are concerned, quite unable to do anything in regard to them. Yet he is efficient with respect to that which is carnal and devilish. Entirely averse to all that is good and holy, his will is desperately set against the truth, but prone to—and in love with—whatever is sinful and evil. He is lying in a horrible pit of corruption, unable to break the cords of sin which hold him fast. He is so infatuated with his iniquities as to regard them as his benefactors (see Hosea 2:5, 12). His heart is so calloused that the mercies of God do not melt him, nor do His threatenings and judgments awe him. Instead of the divine goodness leading him to repentance, it leads him to deeper impenitence, unbelief and presumption; for since he sees the sun shining and the rain falling on the evil and on the good, and God allowing all things to come alike to the one as to the other, he concludes that He will treat them all alike in the next world.

Man's plight is very much worse than is generally recognized, even in those sections of Christendom which are still regarded as being orthodox. Imagine an island affected by some calamity, say, a raging fire, the only escape being a bridge to the mainland. The bridge offers the possibility of escape, of salvation for the entire island population. The realization of the possibility is dependent on the choice of each individual. The bridge does not offer automatic salvation, but simply the opportunity to attain it. If an individual thinks that the fire will die down, and he remains on the island, he forfeits the possibility of escape by the bridge. It is true that he can be carried by force over the bridge to safety.

But, someone says, God does not accomplish the soul's salvation by compulsion. Unless the individual wills to accept God's way of escape, he perishes. He himself must decide to cross the bridge.

But can he do so? Sin has such a stupefying effect on the whole soul of the natural man that he is oblivious to his peril and insensible of his dire need. It loses sight of the fact that the sinner is not only in gross darkness, but has no desire to be enlightened; he is stricken with a deadly malady, and is unwilling to be healed. He is highly displeased if someone tells him of his awful danger, for he resents anything which disturbs his false peace and comfort. Sinners in Bible times could not bear to hear the plain preaching of either God's prophets or His incarnate Son. They stoned the former and crucified the Latter. So it is now; they refuse to give a hearing to one who declares them to be *totally* depraved. The sinner, though mentally convinced of the urgency of his situation, has no eyes to see the "bridge." And if another offered to lead him it would be of no avail, for he lacks strength. True, God does not effect the soul's salvation by compulsion, but He does so by a miracle of grace: making His people willing in the day of His power (Ps. 110:3), imparting life, light and strength to them.

Since man is totally depraved, how great is his need of salvation! The guilt of Adam's transgression is charged to his account, the polluted nature of our first parents transmitted to him. He is shaped in iniquity, conceived in sin, and enters this world a child of wrath, estranged from God from his mother's womb (Ps. 58:3). Born with a heart that is deceitful above all things and desperately wicked, from earliest childhood he pursues a course of self-will and self-pleasing, treasuring up wrath against himself. His iniquities are more in number than the hairs of his head (Ps. 40:12), and his "trespass [guiltiness] is grown up unto the heavens" (Ezra 9:6). He lies beneath the death sentence of the law. That curse cannot be removed until full satisfaction has been rendered to it, and the guilty culprit is utterly powerless to render such satisfaction. Nor can any of his friends—not even his nearest and dearest relatives—discharge his incalculable debt. "None of them can by any means redeem his brother, nor give to God a ransom for him: for the redemption of their soul is precious" (Ps. 49:7-8), or "costly," as the same word is rendered in I Kings 7:9-10. The sinner is a moral bankrupt, with no good thing to his credit, without a penny to discharge his liabilities.

Such a creature is utterly unfit for heaven; even if he were permitted to enter it, he would at once desire to leave, for he would be entirely out of his element, having nothing whatever in common with the ineffable holiness of its atmosphere and society. He is already ripe for hell, fit only for the company of the damned. Thus the natural man is in a perishing condition. Not only does he need delivering from the curse of the law, the wrath of God, and the captivity of the devil; he also needs *saving from himself*: from the guilt, dominion and pollution of his sins. He needs to be saved from his hard, impenitent and unbelieving heart, from his love of the world, from his self-righteousness. Divine justice requires not only that he be clear of any accusation the law can bring against him, but that he possess a perfect obedience which constitutes him righteous before the law, thus giving him title to the reward of endless joy. But his righteousnesses are as filthy rags, and the wearer of them a moral leper. His plight is desperate beyond the power of words to express. There is only a step between him and death, and beyond that lies "the blackness of darkness for ever" (Jude 13).

It is equally evident that the lost sinner is *incapable of contributing toward his salvation*. Can a foul and filthy fountain send forth clear, pure water? Neither can a polluted creature offer anything which is acceptable to the holy One. "The sacrifice of the wicked is an abomination to the Lord" (Prov. 15:8), as He made clear at the beginning, when He did not accept Cain and his offering. Instead of a pleasing service to God, it is an insulting provocation, for it lacks that principle without which it is impossible to please Him. The supplications of the unregenerate are rejected by God. "And when ye spread forth your hands, I will hide mine eyes from you: yea, when ye make many prayers, I will not hear" (Isa. 1:15). Why? Because such "praying" is the howling of those in pain (Hosea 7:14) rather than the breathings of loving devotion. It is the wishings and cravings of those who want their lusts gratified (James 4:3) rather than their souls ministered to. It is the bold presumptions for things unwarranted by the divine promises, for they hope to have mercy without holiness, sins forgiven without forsaking them. Their praying consists of the perfunctory exercises of those who have a form of godliness but are strangers to its power. Likewise are their fastings rejected (Isa. 58:3-7; Zech. 7:5).

Charnock said:

> We can no more be voluntarily serviceable to God while our serpentine nature and devilish habits remain in us, than we can suppose that the Devil can be willing to glorify God while the nature he contracted by his fall works powerfully in him. Our nature and will must be changed, that our actions may regard God as our end, that we may delightfully meditate on Him, and draw the motives of our obedience from love.

The imperative necessity of that radical change in the soul—a change as great and complete as to be like a second birth—was expressed by Christ when He declared, "Ye must be born again," having prefaced the same by stating, "Except a man be born again, he cannot see the kingdom of God. . . . Except a man be born of water and of the Spirit, he cannot enter into the kingdom of God" (John 3:3, 5-7). There must be a spiritual and supernatural principle in us before we can live a spiritual and supernatural life. The new birth is indispensable, yet what can one who is dead in sin do to experience it? As Nicodemus asked, "How can a man be born when he is old?" (v. 4). "Ye must be born again" at once reveals the utter futility of all self-effort. Such a demand withers all fleshly pretensions and bars the gates of heaven against all the unregenerate. It is designed to crush pride and make man realize his helplessness.

As the sinner cannot regenerate himself, neither can he produce any sincere repentance, for "godly sorrow worketh repentance" (II Cor. 7:10), and he has not a spark of godliness. Until he is born again he can neither hate sin nor abhor himself. Nor is he capable of exercising faith. How can he confide in one to whom he is a total stranger, trust in one whom he regards as his enemy, love one with whom he is at odds? The obstacles in the way to salvation are absolutely insurmountable by any efforts of the sinner. He could as easily turn the ocean tide as deliver his soul. That solemn fact was shown by Christ when in answer to His disciples' question "Who then can be saved?" He averred, "With men this is impossible" (Matt. 19:26). What a shattering word that was to all creature sufficiency! How it should bring the sinner to despair of saving himself.

Salvation Only by God's Grace

Since man is totally depraved it necessarily follows that if ever he is to be saved it can be only *by divine grace and power*. Grace is a truth which is peculiar to divine revelation. It is a concept to which the unaided powers of the human mind can never stretch. Proof of that is found in the fact that where the Bible has not gone it is quite unknown. But grace is not only taught in God's Word; it is given great prominence there. Holy Writ declares that salvation is by grace from first to last: it issued from grace, it is received by grace, it is maintained by grace, it is perfected by grace. Divine grace is bestowed on those who have no merits, and from whom no recompense is demanded. More than that, it is given to those who are full of demerit and blame. How thoroughly grace sets aside every thought of worthiness in its object is evident from a single quotation: "Being justified *freely* by his grace" (Rom. 3:24). The Greek word is even more impressive and emphatic, and might be rendered "gratuitously," "for nothing." The same term is translated "for nought" in II Thessalonians 3:8, and "without a cause" in John 15:25. There is nothing whatever in the beneficiary to make it attractive, but rather everything to make it repulsive. "None eye pitied thee . . . to have compassion upon thee. . . . When I passed by thee and saw thee polluted in thy blood, I said unto thee . . ., Live" (Ezek. 16:5-6).

Divine grace is the sinner's only hope, for it is not searching for good men whom it may approve, but for the guilty and lost whom it may save. It comes not to those who have done their best and are quite presentable, but rather to those who have done their worst and are in rags and tatters. Grace ever draws near to the sinner with his condition fully exposed. Grace recognizes no distinctions either social or moral: the chaste virgin is on the same level as the confirmed harlot, the religious moralist with the wildest profligate. Grace is God's provision for those who are so corrupt that they cannot help their conduct, so averse to God that they cannot turn to Him, so dead that He must open their graves and bring them onto resurrection ground. Unless men are saved by grace they cannot be saved at all. It is equally true that the salvation of sinners must be by divine power. Their ignorance and insensibility are irremovable by any human means. Nothing but God's might can dispel the darkness from their minds, take away their hearts of stone or free their sin-enslaved wills. All the faculties of the natural man are opposed to the offers and operations of divine grace until divine power saves him from himself. None ever turned to God except God turned him.

By this time it should be quite apparent that *the sinner lies entirely at God's disposal.* If He sees fit to leave him in his sins, he is undone forever; yet God has a perfect right to do so. Had He precipitated the whole race to hell, as He did the fallen angels the day they sinned, it would have been no excess of severity but simply an act of justice, for they deserved eternal damnation. In its ultimate analysis salvation is a matter of God's choice and not ours, for we are merely clay in His hands to be molded into a vessel of honor or dishonor entirely as He pleases (Rom. 9:21). Sinners are in the sovereign hand of God to save or to destroy according to His own will. That is His divine prerogative. "Therefore hath he mercy on whom he will have mercy, and whom he will he hardeneth" (Rom. 9:18). Far from offering any apology, He bids us observe and ponder that solemn fact: "See now that I, even I, am he, and there is no god with me: I kill, and I make alive; I wound, and I heal: neither is there any that can deliver out of my hand" (Deut. 32:39). Such a One is not to be spoken lightly about, but to be held in the utmost awe.

In the very nature of the case, mercy is not something which can be claimed as a right—least of all from Him whom we have wronged far above all others —but lies entirely at the discretion of the one who is pleased to exercise it.

Robert Erskine stated: "Because He is a sovereign God, infinitely happy in Himself without us, it is at His option to manifest mercy or not, to save or not, as much as it was His option to make man or not." "He doeth according to *his will* in the army of heaven, and among the inhabitants of the earth: and none can stay his hand, or say unto him, What doest thou?" (Dan. 4:35). Therefore He exercises sovereignty in His reason for showing mercy, because He "will shew mercy." God is sovereign not only as to the ones He saves, but as to the time, the instrument, and the means by which He saves them.

Such teaching alone accords to God His proper place, as it likewise cuts away all ground for human merits and boasting; and at the same time it deepens the wonderment and gratitude of the redeemed. God can never act unjustly, but He can and does bestow His favors on whom He pleases, and in so doing exercises His high prerogative: "Is it not lawful for me to do what I will with mine own?" (Matt. 20:15).

The exemption of any sinner from everlasting condemnation is an act of sovereign mercy and free grace; therefore God consults none but exercises His own good pleasure as to those on whom He bestows this grace. "Many widows were in Israel in the days of Elias . . . when great famine was throughout all the land; but unto none of them was Elias sent, save unto Sarepta, a city of Sidon, unto a woman that was a widow. And many lepers were in Israel in the time of Eliseus the prophet; and none of them was cleansed, saving Naaman the Syrian" (Luke 4:25-27). If some are brought to believe in Christ, while others are left in their unbelief, it is sovereign grace alone which makes the one differ from the other. And if it is right for God to make such a difference in time, it could not be wrong for Him to purpose doing so from eternity. They who balk at sovereign and unconditional election believe in neither the total depravity of man nor the God of the Bible. On the one hand, He hides these things from those who are wise and prudent in their own conceit. On the other, He reveals them to babes (Matt. 11:25). There cannot be an election without a rejection: "The one shall be taken, and the other left" (Matt. 24:40-41). "The election hath obtained it, and the rest were blinded" (Rom. 11:7). "Jacob have I loved, but Esau have I hated" (9:13).

Inasmuch as the sinner's will is enslaved by sin, *God must overcome* his opposition before he will submit to Him. But both Scripture and observation make it evident that He does not bring all rebels into subjection, but only a favored few. As Psalm 110:3 declares, "Thy people shall be willing in the day of thy power." Though "by nature the children of wrath, even as others" (Eph. 2:3), equally depraved and guilty, yet these few even in their unregenerate state are "God's people." They are His by sovereign election, His by eternal decree, His by covenant relationship. He loved them with an everlasting love (Jer. 31:3), chose them in Christ before the foundation of the world (Eph. 1:4), predestinated them to be conformed to the image of His Son (Rom. 8:29). Accordingly, in the day of His power He quickens them into newness of life, and puts the soul into a condition to receive the truth and cordially embrace it. That putting forth of divine power upon and within the "vessels of mercy" takes place at a definite season, for there is a set time for God to show favor to the members of Zion (Ps. 102:13). As the length of Israel's captivity in Babylon was so divinely fixed that none could any longer detain them when that time had expired, likewise must His elect be delivered from their bondage to sin and Satan when the appointed moment arrives. He who ordered the moment of our birth and death (Eccles. 3:2) does not leave us to decide the day of our conversion—still less whether we shall be converted or not.

"Thy people shall be willing" to whom? To do what? Willing for that to which previously they were completely averse. Willing to submit their intellect wholly to God's Word, so that they receive with childlike simplicity all that is revealed there. Willing to lean no more to their own understanding, but to accept without question the mysteries of the faith. High imaginations and lofty reasonings against the knowledge of God are cast down, and every thought brought into captivity to the obedience of Christ. Miracles which infidels scoff at, aspects of truth which critics term contradictory, precepts which run counter to the lusts of the flesh, are meekly accepted. The elect are willing to bow to God's way of salvation, so that they freely abandon their idols, renounce the world, repudiate all merits of their own, and come as empty-handed beggars, acknowledging themselves to be deserving only of hell. Willing to receive Christ as Prophet to instruct, as Priest to atone for their sins, as King to rule over them. Willing to receive Him as their Lord, to take His yoke upon them, to follow the example He has left them. Willing to bear reproach for His sake, to be given the cold shoulder, to be hated and persecuted. Willing to be on the side of the minority, to be cast out of the organized church if need be, to lay down their lives rather than deny Him.

Obviously, a miracle of grace must be effected within them before they will choose what is so contrary to fallen human nature. That wonderful change from unwillingness to willingness is not the result of creature effort, but of divine operation; it is not of self-improvement, but the effect of God's work in the soul. Thus we read of "the exceeding greatness of his power to us-ward who believe, according to the working of his mighty power" (Eph. 1:19). That putting forth of His power does not violate man's constitution or responsibility. Instead of destroying the freedom of his will, it liberates it from its native bondage. God's people are not dragged to Christ, but drawn (John 6:44) by "bands of love" (Hosea 11:4). That action of His power has reference to that blessed time when the effectual inworking of the Spirit delivers the soul from the dominion of sin and Satan, when the influences of grace prevail over the corruptions of the flesh, when the Lord opens the heart to receive His Word (Acts 16:14), when the affections are turned from the world to Christ, and the soul gladly gives up itself to Him. This power is life-giving and liberating, and delivers from death in sin. It communicates a new disposition which causes its recipient cordially to yield himself to God. This convincing power convicts the individual of his wickedness, wretchedness and need. God's power works in him "both to will and to do of his good pleasure" (Phil. 2:13). As the Christian reflects on all that this power has accomplished in him, he sings:

> O happy day that fixed my choice
> On Thee, my Saviour and my God!
> Well may this glowing heart rejoice,
> And tell its raptures all abroad.

'Tis done, the great transaction's done;
I am my Lord's, and He is mine;
He drew me, and I followed on,
Charmed to confess the voice divine.

Marvel of Christ's Mediation

The vile condition of mankind *heightens the marvel of Christ's mediation.*
It was by no means incumbent upon God to recover those who had turned
their backs on Him. As He was not obligated to prevent their defection, neither
was He obliged to restore any of those who had revolted. When He permitted
the whole human race to offend in Adam, had He left them to be buried in
the ruins of their fall, to sink utterly beneath the weight of their iniquities,
it would have been no undue severity on His part. He might well have reserved all men in those chains which they fully deserved, and left them to
feed on the fruits of their evil doings, without lifting a finger for their deliverance. To go farther back, as God might forever have left men in their nothingness without bringing them into being, so He could have left them all in their
contracted misery. There was no more reason why the Lord should save any
of Adam's posterity than there was for Him to bring back the fallen angels to
their original obedience and bliss. The blessedness of God Himself would
have been no more infringed upon by the eternal destruction of our entire
race than it was by the everlasting ruin of devils. It was wholly at God's own
option whether He provided a Saviour or withheld Him.

There was no reason why God should not have abandoned all mankind. He
certainly was not bound in justice to intervene on their behalf, for as the
righteous Governor of the world He might well have proceeded to uphold the
majesty of His law by executing its penalty on the disobedient, thereby
making them an example of vengeance to all other intelligences in the universe. Nor did His goodness oblige Him to rescue His refractory subjects
from their misery, for He had previously given full proof of that goodness in
their creation, as is still made manifest in the happiness enjoyed by all His
loyal subjects. Nor did any consideration of *His glory* require that He should
show them mercy. God's glory is not dependent on the manifestation of any
one attribute, but on the manifestation of each in its proper time and place,
and in full harmony with the others. God is glorified when He sends blessings
on the righteous; He is equally glorified when He sends punishment on the
wicked. What would the loss of this world be to Him in whose sight it is
nothing, yes, less than nothing and vanity? The provision of a Saviour was a
matter of His free grace, and *grace* is something which none can claim as a
right.

God was pleased to act in a manner which will cause both the holy angels
and redeemed sinners forever to marvel and adore. His way of salvation is
the wonder of all wonders, whether we consider the dignity of the Mediator's
person, the nature of His work, the things it accomplished, or its beneficiaries.
The Saviour was none other than the Lord of glory, the Coequal and the
Beloved of the Father. His work necessitated a journey from heaven to earth,

the assumption of human nature, being made under the law, and enduring unspeakable humiliation. It required Him to become the Man of sorrows, so that the whole of His life in this scene was one of suffering and grief. It involved His becoming the Substitute of His people; the iniquity of them all was placed upon Him, and He took the wages due them. It entailed laying down His life to ransom them, dying a cruel, shameful and accursed death, during which He was separated from God Himself. So infinitely meritorious and efficacious was Christ's death that it appeased the wrath of God against His people, satisfied every demand of His justice, removed the guilt of their transgressions from them as far as the East is from the West, conquered Satan and spoiled him of his dominion over them, procured the Spirit to quicken and indwell them, opened heaven for them so that they might have access to and fellowship with God, ensured their preservation in time and fullness of joy for eternity.

And on whose behalf did the Son of God suffer such awful indignities? Not for the fallen angels, whose original habitat was heaven, but for creatures of the earth who are but breathing dust and animated clay. These best of men compared with Christ are less in His sight than a worm is in ours. In Job 25:6 He actually terms them worms. It was for the unworthy, the unholy, the unlovely, that Christ's sacrifice was ordained. What an amazing thing that the Lord should set His heart on those who in their fallen estate were incapable of doing anything to please or honor Him. The objects of Christ's mediation were despicable not only in their beings but in their actions also. As man is nothing comparatively, so he can do nothing to glorify Christ, though he can do much to provoke and dishonor Him. How can one who is lame and blind walk or work, or one who is dead act? Such were the Lord's people when He entertained thoughts of mercy toward them: destitute of any good qualities or fruit, and lacking any spiritual principle or nature to yield one or the other. And after Christ has bestowed such a principle and nature on His people, they cannot act except as they are acted upon. They cannot stand, except as He upholds them. They cannot move unless He draws them. Christ must work all their works in them (Isa. 26:12).

Man is not only impotent but poverty-stricken. He is nothing, can do nothing, has nothing. He not only has "no money" (Isa. 55:1) but is heavily in debt. He is in a famishing condition, feeding on nothing but wind and husks, on the vanities and pleasures of this world. He has nothing with which to cover his shame; though he may, like the Laodiceans, imagine himself to be rich and in need of nothing, yet in God's sight he is poor and naked. He cannot rightly say that his soul is his own, for he has given it over to Satan, sold himself to work wickedness. What a marvel that Christ should love such a forlorn creature! But more: man is not only a bankrupt spectacle but a hideous one. Poverty will not hinder love, especially if there is beauty; but who can admire deformity? Yet the sinner, in the eyes of holiness, is full of revolting loathsomeness. No human pen can depict the obnoxiousness of defiled man. He was created fair and very good, adorned with the beauty of

God's image; but not only is all of that erased, but the horrible image of Satan has displaced it. Man's light has been turned into darkness, his comeliness into corruption; instead of a sweet savor there is a stench and burning instead of beauty (Isa. 3:24).

That which makes the soul most unlovely is its being *dead*. When life expires all beauty expires with it. A dead soul is as repulsive to God as a dead body is to us. But men are not only hateful to Christ but *haters of Him*. They hate His person, His offices, His precepts. They hate His very image, and the more resemblance to Him any of His followers have the more they are detested. Yet there is not the least occasion of hatred in Christ. He is altogether lovely—divinely glorious, humanly perfect. Nor does He give any cause to be hated. All His administrations are righteous, so that His justice ought to be admired as much as His mercy. But men hate Christ with an unmixed hatred, without any degree of love, without the slightest inclination or tendency toward Him. This hatred was so deadly that when He was delivered into their hands they murdered Him. This hatred remains unvarying and inveterate, firmly rooted in men's hearts, expressed by continual acts of rebellion against God. What a truly amazing thing it is that Christ should voluntarily lay down His life for such creatures! Yet "when we were enemies, we were reconciled to God by the death of his Son" (Rom. 5:10). Behold such love. Behold and wonder.

Opposition to the Gospel

The total depravity of all mankind explains the opposition which the gospel encounters. When one considers what the gospel is in itself—a message of good news to lost sinners—one would naturally suppose that it would be universally and cordially received. Will not those condemned to eternal damnation welcome a reprieve? Will not those dying from a deadly malady be glad to avail themselves of an effectual remedy? Will the naked scorn the garments of salvation, the poverty-stricken refuse the unsearchable riches of Christ, the famishing decline an invitation to a feast? One would not think so. The evangel contains the most illustrious display of the divine character which has ever been given to this world, and thus it is called "the glorious gospel of the blessed God" (I Tim. 1:11). It makes known to us how divine wisdom has so perfectly adjusted His attributes that God can at the same time be both just and merciful in saving a hell-deserving sinner, that He can lavish on him the riches of grace without in any way compromising His holiness. Such a marvel is so far beyond human conception that it evidences itself to be truly divine. It is indeed "worthy of all acceptation." It announces the inestimable blessings of pardon, holiness and joy, and therefore should be cordially welcomed by all who hear it.

The love of God which the gospel publishes, and the sufferings of Christ for sinners, ought to melt the hardest heart and cause every hearer fervently to cry, "Thanks be unto God for his unspeakable gift." This message of glad tidings proclaims peace. It tells of deliverance from condemnation, and promises eternal life to all who receive it. Yet the fact remains that the great majority of those who hear it are scarcely affected and obtain no lasting advantage to their souls; and *that* perplexes many Christians. But the total depravity of man fully explains that lamentable state. In a heart that is desperately wicked there is nothing whatever on which the gospel can seize that will evoke any echo to it. Its message is directly opposed to the opinions and inclinations of the fallen creature. If it informed men of how great worldly honors could be secured gratis, or how large sums of money could be obtained for nothing, it would be heartily welcomed. If it assured men how they could indulge their lusts with impunity and live in sin without fear of death and hell, it would indeed be good news to them. But a holy gospel does not appeal to them, being foreign to their tastes.

If God were to leave men entirely to themselves in their response to the gospel, it would be universally rejected. There is a deeply rooted contrariety to God in men's very nature which makes them turn a deaf ear to His voice, though they are ready enough to listen to the least whisper of Satan. As there are plants which are attractive to the eye but poisonous to the stomach, so even though the gospel is a pleasant sound to the ear it is repulsive to a corrupt heart. The gospel requires men to renounce their own wisdom and become as little children, to repudiate their own righteousness and accept that of Another, to turn from self-pleasing and submit to the will of God. The gospel is designed to transform the inner man and regulate the outer man, and that is quite unacceptable to the unregenerate. No exhortations will reconcile a wolf and a lamb. No logical arguments will tame a fierce lion. Though man is a rational creature, he follows the promptings of his lusts rather than the dictates of his judgment. One who is wholly in love with sin and Satan does not desire to enter the service of Christ. To turn to God in Christ is altogether contrary to the stream of corrupt nature, and therefore it needs to be overcome by a flood of almighty grace, as the stream of the river is overcome by the tide of the sea.

Certain writers represent the heart of fallen man as painfully conscious of its burden and sighing for deliverance. But the statement that the natural man is eager to escape from the ruin and degradation to which sin has reduced him is a figment of fancy, unsupported by a single fact of experience. The natural man does indeed encounter conflicts, yet his struggles are not for deliverance from indwelling corruption, but to escape the accusations of conscience. Man's misery is that he cannot sin without unpleasant consequences. There is nothing whatever in him that predisposes him to welcome the gospel or to give it joyful acceptance when it is made known to him. The heart of man is more unwilling to embrace the evangel than it is to acknowledge the equity of the law. Charnock stated:

> The Law puts man upon his own strength, the Gospel takes him off from his own footing. The Law acknowledges him to have a power in himself, and to act for his own reward; the Gospel strips him of all his proud and towering thoughts (II Cor. 10:5), brings him to his due place, the

foot of God, and orders him to deny himself as his own rule, righteousness, and end, and henceforth not to live unto himself (II Cor. 5:14).
This is the reason why men are more against the Gospel than against
the Law: because it doth more deify God and debase man.

As there needed to be a forerunner for Christ to prepare the way before
Him, so the Holy Spirit must first work upon the heart before it is ready
to receive the gospel. Not until He renews the soul is any real sense of need
awakened; and until its sickness is felt the great Physician is not desired.
Before the heart has been divinely prepared for its reception, the Word of
God can find no permanent place in it. That is very evident from our Lord's
parable of the sower, wherein He likened those who heard the Word to several kinds of ground. The seed sown was the same in each case; it was the
soils that differed. The seed which fell by the wayside, on the stony ground
and on the thorny ground was abortive. The heart has to be made "honest
and good" (Luke 8:15) before there will be any increase or fruit. None but
the Holy Spirit can produce in the soul a hatred of sin, and the desire to be
saved from it because of its intrinsic vileness. Only because of the distinguishing and astonishing grace of God are *any* brought to repent and believe the
gospel. One whose affections are chained to the things of earth cannot seek
those things which are above. Nothing more clearly demonstrates the certainty of human depravity than the fact that without a special and divine
operation no heart ever did or ever will savingly receive the gospel.

In view of the total depravity of man *we need not be the least surprised
at what we observe in Christendom itself*. A change of clothes effects no
alteration in the character of the wearer, neither does a person's taking on
a profession of religion better his heart. It may indeed foster a spirit of
hypocrisy, and cause him to take more pains to hide from the eyes of his
fellowmen what he is by nature; but it will not cleanse his soul from indwelling sin. Thus, while there is more open wickedness in the profane world,
there is far more secret and cloaked wickedness in the professing world.
Error is bound to be much more popular than truth to the unregenerate;
therefore, to make the truth in any way acceptable to them it has to be
watered down, wrested and perverted. And there are always those who, for
the sake of filthy lucre, are ready to perjure their souls. Hence heretical sects
and systems abound on every side. What delusions are cherished about the
character of God! What erroneous ideas are entertained about His way of
salvation! What false opinions are held of man's dignity, greatness, free will,
even by many who call themselves Christians! Because of the unbelief, selfishness and impiety of men's hearts, the false prophets, who speak smooth and
flattering things, are assured of a ready hearing.

Here, then, is the explanation of the babel of tongues which is now heard
in Christendom. When the natural man takes it on him to handle the things
of God, they are sure to be corrupted. How can those who are devoid of
divine grace and in love with sin faithfully communicate the gospel which
unsparingly condemns sin? For the same reason, those who are without true

piety will prefer to hear and follow those whose preaching gives them the most license to gratify their carnality. Moreover, Satan will see to it that his emissaries cater to the worldly minded. What are Universalism and annihilationism but opiates to remove the dread of eternal punishment? What is Antinomianism, with its bald fatalism and repudiation of the moral law as the believer's rule of life, but an attempt to set aside the unpalatable truth of man's responsibility? What are the great majority of present-day "missions" and "revivals," with their musical attractions and sensational methods, but a pandering to those who love emotionalism and sensationalism? Higher criticism and modernism are simply devices to banish the authority of Holy Writ and get rid of the supernatural. Extreme Arminianism panders to human pride, for it is virtually the deification of man, making him the architect of his life and the determiner of his destiny.

Infinite Patience of God

The depravity of mankind *makes evident the infinite patience of God.* "The LORD is slow to anger, and great in power" (Nahum 1:3). How significant is the conjunction of those divine perfections! It is not because God is indifferent to men's wickedness that He does not speedily take vengeance on them; still less because He lacks the ability to do so. God is not at the command of His passions as men are. He can restrain His anger when under great and just provocation to exercise it. His power over Himself is the cause of His slowness to execute wrath; nevertheless, His might to punish is as great as His patience to spare. What fearful provocations, insults and injuries God meets with daily from mankind. Charnock well states:

> How many millions of practical atheists breathe every day in God's air and live upon His bounty, who deserve to be inhabitants of hell rather than possessors of earth! An infinite holiness is opposed, and infinite justice provoked, yet an infinite patience forbears the punishment, and infinite goodness relieves our wants.

What a wonder it is that God has protracted human history until now, and that He still "maketh his sun to rise on the evil and on the good, and sendeth rain on the just and unjust." Patience is as truly a divine attribute as are holiness, wisdom and faithfulness.

What a mercy that God does not strike dead those who brazenly defy Him and take His holy name in vain! Why does He not suddenly cut off every blatant infidel, as He did Ananias and Sapphira? Why does He not cause the earth to open her mouth and swallow the persecutors of His people, as He did when Dathan and Abiram rebelled against Moses and Aaron? Why does He tolerate the countless abominations in Christendom which are being perpetrated under the holy name of Christ? Only one answer is possible: Because He endures "with much longsuffering the vessels of wrath fitted to destruction" (Rom. 9:22). There are many ways in which the patience of God is manifested in this world. First, by publishing His vengeance before

He strikes. "Because there is wrath, beware lest he take thee away with his stroke: then a great ransom cannot deliver thee" (Job 36:18), thereby affording them space to repent. Second, by delaying the judgments which He has threatened. Recall how long the ark was being prepared before He sent the great deluge (Gen. 6:3)! Third, in executing His judgments by degrees, as He sent plague after plague upon Egypt before He commissioned the angel of death to kill all her firstborn; and as the Shekinah glory departed slowly from apostate Israel, retiring stage by stage (Ezek. 9:3; 10:4, 19; 11:23), as though reluctant to leave.

Consider how great our provocations against the Most High—against His authority and majesty. Consider how many are our transgressions against the law. Consider how long they have been continued. Each succeeding generation has been as bad as the former, or worse, "evil men and seducers waxing worse and worse." Consider how fearfully God is insulted and offended by the world's treatment of His gospel. He proclaims mercy to the worst of sinners, but they scoff at it. He entreats them to turn to Him that they may live, but they are determined to destroy themselves. What an indescribably dreadful state men must be in who prefer their idols to Christ, and have no desire to be saved from their sins! What proof of His long-suffering that God has already prolonged this day of salvation for almost five hundred years more than the Mosaic economy lasted! Yet far from appreciating such clemency the unregenerate misinterpret and abuse it. How it should astonish us that God not only preserves in this life such a multitude of monsters, but continues to spread their tables!

Sure Wrath of God

How clearly the depravity of mankind *demonstrates the necessity for hell!* What can be the future of stout-hearted rebels who throughout life defy their Maker and Ruler and die in impenitence? Shall such a Being be despised with impunity? If, by the common consent of all right-minded people, one who is guilty of treason against an earthly monarch is worthy of death, what punishment can be too great for those who prefer themselves to the King of kings, and daily invade His prerogatives? Sin is a challenge to the government of God, and insurrectionists must be dealt with. Sin has to be paid the wages which it has earned. Equity requires that each one should reap as he has sown. The time of God's patience has an end. He has wrath to punish as well as patience to bear. Because God is holy He hates all sin, and as the moral Governor it becomes Him to deal with revolters. How could He be the sum of all excellence were He to make no distinction between good and evil and to treat virtue and vice alike? Christ bade His hearers, "Fear him, which after he hath killed hath power to cast into hell; yea, I say unto you, Fear him" (Luke 12:5). He knew as none other did that God is the Enemy of sin and the Avenger of those who despise His counsels.

God will yet fully vindicate His throne and make evident what a fearful thing it is to despise Him. It is right that He should display His governmental supremacy and subdue all those who rise up against Him. Though He "endures [not 'loves'!] with much longsuffering the vessels of wrath, fitted to destruction," yet in the day to come He will show His wrath, and make known His power; and that wrath will be no greater than the mercy which men abused. The highest contempt merits the greatest anger, and it is fitting that those who refuse to make God their happiness should be made to feel everlastingly the misery of their separation from Him. Eternal life and eternal death were plainly set before them, and since they chose the latter they cannot justly blame any but themselves when they are consigned to it. God's veracity requires Him to fulfill His threatenings; and His very goodness requires Him to separate eternally the wicked from the righteous, for the latter could not enjoy perfect peace and happiness if they lived forever with the reprobate. It is just that those who freely serve the devil should be cast into the same prison and tormented with him. How could those who hate God, whose very natures are averse to Him, be admitted into heaven? What *must be* the portion of those who would destroy the Deity were it in their power to do so?

The total depravity of our race *sheds much light on Providence.* Many of God's dealings with men present insoluble riddles unto carnal reason. There is a divine handwriting on the wall of human affairs which, like that in Belshazzar's palace, is indecipherable by human wisdom. To those who are unacquainted with what is recorded in Genesis 3, God's ways with our race cannot but be most mysterious. But the whole subject is at once illumined when the doctrine of human depravity is understood. The whole brood of ills which now afflicts mankind has sprung from the pregnant womb of sin. The wrecked and wretched condition in which man now finds himself is the inevitable consequence of his fall. The frowning aspect of Providence which so often darkens this scene and appalls us receives its only adequate solution in the fact that Adam's offense fearfully changed the relation of God and the creature. Our nature being what it is, we cannot expect history to be written in any other inks than those of tears and blood. Hospitals and prisons, the discords and strifes among men, the warring between nations, unprincipled politicians, conscienceless preachers—all are the effects of the corruption of human nature.

Here is the key to the problem of suffering. All the misery in the world proceeds from sin. But not only are the governmental ways of God with men what they are because of what the race is, they are also designed to make more evident the real character of fallen man. While Providence sets bounds to the exercise of human depravity, at the same time it permits sufficient manifestations thereof to leave no candid observer in doubt. God causes men to reveal what they are by suffering their insubjection to His law, their rejection of His gospel, their perverting of His truth, their persecutions of His people. How many others, who were regarded as upright, are by some sudden temptation shown to have been all along corrupt at heart. Many a merchant, lawyer, bank official, even minister of the gospel, who was highly respected is permitted to fall into open sin, that the long-cherished depravity of his soul might be exposed. How remarkably does Providence often bring to light the hidden things of darkness, as in the case of Abraham's deception, of Joseph's brethren's hatred, of Judah's secret sin, as well as Achan's and David's.

Belief of this doctrine *ought to have a beneficial effect on the children of God.* A sense of our native depravity should engender deep humility. What a state we were in when God plucked us as brands from the burning! The realization of that ought to make us take and maintain a very lowly place before Him. "That thou mayest remember, and be confounded, and never open thy mouth any more [in self-praise] because of thy shame, when I am pacified toward thee for all that thou hast done, saith the Lord GOD" (Ezek. 16:63). We have no reason for being proud. That acknowledgment of Jacob's should be our constant confession: "I am not worthy of the least of all the mercies, and of all the truth, which thou hast shewed unto thy servant" (Gen. 32:10). As we look back to the pit from which we were dug, what fervent praise and thanksgiving should be awakened in our hearts! How we should adore the One who opened our prison doors, for none but His hand could loose the bolts and open the many locks which held us captive. Our hearts should be melted and filled with wonderment at the amazing grace which has saved us from the dominion of Satan and made us kings and priests to God, which has elevated beggars to be "heirs of God, and joint-heirs with Christ."

This solemnizing doctrine ought to convince the saint that he cannot keep himself alive. If, being a mutable creature, sinless Adam, when left to himself, brought about his destruction, how much more would the mutable believer, with a fallen and corrupt nature still within him, unless an Almighty hand preserved him! So perverse are we by nature, and so weak as Christians, that without Christ we can do no good thing (John 15:5). Sustaining and preserving grace must be sought by us hourly. We are treading a slippery path and need to pray, "Hold thou me up, and I shall be safe" (Ps. 119:117). Finally, the knowledge of this truth ought to produce in us a spirit of complete dependence on God. How beautifully is that state depicted in the description given of the church: "Who is this that cometh up from the wilderness, leaning upon her beloved?" (Song of Sol. 8:5). So ignorant and wayward are we that "we know not what we should pray for as we ought" (Rom. 8:26). Only by the gracious operations of the Spirit are our affections raised above this world, is our faith strengthened, are we enabled to lay hold of a divine promise. So shut up are we to God that in all things He must work in us "both to will and to do of his good pleasure."

Chapter 13

REMEDY

PERHAPS SOME READERS are inclined to demur thus: "Why devote a separate section to this? We already know all about it. The remedy for ruined man is to be found in God's salvation." But that is a very superficial view, and a wrong one too; for the greatest and grandest of all the wonderful works of God ought never to be spoken of so lightly or dismissed so cursorily. Moreover, the matter is far from being as simple as that; and since there is such widespread ignorance concerning the disease itself it is necessary to examine closely and in some detail a description of its cure. The fact needs to be deeply realized at the outset that as far as all natural wit is concerned the condition of fallen man is beyond repair, that as far as self-help or human skill is concerned his case is hopeless. None other than the Son of God Himself declared, "With men this is impossible" (Matt. 19:26); and it is only as we perceive, to some extent at least, the various respects in which that impossibility lies that we can begin to appreciate the miracle of grace which secures the recovery of lost sinners.

Man's Deadly Disease

The deadly disease which has seized man is not a simple but a compound one, consisting of not a single element but a combination, each of which is fatal in itself. Look at some of them. Man's very nature is thoroughly corrupt, yet he is in no way horrified because of it. Not only is sin part and parcel of his being, but he is deeply in love with it. He is filled with enmity against God, and his heart is as hard as a stone. He is wholly paralyzed Godward, and completely under the dominion and sway of Satan. He is devoid of righteousness, a guilty sinner without a spark of holiness, a moral leper. He is utterly incapable of helping himself, for he is "without strength" (Rom. 5:6). The wrath of God abides on him, and he is dead in trespasses and sins. Fallen man is not merely in danger of ruin and destruction, but is already sunk in them. He is like a brand on the very edge of a raging fire, which will swiftly be consumed unless the divine hand plucks him out (Zech. 3:2). His condition is not only wretched but desperate, inasmuch as he is altogether incapable of devising any expedient for his cure.

The sinner is guilty, and no creature can make an atonement for him. He is an outcast from God, terrified by His very perfections; therefore he does his best to banish Him from his thoughts. No tongue can express or heart be

185

suitably affected with the woeful plight and abject misery of the natural man. And such will be his condition forever unless God intervenes. Yet all of this presents only one side of the problem—the easier one—which stands in the way of man's recovery. To finite intelligence it would seem that a creature so vile and polluted, so wayward and rebellious, so obnoxious to the righteous God, is beyond all hope; surely it would not comport with the divine honor to save such a wretch. How a transgressor could be pardoned consistently with the requirements of that law which he had despised and flouted, and be delivered from the penalty which it justly demands, and how he could be brought back into God's favor in concord with the maintaining of the divine government, presented a difficulty which no angelic wisdom could solve. It was a secret hidden in God till He was pleased to make it known.

There are those—with no regard to the Word of truth—who suppose that God must pardon and receive into favor those who throw down the weapons of their rebellion against Him and ask for mercy. But the solution to the problem is far from being as simple as that. Human reason can advance no valid and sufficient argument why God should forgive the sinner merely because he repents, or that this could be done consistently with His moral government. Rather the contrary is evident. The contrition of a criminal will not exonerate him in a human court of law, for it offers no satisfaction and reparation for his crimes. Any sinner who cherishes the idea that his repentance gives him a claim to divine clemency and favor demonstrates that he is a total stranger to true repentance; and he will never repent until he abandons such presumption. Universal experience and observation, as well as Scripture, fully attest the fact that no one ever repents while he is left to himself. He is not made the subject of those divine operations to which he has no claim, and which mere reason is incapable of concluding that God will grant.

It is obvious that an adequate remedy for the complicated and fatal malady by which man is stricken must be *of God*. It must be of His devising, His providing, His applying, His making effectual. That is another way of saying it must be *wholly of Him* from start to finish, for if any part is left to the sinner, at any stage, it is certain to fail. Yet it must be pointed out once more that God was under no obligation whatever to make such provision, for when man deliberately apostatized from Him he forfeited all favorable regard from his Maker. Not only might God righteously inflict the full penalty of His broken law on the entire human race; consistent with His holy nature He could have left all mankind to perish eternally in that condemnation into which they had cast themselves. Had He utterly forsaken the whole of Adam's apostate posterity and left them as remediless as the fallen angels, it would have been no reflection whatever on His goodness, but rather a display of His inexorable justice. Therefore, whenever redemption is mentioned, it is constantly described as proceeding from sovereign grace and mere mercy (Eph. 1:3-11).

Yet something more than a gracious design was required on God's part in order for any sinner to be saved. Grace was indeed the source of God's action, yet it was not sufficient of itself. One may have the most admirable intentions, yet be unable to carry them out. How often is the deep love of a mother impotent in the presence of her suffering child! There has to be the putting forth of divine *power* also if the purpose of grace is to be accomplished. And it can be no ordinary power, but, as Scripture affirms, "the exceeding greatness of his power to us-ward who believe, according to the working of his mighty power" (Eph. 1:19). It calls for the exercise of far more might to re-create a fallen creature than it did to create the universe out of nothing. Why so? Because in *that* there was no opposition, nothing to resist God's working; whereas in the case of fallen man there is the hostility of his will, the alienation of his heart, the inveterate enmity of his carnal mind, to be overcome. Furthermore, the malice and opposition of Satan must be neutralized, for he endeavors with all his might to retain his hold on his victims. The devil must be despoiled of the advantage which he had gained, for it is not consistent with the glory of God that he should be left to triumph.

But something more than the exercise of God's power was still required. Omniscience must be exercised as well as omnipotence. Strength itself will not build a house; there must also be art to contrive and proportion the materials. *Skill* is the chief requirement of an architect. Let that faintly illustrate what we are here trying to express. Those who are saved are not only the products of God's amazing grace and almighty power but also "his workmanship" (Eph. 2:10). God's *wisdom* wonderfully appears in the beautiful fabric of His grace, in the spiritual temple which He erects for His own residence. He has "wrought for us the selfsame thing" (II Cor. 5:5). As stones are carved and polished, so believers are made "living stones" in that edifice in which God will dwell forever. Now that which is exquisite in execution points to the excellent skill in its planning. The counterpart of God's law in the hearts of His quickened children is no less the fruit of His wisdom than the writing of it on the tables of stone. His wisdom was shown in the first framing of it; His wisdom is apparent also in the imprinting of it upon the understanding and the affections.

God's Redemptive Cure

The depths and riches of *God's wisdom* are to be found neither in the marvels of creation nor in the mysteries of providence. Rather they are most fully and illustriously revealed in the plan and fruits of redemption. This is clear from several scriptures. In the God-Man Mediator "are hid all the treasures of wisdom and knowledge" (Col. 2:3). He is expressly designated "the wisdom of God" (I Cor. 1:24). "Unto the principalities and powers in heavenly places" is now being made known by means of "the church the manifold wisdom of God" (Eph. 3:10). The devising of a method whereby a part of mankind should be recovered out of their miserable state is indeed the masterpiece of divine wisdom. Nothing but Omniscience could have found a way to effect such a triumph in a manner suited to all the divine perfections. The wise men of this world are termed "princes" (I Cor. 2:6, 8),

but angels are designated "principalities and powers in the heavenlies" because of their superior dignity, wisdom and strength. Yet though they are so
great in intelligence, always beholding the face of the Father, a new and
grander discovery of God's wisdom is made to them through the church, for
His work in the redemption of it far transcends their understanding.

The celestial hierarchies had witnessed the dishonor done to the authority
of God and the discord brought into the sphere of His government by the sin
and rebellion of Adam. It was therefore necessary, morally speaking, that the
defiance of God's rule should be dealt with, and that the affront to His throne
should be rectified. This could not be done except by the infliction of that
punishment which in the unalterable rule and standard of divine justice was
necessary. The dismissal of sin on any other terms would leave the rule of
God under unspeakable dishonor and confusion. As John Owen stated:

> For where is the righteousness of government if the highest sin and
> provocation that our nature was capable of, and which brought confusion
> on the whole creation below, should for ever go unpunished? The first
> express intimation that God gave of His righteousness in the government
> of mankind was His threatening punishment equal unto the demerit of
> disobedience if man should fall into it: "In the day that thou eatest
> thereof thou shalt surely die." If He revoke and disannul this sentence,
> how shall the glory of His righteousness in the rule of all be made
> known? But how this punishment should be undergone, which consisted
> in man's eternal ruin, and yet man be eternally saved, was a work for
> Divine wisdom to contrive.

Not only was it necessary for the honor of God's righteousness, as He is the
moral Governor and supreme Judge of all the earth, that sin should be sum-
marily punished; it was required that there should be obedience to God, such
obedience as would bring more glory to Him than the dishonor and reproach
which resulted from the disobedience of man. We again quote Owen:

> This was due unto the glory of His holiness in giving the Law. Until this
> was done, the excellency of that Law as becoming the holiness of God, and
> as an effect thereof, could not be made manifest. For if it were never
> kept in any instance, never fulfilled by any one person in the world, how
> should the glory of it be declared? How should the holiness of God be
> represented by it? How should it be evident that the transgression of it
> was not rather from some defect in the Law itself, than from any evil in
> them that should have yielded obedience unto it? If the Law given unto
> man should never be complied withal in perfect obedience by any one
> whatever, it might be thought that the Law itself was unsuited unto our
> nature, and impossible to be complied withal.

It did not become the Rector of the universe to give man a law whose spirituality and equity should never be exemplified in obedience. That law was
not imposed, primarily, that man might suffer justly for its transgression, but
rather that God should be glorified in its performance. But since Adam's
offense brought ruin upon all his posterity, so that they are incapable of meeting its requirements, how could perfect obedience be rendered to it? Omniscience alone could supply the answer.

It is truly amazing that the wisdom of God has, by our redemption, made that which is the greatest possible dishonor to Him the occasion of His greatest glory. Yet this is indeed the case. Nothing is so displeasing to the Most High as sin, nothing so dishonoring to Him, for it is in its very nature enmity against Him, contempt of Him. Sin is a reproach to His majesty, an insult to His holiness, an insurrection against His government. And yet this "abominable thing" which He hates (Jer. 44:4), upon which He cannot look but with infinite disfavor (Hab. 1:13), is made the occasion of the greatest possible good. What a miracle of miracles that the Lord makes the wrath of man to praise Him (Ps. 76:10), that the very evil which aims at dethroning Him is transmuted into the means of magnifying Him; indeed, that thereby He has made the grandest manifestation of His perfections. Sin casts contempt upon the law of God, yet through redemption that law is made supremely honorable. Never was the King of heaven so grievously slighted as when those made in His image and likeness revolted against Him. Never was such honor paid Him as by the way He chose to effect the salvation of His people. Never was the holiness of God so slighted as when man preferred to give allegiance to that old serpent the devil. Never did God's holiness shine forth so illustriously as in the victory He gained over Satan.

It is equally wonderful that God contrived a way whereby a flagrant transgressor should become not guilty, and that he who was completely destitute of righteousness should be justified, or pronounced righteous, by the Judge of all the earth. Had such things as these been submitted for solution, they had forever appeared to be irreconcilable contradictions to all finite understandings. It seems to be utterly impossible for a condemned culprit to be cleared of any charge against him. Sin necessarily entails punishment; how then can any committer of it escape the "due reward" of his deeds (Luke 23:41) except by a manifest violation of justice? God has declared plainly that He "will by no means clear the guilty" (Exodus 34:7). He has determined by an unalterable decree that sin shall be paid its wages. Then how can the guilty be exempted from the sentence of death? Nor is the problem any less formidable of how God can, with perfect equity, declare righteous those who have not themselves met the requirements of the law. To judge as entitled to the reward of obedience those whose record is a lifelong disobedience appears to be worse than an irregularity. Nevertheless, Omniscience contrived a solution to both of these problems, a solution which is in every respect a perfect and a glorious one.

Without that solution, the restoration of any of mankind to favor and fellowship with God and to enjoyment of Him was utterly impossible. It was so not only because of the total depravity of man himself, but because of the concernment of the glory of the divine perfections in our sin and apostasy. Not only was man stricken with a fatal disease, from which there was not the slightest hope of deliverance unless a supernatural remedy be provided, but the government of God had been so grievously outraged by man's revolt that full compensation must be made to His insulted scepter, and complete satisfaction offered to His broken law, before the throne of heaven could be satisfied. Great beyond conception to finite intelligence was the difficulty of repairing the damage worked in the whole of our constitution by sin, yet greater far were the obstacles which stood in the way of the exercise of God's grace and mercy in restoring the outcast. That way of restoration must be one wherein God was magnified. His justice must be vindicated, His threatenings realized, His holiness glorified. The manner in which all of those ends were achieved and those results secured is the adoring marvel alike of the redeemed and of the angels.

As others before us have pointed out, if the divine government was to be vindicated the whole work of our recovery must be performed *in our nature.* The very nature of those who had sinned was to be recovered from the ruin of the fall and brought to everlasting well-being. Human nature was not only to be freed of any pollution, but made intrinsically holy. In order to effect the salvation of sinners, no satisfaction could be made to the glory of God for the vitiation of apostate man's nature with all its evil fruits, but only in the nature of those who had sinned and were to be saved. Since God's giving of the law to our first parents was itself an effect of His wisdom and holiness, wherein could the glory of them be exalted if that rule of righteousness were complied with by a nature of a totally different kind? Should an *angel* fulfill it, his obedience would be no proof that the law was suited to man's nature, to which it was originally prescribed; rather would an angel's compliance with the law have been a reflection on the divine goodness in giving it to men. Nor could there have been the necessary *relation* between the nature of the substitute and those on whose behalf he acted and suffered; and therefore such an arrangement would not have magnified the divine wisdom, but would have been at best an unsatisfactory expedient.

God's Representative

The Scriptures are very explicit in their teaching about the necessity of the same nature in the representative and in those whom he represented, as being consistent with God's wisdom. Speaking of the way of our relief, the apostle declared, "Forasmuch then as the children are partakers of flesh and blood, he [the Deliverer] also himself likewise took part of the same" (Heb. 2:14). It was human nature—here expressed by "flesh and blood"—that was to be delivered, and therefore it was human nature in which this deliverance was to be wrought. The apostle entered into considerable detail on this point in Romans 5:12-21, the sum of which is in verse 19: "As by one man's disobedience many were made sinners, so by the obedience of one ['by one man,' v. 15] shall many be made righteous." The same nature that transgressed must work out the remedy. This truth is reiterated in I Corinthians 15:21: "For since by man came death, by man came also the resurrection of the dead." Our ruin could not be retrieved, nor deliverance from our guilt be effected, except by one in our own nature.

Observe that the deliverance needed to be accomplished by one whose substance was derived from the common stock *of our first parents*. It would not have met the exigencies of the case for God to create a second man out of the dust of the ground, or out of anything which was different in nature from ourselves; in such a case there would have been no relation between him and us, therefore we could have been in no way concerned in anything he did or suffered. That alliance depended solely on the fact that God "hath made of one blood all nations of men" (Acts 17:26). But another difficulty was presented, one which also would have proved insurmountable to all created intelligences had not "the only wise God" revealed His provision for resolving it. Any deliverer of sinful men must derive his nature from their original stock, yet he must not bring along with it the least taint of corruption or liability to guilt on his own account; for if his nature were defiled, if it lacked the image of God, it could do nothing that would be acceptable to Him. And were he subject to the penalty of the law on his own account, he could make no satisfaction for the sins of others. But since every descendant of Eve is shaped in sin and conceived in iniquity, how could any of *her seed* be sinless? Only Omniscience could bring an immaculately clean thing out of thorough uncleanness.

We must not lose sight of the grounds on which defilement and guilt adhere to our nature, as they do in all individuals alike. First, our participation in sin was in Adam as our covenant head and federal representative. Therefore his offense was ours also, and justly imputed to us. Because we sinned in him, we became "by nature the children of wrath," the subjects of God's judicial displeasure. Second, we derived our nature from Adam by way of natural generation, so that his defilement is communicated to all his offspring. We are the degenerate plants of a degenerate stock. Thus, still another difficulty was presented: The nature of a deliverer for fallen man must, as to its substance, be derived from our first parents, yet so as *not* to have been in Adam as a legal representative, nor be derived from him by natural generation. But how could it be that his nature should relate as truly to Adam as does ours, while neither partaking of the guilt of Adam's transgression nor participating in his pollution? Such a one was utterly beyond the concept of every finite mind.

We have considered some of the difficulties—yes, seeming impossibilities —which stood in the way of the recovery of any of the fallen sons of Adam, showing that something more than a benign purpose of grace on God's part was required to effect that recovery—something more than the putting forth of His mighty power. The obstacles which needed to be removed were so many and so great that "the manifold wisdom of God" (Eph. 3:10) also needed to be called into play. The difficulty from the human side was the desperate state of the sinner. How could his darkness be changed into light, his enmity into love, his unwillingness into willingness, without any violence being done to his moral agency? The obstacles from the divine side were how the Most High could restore such wretches to His favor, and yet not compromise His perfections; how He could have dealings with moral lepers without sullying His holiness, clear the guilty without repudiating His law, exercise mercy consistently with His justice. To provide a remedy for such a malady, and to do so in a way that honored the throne of God, was far beyond the reach of created intelligence.

In order to save a law-cursed and hell-deserving sinner it was necessary that some method and means be devised whereby he could be delivered from all the consequences of the fall, and at the same time meet all the requirements of the divine government. Sin had to be dealt with unsparingly, yet transgressors be exempted from their merited doom. Full conformity to the law must be accomplished, yet by one in *the same nature* as those who had violated it. That was clearly signified by the Old Testament types: the redeemer had to be a *kinsman* of those he befriended (Lev. 25:25; Ruth 4:4-6). Moreover, the requirements of the law could be met only by one whose nature was derived from *the same stock* as those on whose behalf he transacted, yet his humanity must not be tainted in the least degree by their common defilement. It was necessary that he be a man of the seed of Adam (Luke 3:31) and of Eve (Gen. 3:15), yet an absolutely pure and holy man, for none other could personally and perpetually obey in thought, word and deed. But none such existed: "There is not a just man upon earth, that doeth good, and sinneth not" (Eccles. 7:20); nor would there ever have been one had the human race been left to itself. Nothing but the manifold wisdom and miracle-working power of God could produce him.

Yet one was needed who was *more than man*, indeed, far superior to those heavenly beings who veil their faces in the presence of Deity, in order to discharge the liabilities of depraved sinners, and renew them in holiness. This is evident from several considerations. The most exalted creature, simply because he is a creature, is obligated to give perfect obedience to his Maker, and therefore could merit nothing on behalf of others. If he fully performed his duty, he would indeed work out a righteousness and be entitled to the reward of the law; but he would need that righteousness *on his own account*, and therefore it would not be available for imputation to another—still less to many others. Also, the work he had to do—pay in full that incalculable debt incurred by those who were to be saved, make expiation for all their sins, reconcile them to God, restore them to His favor, make them fit for the inheritance of the saints in light—was far beyond the compass of any mere creature, no matter how high his rank in the scale of being. Moreover, any deliverer of the apostate sons of Adam must be essentially and infinitely holy, for none less qualified could put away the infinite guilt of their countless iniquities.

In order for any portion of mankind to be eternally saved for the glory of God, it was not only necessary that flawless obedience be given to God's law, but that such obedience bring more honor to His holiness than the dishonor brought on it by the disobedience of all. To affirm that it matters little what becomes of the glory of God so long as poor sinners are saved in some way or other is nothing but a fabrication of the carnal mind. Where God is revered and loved above all, the sentiments will be very different: better far that the whole of Adam's race perish than that the character of Deity be sullied and the foundations of His throne undermined. But such obedience could not be given by any mere creature, no matter how pure his nature or how eminent his rank; there must be somewhat of *the divine* in it, in order for his performance to have infinite value. Nor might his obedience be constrained, but rather voluntary, for that which is forced does not proceed from love and is valueless. Also, his conformity to the law could not be one which he was personally responsible to render to it, for in that case it could not be accepted as a due compensation for the disobedience of all.

It was not a single individual who was to be recovered from the fall and be brought to glory, but "ten thousands" (Jude 14), each of them with more sins to his account than the hairs on his head; and every sin had in it immeasurable guilt, since it was committed against the infinite Majesty of heaven. The woe to which all of them were consigned was also infinite, its duration being eternal—everything unspeakably dreadful and painful which our nature is capable of suffering. Nor could they be delivered from the awful consequences of their sin without adequate satisfaction being made to the offended justice of God. To assert the contrary is to say it does not matter to God whether He is obeyed or disobeyed, whether He is honored or dishonored in and by His creatures; and that would be to deny His very being, seeing it is directly contrary to the glory of all His perfections. But where was the person who was qualified and capable of making the requisite propitiation for sin? Where was the one fitted to act as mediator between God and men, between the holy One and the unholy? Where was the one who could bestow life on the dead and merit everlasting blessedness for them?

If a remedy were to be provided for sinners, it must be one that would restore them to the same state and dignity in which they were placed before the fall. To recover them to any lesser honor and blessedness than that which was theirs originally would not consist with either the divine wisdom or bounty. Owen stated: "Seeing it was the infinite grace, goodness and mercy of God to restore him, it seems agreeable unto the glory of the Divine excellencies in their operations that he should be brought into a better and more honourable condition than that which he had lost." In his primitive state man was subject to none but his Maker. Though he was less in dignity than the angels, yet he owed them no obedience; they were his fellow servants of the Lord God. Obviously (as Owen also pointed out), if the sinner were saved by any mere creature, he could not be restored to his first state and dignity, for in such a case he would owe allegiance and subservience to that creature who had redeemed him—he would become the property of the one who bought him. That would not only introduce the utmost confusion, but the sinner would be in a still worse case than he was before the fall, for he would *not* be in the position where he owed subjection and honor to God *alone*.

From the foregoing it will be seen that the only sufficient deliverer of fallen men must be one possessed of infinite dignity and worthiness, in order that he might be capable of meriting infinite blessings. He must be a person of infinite power and wisdom, for the work he must perform could be successfully accomplished by none less. But another requisite was that he should be a person who was infinitely dear to God the Father, in order to give his transactions an infinite value in the Father's esteem, and that the Father's love to him might balance the offense and provocation of our sins. He must also be a person who could act in this matter in his own right, who in himself was not a servant and subject of the Most High; otherwise he could not merit anything for those he wished to save. Moreover, he must be a person possessed of infinite mercy and love, for none other would voluntarily undertake a task so arduous, so humiliating, and involving such unspeakable suffering, for creatures so unworthy and foul as fallen men. But where in all the universe was such a one to be found? No created person possessed the necessary qualifications. When the Apostle John saw the vision of the seven-sealed book, we are told that he wept because no man in heaven or earth was found worthy to open the book (Rev. 5:1-4). Had not the manifold wisdom of God found the solution to all these problems, men and angels alike forever would have been nonplussed by them.

The various elements in the complicated problem of salvation for any of Adam's children are far from being exhausted in those already pointed out. Man was made to serve and glorify God. In spirit and soul and body, in all his faculties and powers, in all that was given to and entrusted with him, he was not his own, but was in the place of a servant. The same was equally the case with the angels. But from that condition and status the human race in Adam revolted, determining to be "as gods"—lords over themselves. There is something of *that* in every sin: a preferring of self-will to the will of the Almighty. By his insurrection, man fell into complete bondage to sin and Satan. In order to free the sinner from his captivity, it was necessary for any deliverer to take the position man originally occupied. He must enter the place of absolute subjection to God, entirely subordinating his own will to His; for in no other way could adequate compensation be made to the outraged government of God, and the damage done by our first parents be repaired. But how could any uncreated being occupy the position of a creature? With what propriety could one possessed of infinite dignity and excellence suffer such humiliation? How could one who was above all law come under the law and give obedience to it?

In his original state man had nothing but what his Creator had given him. Made out of the dust of the ground, he was endowed with intelligence and moral agency—to be employed in the divine service. He was also dependent on his Maker for every breath he drew. But he deliberately left that state of need and dependence, determining to enrich himself and assume absolute dominion. But his awful crime brought upon him and all whom he represented the loss of his original endowments. He lost the image of God, his dominion over the animals, his own soul. Consequently, any savior for him needed to experience the *degradation and poverty* which the sinner had brought on himself. But how was such an experience possible for anyone who was infinitely rich in himself and in his own right? Since Adam stood for and transacted on the behalf of all whom he legally represented, it follows that any savior would need to serve not in a private capacity but as the covenant head of those whom he was to recover. Finally, since God made the first man lord of the earth, giving him dominion over all creatures, which dominion he forfeited upon his fall, then a deliverer must be capable of recovering that lost state. But where was one that was able to purchase so vast an inheritance?

"The things which are impossible with men are possible with God" (Luke 18:27). Omniscience found a solution to all those problems which baffled the minds of men. Scripture places not a little emphasis on this. It is referred to as "the wisdom of God in a mystery, even the hidden wisdom, which God ordained before the world unto our glory [salvation]" (I Cor. 2:7). "In a mystery" connotes that which is undiscoverable by human reason, incomprehensible to the finite capacity, completely concealed until divinely revealed, and even then beyond our powers to comprehend fully. In Ephesians 1:8 we are told of it: "Wherein he hath abounded toward us in all wisdom and prudence." The word "abounded" has the force of gushing out, overflowing. It is called "all wisdom" for its excellence. It was not a single concept or act, but a conjunction of many excellent ends and means to the glory of God. To wisdom is added "prudence." The former refers to the eternal contriving of a way, the latter to the ordering of all things for the accomplishment of God's counsel or purpose—wisdom in devising, prudence in executing. In Ephesians 3:10 it is designated "the manifold wisdom of God" because of its complexity and variety: the salvation of sinners, the defeat of Satan, the full discovery of the blessed Trinity in Their different persons, separate operations, combined actions and expressions of goodness; and because of the vastness of its extent.

That manifold wisdom of God, now exhibited before the angels in the redemption of the church, is said to be "according to the eternal purpose which he purposed in Christ Jesus our Lord" (Eph. 3:11). The eternal Son of God, predestined to be the God-Man Mediator, is the grand medium, means and manifestation of the divine omniscience, and therefore He is called "The Word of God" (Rev. 19:13) and "the wisdom of God" (I Cor. 1:24). "Having made known unto us the mystery of his will, according to his good pleasure which he hath purposed in himself: that in the dispensation of the fulness of times he might gather together in one all things in Christ, both which are in heaven, and which are on earth; even in him" (Eph. 1:9-10). We again quote Owen:

> The mystery of the will of God is His counsels concerning His own eternal glory in the sanctification and salvation of the Church here below, to be united unto that above. The absolute original hereof was in His own good pleasure, or the sovereign acting of His wisdom and will. But

it was all to be effected in Christ, which the apostle twice repeats: He would gather "all things into a head in Christ, even in Him," that is, in Him alone.

Thus it is said of Him with respect unto His future incarnation and work of mediation that "the Lord possessed Me in the beginning of His way, before His works of old. I was set up from everlasting, from the beginning, or ever the earth was" (Prov. 8, 22, 23). The eternal personal existence of the Son of God is supposed in these expressions . . . without it none of these things could be affirmed of Him. But there is a regard in them both unto His future incarnation and the accomplishment of the counsels of God thereby. With respect thereto, God "possessed" Him in the beginning of His way, and set Him up from everlasting. God possessed Him eternally as His essential wisdom, as He was always and is always in the bosom of the Father, in the mutual, ineffable love of the Father and Son, in the eternal bond of the Spirit. But He signally possessed Him "in the beginning of His way" as His wisdom acting in the production of all the ways and works that are outwardly in Him. The beginning of God's way before His works, are His counsels concerning them, even as our counsels are the beginning of our ways with respect unto future works. And He "set Him up from everlasting" as *the foundation* of all the counsels of His will, in and by whom they were to be executed and accomplished.

Proverbs 8 is an exceedingly profound chapter, but a most blessed one. In it, as verse 1 shows, the voice of "wisdom" is heard. That a *person* is in view is evident from verse 12: "I wisdom dwell with prudence" and verse 17: "I love them that love me." That it is a divine person may be seen from verse 15: "By me kings reign." But it is equally clear from the statement "I was brought forth" in verses 24 and 25, and from "I was by him [the Father], as one brought up with him" in verse 30, that such expressions could not be predicated of the Son of God absolutely, that is, as coeternal and coequal with the Father. "Wisdom" is here to be understood as the Son as God-Man Mediator in His *two natures*, as the One ordained to be the incarnate "wisdom of God" (I Cor. 1:24). When He declares, "The LORD possessed me . . . [the Hebrew is without the 'in'] the beginning of his way, before his works of old" (Prov. 8:22) it is the Mediator speaking in the covenant subsistence which He had with God the Father and the Spirit before the universe was called into existence. The eternal Son was from "the beginning" (cf. Rev. 1:8) of the triune God's "way," for in all things He must "have the preeminence" (Col. 1:18).

The *first counsel* of God had respect to the Man Christ Jesus, for He was appointed to be not only the Head of His church but "the firstborn of every creature" (Col. 1:15). The One whom the Lord of hosts addresses as "the man, my fellow" (Zech. 13:7, literal trans.) shared the divine union and glory. He stated, "In the volume [Greek, head] of the book it is written of me" (Heb. 10:7). He was the Object and Subject of God's original decree. Charnock said,

> Our Redeemer came forth of the womb of a decree from eternity, before He came out of the womb of the Virgin in time. He was hid in the will

of God before He was made manifest in the flesh of a Redeemer. He was a Lamb slain in purpose before He was slain upon the cross. He was possessed by God in the beginning or the beginning of His way (the Head of His works), and set up from everlasting to have His delights among the sons of men.

The person of the God-Man Mediator was the origin of the divine counsels. As such, the triune Jehovah "possessed" or embraced Him, as a treasury in which all the divine counsels were laid up, as an efficient Agent for the execution of all His works. Christ was God's first Elect (Isa. 42:1) and then the church was chosen in Him (Eph. 1:4).

"I was set up from everlasting" (Prov. 8:23). That declaration concerns Him not essentially as God the Son, but economically as the Mediator: "set up" or literally "anointed" by a covenant constitution and by divine subsistence. Before all worlds Christ was appointed and anointed to His official character. Before God planned to produce any creature, He first "set up" Christ as the great archetype and original. "Then I was by him, as one brought up with him, and I was daily his delight, rejoicing always before him" (v. 30). It is not the Father's complacence in the second Person in the Trinity (as such) which is there in view, but His satisfaction and joy in the Mediator, as God contemplated Him as the repository of all His designs. The Hebrew word for "brought forth" also signifies "master-builder," and is so rendered in the English Revised Version. How blessedly it describes Him who could be relied upon to carry out the Father's purpose. In God's eternal thoughts the Man Christ Jesus was the object of His love. By Him all things were to be created. By Him vessels were to be formed for His glory. By Him the grand remedy was to be provided for sin's victims.

It is indeed lamentable that so few of the Lord's people have been instructed in these "deep things of God" (I Cor. 2:10), for they have been revealed for their edification and consolation. What we have sought to explain in Proverbs 8 throws light on other passages. For example, many a thoughtful person has been puzzled by John 6:62: "What and if ye shall see the Son of man ascend up where he was before?" In what sense had He been in heaven as Man before He became incarnate? Though *we* are ignorant of this awesome truth, the Old Testament saints were not, as is clear from Psalm 80:17: "Let thy hand be upon the man of thy right hand, upon the son of man whom thou madest strong for thyself." Though the Man Christ Jesus had no historical existence, He had a covenant subsistence with the Father, as taken into union with the second Person of the Trinity. As faith gives a present "substance" (the Greek word means "a real subsistence") in the believer's heart and mind of the things hoped for, so that he has a present enjoyment of things yet future, so in the mind of Him before whom all things are ever present, Christ as incarnate was ever a living reality. Thus when God said, "Let us make man in our image" (Gen. 1:26) the ultimate reference was to the God-Man who is par excellence "the image of the invisible God" (Col. 1:15).

Infinite Wisdom of God

Let us pause here and admire and adore the glorious wisdom of God, which found a way to save His people in a manner that was infinitely becoming and honoring to Himself; and let us bow in wonder and worship before the Lord Jesus who, notwithstanding the unspeakable shame and suffering involved, delighted to do the Father's will. The manifold wisdom of God is seen in *His choice* of the One to be the Head and Saviour of the church, since that One was in every respect fit to perform that office and work, possessed of all the necessary qualifications—in fact He was the *only* person suited to the work. God's great wisdom appeared in His knowing that Christ *was* a fit Person. None but Omniscience could have thought of God's dear Son becoming the Redeemer of hell-deserving sinners.

God's choice of the Person who was to be the Restorer of His honor, the Vanquisher of Satan, the Victor of death, and the Deliverer of His fallen people, was a perfect one. Who but One endowed with infinite wisdom would have thought of selecting his only begotten Son for such a fearful undertaking? For Christ, as God, is one of the eternal Three who were offended by sin, and from whom men had revolted. They were His avowed enemies, and they deserved His infinite vengeance. Who, then, could have conceived of Him as One who would set His heart on depraved wretches, who would exercise infinite love and pity toward them, would be willing to provide an all-sufficient remedy for all their ills? But even if that choice *were made*, seemingly insurmountable difficulties would have stood in the way of its realization. How was it possible for a divine person to enter the place of ruined sinners, to come under the law and give perfect obedience to it, and so work out a perfect righteousness for those who had none? And how could it be possible for the holy One to be made a curse, for the Lord of glory to suffer the penalty of the broken law, for the Beloved of the Father to experience the fires of divine wrath, for the Lord of life to die? Such problems as those would have forever baffled all created intelligences. But divine wisdom found a solution.

First, the manifold wisdom of God ordained that His dear Son should be constituted the last Adam, that as He made a covenant of works with the first man who was of the earth, so He would make a covenant of grace with the second Man, who is the Lord from heaven. As the first Adam stood as the covenant head and federal representative of all his posterity, so the last Adam would stand as the covenant Head and Representative of all His seed. But as the first Adam broke the covenant of works and brought ruin upon all those for whom he acted, so the last Adam would fulfill the terms of the covenant of grace, and thereby secure the everlasting blessedness of all on whose behalf He transacted. Accordingly, a covenant was entered into between the Father and the Son, the Former promising a glorious reward upon the Latter's meeting all the conditions. That wonderful transaction is referred to in Psalm 89:3-5: "I have made a covenant with my chosen, I have

sworn unto [the antitypical] David [which means 'the beloved'] my servant,
Thy seed will I establish for ever, and build up thy throne to all generations.
Selah. And the heavens shall praise thy wonders, O LORD: thy faithfulness
also in the congregation of the saints." That passage, like Proverbs 8, takes
us back to the eternal counsels of God, for verse 19 declares, "Then thou
spakest in vision to thy holy one and saidst, I have laid help upon one that
is mighty." That One was fully able to accomplish heaven's vast and gracious
designs.

That covenant of grace was a mutual compact voluntarily entered into
between the Father and the Son, the One promising a rich reward in return
for the fulfillment of the terms agreed upon; the Other solemnly pledging
Himself to carry out its stipulations. Many are the scriptures which speak of
Christ in connection with the covenant. In Isaiah 42:6 we hear the Father
saying to the Son, "I the LORD have called thee in righteousness, and will . . .
give thee for a covenant of the people." In Malachi 3:1 Christ is designated
"the messenger of the covenant" because He came here to make known its
contents and proclaim its glad tidings. In Hebrews 7:22 He is designated "a
surety of a better testament [covenant]," in 9:15 "the mediator of the new
testament," while in 13:20 we read of "the blood of the everlasting covenant."
In that covenant the Son agreed to be the Head of God's elect, and to do all
that was required for the divine glory and the securing of the elect's eternal
blessedness. Reference is made to that in "his own purpose and grace, which
was given us in Christ Jesus before the world began" (II Tim. 1:9). A
federal relation then existed between God (Christ) and the church, though
this was not made fully manifest until He became incarnate. It was then
that the Son was appointed to the mediatorial office, when He was "set up"
or "anointed," when He was "brought forth" from the everlasting decree
(Prov. 8:23-24) and given a covenant subsistence with the triune God.

It was proposed and freely agreed upon that the Beloved of the Father
should take upon Him the form of a servant and be made in the likeness of
sin's flesh. Accordingly, in the fullness of time He was "made of a woman,"
taking a human spirit and soul and body into perpetual union with Himself.
As the body of Adam was supernaturally made out of the virgin earth by
God's immediate hand, so the body of Christ was supernaturally made out
of the virgin's substance by the immediate operation of the Holy Spirit. So
too the union of soul and body in Adam prefigured the hypostatic union of
our nature with the Son of God, so that He is not two persons in one, but
one Person with two natures—those natures not being confounded, but each
preserving its distinctive properties. Owen's remark is significant:

> His conception in the womb of the Virgin, as unto the integrity of human
> nature, was a miraculous operation of the Divine power. But the preven-
> tion of that nature from any subsistence of its own, by its assumption
> unto personal union with the Son of God, in the first instance of its con-
> ception, is that which is above all miracles, nor can be designated by that
> name. A *mystery* it is, so far above the order of all creating or providen-

tial operations, that it wholly transcends the sphere of them that are most miraculous. Herein did God glorify all the properties of the Divine nature, acting in a way of infinite wisdom, grace and condescension.

He who was the Lord of all and owed no service or obedience to any, being in the form of God and equal with Him, descended into a condition of absolute subjection. As Adam deliberately forsook the place of complete submission to God, which was proper to his nature and acceptable to God, and aspired after lordship, so the Son of God left that state of absolute dominion which was His by right, and took upon Him the yoke of servitude. The Son's descent involved far greater humiliation to Himself than was the glory to which the first man aspired in his pride. As others have shown, this self-abasement of the Lord of glory to an estate of entire subjection is referred to by the apostle in Hebrews 10:5, where Christ is heard saying "A body hast thou prepared me." Those words are an explanatory paraphrase of "Mine ears hast thou opened"—margin "digged"—in Psalm 40:6, which in turn looks back to Exodus 21:6, where a statute was appointed to the effect that one who voluntarily gave himself up to absolute and perpetual service signified it by having his ear bored with an awl. Thus, Hebrews 10:5, in the light of Psalm 40:6 and Exodus 21:6, implies that Christ's body was prepared for Him with the express design of His absolute service for God.

Christ the Mediator

By His assumption of human nature, not only was Christ fitted to render subjection to God, but He became qualified to serve as *Mediator* between God and men. For it is required that a mediator be related to both of the parties he would reconcile, and that he be the equal of each of them. An angel would not be qualified for this office, since he possesses neither the divine nor the human nature. It was necessary for Christ to be real *man* as well as God in order to perform the work of redemption: the former so that He should be susceptible to suffering, qualified to offer Himself as a sacrifice, capable of dying. So too the assumption of human nature fitted Christ to be *the Substitute* of His people, to act not only on their behalf but in their room and stead, actually to take their lawful place and offer full satisfaction to the law by obeying its precepts and enduring its penalty. But that, in turn, required that He be their Surety and Sponsor, that He be so related to them legally and federally that He could fittingly serve as their Substitute. As there was a federal and representative oneness between the first Adam and those he stood for, so there must be a like oneness between the last Adam and those for whom He transacted, that as the guilt of the former was charged to the account of his posterity, so the righteousness of the Latter might be imputed to all His seed.

Yet the truth concerning the position which the Son of God took is not fully expressed by the above statements. It is not sufficient to say that He became their Surety and Substitute. We must go farther back and ask what it was that made it proper that He *should* serve as the Sponsor of His people before their offended Lawgiver and Judge. The answer is *Their covenant union.* Christ served as their Surety and Substitute because He was one with them, and therefore He could and did assume and discharge all their liabilities. In the covenant of grace Christ had said to the Father, "I will declare thy name unto my brethren, in the midst of the church will I sing praise unto thee. And again, I will put my trust in him. And again, Behold I and the children which God hath given me" (Heb. 2:12-13). Most blessedly is that explained in what immediately follows: "Forasmuch then as the children are partakers of flesh and blood, he also himself likewise took part of the same," therefore He is not ashamed to call them brothers. *Federation* is the repository of this amazing mercy, *identification* the key which unlocks it. Christ came not to strangers but to His "brethren"; He assumed human nature, not in order to procure a people for Himself, but to secure a people already His (Matt. 1:21; Eph. 1:4).

Since a union has existed between Christ and His people from all eternity, it inevitably follows that when He came to this earth He took on Himself their debts, and now that He has gone to heaven they must be clothed (Isa. 61:10) with all the rewardableness of His perfect obedience. This is very much more than a technicality of theology, being the strongest buttress of all in the walls of truth which protect the atonement, though it is one of the most frequently and fiercely assailed by its enemies. Men have argued that the punishment of the innocent Christ as though He were guilty was an outrage upon justice. In the human realm, to punish a person for something when he is neither responsible nor guilty is, beyond question, unjust. But that objection is invalid and entirely pointless in connection with the Lord Jesus, for He voluntarily entered the place and lot of His people in such an intimate way that it could be said, "For both he that sanctifieth and they who are sanctified *are all of one*" (Heb. 2:11). They are not only one in nature, but are also so united in the sight of God and before His law as to involve an identification of legal relations and reciprocal obligations and rights. "By the obedience of one shall many be made [legally constituted] righteous" (Rom. 5:19).

It was required of the Surety of God's people that He should not only render full and perfect obedience to the precepts of the law, and thereby provide the meritorious means of their justification, but should also make full satisfaction for their sins by having visited upon Him the curse of the law. But before that penalty could be inflicted, the guilt of the transgressors must be transferred to Him; that is to say, their sins must be judicially imputed to Him. To that arrangement the holy One willingly consented, so that He who "knew no sin" was legally "made sin" for them (II Cor. 5:21). God laid on Him the iniquities of them all, and then the sword of divine justice struck Him (Zech. 13:7), exacting full satisfaction. Without the shedding of blood there is no remission of sin. Blotting out our transgressions, procuring for us the favor of God, purchasing the heavenly inheritance, required the death of Christ. That which demanded the death sentence was the guilt of our sins. Let *that* be removed, and condemnation for us is gone forever. But how could guilt be "removed"? Only by its being transferred to another. The punishment due to the church was borne by her Surety and Substitute. God charged to Him all the sins of His elect, and moved against Him accordingly, visiting on Him His judicial wrath.

How marvelous are the ways of God. As death was destroyed by death— the death of God's Son—so sin by sin—the greatest that was ever committed, the crucifixion of Christ—putting it away as far as the East is from the West. Because God imputed the trespasses of His people to their Surety, He was condemned that they might be acquitted. Christ took upon Him their accumulated and incalculable debt and, by discharging it, made them forever free and solvent. By His precious blood all their iniquities were expiated, so that the triumphant challenge rings out: "Who shall lay any thing to the charge of God's elect?" (Rom. 8:33). Throughout His life and by His death Christ was repaying and repairing all that injury which the sins of the church had done to the demonstrative glory of God. God now remits the sins of all who truly believe in Christ, because Deity has received a vicarious but full satisfaction for them in the person of their Substitute. Through Christ they are delivered from the wrath to come. Necessarily so, for God's acceptance of the Lamb's sacrifice obtained the eternal redemption of all for whom it was offered. Just as a storm cloud empties itself on earth and then melts away under the rays of the sun, so when the storm of divine judgment had exhausted itself upon the cross our sins disappeared from before God's face, and we were received into His everlasting favor.

Wonderful as was the work that the incarnate Son performed *for* His people, something more was still needed in order to provide a *complete* remedy for their complicated ruin, for the former covered only the *legal* aspects of their plight. A miracle of grace needed to be worked *in* them in order to make them experientially worthy of everlasting glory; indeed, such a work was absolutely indispensable to fit them to commune with God in this life. His elect needed to be quickened into newness of life, their enmity against God destroyed, their darkness dispelled, their wills freed, their love of sin and hatred of holiness rectified. In a word, they needed to experience a thorough change of heart, a principle of grace had to be communicated to them, and they needed to be made new creatures in Christ.

That miracle of grace is performed by the Holy Spirit in those who are "by nature the children of wrath, even as others" (Eph. 2:3). But how little this is realized today. Insistence on this fact has all but disappeared from the modern pulpit, even in those who pride themselves on being orthodox. The work of the Spirit *in the saving of sinners* has no place in the creed of many a churchgoer; and where it is nominally acknowledged it possesses no real weight and exerts no practical influence.

In the majority of places where the Lord Jesus is still formally owned as the only Saviour, the current teaching is that He has made it *possible* for men to be saved, but that they themselves must decide whether or not they will be saved; thus the greatest of all God's works is left contingent on the fickle will of men as to whether it is a success or a failure. Narrowing the circle to those places where it is still held that the Spirit has a mission and ministry in connection with the gospel, the general idea prevailing is that, when the Word is faithfully preached, the Spirit convicts men of sin and reveals to them their need of a Saviour; but beyond that, very few are prepared to go. The popular view is that the sinner has to cooperate with the Spirit, that he must yield himself to His "striving," or he will not and cannot be saved. But such a pernicious and God-insulting concept repudiates two cardinal facts. To affirm that the natural man is capable of cooperating with the Spirit is to deny that he is "dead in trespasses and sins," for a dead man is powerless to do any good. To say that the specific operations of the Spirit in a man's heart and conscience are capable of being so resisted as to thwart His endeavors is to deny His omnipotence.

The solemn and unpalatable fact is that were the Spirit of God to suspend His operations, not a single person on earth would savingly benefit from the redemptive work of Christ. The natural man is such an enemy to God and so obstinate in his rebellion that he dislikes a holy Christ, and remains opposed to *His* way of salvation until his heart is divinely renewed. The criminal darkness and delusion which fill every soul in which sin reigns cannot be removed by any agent but God the Spirit—by His giving a new heart and enlightening the understanding to perceive the exceeding sinfulness of sin. There are indeed thousands of people ready to respond to the fatal error that sinners may be saved *without* throwing down the weapons of their warfare against God. There are many who receive Christ as their Saviour, but are unwilling to surrender to Him as their Lord. They would like His rest, but they refuse His yoke, without which His rest cannot be had. His promises appeal to them, but they have no heart for His precepts. They will believe in an imaginary Christ who is suited to their corrupt nature, but they despise and reject the Christ of God. Like the multitudes of old, they are pleased with His loaves and fishes; but for His heart-searching, flesh-withering, sin-condemning teaching they have no appetite. Nothing but the miracle-working power of the Spirit can change them.

C. H. Spurgeon stated:

> Man is utterly and entirely averse to everything that is good and right. "The carnal mind is enmity against God, for it is not subject to the law of God, neither indeed can be" (Romans 8, 7). Turn you all Scripture through, and you will find continually the will of man described as being contrary to the things of God. What said Christ in that text so often quoted by the Arminian to disprove the very doctrine which it clearly states? What did Christ say to those who imagined that men would come *without* Divine influence? He said, first, "No man can come unto Me, except the Father which hath sent Me draw him"; but He said something more strong—"Ye *will not* come unto Me that ye might have life." Herein lies the deadly mischief: not only that he is powerless to do good, but that he is powerful enough to do that which is wrong, and that his will is desperately set against everything that is right. Men *will not* come; you

cannot force them to by all your invitations. Until the Spirit draw them, come they neither will, nor can.

The manifold wisdom of God is just as evident in the official task assigned the Holy Spirit as in the work that the Son was commissioned to perform. The miracles of regeneration and sanctification are as wonderful as were the obedience and sufferings, the death and resurrection, of Christ; and the saint is as truly and as deeply indebted to the One as he is to the Other. If it was an act of amazing condescension for God the Son to leave heaven's glory and assume human nature, it was equally so for God the Spirit to descend to this earth and take up His abode in fallen men and women; and if God pointed up the marvel and importance of the one by mighty wonders and signs, so did He in connection with the latter—the song of the angelic choir (Luke 2:13) having its counterpart in the "sound from heaven" (Acts 2:2), the Shekinah "glory" (Luke 2:9) in the "tongues like as of fire" (Acts 2:3). If we admire the gracious and mighty works of Christ in cleansing the leper, strengthening the palsied, giving sight to the blind and imparting life to the dead, no less is the Spirit to be adored for His supernatural operations in quickening lifeless souls, illuminating their minds, delivering them from the dominion of sin, removing their enmity against God, uniting them to Christ and creating in them a love of holiness.

How complete and perfect is the remedy which the grace and wisdom of God have provided for His people. As they were federally in Adam, and therefore held responsible for what he did, so they are federally in Christ, and therefore enjoy all the benefits of His meritorious work. As they were ruined by the breaking of one covenant, so they are restored by the keeping of another. As they were made guilty by Adam's disobedience being charged to their account, so they are justified before the throne of God because the righteousness of their Surety is imputed to them. As they fell under the curse of the law, were alienated from God and became children of wrath, through Christ's redemption they are entitled to the reward of the law, reconciled to God and restored to His favor. As they inherited a corrupt nature from their first head, so they receive a holy nature from their second Head. In every respect the remedy answers to the malady.

Chapter 14

SUMMARY

THE ENTRANCE OF EVIL into the domain of God is admittedly a deep mystery, nevertheless sufficient is revealed in the Scriptures to prevent our forming erroneous views. For instance, it is contrary to the Word of truth to entertain the notion that either the fall of Satan and his angels or that of our first parents took God by surprise or wrecked His plans. For all eternity God designed that this earth should be the stage on which He would display His perfections: in creation, in providence and in redemption (I Cor. 4:9). Accordingly, He foreordained everything which comes to pass in this scene (Acts 15:18; Rom. 11:36; Eph. 1:11). God is not idly looking on from a far-distant world at the happenings of this earth, but is Himself ordering and shaping everything to the ultimate promotion of His glory—not only in spite of the opposition of men and Satan, but by means of them, everything being made to serve His purpose. Nor did the introduction of evil into the universe take place simply by the bare permission of the Most High, for nothing can come to pass that is contrary to His decreed will. Rather, for wise and holy reasons, God foreordained to allow His mutable creatures to fall, thereby affording an occasion for Him to make a further and fuller exhibition of His attributes.

God's Overruling

From *God's* standpoint the result of Adam's probation was left in no uncertainty. Before He formed him out of the dust of the ground and breathed into his nostrils the breath of life, He knew exactly how the appointed testing of Him would eventuate. But more: God had *decreed* that Adam should eat of the forbidden fruit. That is certain from I Peter 1:19-20, which tells us that the shedding of Christ's blood was verily "foreordained before the foundation of the world" (cf. Rev. 13:8). As Witsius rightly affirmed of Adam's sin, "If foreknown it was also predestinated: thus Peter joins together 'the determinate counsel and foreknowledge of God' (Acts 2, 23)." In full harmony with that fact, note that it was God Himself who placed in Eden the tree of the knowledge of good and evil. Moreover, as Twisse, the celebrated moderator of the Westminster Assembly, asked in 1653, "Did not the Devil provoke Eve and Adam to sin against God in paradise? Could not God have kept the Devil off? Why did He not? Doth it not manifestly appear that it

205

was God's will to have them tempted, to have them provoked unto sin? And why not?" God overruled it for a higher manifestation of His glory. Just as without night we could not admire the beauty of day, so sin was necessary as a dark background on which the divine grace and mercy should shine forth more resplendently (Rom. 5:20).

It has been asserted dogmatically by some that God could not have prevented the fall of our first parents without reducing them to mere machines. It is argued that since the Creator endowed man with a free will he must be left entirely to his own volitions, that he cannot be coerced, still less compelled, without destroying his moral agency. That may seem to be good reasoning, yet it is refuted by Holy Writ. God declared to Abimelech concerning Abraham's wife, "I also *withheld thee* from sinning against me: therefore suffered I thee not to touch her" (Gen. 20:6). It is *not impossible* for God to exert His power over man without destroying his responsibility, for *there* is a case in point where He restricted man's freedom to do evil and prevented him from committing sin. In like manner, He prevented Balaam from carrying out the wicked desires of his heart (Num. 22:38; 23:3, 20). Also, He prevented kingdoms from making war on Jehoshaphat (II Chron. 17:10). Why, then, did not God exert His power and prevent Adam and Eve from sinning? Because their fall served His own wise and blessed designs.

But does that make God the Author of sin? The culpable Author, no; for as Piscator long ago pointed out, "Culpability is failing to do what ought to be done." Clearly it was the divine will that sin should enter this world, or it would not have done so. God had the power to prevent it. Nothing ever comes to pass except what He has decreed. As John Gill said, "Though God's decree made Adam's fall infallibly necessary *as to the event*, yet not by way of efficiency, or by force and compulsion on the will." Nor did God's decree in any way excuse the wickedness of our first parents or exempt them from punishment. They were left entirely free to the exercise of their nature, and therefore were fully accountable and blameworthy for their actions. While the tree of the knowledge of good and evil and the solicitations of the serpent to eat its fruit were *the occasion* of their sinning, yet they were *not the cause.* *That* lay in their voluntarily ceasing to be in subjection to the will of their Maker and rightful Lord. God is the efficient Author of whatever works of holiness men perform, but He is not the Author of their sins.

God's decree that sin should enter this world was a secret hid in Himself. Our first parents knew nothing of it, and that made all the difference so far as their responsibility was concerned. Had they been informed of the divine purpose and the certainty of its fulfillment by their actions, the case would have been radically altered. They were unacquainted with the Creator's secret counsels. What concerned them was God's revealed will, and *that* was quite plain. He had forbidden them to eat of a certain tree, and that was enough. But He went further, even warning Adam of the dire consequences which should follow his disobedience. Death would be the penalty. Thus, transgression on his part was without excuse. God created Adam morally "upright," without any bias toward evil. Nor did He inject any evil thought or desire into Eve. "God cannot be tempted with evil, neither tempteth he any man" (James 1:13). Instead, when the serpent came and tempted Eve, God caused her to remember His prohibition. Consider the wonderful wisdom of God, for though He had predestinated the fall of our first parents, yet in no sense was He the Instigator or Approver of their sins, and their accountability was left entirely unimpaired.

These two things we must believe if the truth is not to be repudiated: that God has foreordained everything that comes to pass; that He is in no way blamable for any of man's wickedness, the criminality thereof being wholly his. The decree of God in no way infringes on man's moral agency, for it neither forces nor hinders man's will, though it orders and bounds its actions. Both the existence and operations of sin are subservient to the counsels of God's will, yet that does not lessen the evil of its nature or the guilt of its committers. Someone has said that though God does not esteem evil to be good, yet He accounts it good that evil should be. Nevertheless sin is that "abominable thing" (Jer. 44:4) which the holy One always hates. In connection with the crucifixion of Christ there was the agency of God (John 19:11; Acts 4:27-28), the agency of Satan (Gen. 3:13; Luke 22:53) and the agency of men. Yet God neither concurred nor cooperated with the internal actions of men's wills, charging them with the wickedness of their deed (Acts 2:23). God overrules evil for good (Gen. 45:8; Ps. 76:10), and therefore He is as truly sovereign over sin and hell as He is over holiness and heaven.

God's Perfect Plan

God cannot will or do anything that is wrong: "The LORD is righteous in all his ways, and holy in all his works" (Ps. 145:17). He therefore stands in no need whatsoever of vindication by any of His puny creatures. Yet even the finite mind, when illumined by the Spirit of truth, can perceive how God's admittance of evil into this world provided an occasion for Him to display His ineffable perfections in the fullest manner and to the greatest degree. He thus magnified Himself by bringing a clean thing out of an unclean, and by securing to Himself a return of praise from redeemed sinners such as He does not receive from the unfallen angels. Horrible and terrible beyond words was the revolt of man against his Maker, and fearful and total the ruin which it brought upon him and all his posterity. Nevertheless, the wisdom of God contrived a way to save a part of the human race in a manner by which He is more glorified than by all His works of creation and providence; also, the misery of sinners is made the occasion of their greater happiness. This is a never ending wonder.

That way of salvation, determined and defined in the terms of the everlasting covenant of grace, was one by which each of the divine Persons is exceedingly honored. Jonathan Edwards long ago pointed out:

Herein the work of redemption is distinguished from all the other works of God. The attributes of God are glorious in His other works; but the three persons of the Trinity are *distinctly glorified* in no other work as in this of redemption. In this work every distinct person has His distinct parts and offices assigned personal properties, relations, and economical offices. The redeemed have an equal concern with and dependence upon each person in this affair, and owe equal honour and praise to each of Them. The Father appoints and provides the Redeemer, and accepts the price of redemption. The Son is the Redeemer and the price—He redeems by offering up Himself. The Holy Spirit immediately communicates to us the thing purchased; yea, and He is the good purchased. The sum of what Christ purchased for us is holiness and happiness. Christ was "made a curse for us . . . that we might receive the promise of the Spirit through faith" (Gal. 3:13, 14). The blessedness of the redeemed consists in partaking of Christ's fulness, which consists in partaking of that Spirit which is not given by measure unto Him. This is the oil that was poured upon the Head of the Church, which ran down to the members of His body (Psalm 133, 2).

It is a serious mistake to regard the Lord Jesus as our Saviour to the exclusion of the saving operations of both the Father and the Spirit. Had not the Father eternally purposed the salvation of His people, chosen them in Christ and bestowed them on Him; had He not entered into an everlasting compact with Him, commissioned Him to become incarnate, and redeemed them, His Beloved never would have left heaven in order that He might die, the just for the unjust. Accordingly, we find that He who loved the world so much that He gave His only begotten Son has ascribed to Him the salvation of the church: "Who hath *saved* us, and called us . . . according to his own purpose and grace, which was given us in Christ Jesus before the world began" (II Tim. 1:9). Equally necessary are the operations of the Holy Spirit to actually apply to the hearts of God's elect the good of what Christ did for them. He is the One who convicts of sin and imparts faith to them. Therefore their salvation is also ascribed to Him: "God hath from the beginning chosen you to salvation *through* sanctification of the Spirit and belief of the truth" (II Thess. 2:13). A careful reading of Titus 3:4-6 shows the three Persons acting together in this connection: "God our Saviour" in verse 4 is plainly the Father. "He saved us, by the washing of regeneration, and renewing of the Holy Ghost" (v. 5), "which he shed on us abundantly through Jesus Christ our Saviour" (v. 6). Compare the doxology of II Corinthians 13:14.

It is very profitable to ponder the many *promises* which the Father made to and respecting Christ. Upon the Son's acceptance of the exacting terms of the covenant of grace, the Father agreed to invest Him with a threefold office, thereby authenticating His mission with the broad seal of heaven: the prophetic office (Deut. 18:15, 18; cf. Acts 3:22), the priestly office (Heb. 5:5; 6:20) and the kingly office (Jer. 23:5; Ps. 89:27). Thus Christ did not run without being sent. God the Father promised to furnish and equip the Mediator with a plentiful effusion of the graces and gifts of the Holy Spirit (Isa. 42:1-2; cf. Matt. 12:27; Acts 10:38). He promised to strengthen Christ, supporting and protecting Him in His execution of the tremendous work of redemption (Isa. 42:1, 6; Ps. 89:21). This undertaking would be attended with such difficulties that creature power, though unimpaired by sin, would have been quite inadequate for it. Therefore the Father assured Christ of all needed help and power to carry Him through the opposition and trials He would encounter. Note how the incarnate Son rested upon those promises (Ps. 16:1; 22:10; Isa. 50:6-8; 69:4-7).

The Father promised to raise the Messiah from the dead (Ps. 21:8; 102:23-24; Isa. 53:10), and it is blessed to observe how Christ laid hold of the promise (Ps. 16:8-11). Promise of His ascension was also made to Christ (Ps. 24:3, 7; 68:18; 89:27; Isa. 52:13). That promise too was appropriated by the Saviour while still on earth (Luke 24:26). Having faithfully fulfilled the terms of the covenant, Christ was highly exalted by God, and made to be Lord and Christ (Acts 2:36), God seating Him at His own right hand. That is an economical lordship, a dispensation committed to Christ as the God-Man. God has crowned with glory and honor the One whom men crowned with thorns. The "government" is upon His shoulder.

Christ was assured of a "seed" (Isa. 53:10). His crucifixion must not be regarded as a dishonor to Him, since it was the very means ordained of God whereby He should propagate numerous spiritual progeny. He referred to this in John 12:24. The "seed" promised Christ occupies a prominent place in Psalm 89 (see vv. 3-4, 29-36; cf. 22:30). Thus, from the outset Christ was assured of the success of His undertaking.

As there were two parts to the covenant, so the elect were given to Christ in a twofold manner. As He was to fulfill its terms, they were entrusted to Him as a *charge*; but in fulfillment of the covenant, the Father promised to bestow them on Him as a *reward*. In the former sense, they were regarded as fallen, and Christ was held responsible for their salvation. They were committed to Him as lost and straying sheep (Isa. 53:6) whom He must seek out and bring into the fold (John 10:16). In the latter sense, they are viewed as the fruit of His travail, the trophies of His victory over sin, Satan and death; as His crown of rejoicing in the day to come, when He shall be "glorified in his saints, and . . . admired in all them that believe" (II Thess. 1:10); as the beloved wife of the Lamb.

Finally, God made promise of the Holy Spirit to Christ. The Spirit was with Christ during the days of His flesh, anointing Him to preach the gospel (Isa. 61:1) and work miracles (Matt. 12:28). But He received the Spirit in another manner (Ps. 45:7; Acts 2:33) and for a different purpose after His ascension. He, as the God-Man Mediator, was given the administration of the Spirit's activities and operations toward the world in providence and toward the church in grace. John 7:39 and 16:7 make it clear that the Spirit's advent was dependent on Christ's exaltation. That assurance was also appropriated by Christ before He left this scene. On the point of His departure, He said to His disciples, "Behold, I send the promise of my Father upon you" (Luke 24:49), which was duly accomplished ten days later. In full accord with what has just been pointed out, we hear the Saviour saying from heaven, "These things saith he that hath the seven Spirits of God" (Rev. 3:1). He "hath," to communicate to His redeemed individually and to His churches corporately.

The grand design in the Spirit's descent to this earth was to glorify Christ (John 16:14). He is here to witness to the Saviour's exaltation, Pentecost being God's seal upon the Messiahship of Jesus. The Spirit is here to take Christ's place. That is clear from Christ's words to the apostles: "I will pray the Father, and he shall give you *another* Comforter, that he may abide with you for ever" (John 14:16). Until then the Lord Jesus had been their Comforter, but He was on the eve of returning to heaven. Nevertheless, He graciously assured them, "I will not leave you orphans: I will come to you" (John 14:18, margin). This promise was fulfilled spiritually in the advent of His Deputy. The Spirit is here to further Christ's cause. The word Paraclete (translated "Comforter" in John's gospel) is rendered "advocate" at the beginning of the second chapter of his first epistle, and an advocate is one who appears as the representative of another. The Spirit is here to interpret and vindicate Christ, to administer for Christ in His kingdom and church. He is here to make good His redeeming purpose, by applying the benefits of His sacrifice to those in whose behalf it was offered. He is here to endue Christ's servants (Luke 24:49).

It is of first importance to recognize and realize that the Lord Jesus obtained for God's people not only redemption from the penal consequences of sin, but also their personal sanctification. How little this is emphasized today. In far too many instances those who think and speak of the "salvation" which Christ has purchased attach no further idea to the concept than that of deliverance from condemnation, omitting deliverance from the love, dominion and power of sin. But the latter is no less essential, and is as definite a blessing as the former. It is just as necessary for fallen creatures to be delivered from the pollution and moral impotence which they have contracted as it is to be exempted from the penalties which they have incurred, so that when reinstated in the favor of God they may at the same time be capacitated to love, serve and enjoy Him forever. And in this respect also the divine remedy meets all the requirements of our sinful malady (see II Cor. 5:15; Eph. 5:25-27; Titus 2:14; Heb. 9:14). This is accomplished by the gracious operations of Christ's Spirit, begun in regeneration, continued throughout their earthly lives, consummated in heaven.

God's Honor

Not only is the triune God more honored by redemption than He was dishonored by the defection of His creatures, but His people also are greatly the gainers. That too magnifies the divine wisdom. It would have been wonderful indeed had they been merely restored to their original state; but it is far more wonderful that they should be brought to a much higher state of blessedness—that the fall should be the occasion of their exaltation! Their sin deserved eternal wretchedness, yet everlasting bliss is their portion. They are now favored with a greater manifestation of the glory of God and a fuller discovery of His love than they would have had otherwise, and in those two things their happiness principally consists. They are brought into a much closer and endearing relation to God. They are now not merely holy creatures but heirs of God and joint heirs with Christ. The Son having taken their nature upon Him, they have become His "brethren," members of His body, His spouse. They are thereby provided with more powerful motives and inducements to love and serve Him than they had in their unfallen condition. The more of God's love we apprehend, the more we love Him in return. Throughout eternity the knowledge of God's love in giving His dear Son to and for us, and Christ's dying in our stead, will fix our hearts upon Him in a manner which His favors to Adam never could have done.

It is in the gospel that the wonderful remedy for all our ills is made known. That glorious gospel proclaims that Christ is able to save to the uttermost them that come to God by Him. It tells us that the Son of Man came to seek and to save that which was lost. It announces that sinners, even the chief of sinners, are the ones that are freely invited to come. It publishes liberty to Satan's captives and the opening of doors to sin's prisoners. It reveals that God has chosen the greatest of sinners to be the everlasting monuments of His mercy. It declares that the blood of Jesus Christ, God's Son, cleanses believers from all sin. It furnishes hope to the most hopeless cases. The miracles which Christ performed in the bodies of men were types of His miracles of grace on sinners' souls. No case was beyond His healing. He not only gave sight to the blind and cleansing to the leper, but delivered the demon-possessed and bestowed life on the dead. He never refused a single appeal made to His compassion. Whatever the sinner's record, if he will trust in the atoning sacrifice of Christ he will be saved, now and forever.

Part II

THE DOCTRINE OF MAN'S IMPOTENCE

Chapter 15

INTRODUCTION

THE TITLE of this second section of our book may occasion a raising of the eyebrows. That we should designate the spiritual helplessness of fallen man a "doctrine" is likely to cause surprise, for it is certainly not so regarded in most circles today. Yet this is hardly to be wondered at. Didactic preaching has fallen into such general disuse that more than one important doctrine is no longer heard from the pulpits. If on the one hand there is a deplorable lack of a clear and definite portrayal of the character of God, on the other there is also a woeful absence of any lucid and comprehensive presentation of the teaching of Scripture concerning the nature and condition of man. Such failure at either point leads to the most disastrous consequences. A study of this neglected subject is therefore timely and urgent.

Timely and Urgent Study

It is of the utmost importance that people should clearly understand and be made thoroughly aware of their spiritual impotence, for thus alone is a foundation laid for bringing them to see and feel their imperative need of divine grace for salvation. So long as sinners think they have it in their own power to deliver themselves from their death in trespasses and sins, they will never come to Christ that they might have life, for "the whole need not a physician, but they that are sick." So long as people imagine they labor under no insuperable inability to comply with the call of the gospel, they never will be conscious of their entire dependence on Him alone who is able to work in them "all the good pleasure of his goodness, and the work of faith with power" (II Thess. 1:11). So long as the creature is puffed up with a sense of his own ability to respond to God's requirements, he will never become a suppliant at the footstool of divine mercy.

A careful perusal of what the Word of God has to say on this subject leaves us in no doubt about the awful state of spiritual serfdom into which the fall has brought man. The depravity, blindness and deafness of all mankind in things of a spiritual nature are continually inculcated and emphatically insisted on throughout the Scriptures. Not only is the total inability of the natural man to obtain salvation by deeds of the law frequently asserted, but his utter helplessness in himself to comply with the terms of the gospel is also strongly affirmed—not indirectly and occasionally, but expressly and continually. Both in the Old Testament and in the New, in the declarations

215

of the prophets, of the Lord Christ, and of His apostles, the bondage of the natural man to Satan is often depicted, and his complete impotence to turn to God for deliverance is solemnly and unequivocally set forth. Ignorance or misconception on the matter is therefore inexcusable.

Nevertheless the fact remains that this is a doctrine which is little understood and rarely insisted upon. Notwithstanding the clear and uniform testimony of the Scriptures, the actual conditions of men, their alienation from God, their sinful inability to return to Him, are but feebly apprehended and seldom heard even in orthodox quarters. The fact is that the whole trend of modern thought is in the very opposite direction. For the past century, and increasingly so during the last few decades, the greatness of man—his dignity, his development and his achievements—has been the predominant theme of pulpit and press. The antiscriptural theory of evolution is a blank detail of the fall and its dire consequences, and even where the Darwinian hypothesis has not been accepted, its pernicious influences have been more or less experienced.

The evil effects from the promulgation of the evolutionary lie are far more widespread than most Christians realize. Such a philosophy (if it is entitled to be called that) has induced multitudes of people to suppose that their state is far different from, and vastly superior to, the fearful diagnosis given in Holy Writ. Even among those who have not accepted without considerable reservation the idea that man is slowly but surely progressing, the great majority have been encouraged to believe that their case is far better than it actually is. Consequently, when a servant of God boldly affirms that all the descendants of Adam are so completely enslaved by sin that they are utterly unable to take one step toward Christ for deliverance, he is looked upon as a doleful pessimist or a crazy fanatic. To speak of the spiritual impotence of the natural man is, in our day, to talk in an unknown tongue.

Not only does the appalling ignorance of our generation cause the servant of God to labor under a heavy handicap when seeking to present the scriptural account of man's total inability for good; he is also placed at a serious disadvantage by virtue of the marked distastefulness of this truth. The subject of his moral impotence is far from being a pleasing one to the natural man. He wants to be told that all he needs to do is exert himself, that salvation lies within the power of his will, that he is the determiner of his own destiny. Pride, with its strong dislike of being a debtor to the sovereign grace of God, rises up against it. Self-esteem, with its rabid repugnance of anything which lays the creature in the dust, hotly resents what is so humiliating. Consequently, this truth is either openly rejected or, if seemingly received, is turned to a wrong use.

Moreover, when it is insisted on that man's bondage to sin is both voluntary and culpable, that the guilt for his inability to turn to God or to do anything pleasing in His sight lies at his own door, that his spiritual impotence consists in nothing but the depravity of his own heart and his inveterate enmity against God, then the hatefulness of this doctrine is speedily demonstrated.

While men are allowed to think that their spiritual helplessness is involuntary rather than willful, innocent rather than criminal, something to be pitied rather than blamed, they may receive this truth with a measure of toleration; but let them be told that they themselves have forged the shackles which hold them in captivity to sin, that God counts them responsible for the corruption of their hearts, and that their incapability of being holy constitutes the very essence of their guilt, and loud will be their outcries against such a flesh-withering truth.

However repellent this truth may be, it must not be withheld from men. The minister of Christ is not sent forth to please or entertain his congregation, but to declare the counsel of God, and not merely those parts of it which may meet with their approval and acceptance, but *"all* the counsel of God" (Acts 20:27). If he deliberately omits that which raises their ire, he betrays his trust. Once he starts whittling down his divinely given commission there will be no end to the process, for one class will murmur against this portion of the truth and another against that. The servant of God has nothing to do with the response which is made to his preaching; his business is to deliver the Word of God in its unadulterated purity and leave the results to the One who has called him. And he may be assured at the outset that unless many in his congregation are seriously disturbed by his message, he has failed to deliver it in its clarity.

A Resented Doctrine

No matter how hotly this doctrine of man's spiritual impotence is resented by both the profane and the religious world, it must not be withheld through cowardice. Christ, our supreme Exemplar, announced this truth emphatically and constantly. To the Pharisees He said, "O generation of vipers, how can ye, being evil, speak good things? For out of the abundance of the heart the mouth speaketh" (Matt. 12:34). Men's hearts are so vile, it is utterly impossible that anything holy should issue from them. They can no more change their nature by an effort of will than a leper might heal himself by his own volition. Christ further said, "How can ye believe, which receive honour one of another, and seek not the honour that cometh from God only?" (John 5:44). It is a moral impossibility—pride and humility are opposites. Those who seek to please self and those who sincerely aim at the approbation of God belong to two entirely different stocks.

On another occasion the Lord Christ asked, "Why do ye not understand my speech?" to which He Himself answered, "Even because ye cannot hear my word" (John 8:43). There is no mistaking His meaning here and no evading the force of His solemn utterance. The message of Christ was hateful to their worldly and wicked hearts and could no more be acceptable to them than would wholesome food to birds accustomed to feed on carrion. Man cannot act contrary to his nature; one might as well expect fire to burn downward or water flow upward. "Ye are of your father the devil, and the lusts of your father ye will do" (John 8:44) said the Saviour to the Jews. And what was their response? "Say we not well that thou art a Samaritan, and has a devil?" (v. 48). Sufficient for the servant to be as his Master.

Now if such is the case with the natural man that he can no more break the bonds which hold him in captivity to Satan than he could restore the dead to life, ought he not to be faithfully informed of his wretched condition? If he is so helpless and hopeless in himself that he cannot turn from sin to holiness, that he cannot please God, that he cannot take one step toward Christ for salvation, is it not a kindness to acquaint him with his spiritual impotence, to shatter his dreams of self-sufficiency, to expose the delusion that he is lord of himself? In fact, is it not positively cruel to leave him alone in his complacency and make no effort to bring him face to face with the desperateness of his depravity? Surely anyone with a vestige of charity in his heart will have no difficulty in answering such questions.

It is far from a pleasant task for a physician to tell an unsuspecting patient that his or her heart is organically diseased or to announce to a young person engaging in strenuous activities that his lungs are in such a condition he is totally unfit for violent exertions; nevertheless it is the physician's duty to break such news. Now if this principle holds good in connection with our mortal bodies, how much more so with regard to our never dying spirits. True, there are some doctors who persuade themselves that there are times when it is expedient for them to withhold such information from their patients, but a true physician of souls is never justified in concealing the more distasteful aspect of the truth from those who are under his care. If he is to be free from their blood, he must unsparingly expose the plague of their hearts.

The fact of fallen man's moral inability is indissolubly bound up with the doctrine of his total depravity, and any denial of the one is a repudiation of the other, as any attempt to modify the former is to vitiate the latter. In like manner, the fact of the natural man's impotence to deliver himself from the bondage of sin is inseparably connected with the truth of regeneration; for unless we are without strength in ourselves, what need is there for God to work a miracle of grace in us? It is, then, the reality of the sinner's helplessness which provides the dark background necessary for the gospel, and just in proportion as we are made aware of our helplessness shall we really value the mercy proffered us in the gospel. On the other hand, while we cherish the delusion that we have power to turn to God at any time, just so long we shall continue procrastinating and thereby despise the gracious overtures of the gospel.

William Shedd stated:

> A sense of danger excites; a sense of security puts to sleep. A company of gamblers in the sixth story are told that the building is on fire. One of them answers, "We have the key to the fire escape," and all continue the game. Suddenly one exclaims, "The key is lost"; all immediately spring to their feet and endeavour to escape.

Just so long as the sinner believes—because of his erroneous notion of the freedom of his will—that he has the power to repent and believe at any moment, he will defer faith and repentance; he will not so much as beg God to work these graces in him.

The first office of the preacher is to stain the pride of all human glory, to bring down the high looks of man, to make him aware of his sinful perversity, to make him feel that he is unworthy of the least of all God's mercies. His business is to strip him of the rags of his self-righteousness and to shatter his self-sufficiency; to make him conscious of his utter dependence on the mere grace of God. Only he who finds himself absolutely helpless will surrender himself to sovereign grace. Only he who feels himself already sinking under the billows of a justly deserved condemnation will cry out, "Lord, save me, I perish." Only he who has been brought to despair will place the crown of glory on the only head entitled to wear it. Though God alone can make a man conscious of his impotence, He is pleased to use the means of the truth—faithfully dispensed, effectually applied by the Spirit—in doing so.

Chapter 16

REALITY

THE SPIRITUAL IMPOTENCE of the natural man is no mere product of theological dyspepsia, nor is it a dismal dogma invented during the Dark Ages. It is a solemn fact affirmed by Holy Writ, manifested throughout human history, confirmed in the conscious experience of every genuinely convicted soul. The moral powerlessness of the sinner is not proclaimed in the pulpit today, nor is it believed in by professing Christians generally. When it is insisted that man is so completely the bondslave of sin that he cannot move toward God, the vast majority will regard the statement as utterly unreasonable and reject it with scorn. To tell those who consider themselves to be hale and hearty that they are without strength strikes them as a preposterous assumption unworthy of serious consideration.

Objections of Unbelief

When a servant of God does press this unwelcome truth on his hearers, the fertile mind of unbelief promptly replies with one objection after another. If we are totally devoid of spiritual ability, then assuredly we must be aware of the fact. But that is far from being the case. The skeptic says we are very much aware of our power to do that which is pleasing in God's sight; even though we do not perform it, we *could* if we would. He also contends that were we so completely the captives of Satan as is declared, we should not be free agents at all. Such a concept as that we will not allow for a moment. Another point of the skeptic is that if man has no power to do that which God requires, then obviously he is not a responsible creature, for he cannot justly be held accountable to do that which is beyond his powers to achieve.

We must establish the fact of man's spiritual impotence and show that it is a solemn reality; for until we do this, it is useless to discuss the nature of that impotence, its seat, its extent or its cause. And it is to the inspired Word of God alone that we shall make our appeal; for if the Scriptures of truth plainly teach this doctrine, then we are on sure ground and may not reject its testimony even though no one else on earth believed it. If the divine oracles affirm it, then none of the objections brought against it by the carnal mind can have any weight with us, though in due course we shall endeavor to show that these objections are as pointless as they are groundless.

In approaching more definitely the task now before us it should be pointed out that, strictly speaking, it is the subject of human depravity which we are going to write on; yet to have so designated this section would be rather misleading as we are going to confine ourselves to only one aspect of it. The spiritual impotence of the natural man forms a distinct and separate branch of his depravity. The state of evil into which the fall has plunged us is far more dreadful and its dire consequences far more wide-reaching than is commonly supposed. The common idea is that though man has fallen he is not so badly damaged but that he may recover himself, providing he properly exercises his remaining strength or with due attention improves the help proffered him. But his case is vastly more serious than that.

A. A. Hodge said:

> The three main elements involved in the consequences entailed by the sin of Adam upon his posterity are these: First, the guilt, or just penal responsibility of Adam's first sin or apostatising act, which is imputed or judicially charged upon his descendants, whereby every child is born into the world in a state of antenatal forfeiture or condemnation. Second, the entire depravity of our nature, involving a sinful innate disposition inevitably leading to actual transgression. Third, the entire inability of the soul to change its own nature, or to do any thing spiritually good in obedience to the Divine Law.

God's Word on the Subject

Let us consider some of the solemn declarations of our Lord on the third of these dire consequences of the fall. "Verily, verily, I say unto thee, Except a man be born again, he cannot see the kingdom of God" (John 3:3). Until a man is born again he remains in his natural, fallen and depraved state, and so long as that is the case it is utterly impossible for him to discern or perceive divine things. Sin has both darkened his understanding and destroyed his spiritual vision. "The way of the wicked is as darkness: they know not at what they stumble" (Prov. 4:19). Though divine instruction is supplied them, though God has given them His Word in which the way to heaven is plainly marked out, still they are incapable of profiting from it. Moses represented them as groping at noonday (Deut. 28:29), and Job declares, "They meet with darkness in the daytime, and grope in the noonday as in the night" (5:14). Jeremiah depicts them as walking in "slippery ways in the darkness" (23:12).

Now this darkness which envelops the natural man is a moral one, having its seat in the soul. Our Saviour declared, "The light of the body is the eye: if therefore thine eye be single, thy whole body shall be full of light. But if thine eye be evil, thy whole body shall be full of darkness. If therefore the light that is in thee be darkness, how great is that darkness!" (Matt. 6:22-23). The heart is the same to the soul as the eye is to the body. As a sound eye lets in natural light, so a good heart lets in spiritual light; and as a blind eye shuts out natural light, so an evil heart shuts out spiritual light. Accordingly we find the apostle expressly ascribing the darkness of the understanding to the blindness of the heart. He represents all men as "having the understanding darkened, being alienated from the life of God through the ignorance that is in them, because of the blindness of their heart" (Eph. 4:18).

While sinners remain under the entire dominion of a wicked heart they are altogether blind to the spiritual excellence of the character, the works and the ways of God. "Hear now this, O foolish people, and without understanding; which have eyes, and *see not;* which have ears, and hear not" (Jer. 5:21). The natural man is blind. This awful fact was affirmed again and again by our Lord as He addressed hypocritical scribes thus: "blind leaders of the blind," "ye blind guides," "thou blind Pharisee" (Matt. 15:14; 23:24, 26). Paul said: "The god of this world hath blinded the minds of them which believe not" (II Cor. 4:4). There is in the unregenerate mind an incompetence, an incapacity, an inability to understand the things of the Spirit; and Christ's repeated miracle in restoring sight to the naturally blind was designed to teach us our imperative need of the same divine power recovering spiritual vision to our souls.

A question has been raised as to whether this blindness of the natural man is partial or total, whether it is simply a defect of vision or whether he has no vision at all. The nature of his disease may best be defined as spiritual myopia or shortsightedness. He is able to see clearly objects which are nearby, but distant ones lie wholly beyond the range of his vision. In other words, the mind's eye of the sinner is capable of perceiving natural things, but he has no ability to see *spiritual* things. Holy Writ states that the one who "lacketh these things," namely, the graces of faith, virtue, knowledge, and so forth, mentioned in II Peter 1:5-7, is "blind, and cannot see afar off" (v. 9). The Book therefore urges him to receive "eyesalve" from Christ, that he may see (Rev. 3:18).

For this very purpose the Son of God came into the world: to give "deliverance to the captives, and recovering of sight to the blind" (Luke 4:18). Concerning those who are the subjects of this miracle of grace it is said, "Ye were sometimes darkness, but now are ye light in the Lord" (Eph. 5:8). This is the fulfillment of our Lord's promise: "I am the light of the world: he that followeth me shall not walk in darkness, but shall have the light of life" (John 8:12). God is light, therefore those who are alienated from Him are in complete spiritual darkness. They do not see the frightful danger to which they are exposed. Though they are led captive by Satan from day to day and year to year, they are totally unaware of his malignant influence over them. They are blind to the nature and tendency of their religious performances, failing to perceive that no matter how earnestly they engage in them, they cannot be acceptable to God while their minds are at enmity against Him. They are blind to the way and means of recovery.

The awful thing is that the natural man is quite blind to the blindness of his heart which is insensibly leading him to "the blackness of darkness for ever" (Jude 13). That is why the vast majority live so securely and peacefully. It has always appeared strange to the godly why the ungodly can be so unconcerned while under sentence of death, and conduct themselves so frivolously and gaily while exposed to the wrath to come. John was surprised to see the wicked spending their days in carnality and feasting. David was grieved at the prosperity of the wicked and could not account for their not being in trouble as other men. Amos was astonished to behold the sinners in Zion living at ease, putting the evil day far from them, lying on beds of ivory. Nothing but their spiritual blindness can explain the conduct of the vast majority of mankind, crying peace and safety when exposed to impending destruction.

Man's Opposition

Since all sinners are involved in such spiritual darkness as makes them unaware of their present condition and condemnation, it is not surprising that they are so displeased when their fearful danger is plainly pointed out. Such faithful warning tends to disturb their present peace and comfort and to destroy their future hopes and prospects of happiness. If they were once made to truly realize the imminent danger of the damnation of hell, their ease, security and joy would be completely dispelled. They cannot bear, therefore, to hear the plain truth respecting their wretchedness and guilt. Sinners could not bear to hear the plain teachings of the prophets or Christ on this account; this explains their bitter complaints and fierce opposition. They regard as enemies those who try to befriend them. They stop their ears and run from them.

That the natural man—even the most zealous religionist—has no perception of this spiritual blindness, and that he is highly displeased when charged with it, is evident: "Jesus said, For judgment I am come into this world, that they which see not might see; and that they which see might be made blind. And some of the Pharisees which were with him heard these words, and said unto him, Are we blind also? And Jesus said unto them, If ye were blind, ye should have no sin: but now ye say, We see; therefore your sin remaineth" (John 9:39-41). God's Son became incarnate for the purpose of bringing to light the hidden things of darkness. He came to expose things, that those made conscious of their blindness might receive sight, but that they who had spiritual sight in their own estimation should be "made blind"—judicially abandoned to the pride of their evil hearts. The infatuated Pharisees had no desire for such an experience. Denying their blindness, they were left in their sin.

"Verily, verily, I say unto thee, Except a man be born again, he cannot see the kingdom of God" (John 3:3). He cannot see the things of God because by nature he is enveloped in total spiritual darkness; even though external light shine on him, he has no eyes with which to see. "The light shineth in darkness; and the darkness comprehended it not" (John 1:5). When the Lord of life and light appeared among them, men had no eyes to see His beauty, but despised and rejected Him. And so it is still; every verse in Scripture which treats of the Spirit's illumination confirms this solemn fact. "For God, who commanded the light to shine out of darkness, hath shined in our hearts, to give the light of the knowledge of the glory of God in the face of Jesus Christ" (II Cor. 4:6). This giving of light and knowledge is by divine power, being analogous to that power by which the light at the first creation was provided. As far as spiritual, saving knowledge of the truth is concerned, the mind of fallen man is like the chaos before God said "Let there be light." "Darkness was upon the face of the deep," and in that state it is impossible for men to understand the things of the Spirit.

Not only is the understanding of the natural man completely under the dominion of darkness, but his will is paralyzed against good; and if that is so, the sinner is indeed impotent. This fact was made clear by Christ when He affirmed, "No man can come to me, except the Father which hath sent me draw him" (John 6:44). And why is it that the sinner cannot come to Christ by his own unaided powers? Because he has no inclination to do so and, therefore, no volition in that direction. The Greek might be rendered "Ye will not come to me." There is not the slightest desire in the unregenerate heart to do so.

The will of fallen man is depraved, being completely in bondage to sin. There is not merely a negative lack of inclination, but there is a positive disinclination. The unwillingness consists of aversion: "The carnal mind is enmity against God: for it is not subject to the law of God, *neither indeed can be*" (Rom. 8:7). And not only is there an aversion against God, there is a hatred of Him. Christ said to His disciples, "If the world hate you, ye know that it hated me before it hated you" (John 15:18). This hatred is inveterate obstinacy: "The LORD said unto Moses, I have seen this people, and, behold, it is a stiffnecked people" (Exodus 32:9). "All day long I have stretched forth my hands unto a disobedient and gainsaying people" (Rom. 10:21). Man is incorrigible and in himself his case is hopeless. "Thy people shall be willing in the day of *thy power*" (Ps. 110:3) because they have no power whatever of their own to effect such willingness.

Since we have demonstrated from the Scriptures of truth that the natural man is utterly unable to discern spiritual things, much less to choose them, there is little need for us to labor the point that he is quite incompetent to perform any spiritual act. Nor is this only a logical inference drawn by theologians; it is expressly affirmed in the Word: "So then they that are in the flesh cannot please God" (Rom. 8:8). There is no denying the meaning of that terrible indictment, as there is no likelihood of its originating with man himself. Jeremiah said, "O LORD, I know that the way of man is not in himself: it is not in man that walketh to direct his steps" (10:23). All power to direct our steps in the paths of righteousness was lost by us at the fall, and therefore we are entirely dependent on God to work in us "both to will and to do of his good pleasure" (Phil. 2:13).

Little as this solemn truth of man's moral impotence is known today and widely as it is denied by modern thought and teaching, there was a time when it was generally contended for. In the Thirty-nine Articles of the Church of

England (to which all her ministers must still solemnly and formally subscribe) the Tenth reads thus:

> The condition of man after the fall of Adam is such, that he cannot turn and prepare himself, by his own natural strength and good works to faith and calling upon God. Wherefore we have no power to do good works pleasant and acceptable to God.

In the Westminster Confession of Faith chapter 6 begins thus:

> Our first parents being seduced by the subtilty and temptation of Satan, sinned in eating the forbidden fruit. This their sin God was pleased, according to His wise and holy counsel, to permit, having purposed to order it to His own glory. By this sin they fell from their original righteousness and communion with God, and so became dead in sin, and wholly defiled in all the faculties and parts of soul and body. They being the root of all mankind, the guilt of this sin was imputed, and the same death in sin and corrupted nature conveyed to all their posterity, descending from them by ordinary generation. From this original corruption, whereby we are *utterly indisposed*, disabled, and made opposite to all good, and wholly inclined to all evil, do proceed all actual transgressions.

Chapter 17

NATURE

THE DOCTRINE we are now considering is a most solemn and forbidding one. Certainly it is one which could never have been invented by man, for it is far too humbling and distasteful. It is one which is most offensive to human pride, and at complete variance with the modern idea of the progress of the human race. Nevertheless, if we accept the Scriptures as a divine revelation, we have no choice but to uncomplainingly receive this truth. The ruined and helpless state of the sinner is fully attested by the Bible. There fallen man is represented as so utterly carnal and sold under sin as to be not only "without strength" (Rom. 5:6) but lacking the least inclination to move toward God. Very dark indeed is this side of the truth, but its supplement is the glory of God in rich grace, for it furnishes a real but necessary background to the blessed contents of the gospel.

Clear Teaching of Scripture

The Scriptures plainly teach that man is a fallen being, that he is lost (Luke 19:10), that he cannot recover himself from his ruin, that despite the fact of an all-sufficient Saviour presented to him, he cannot come to Him until he is moved upon by the Spirit of God. Thus it is quite evident that if a sinner is saved, he owes his salvation entirely to the free grace and effectual power of God, and not to any good in or from or by himself. "Not unto us, O LORD, not unto us, but thy name give glory, for thy mercy" (Ps. 115:1) is the unqualified acknowledgment of all the redeemed. Scripture speaks in no uncertain language on this point. If one man differs from another on this all-important matter of being saved, then it is God who has made him to differ (I Cor. 4:7) and not himself.

Nor is the sinner's salvation to be in any way attributed to either pliability of heart or diligence in the use of means. "So then it is not of him that willeth, nor of him that runneth, but of God that sheweth mercy." "Therefore hath he mercy on whom he will have mercy" (Rom. 9:16, 18). The context of John 6:44 indicates that our Lord was thus accounting for the enmity of the murmuring Jews: "No man can come to me, except the Father which hath sent me draw him." By those words Christ intimated that, considering what fallen human nature is, the conduct of His enemies is not to be wondered at; that they acted in no other way than will all other men when left to themselves; that His own disciples would never have obeyed and followed Him had not a gracious divine influence been exercised on them.

Man's Strong Objection

But as soon as this flesh-withering truth is pressed upon the unregenerate, they raise an outcry and voice their objections against it. If the spiritual condition of fallen man is one of complete helplessness, then how can the gospel ask him to turn from his sins and flee to Christ for refuge? If the natural man is unable to repent and believe the gospel, then how can he be justly punished for his impenitence and unbelief? On what ground can man be blamed for not doing what is morally impossible? Notwithstanding these difficulties the point of doctrine which we shall insist upon is that no one is able to comply with the terms of the gospel until he is made the subject of the special and effectual grace of God, that is, until he is divinely quickened, made willing, so that he actually does comply with its terms.

Nevertheless, we shall endeavor to show that sinners are not unjustly condemned for their depravity, but that their inability is blameworthy. Great care needs to be taken in stating this doctrine accurately. Otherwise men will be encouraged to put it to wrong use, making it a comfortable resting place for their corrupt hearts. By a misrepresentation of this doctrine more than one preacher has "strengthened the hands of the wicked, that he should not return from his wicked way" (Ezek. 13:22). The truth of man's spiritual impotence has been so distorted that many sinners have been made to feel that they are to be pitied, that they are sincere in desiring a new heart— which has not yet been granted them. Many, while excusing their helplessness, suppose this to be consistent with a genuine longing to be renewed. It is the duty of the minister to make his hearers realize they are under no inability except the excuseless corruption of their own hearts.

Need for Understanding the Doctrine

There is a real need for us to look closely at the precise *nature* of man's spiritual inability, as to *why* he cannot come to Christ unless he be divinely drawn. But first let us notice some of the tenets of others on this point. These fall into two main classes, Pelagians and Semi-Pelagians—Pelagius being the principal opponent of the godly Augustine in the fifth century.

A. A. Hodge in his *Outlines of Theology* has succinctly summarized the Pelagian dogmas on the subject of man's ability to fulfill the law of God. Here is the essence of his four points: (1) Moral character can be predicated only of volitions. (2) Ability is always the measure of responsibility. (3) Hence every man has always plenary power to do all that it is his duty to do. (4) Hence the human will alone, to the exclusion of the interference of any internal influence from God, must decide human character and destiny. The only divine influence needed by man or consistent with his character as a self-determining agent is an external, providential and educational one.

Semi-Pelagians believe thus: (1) Man's nature has been so far weakened by the fall that it cannot act right in spiritual matters without divine assistance. (2) This weakened moral state which infants inherit from their parents is the cause of sin, but not itself sin in the sense of deserving the wrath of God. (3) Man must strive to do his whole duty, when God meets him with cooperative grace and makes his efforts successful. (4) Man is not responsible for the sins he commits until after he has enjoyed and abused the influences of grace.

Arminians are Semi-Pelagians, many of them going the whole length of the error in affirming the freedom of fallen man's will toward good. But their practical contention may fairly be stated thus: Man has certainly suffered considerably from the fall, so much so that sinners are unable to do much, if anything, toward their salvation merely of themselves. Nevertheless sinners are able, by the help of common grace (supposed to be extended by the Spirit to all who hear the gospel) to do those things which are regarded as fulfilling the preliminary conditions of salvation (such as acknowledging their sins and calling on God for help to forsake them and turn to Christ). And if sinners will thus pray, use the means of grace, and put forth what power they do have, then assuredly God will meet them halfway and renew their hearts and pardon their iniquities.

We object to this belief. First, far from the Scriptures representing man as being partially disabled by the fall, they declare him to be completely ruined—not merely weakened, but "without strength" (Rom. 5:6). Second, to affirm that the natural man has any aspiration toward God is to deny that he is totally depraved, that "every imagination of the thoughts of his heart . . . [is] only evil continually" (Gen. 6:5; cf. 8:21), that "there is none that seeketh after God" (Rom. 3:11). Third, if it were true that God could not justly condemn sinners for their inability to comply with the terms of the gospel, and that in order to give every man a "fair chance" to be saved He extends to all the common help of His Spirit, that would not be "grace" but a *debt* which He owed to His creatures. Fourth, if such a God-insulting principle were granted, the conclusion would inevitably follow that those who improved this "common grace" could lawfully boast that they made themselves to differ from those who did not improve it.

But enough of these shifts and subterfuges of the carnal mind. Let us now turn to God's own Word and see what it teaches us concerning the nature of man's spiritual impotence. First, it represents it as being a *penal* one, a judicial sentence from the righteous Judge of all the earth. Unless this is clearly grasped at the outset we are left without any adequate explanation of this dark mystery. God did not create man as he now is. God made man holy and upright, and by man's own apostasy he became corrupt and wicked. The Creator originally endowed man with certain powers, placed him on probation, and prescribed a rule of conduct for him. Had our first parents preserved their integrity, had they remained in loving and loyal subjection to their Maker and Ruler, all would have been well, not only for themselves but also for their posterity. But they were not willing to remain in the place of subjection. They took the reins into their own hands, rebelling against their Governor. And the outcome was dreadful.

The sin of man was extreme and aggravated. It was committed contrary to knowledge and, through the beneficence of the One against whom it was directed, in the face of great advantages. It was committed against divine warning, and against an explicit declaration of the consequence of man's transgression. In Adam's fearful offense there were unbelief, presumption, ingratitude, rebellion against his righteous and gracious Maker. Let the dreadfulness of this first human sin be carefully weighed before we are tempted to murmur against the dire consequences which accompanied it. Those dire consequences may all be summed up in the fearful word "death," for "the wages of sin is death." The full import of that statement can best be ascertained by considering all the evil effects which have since come to man. A just, holy, sin-hating God caused the punishment to fit the crime.

Probation of Human Race in Adam

When God placed Adam on probation it pleased Him to place the whole human race on probation, for Adam's posterity were not only in him seminally as their natural head, but they were also in him legally and morally as their legal and moral head. In other words, by divine constitution and covenant Adam stood and acted as the *federal representative* of the whole human race. Consequently, when he sinned, *we* sinned; when he fell, *we* fell. God justly imputed Adam's transgression to all his descendants, whose agent he was: "By the offence of one judgment came upon all men to condemnation" (Rom. 5:18). By his sin Adam became not only guilty but corrupt, and that defilement of nature is transmitted to all his children. Thomas Boston said, "Adam's sin corrupted man's nature and leavened the whole lump of mankind. We putrefied in Adam as our root. The root was poisoned, and so the branches were envenomed."

"Wherefore, as by one man sin entered into the world, and death by sin; and so death passed upon all men, for that all sinned" (Rom. 5:12). We repeat that Adam was not only the father but the federal representative of his posterity. Consequently justice required that *they* should be dealt with as sharing in his guilt, that therefore the same punishment should be inflicted on them, which is exactly what the vitally important passage in Romans 5:12-21 affirms. "By one man [acting on behalf of the many], sin entered [as a foreign element, as a hostile factor] into the world [the whole system over which Adam had been placed as the vicegerent of God: blasting the fair face of nature, bringing a curse upon the earth, ruining all humanity], and death by sin [as its appointed wages]; and so death [as the sentence of the righteous Judge] passed upon all men [because all men were seminally and federally in Adam]."

It needs to be carefully borne in mind that in connection with the penal infliction which came upon man at the fall, he lost no moral or spiritual faculty, but rather *the power to use them right*. In Scripture "death" (as the wages of sin) does not signify annihilation but separation. As physical death is the separation of the soul from the body, so spiritual death is the separation of the soul from its Maker. Ephesians 4:18 expresses it as "being alienated from the life of God." Thus, when the father said of the prodigal, "This my son was dead" (Luke 15), he meant that his son had been absent from him—away in the "far country." Hence when, as the Substitute of His people, Christ was receiving in their stead the wages due them, He cried, "My God, my God, why hast thou *forsaken* me?" This is why the lake of fire is called "the second death"—because those cast there are "punished with everlasting destruction *from the presence of the Lord*" (II Thess. 1:9).

We have said that all of Adam's posterity shared in the guilt of the great transgression committed by their federal head, and that therefore the same punishment is inflicted on them as on him. That punishment consisted (so far as its present character is concerned) in his coming under the curse and wrath of God, the corrupting of his nature, and the mortalizing of his body. Clear proof of this is found in that inspired statement "And Adam lived a hundred and thirty years, and begat a son in *his own likeness*, after his image" (Gen. 5:3), which is in direct antithesis to his being created "in the image of God" (Gen. 1:27). That Adam's first son was morally depraved was clearly evidenced by his conduct; and that his second son was also depraved was fully acknowledged by the sacrifice which he brought to God.

As a result of the fall man is born into this world so totally depraved in his moral nature as to be entirely unable to do anything spiritually good; furthermore, he is not in the slightest degree disposed to do good. Even under the exciting and persuasive influences of divine grace, the will of man is completely unfit to act right in cooperation with grace until the will itself is by the power of God radically and permanently renewed. The tree itself must be made good before there is the least prospect of any good fruit being borne by it. Even after a man is regenerated, the renewed will always continues dependent on divine grace to energize, direct and enable it for the performance of anything acceptable to God, as the language of Christ clearly shows: "Without me ye can do nothing" (John 15:5).

But let it be clearly understood that though man has by the fall lost all power to do anything pleasing to God, yet his Maker has not lost His authority over him nor forfeited His right to require that which is due Him. As creatures we were bound to serve God and do whatever He commanded; and the fact that we have, by our own folly and sin, thrown away the strength given to us cannot and does not cancel our obligations. Has the creditor no right to demand payment for what is owed him because the debtor has squandered his substance and is unable to pay him? If God can require of us no more than we are now able to give Him, then the more we enslave ourselves by evil habits and still further incapacitate ourselves the less our liabilities; then the deeper we plunge into sin the less wicked we would become. This is a manifest absurdity.

Even though by Adam's fall we have become depraved and spiritually helpless creatures, yet the terrible fact that we are enemies to the infinitely glorious God, our Maker, makes us infinitely to blame and without the vestige of a legitimate excuse. Surely it is perfectly obvious that nothing can make it right for a creature to voluntarily rise up at enmity against One who is the sum of all excellence, infinitely worthy of our love, homage and obedience. Thus, for man—whatever the origin of his depravity—to be a rebel against the Governor of this world is infinitely evil and culpable. It is utterly vain for us to seek shelter behind Adam's offense while every sin we commit is voluntary and not compulsory—the free, spontaneous inclination of our hearts. This being the case, every mouth will be stopped, and all the world stand guilty before God (Rom. 3:19).

To this it may be objected that the writer of Romans argued that he was not personally and properly to blame for the corruptions of his heart: "It is no more I that do it, but sin that dwelleth in me" (7:17, 20). But there is no justification for perverting the language in that passage. If the scope of the words is noted, such a misuse of them is at once ruled out. The writer was showing that divine grace and not indwelling sin was the governing principle within him—as he had affirmed previously: "Sin shall not have dominion over you: for ye are not under the law, but under grace" (6:14). Far from insinuating that he did not feel wholly blamable for his remaining corruption, he declared, "I am carnal, sold under sin" (7:14), and cried as a brokenhearted penitent, "O wretched man that I am!" (v. 24). It is perfectly obvious that he could not have *mourned* for his remaining corruption as being *sinful* if he had not felt he was to *blame* for them.

Man's spiritual impotence is not only penal but *moral*, by which we mean that he is now unable to meet the requirements of the moral law. We employ this term "moral," first of all, in contrast with "natural," for the spiritual helplessness of fallen man is unnatural, inasmuch as it does not pertain to the nature of man as created by God. Man (in Adam) was endowed with full ability to do whatever was required of him, but he lost that ability by the fall. We employ this term "moral," in the second place, because it accurately defines the character of fallen man's malady. His inability is purely moral, because while he still possesses all moral as well as intellectual faculties requisite for right action, yet the *moral state* of his faculties is such as to render right action impossible. A. A. Hodge said, "Its *essence* is in the inability of the soul to know, love, or choose spiritual good; and its *ground* exists in that moral corruption of soul whereby it is blind, insensible, and totally averse to all that is spiritually good."

The affirmation that fallen man is morally impotent presents a serious difficulty for many. They suppose that to assert his inability to will or do anything spiritually good is utterly incompatible with human responsibility or the sinner's guilt. These difficulties are later considered at length. But it is necessary for us to allude to these difficulties at the present stage because the effort to show the reconcilability of fallen man's inability with his responsibility has led not a few defenders of the former truth to make predications which were unwarrantable and untrue. They have felt that there is, there must be, some sense or respect in which even fallen man may be said *to be able* to will and do what is required of him; and they have labored to show in what sense this ability exists, while at the same time man is, in another sense, unable.

Many Calvinists have supposed that in order to avoid the awful error of antinomian fatalism it was necessary to ascribe some kind of ability to fallen man, and therefore they have resorted to the distinction between natural and moral inability. They have affirmed that though man is now morally unable to do what God requires, yet he *has* a natural ability to do it, and therefore is responsible for not doing it. In the past we ourselves have made use of this distinction, and we still believe it to be a real and important one, though we are now satisfied that it is expressed faultily. There is a radical difference between a person being in possession of natural or moral faculties, and his possessing or not possessing *the power to use* those faculties right. And in the accurate stating of these considerations lies the difference between the preservation of the doctrine of man's depravity and moral impotence, and the repudiation or at least the whittling down of it.

At this very point many have burdened their writings with a metaphysical discussion of the human *will*, a discussion so abstruse that comparatively few of their readers possessed the necessary education or mentality to intelligently follow it. We do not propose to discuss such questions as Is the will of fallen man free? If so, in what sense? To introduce such an inquiry here would divert attention too much from the more important query, Can man by any efforts of his own recover himself from the effects of the fall? Suffice it, then, to insist that the sinner's unwillingness to come to Christ is far more than a mere negation or a not putting forth of such a volition. It is a positive thing, an active aversion to Him, a terrible and inveterate enmity against Him.

Impossibility of Moral Obedience

The term "ability," or "power," is not easy to define, for it is a relative term, having reference to something to be done or resisted. Thus when we meet with the word, the mind at once asks, Power to do what? Ability to resist what? The particular kind of ability necessary is determined by the particular kind of action to be performed. If it is the lifting of a heavy weight, physical ability is needed; if the working out of a sum in arithmetic, mental power; if the choosing between good and evil, moral power. Man has sufficient physical and intellectual ability to keep many of the precepts of the moral law, yet no possible expenditure of such power could produce *moral obedience*. It may be that Gabriel has less natural and intellectual power than Satan. Suppose it is so, then what? The conclusion is simply that no amount of ability can go beyond its own kind. Love to God can never proceed from the powers possessed by Satan.

Let us now consider what the Scriptures teach concerning the bodily, mental and moral abilities of fallen man. First, they teach that his *bodily* faculties are in a ruined state, that his physical powers are enfeebled, and this as a result of sin. "By one man sin entered into the world, and death by sin" (Rom. 5:12). None of our readers is likely to deny that this includes physical death. Now death necessarily implies a failure of the powers of the body. Sickness, feebleness, the wasting of the physical energies and tissues are included. And all of these originate in sin as their moral cause, and are the penal results of it. Every aching joint, every quivering nerve, every pang of pain we experience, is a reminder and mark of God's displeasure on the original misuse of our bodily powers in the garden of Eden.

Second, man's *intellectual* powers have suffered by the fall. "Having the understanding darkened, being alienated from the life of God through the ignorance that is in them, because of the blindness of their heart" (Eph. 4:18). A very definite display of this ignorance was made by our first parents after their apostasy. Their sin consisted in allowing their affections to wander after a forbidden object, seeking their happiness not in the delightful communion of God but in the suggestion presented to them by the tempter. Like their descendants ever since, they loved and served the creature more than the Creator. Their conduct in hiding from God showed an alienation of affections. Had their delight been in the Lord as their chief good, then desire for concealment could not have possessed their minds. That foolish attempt to hide themselves from the searching eye of God betrayed their ignorance as well as their conscious guilt. Had not their foolish hearts been darkened, such an attempt would not have been made. "Professing themselves to be wise, they became fools" (Rom. 1:22).

This mental darkness, this ignorance of mind, is insuperable to man unaided by supernatural grace. Fallen man never would, never could, dispel this darkness, overcome this ignorance. He labors under mental paucity to such a degree as to make it impossible for him to attain to the true knowledge of God and to understand the things of the Spirit. He has an understanding by which he may know natural things: he can reason, investigate truth, and learn much of God's wisdom as it is displayed in the works of creation. He is capable of knowing the moral truths of God's Word as mere abstract propositions; but a true, spiritual, saving apprehension of them is utterly beyond his unaided powers. There is a positive defect and inability in his mind. "The natural man receiveth not the things of the Spirit of God: for they are foolishness unto him: neither can he know them, because they are spiritually discerned" (I Cor. 2:14).

The Natural Man

By the "natural man" is unquestionably meant the unrenewed man, the man in whom the miracle of regeneration and illumination has not been effected. The context makes this clear: "Now we [Christians] have received, not the spirit of the world, but the Spirit which is of God" (v. 12). And for what end had the Spirit been given to them? That they might be delivered from their chains of ignorance, that their inability of mind might be removed so that they "*might know* the things that are freely given to us of God." "Which things [of the Spirit] also we speak, not in the words which man's wisdom teacheth, but which the Holy Ghost teacheth; comparing spiritual things with spiritual" (v. 13). Here is a contrast between man's wisdom and its teachings, and the Spirit's wisdom and His teachings. That the "natural man" of verse 14 is unregenerate is further seen from contrasting him with the "spiritual" man in verse 15.

A divine explanation is here given as to *why* the natural man does not receive the things of the Spirit of God. It is a most cogent and solemn one: "For they are foolishness unto him." That is, he rejects them because they are absurd to his apprehension. It is contrary to the very nature of the human mind to receive as truth that which it thinks is preposterous. And why do the things of the Spirit of God appear as foolishness to the natural man? Are they not in themselves the consummation of wisdom? Wisdom is not folly; no, yet it may *appear* as such and be so *treated*, even by minds which in other matters are of quick and accurate perception. The wisdom of the higher mathematician is foolishness to the illiterate. Why? Because he cannot understand it; he does not have the power of mind to comprehend the mighty thoughts of a Newton.

Why are the things of the Spirit of God beyond the comprehension of the natural man? Do not many of the unregenerate possess vigorous and clear-thinking minds? Can they not reason accurately when they have perceived clearly? Have not some of the unconverted given the most illustrious displays of the powers of the human intellect? Why, then, cannot they know the things of the Spirit? This too is answered by I Corinthians 2:14. Those things require a peculiar power of discernment, which the unrenewed have not: "They are *spiritually* discerned." And the natural man is *not* spiritual. Until the natural man is taught of God—until the eyes of his understanding are enlightened (Eph. 1:18)—he will never see any beauty in the Christ of God or any wisdom in the Spirit of God.

If further proof of the mental inability of the natural man is needed, it is furnished in those passages which speak of the Spirit's illumination. "God, who commanded the light to shine out of darkness, hath shined in our hearts, to give the light of the knowledge of the glory of God in the face of Jesus Christ" (II Cor. 4:6). Hence, "the spirit of wisdom and revelation in the knowledge of him" is said to be the gift of the Father (Eph. 1:17). Previous to that gift, "ye were sometimes darkness, but now are ye light in the Lord" (Eph. 5:8). "But the anointing which ye have received of him abideth in you, and ye need not that any man teach you" (I John 2:27). From these passages it is evident (1) that the mind of man is in a state of spiritual darkness; (2) that it continues, and will continue so, until the Spirit of God gives it light or knowledge; (3) that this giving of light or knowledge is by divine power, a miracle of grace, as truly a miracle as when at the beginning the Lord said, "Let there be light."

Some have objected that man possesses the *organ* of vision, and therefore he has the ability to see, although he does not have the light. Simply remove the obstructing shutters and the prisoner in his dungeon will see. But let us not be deceived by such sophistry. It is not true that man having a sound eye has the ability to see. It is often contrary to facts, both naturally and spiritually. Without light he cannot see, he has not the ability to do so. Indeed, those with sound eyes *and* light cannot see *all* things, even things which are perceptible to others; myopia, or nearsightedness, hinders. A man who may be able to see with the mind's eye a simple proposition cannot see the force of a profound argument.

Third, the moral powers of man's soul are paralyzed by the fall. Darkness on the understanding, ignorance in the mind, corruption of the affections, must of necessity radically affect motives and choice. To insist that either the mind or the will has a power to act contrary to motive is a manifest absurdity, for in that case it would not be a *moral* act at all. The very essence of morality is a capacity to be influenced by considerations of right and wrong. Were a rational mind to act without any motive—a contradiction in terms—it certainly would not be a moral act. Motives are simply the mind's view of things, influencing to action; and since the understanding has been blinded by sin and the affections so corrupted, it is obvious that until man is renewed he will reject the good and choose the evil.

Man's Bias Toward Evil

As we have already pointed out, man is unwilling to choose the good because he is *disinclined* to it, and he chooses evil because his heart is *biased* toward it. Men love darkness rather than light. Surely no proof of such assertions is needed; all history too sadly testifies to their verity. It is a waste of breath to ask for evidence that man is inclined to evil as the sparks fly upward. Common observation and our own personal consciousness alike bear witness to this lamentable fact. It is equally plain that it is the derangement of the mind by sin which affects the moral power of perceiving right and wrong enfeebling or destroying the force of moral motives.

An unregenerate and a regenerate man may contemplate the same subject matter, view the same objects; but how different their moral perceptions! Therefore their motives and actions will be quite different. The things seen by their minds being different, diverse effects are necessarily produced on them. The one sees a "root out of a dry ground" in which there is "no form nor comeliness," whereas the other sees One who is "altogether lovely." In consequence, our Lord is despised and rejected by the former, whereas He is loved and embraced by the latter. While such are the views (perceptions) of the two individuals, respectively, such *must* be their choice and conduct. It is impossible to be otherwise. Their moral perception must be changed before it is possible for their volitions to be altered.

Such is the ruined condition of the fallen creature. No human power is able to effect any alteration in the moral perceptions of sinful men. "Can the Ethiopian change his skin, or the leopard his spots? *Then* may ye also do good, that are accustomed to do evil" (Jer. 13:23). Nothing short of the sinner, mentally and morally blind to divine light. Here, then, lies the moral inability of the natural man: it consists in the lack of adequate powers of moral perception. His moral sense is prostrated, his mind unable to properly discern between good and evil, truth and falsehood, God and Mammon, Christ and Belial. Not that he can perceive no difference, but that he cannot appreciate in any tolerable degree the excellence of truth or the glory of its Author. He cannot discern the real baseness of falsehood or the degradation of vice.

It is a great mistake to suppose that fallen man possesses adequate faculties for such moral perception, and lacks only the necessary moral light. The very opposite is the actual case. Moral light shines all around him, but his powers of vision are gone. He walks in darkness while the midday splendors of the sun of righteousness shine all around him. Fables are regarded as truth, but the truth itself is rejected. Shadows are chased, but the substance is ignored. The gospel is *"hid* to them that are lost"* (II Cor. 4:3). When the Lord is presented to sinners, they "see in him no beauty that they should desire him." So blind is the natural man that he gropes in the noonday and stumbles over the rock of ages. And unless a sovereign God is pleased to have mercy on him, his moral blindness continues until he passes out into the "blackness of darkness for ever."

The deprivation of our nature consists not in the absence of intelligence, but in the ability to *use* our reason in a wise and fit manner. That which man lost at the fall was not a faculty but a principle. He still retains everything which is requisite to constitute him a rational, moral and responsible being; but he threw away that uprightness which secured the approbation of God. He lost the principle of holiness and, with it, all power to keep the moral law. Nor is this all; a foreign element—an element diametrically opposed to God—entered into man, corrupting his whole being. The principle of holiness was supplanted by the principle of *sin,* and this has rendered man utterly unable to act in·a spiritual manner. True, he may mechanically or imitatively perform spiritual acts (such as praying), yet he cannot perform them in a spiritual manner—from spiritual motives and for spiritual ends. He has no moral ability to do so. True, he can do many things, but none *rightly*—in a way pleasing to God.

Spiritual good is holiness, and holiness consists in supreme love of God and equal love of men. Fallen man, alone and of himself, is utterly unable to love God with all his soul and strength, and his neighbor as himself. This principle of holy love is completely absent from his heart, nor can he by any effort beget such an affection within himself. He is utterly unable to originate within his will any inclination or disposition that is spiritually good; he has not the moral power to do so. Moral power is nothing more nor less than a holy nature with holy dispositions; it is the perception of the beauty of God and the response of the heart to the excellence and glory of God, with the consequent subjection of the will to His royal law of liberty. J. Thornwell said, "Spiritual perceptions, spiritual delight, spiritual choice, these and these alone, constitute ability to good."

In our efforts to carefully define and describe the precise character of fallen man's inability to do anything which is pleasing to God, we have shown, first, that the impotence under which he now labors is a *penal* one, judicially inflicted upon him by the righteous Judge of all the earth, because of his misuse of the faculties with which he was originally endowed in Adam. Second, we noted that his spiritual helplessness is a *moral* one, having its seat in the soul or moral nature. The principle of holiness was lost by man when he apostatized from his Maker and Governor, and the principle of sin entered his soul, corrupting the whole of his being, so that he is no longer capable of rendering any spiritual obedience to the moral law; that is, he is incapable of obeying it from spiritual motives and with spiritual designs.

We pass on now to show, third, that fallen man's inability is *voluntary*. Some of our readers who have had no difficulty in following us through the first two sections are likely to demur here. We refer to hyper-Calvinists who have such a one-sided conception of man's spiritual helplessness that they have lapsed into serious error. They look upon the condition and case of the sinner much as they do those people who have suffered a stroke which has paralyzed their limbs: as a calamity and not the result of a crime, as something which necessitates a state of inertia and inactivity, as something which annuls their responsibility. They fail to see that the moral impotence of the natural man is *deliberate* and therefore highly culpable.

Before appealing to the Scriptures for proofs of this third point, we must explain the sense in which we use our term. In affirming that the moral and sinful inability of fallen man is a voluntary one, we mean that he acts freely and spontaneously, unforced either from within or without. This is an essential element of an accountable being, everywhere recognized and acknowledged among men. Human law (much less divine) does not hold a person to be guilty if he has been *compelled* by others to do wrong against his own will and protests. In all moral action the human will is self-inclined, acting freely according to the dictates of the mind, which are in turn regulated by the inclination of the heart. Though the mind be darkened and the heart corrupted, nevertheless the will acts freely and the individual remains a voluntary agent.

Some of the best theologians have drawn a distinction between the liberty and ability of the sinner's will, affirming the former but denying the latter. We believe this distinction to be accurate and helpful. Unless a person is free to exercise volitions as he pleases, he cannot be an accountable being. Nevertheless, fallen man cannot, by any exercise of will, change his nature or make any choice contrary to the governing tendencies of indwelling sin. He totally lacks any disposition to meet the requirements of the moral law, and therefore he cannot make himself willing to do so. The affections of the heart and the perceptions of the mind regulate our volitions, and the will has no inherent power to change our affections; we cannot by any resolution, however strong or prolonged, make ourselves love what we hate or hate what we love.

Because the sinner acts without any external compulsion, according to his own inclinations, his mind is free to consider and weigh the various motives which come before it, making its own preferences or choices. By motives we mean those reasons or inducements which are presented to the mind tending to lead to choice and action. The power or force of these inducements lies not in themselves (abstractedly considered), but in the state of the person who is the subject of them; consequently that which would be a powerful motive in the view of one mind would have no weight at all in the view of another. For example, the offer of a bribe would be a sufficient motive to induce one judge to decide a case contrary to law and against the evidence; whereas to another such an offer, far from being a motive to such an evil course, would be highly repulsive.

Let this be clearly grasped by the reader: Those external inducements which are presented to the mind affect a person according to the state of his or her heart. The temptation presented by Potiphar's wife, which was firmly refused by Joseph, would have been a motive of sufficient power to ruin many a youth of less purity of heart. External motives can have no influence over the choice and conduct of men except as they make an appeal to desires already existing in the mind. Throw a lighted match into a barrel of gunpowder and there is at once an explosion; but throw that match into a barrel of water and no harm is done. "The prince of this world cometh, and hath nothing *in* me" (John 14:30) said the holy One of God. None among the children of men can make such a claim.

Freedom of Human Will

All the affections of the human heart are, in their very nature, free. The idea of *compelling* a man to love or hate any object is manifestly absurd. The same holds good of all his faculties. Conscience may be enlightened and made more sensitive, or it may be resisted and hardened; but no man can be compelled to act contrary to its dictates without depriving him of his freedom, and at the same time of his responsibility. So of his will or volition: two or more alternatives confront a man, conflicting motives are presented to his mind, and his will is quite free in making a preference or choice between them. Nevertheless, it is the very nature of his will to choose that which is preferable, that which is most agreeable to his heart. Consequently, though the will acts freely, it is *biased* by the corruptions of the heart and therefore is unable to choose spiritual good. The heart must be changed before the will chooses God.

Against our assertion that the spiritual impotence of fallen man is a voluntary one, it may be objected that the sinner is so strongly tempted, so powerfully influenced by Satan and so thoroughly under his control that (in many instances, at least) he cannot help himself, being irresistibly drawn into sinning. That there is some force in this objection is readily granted, but we can by no means allow the length to which it is carried. However subtle the craft, however influential the sophistry, however great the power of the devil, these must not be used to repudiate our personal responsibility and criminality in sinning, nor must we construe ourselves into being his innocent dupes or unwilling victims. Never does Scripture so represent the matter; rather, we are told "Resist the devil, and he will flee from you" (James 4:7). And if we seek grace to meet the conditions (specified in I Peter 5:8-9), God will assuredly make good His promise.

Satan's power is not physical but moral. He has intimate access to the faculties of our souls, and though he cannot (like the Holy Spirit) work at their roots so as to change and transform their tendencies, he can ply them with representations and delusions which effectually incline them to will and do according to his good pleasure. He can cheat the understanding with appearances of truth, fascinate the fancy with pictures of beauty, and mock the heart with semblances of good. By a secret suggestion he can give an impulse to our thoughts and turn them into channels which serve the purposes of his malignity. But in all of this he does no violence to the laws of our nature. He disturbs neither the spontaneity of the understanding nor the freedom of the will. He cannot make us do a thing without our own consent, thus *in* consenting to his evil suggestions lies our guilt.

That sinners act freely and voluntarily in all their wrongdoing is taught throughout the Scriptures. Take, first of all, the horrible state of the heathen, a dark picture of whom is painted for us in Romans 1. There we see the consummation of human depravity. Heathenism is the full development of the principle of sin in its workings upon the intellectual, moral and religious nature of man. In Romans 1 we are shown that the dreadful condition in which the heathen now lie (and missionaries bear clear witness that what comes before their notice accurately corresponds to what is here stated) is the consequence of their own voluntary choice. "When they knew God, they glorified him not as God" (v. 21). They "changed the glory of the uncorruptible God into an image made like to corruptible man" (v. 23). They "changed the truth of God into a lie" (v. 25). They "*did not like to* retain God in their knowledge" (v. 28).

Nor was it any different with the favored people of Israel. So averse were they to God and His ways that they hated, persecuted and killed those messengers whom He sent to reclaim them from their wickedness. "They kept not the covenant of God, and *refused* to walk in his law" (Ps. 78:10). They said, "I have loved strangers, and after them *will I* go" (Jer. 2:25). "Thus saith the LORD, Stand ye in the ways, and see, and ask for the old paths, where is the good way, and walk therein, and ye shall find rest for your souls. But they said, We *will not* walk therein. Also I set watchmen over you saying, Hearken to the sound of the trumpet. But they said, We *will not* hearken" (Jer. 6:16-17). The Lord called to them, but they "refused." He stretched forth His hand, but "no man regarded." They set at nought all His counsel, and would heed none of His reproofs (Prov. 1:24-25). "The LORD God of their fathers sent to them by his messengers, rising up betimes, and sending. . . . But they mocked the messengers of God, and despised his words, and misused his prophets, until the wrath of the LORD rose against his people, till there was no remedy" (II Chron. 36:15-16).

Mistreatment of Christ

God's blessed Son did not receive any better treatment at their hands. Though He appeared before them in "the form of a servant," He did not appeal to their proud hearts. Though He was "full of grace and truth," they despised and rejected Him. Though He sought only their good, they returned Him nought but evil. Though He proclaimed glad tidings for them, they refused to listen. Though He worked the most wonderful miracles before them, yet they would not believe Him. "He came unto his own, and his own received him not" (John 1:11). Their retort was "We *will not* have this man to reign over us" (Luke 19:14). It was a voluntary and deliberate refusal of Him. It is this very voluntariness of their sin which shall be charged against them in the day of judgment, for then shall He give order thus: "But those mine enemies, which *would not* that I should reign over them, bring hither, and slay them before me" (Luke 19:27).

And from whence did such wicked treatment of the Son of God proceed? From the vile corruptions of their own hearts. "They hated me without a cause" (John 15:25) declared the incarnate Son of God. There was absolutely nothing whatever either in His character or conduct which merited their wicked contempt and enmity. Did anyone *force* them to be of such an abominable disposition? Surely not; they were *hearty* in it. Were they of such bad temper *against* their wills? No indeed. They were voluntary in their wicked hatred of Christ. They loved darkness. They were infatuated by their corruptions and delighted in gratifying them. They were highly pleased with false prophets, because they preached in their favor, flattering them and gratifying their evil hearts. But they hated whatever was disagreeable to their evil ways.

Mistreatment of Christ's Followers

It was the same with those who heard the ambassadors of Christ, except for those in whom the sovereign God wrought a miracle of grace. Jews and Gentiles alike willfully opposed and rejected the gospel. In some cases their hatred of the truth was less openly manifested than in others; nevertheless, it was just as real. And the disrelish of and opposition to the gospel was entirely voluntary on the part of its enemies. Did not the Jewish leaders act freely when they threw Peter and John into prison? Did not the murderers of Stephen act freely when they "stopped their ears, and ran upon him with one accord" (Acts 7:57)? Did not the Philippians act freely when they "rose up together" against Paul and Silas, beat them, and cast them into prison?

The same thing obtains everywhere today. If the gospel of Christ is preached in its purity and all its glory, it does not gain the regard of the masses who hear it. Instead, as soon as the sermon is over, like the generality of the Jews in our Lord's day, they make light of it and go their ways, "one to his farm, another to his merchandise" (Matt. 22:5). They are too indifferent to seek after obtaining even a doctrinal knowledge of the truth. There are many who regard this dullness of the unsaved as mere indifference, but it is actually something far worse: it is dislike of the heart for God, deliberate opposition to Him. "They are like the deaf adder that stoppeth her ear; which *will not* hearken to the voice of charmers, charming never so wisely" (Ps. 58:4-5). As Paul declared in his day, "The heart of this people is waxed gross, and their ears are dull of hearing, and their eyes have *they* closed; lest they should see with their eyes, and hear with their ears, and understand with their heart, and should be converted" (Acts 28:27).

"They say unto God, Depart from us; for we desire not the knowledge of thy ways" (Job 21:14). Such is the desperately wicked state of man's heart, diametrically opposite to the divine excellences. Yet when this solemn truth is pressed on the unregenerate, many of them will strongly object, denying that there is any such contrariety in their hearts, saying, "I have never hated God, but have always loved Him." Thus they flatter themselves and seek to make themselves out to be far different from what they are. Nor are they wittingly lying when they make such a claim; rather, they are utterly *misled* by their deceitful hearts. The scribes and Pharisees truly thought that *they* loved God and that, had they lived in the days of their forefathers, they would not have put the prophets to death (Matt. 23:29-30). They were altogether insensible to their fearful and inveterate enmity against God; nevertheless it was there, and it later unmistakably displayed itself when they hounded the Son of God to death.

Why was it that the scribes and Pharisees were quite unconscious of the opposition of their hearts to the divine nature? It was because they had erroneous notions of the divine Being and loved only that false image which they had framed in their own imaginations; therefore they had false conceptions of the prophets which their fathers hated and murdered, and hence supposed *they* would have *loved* them. But when God was manifested in Christ, they hated Him with bitter hatred. In like manner there are multitudes of sinners today, millions in Christendom who persuade themselves that they truly *love God*, when in reality they hate Him; and the hardest of all tasks confronting the ministers of Christ is to shatter this cherished delusion and bring their unsaved hearers face to face with the horrible reality of their unspeakably vile condition.

Loudly as our deluded fellow creatures may boast of their love of the divine nature, as soon as they pass out of time into eternity and discover what God is, their spurious love immediately vanishes and their enmity bursts forth in full force. Sinners today do not perceive their contrariety to the divine nature because they are utterly ignorant of the true God. It must be so, for a sinful nature and a holy nature are diametrically opposite. Christendom has invented a false "God," a "God" without any sovereign choice, a "God" who loves all mankind, a "God" whose justice is swallowed up in His mercy. Were they acquainted with the God of Holy Writ—who "hatest all workers of iniquity" (Ps. 5:5), who will one day appear "in flaming fire taking vengeance on them that know not God, and that obey not the gospel of our Lord Jesus Christ: who shall be punished with everlasting destruction from the presence of the Lord" (II Thess. 1:8-9)—they, if they honestly examined their hearts, would be conscious of the hatred they bear Him.

Guilt of Natural Man

The spiritual inability of the natural man is a *criminal* one. This follows inevitably from the fact that his impotence is a moral and voluntary one. It is highly important that we should be brought to see, feel and own that our spiritual helplessness is culpable, for until we do so we shall never truly justify God nor condemn ourselves. To realize oneself to be equally "without strength" and "without excuse" is deeply humiliating, and fallen man will strive with all his might to stifle such a conviction and deny the truth of it. Yet until we place the blame of our sinfulness where it really belongs, we shall not, we cannot, either vindicate the righteousness of the divine law or appreciate the marvelous grace made known in the gospel. To condemn ourselves as God condemns us is the one prerequisite to establish our title to salvation in Christ.

John Newton wrote:

> We cannot ascribe too much to the grace of God; but we should be careful that, under a semblance of exalting His grace, we do not furnish the slothful and unfaithful (Matt. 25:16) with excuses for their wilfulness and wickedness. God is gracious; but let man be justly responsible for his own evil and not presume to state his case so as would, by just consequence, represent the holy God as being the cause of the sin which He hates and forbids.

That was indeed a timely word. Unfortunately, some who claim to be great admirers of Newton's works have sadly failed to uphold the responsibility of the sinner, and have so expressed his spiritual inability as to furnish him with much excuse for his sloth and infidelity. Only by insisting on the criminality of fallen man's impotence can such a deplorable snare be avoided.

Inexorably as man's criminality attaches to his free agency in the committing of sin, yet the sinner will strive with might and main to avoid such a conclusion and seek to throw the blame on someone else. He will haughtily ask, "Would any right-minded person blame a man whose arms had been broken because he could no longer perform manual labor, or condemn a blind man because he did not read? Then why should I be held guilty for not performing spiritual duties which are altogether beyond my powers?"

To this difficulty several replies may be made: (1) There is no analogy in the cases advanced. Broken arms and sightless eyes are incompetent members; but the intellectual and moral faculties have not been destroyed, and it is because of misuse of these that the sinner is justly held culpable. (2) Not only does he fail to use his moral faculties in the performing of spiritual good, but he employs them in the doing of moral evil; and the excuse that he cannot help himself is an idle one.

Apply that principle to the commercial transactions of society, and what would be the result? A man contracts a debt within the compass of his present financial ability to meet. He then perversely and wickedly squanders his money and gambles away his property, so that he is no longer able to pay what he owes. Is he *therefore* not bound to pay? Has his reckless prodigality freed him from all moral obligation to discharge his debts? Must justice break her scales and no more hold an equal balance because he chooses to be a villain? No indeed; unregenerate men would not allow such reasoning.

To this it may be objected, "I did not bring this depravity upon myself, but was born with it. If my heart is altogether evil and I did not make it so, if such a heart was given me without my choice and consent, then how can I be to blame for its inevitable issues and actions?" Such a question betrays the fact that a wicked heart is regarded as a calamity which man did not choose, but which must be endured. It is contemplated as a thing not at all faulty *in its own nature*; if there is any blame attaching to it, it must be for something previous to it and of quite another kind. A person born diseased is not personally to blame, but if the disease is the result of his own indiscretion it *is* a just retribution. But to reason thus about sin is utterly erroneous, as if it were no sin to be a sinner or to commit sin when one has an inclination to do so, but to bring a sinful predisposition upon oneself would be a wicked thing.

Stripped of all disguise and ambiguity, the above objection amounts to this: Adam was in reality the only *sinner*; and we, his miserable offspring, being by nature depraved, are under a necessity of sinning, therefore cannot be to blame for it. The fact that sin itself is sinful is lost sight of. Scripture traces all our evil acts back to a sinful heart, and teaches that this is a blamable thing in itself. A depraved heart is a moral thing, being something quite different from a weak head, a bad memory or a frail constitution. A man is not to blame for these infirmities, providing he has not brought them upon himself. To say that I cannot help hating God and opposing my neighbor, and that therefore I am not to blame for doing so, certainly makes me out to be a vile and insensible scoundrel.

In order for a fallen creature to be blameworthy for his evil tendencies, it is not necessary that he should first be virtuous or free from moral corruption. If a person now finds that he is a sinner, and that from the heart he approves and chooses rebellion against God and His law, he is not the less a sinner because he has been of the same disposition for many years and has always sinned from his birth. His having sinned from the beginning, and having done nothing else, cannot be a legitimate excuse for sinning now. Nor is man's guilt the less because sin is so deeply and so thoroughly fixed in his heart. The stronger the enmity against God, the greater its heinousness. Disinclination Godward is the very essence of depravity. When we rightly define the *nature* of man's inability to do good—namely, a moral and a voluntary inability (not the absence of faculties, but the misuse of them)—then this excuse of blamelessness is at once exposed.

But the carnal mind will still object. We are natively no other way than

God has made us; therefore if we are born sinful and God has created us thus, then He, not ourselves, is the Author of sin. To such awful lengths is the enmity of the carnal mind capable of going: shifting the onus from his own guilty shoulders and throwing the blame upon the thrice holy God. But this objection was earlier obviated. God made man upright, but he apostatized. Man ruined himself. God endowed each of us with rationality, with a conscience, with a will to refuse the evil and choose the good. It is by the free exercise of our faculties that we sin, and we have no more justification for transferring the guilt from ourselves to someone else than Adam had to blame Eve or Eve the serpent.

But is it consistent with the divine perfections to bring mankind into the world under such handicapped and wretched circumstances? "Nay but, O man, who art thou that repliest against God? Shall the thing formed say to him that formed it, Why hast thou made me thus?" (Rom. 9:20). It is blasphemous to say that it is not consistent with the divine perfections for God to do what in fact He does. It is a matter of fact that we are born into the world destitute of the moral image of God, ignorant of Him, insensible of His infinite glory. It is a plain matter of fact that in consequence of this deprivation we are disposed to love ourselves supremely, live to ourselves ultimately, and wholly delight in what is not of God. And it is clearly evident that this tendency is in direct contrariety to God's holy law and is exceedingly sinful. Whether or not we can see the justice and wisdom of this divine providence, we must remember that God is "holy in all his ways, and righteous in all his works."

But how can the sinner possibly be to blame for his evil inclination when it was Adam who corrupted human nature? The sinner is an enemy to the infinitely glorious God, and that voluntarily; therefore he is infinitely to blame and without excuse, for nothing can make it right for a creature to be deliberately hostile to his Creator. Nothing can possibly extenuate such a crime. Such hostility is in its own nature infinitely wrong, and therefore the sinner stands guilty before God. The very fact that in the day of judgment every mouth will be stopped (Rom. 3:19) shows there is no validity or force to this objection. It is for the acting out of his nature—instead of its mortifying—that the sinner is held accountable. The fact that we are born traitors to God cannot cancel our obligation to give Him allegiance. No man can escape from the righteous requirements of law by a voluntary opposition to it.

The fact that man's sinful nature is the direct consequence of Adam's transgression does not in the slightest degree make it any less *his own* sin or render him any less blameworthy. This is clear not only from the justice of the principle of representation (Adam's acting as our federal head), but also from the fact that each of us approves of Adam's transgression by emulating his example, joining ourselves with him in rebellion against God. That we go on to break the covenant of works and disobey the divine law demonstrates that we are righteously condemned with Adam. Because each descendant of Adam voluntarily prolongs and perpetuates in himself the evil inclination originated by his first parents, he is *doubly* guilty. If not, why do we not repudiate Adam and refuse to sin—stand out in opposition to him, and be holy? If we resent our being corrupted through Adam, why not break the involvement of sin?

But let us turn from these objections to the positive side of our subject. The Scriptures uniformly teach that fallen man's moral and voluntary inability is a *criminal* one, that God justly holds him guilty both for his depraved state and for all his sinful actions. So plain is this, so abundantly evidenced, that there is little need for us to labor the point. The first three chapters of Romans are expressly devoted to this solemn theme. There it is declared, "The wrath of God is revealed from heaven against all ungodliness and unrighteousness of men, who hold the truth in unrighteousness" (1:18). The reason for this is given in verses 19-20, ending with the inexorable sentence "They are without excuse." Chapter 2 opens with "Therefore thou art inexcusable, O man," and in 3:19 the apostle shows that the ruling of the divine law is such that, in the day to come, "every mouth may be stopped, and all the world may become guilty before God."

The criminality of the sinner's depravity and moral impotence is clearly brought out in Matthew 25:14-30. The general design of that parable is easily perceived. The "lord" of the servants signifies the Creator as the Owner and Governor of this world. The "servants" represent mankind in general. The different "talents" depict the faculties and powers with which God has endowed us, the privileges and advantages by which He distinguishes one person from another. The two servants who faithfully improved their talents picture the righteous who serve God with fidelity. The slothful and unfaithful servant portrays the sinner, who entirely neglects the service of God and blames Him rather than himself for his negligence. His grievance in verses 24-25 expresses the feelings of every impenitent sinner, who complains that God requires from him (holiness) what He has not given to him (a holy heart). This servant's condemnation was on the ground that he did not improve what he *did* have (v. 27)—his rational faculties and moral powers. "Cast ye the unprofitable servant into outer darkness" (v. 30) shows the justice of his condemnation.

Excuses of Natural Man

The excuse that we cannot help being so perverse is further ruled out of court by Christ's declarations to the scribes and Pharisees. They had no heart either for Christ or His doctrine. He told them plainly, "Why do ye not understand my speech? Even because ye cannot hear my word" (John 8:43). But their inability was no excuse for them in His accounting, for He affirmed that all their impotence rose from their evil hearts, their lack of a holy makeup: "Ye are of your father the devil, and the lusts of your father ye will [desire to] do" (v. 44). Though they had no more power to help themselves than we have, and were no more able to transform their hearts than we are, nevertheless our Lord judged them to be wholly to blame and altogether inexcusable, saying of them, "If I had not come and spoken unto them, they had not had sin: but now they have . . . [*no excuse*] for their sin" (John 15:22).

Let it be specifically pointed out that when Scripture affirms the inability of a man to do good, it never does so by way of excuse. Thus, when Jehovah asked Israel, "Can the Ethiopian change his skin, or the leopard his spots? Then may ye also do good, that are accustomed to do evil" (Jer. 13:23), it was not for the purpose of mitigating their guilt, but with the object of showing how it aggravated their obstinacy of heart and to evince that no external means could effect their recovery. Just as likely was an Ethiopian to be moved by exhortation to change the color of his skin as were rebels against God to be moved by appeals to renounce their iniquities.

"Because I tell you the truth, ye believe me not. Which of you convinceth me of sin? And if I say the truth, why do ye not believe me? He that is of God heareth God's words: ye therefore hear them not, because ye are not of God" (John 8:45-47). Those cutting interrogations of our Lord proceeded on the supposition that His listeners could have received the teaching of Christ if it had been agreeable to their corrupt nature; it being otherwise, they could not understand or receive it. In like manner, when He affirmed, "No man can come to me, except the Father which hath sent me draw him," Christ did not intimate that any natural man honestly desired to come to Him, but was deterred from doing so *against* his will; rather, He meant that man is incapable of freely doing that which is inconsistent with his corruptions. They were averse to come to the holy Redeemer because they were in love with sin.

The excuse that I cannot help doing wrong is worthless. To plead my inability to do good simply because I lack the heart to do it would be laughed out of court even among men. Does anyone suppose that only the lack of a will to earn his living excuses a man from doing so, just as bodily infirmity does? Does anyone imagine that the covetous miser, who has no heart to give a penny to the poor, is for that reason excused from deeds of charity as one who has nothing to give? A man's heart being fully set to do evil does not render his wicked actions the less evil. If it did, it would necessarily follow that the worse any sinner grows, the less he is to blame. Nothing could be more absurd.

Let us show yet further the utter worthlessness of those evasions by which the sinner seeks to deny the criminality of his moral impotence. Men never resort to such silly reasonings when they are wronged by others. When treated with disrespect and animosity by their associates, they never offer the excuses for *them* behind which they seek to hide their *own* sins. If someone deliberately robbed me, would I say, "Poor fellow, he could not help himself; Adam is to blame"? If someone wickedly slandered me, would I say, "This person is to be pitied, for he was born into the world with this evil disposition"? If someone whom I had always treated honorably and generously returned my kindness by doing all he could to injure me, and then said, "I could not help hating you," far from accepting that as a valid extenuation, I would rightly consider that his enmity made him all the more to blame.

When a sinner is truly awakened, humbled and broken before God, he realizes that he *deserves* to be damned for his vile rebellion against God, and freely acknowledges that he is what he is voluntarily and not by compulsion. He realizes that he has had no love for God, nor any desire to love Him. He admits that he is an enemy to Him in his very heart, and voluntarily so; that all his fair pretenses, promises, prayers and religious performances were mere hypocrisy, arising only from self-love, guilty fears and mercenary hopes. He feels himself to be *without excuse* and owns that eternal judgment is His just due. When truly convicted of sin by the Holy Spirit, the sinner is driven out of all his false refuges and owns that his inability is a criminal one, that he is guilty.

Chapter 18

ROOT

As NO HEART can sufficiently conceive, so no voice or pen can adequately portray the awful state of wretchedness and woe into which sin has cast guilty man. It has separated him from God and so has severed him from the only Source of holiness and true happiness. It has ruined him in spirit and soul and body. By the fall man not only plunged himself into a state of infinite guilt from which there is no deliverance unless sovereign grace unites him with the Mediator; by his apostasy man also lost his holiness and is wholly corrupt and under the dominion of dispositions or lusts which are directly contrary to God and His law (Rom. 8:7). The fall has brought man into love of sin and hatred of God. The corruption of man's being is so great and so entire that he will never truly repent or even have any right responses toward God and His law unless and until he is supernaturally renewed by the Holy Spirit.

Corruption of Human Nature

If any reader is inclined to think we have painted too dark a picture or have exaggerated the case of the fallen creature, we ask him to carefully ponder the second half of Romans 7 and note how human nature is there represented as so totally depraved as to be utterly unable not merely to keep God's law perfectly, but to do anything agreeable with it. "The law is spiritual: but I am carnal, sold under sin. For I know that in me (that is, in my flesh,) dwelleth *no* good thing: for to will is present with me; but how to perform that which is good I find not. But I see another law in my members, warring against the law of my mind, and bringing me into captivity to the law of sin which is in my members" (vv. 14, 18, 23). How completely at variance is that language from the sentiments which prevail in Christendom today. Paul, that most eminent Christian, nothing behind the chief apostles, when he considered what he was in himself, confessed that he was "sold under sin."

The apostle's phrase "*in my flesh*," as may be seen by tracing it through the New Testament, means "in me by nature." He was saying, "There is nothing in me naturally good." But before proceeding further let us seek to carefully define what is signified by the term "the natural man," or "man by nature." It does not mean the human nature itself, or man as a tripartite being of spirit and soul and body, for then we should include the Lord Jesus

248

Christ, who truly and really assumed human nature, becoming the Son of Man. No, this term connotes not man as *created*, but man as *corrupted*. God did not in creation plant in us a principle of contrariety to Himself, for He fashioned man after His own image and likeness. He made him upright, holy. It was our defection from Him which plunged us into such immeasurable wretchedness and woe, which polluted and defiled all the springs of our being and corrupted all our faculties.

As a result of the fall man is the inveterate enemy of God, not only because of what he does, but because of what he now *is* in himself. Stephen Charnock said:

> What kind of enmity this is. First, I understand it of nature, not of actions only. Every action of a natural man is an enemy's action, but not an action of enmity. A toad doth not envenom every spire of grass it crawls upon nor poison every thing it toucheth, but its nature is poisonous. Certainly every man's nature is worse than his actions: as waters are purest at the fountain, and poison most pernicious in the mass, so is enmity in the heart. And as waters partake of the mineral vein they run through, so the actions of a wicked man are tinctured with the enmity they spring from, but the mass and strength of this is lodged in his *nature*. There is in all our natures such a diabolical contrariety to God, that if God should leave a man to the current of his own heart, it would overflow in all kinds of wickedness.

It is quite true that their deep enmity against God is less openly displayed by some than others, but this is not because they are any better in themselves than those who cast off all pretenses of decency. Their moderation in wickedness is to be attributed to the greater restraints which God places upon them either by the secret workings of His Spirit upon their hopes and fears or by His external providences—such as education, religious instruction, the subduing influence of the pious. But none is born into this world with the slightest spark of love to God in him. "The wicked are estranged from the womb: they go astray as soon as they be born, speaking lies. Their poison is like the poison of a serpent" (Ps. 58:3-4). The poison of a serpent is radically the same in all of its species.

"That which is born of the flesh is flesh" (John 3:6). These words make it clear that inherent corruption is imparted to us by birth. This is evident from the remainder of the verse: "and that which is born of the Spirit is spirit." The "spirit" which is begotten differs from the Spirit who is the Begetter, and signifies that new creation of holiness which is effected and inbred in the soul and therefore is called "the seed of God" (I John 3:9). As the spirit here unquestionably denotes the new nature or principle of holiness, so the flesh in John 3:6 stands for the old nature or principle of sin. This is further established by Galatians 5:17: "For the flesh lusteth against the Spirit, and the Spirit against the flesh: and these are contrary the one to the other: so that ye cannot do the things that ye would." Flesh and spirit are there put as two inherent qualities conveyed by two several births, and so are in that respect opposed. That the flesh refers to our very nature as corrupt is seen from the fact that it has works or fruits. The flesh is a principle from which operations issue, as buds from a root.

The *scope* of Christ in John 3 shows that flesh has reference to the corruption of our *nature*. His evident design in those verses was to show what imperative need there is for fallen man to be regenerated. Now regeneration is nothing else but a working of new spiritual dispositions in the whole man, called there "spirit," without which it is impossible that he should enter the kingdom of God. Christ said, "That which is born of the flesh is flesh" (v. 6), by which statement He made it the direct opposite of the spirit of holiness which is wrought in the soul by the Holy Spirit. Had we derived only guilt from Adam we would need only justification; but since we also derived corruption of nature we need regeneration too.

There is, then, in every man born into this world a mass of corruption which inheres in and clings to him and which is the principle and spring of all his activities. This may justly be termed his nature, for it is the predominant quality which is in all and which directs all that issues from him. Let us now proceed to *the proof* of this compound assertion. First, it is a mass of corruption, for that which our Lord called flesh in John 3:6 is called "the old *man*, which is corrupt" by His apostle in Ephesians 4:22. Observe carefully what is clearly implied by this term, and see again how perfectly one part of Scripture harmonizes with another. Corruption necessarily denotes something which was previously *good*, and so it is with man. God made him righteous; now he is defiled. Instead of having a holy soul, it is depraved; instead of an immortal body, it has within it even now the seeds of putrefaction.

Second, we have said that this corruption cleaves to man's very nature. It is expressly said to be within him: "Now then it is no more I that do it, but sin that *dwelleth in me.* For I know that in me (that is, in my flesh,) dwelleth no good thing" (Rom. 7:17-18). Man, then, has not only acts of sin which are transient, which come from him and go away, but he has a root and spring of sin dwelling with him, residing in him, not only adjacent to but actually inhabiting him. Not simply our ways and works are corrupt; "the *heart* is deceitful above all things, and desperately wicked" (Jer. 17:9). Nor is this something which we acquire through association with the wicked; rather it is that which we bring with us into the world: "Foolishness is bound in the heart of a child" (Prov. 22:15).

Third, we have stated that this indwelling corruption is the predominant principle of all the actions of unregenerate man, that from which all proceeds. Surely this is clear from "Now the *works of the flesh* are manifest, which are these: adultery, fornication, uncleanness, lasciviousness, idolatry, witchcraft, hatred, variance, emulations, wrath, strife" (Gal. 5:19-21). The flesh is here said to have works or fruits, and this quality of fruit-bearing exists in man's nature. Note that hatred and wrath are not deeds of the body, but dispositions of the soul and affections of the heart; thus the flesh cannot be restricted to our physical structure. This evil principle or corruption is divinely labeled a root: "Lest there should be among you a *root* that beareth gall and wormwood" (Deut. 29:18; cf. Heb. 12:13). It is a root which brings forth "gall and wormwood," that is, the bitter fruits of sin; in fact, it is said to "bring forth fruit unto death" (Rom. 7:5).

Fourth, we have affirmed that there is a *mass* of this corruption which thoroughly affects and defiles man's being. This is confirmed by the fact that in Colossians 2:11 it is called a body, which has many members: "In whom also ye are circumcised with the circumcision made without hands, in putting off *the body* of the sins of the flesh by the circumcision of Christ." This body of the sins of the flesh is of abounding dimensions, a body which has internal and external manifestations, gross and more secret lusts. Among these are atheism and contempt or hatred of God, which is not fully perceived by man until the Holy Spirit pierces him to the dividing asunder of soul and spirit. That this corruption lies in the very nature of man appears from the psalmist's statement "Behold, I was shapen in iniquity; and in sin did my mother conceive me" (51:5). David was there confessing the *spring* from which his great act of sin sprang. In essence he said, "I have not only committed the awful act of adultery, but there is sin even in my inward parts, defiling me from the moment I was conceived" (cf. v. 6).

Finally, we have declared that this corruption may in a very real sense be termed the *nature* of man. Once more we appeal to John 3:6 in proof, for there it is predicated in the abstract, which implies more than a simple quality, even that which explains the very definition and nature of man. The Lord Jesus did not say merely, "That which is born of the flesh is fleshly"; He said it "is flesh." In that statement Christ framed a new definition of man, beyond any the philosophers have framed. Philosophers define man as a rational animal; the Son of God announces him to be flesh, that is, sin and corruption contrary to grace and holiness, this being his very nature as a fallen creature in the sight of God. The very fact that this definition of man's nature is, as it were, in the abstract argues that it is a thing *inherent* in us. But let us enlarge a little on this point.

Definitions are taken from things brought out in nature, and none but essential properties are ingredients in definitions. Definitions are taken from the most predominant qualities. Sinful corruption is a more predominant principle in man's nature than is reason itself, for it not only guides reason, but it resides in every part and faculty of man, while reason does not. This corruption is so inbred and predominant and so diffused through the whole man that there is mutual expression between man and it. In John 3:6 the whole of man's nature is designated flesh; in Ephesians 4:22 this corruption is called man: "Put off . . . the old man, which is corrupt." Obviously we cannot put off our essential substance or discard our very selves, only that which is sinful and foul. It is called the *old* man because it is inherited from Adam, and because it is contrasted with our new nature.

Bondage of Corruption

Man's nature, then, which has become corrupt and termed flesh, is a bundle of foolishness and vileness, and it is this which renders him totally impotent to all that is good. Thus Scripture speaks of "the bondage of corruption" (Rom. 8:21) and declares men to be "the servants [Greek, 'slaves'] of corruption" (II Peter 2:19). Reluctant as any are to acknowledge this humbling truth, the solemn fact that the very nature of man is corrupt and that it defiles everything which issues from him is clearly and abundantly demonstrated. First, the human creature sins *from earliest years*. The first acts which evidence reason have sin also mingled with them. Take any child and observe him closely, and it will be found that the first dawnings of reason are corrupt. Children express reason selfishly—as in rebellion when thwarted, in readiness to please themselves, in doing harm to others, in excusing themselves by lying, in pride of apparel.

John Bunyan said:

> To speak my mind freely: I do confess it is my opinion that children come polluted with sin into the world, and that oftentimes the sins of their youth—especially while they are very young—are rather by virtue of indwelling sin than by examples that are set before them by others: not but what they *learn* to sin by example too, but example is not the root but rather the *temptation* to wickedness.

How can we believe otherwise when our Lord has expressly affirmed, "For from within, out of the heart of men [and not from association with degenerates], proceed evil thoughts, adulteries, fornications, murders, thefts, covetousness, wickedness, deceit, lasciviousness, an evil eye, blasphemy, pride, foolishness: all these things come from within, and defile the man" (Mark 7:21-23). It is true that evil habits may be acquired through contact with evildoers, but they are the occasion and not the radical cause of the habits.

This pollution of our very nature, this indwelling corruption, holds men in complete bondage, making them utterly impotent to do that which is good. In further proof of this, let us turn again to Romans 7. In his explanation of why he was unable to perform that obedience which God required, the apostle said, "I find then a *law*, that, when I would do good, evil is present with me. For I delight in the law of God after the inward man: but I see another law in my members, warring against the law of my mind, and bringing me into captivity to *the law of sin* which is in my members" (vv. 21-23). Indwelling sin is here called a law. Literally, a law is a moral rule which directs and commands, which is enforced with rewards and penalties, which impels its subjects to do the things ordered and to avoid the things forbidden. Figuratively, law is an inward principle that moves and inclines constantly to action. As the law of gravity draws all objects to their center, so sin is an effectual principle and power inclining to actions according to its own evil nature.

When the apostle says, "I see another law in my members" (that is, in addition to the principle of grace and holiness communicated at the new birth), he refers to the presence and being of indwelling sin; when he adds "bringing me into captivity" he signifies its power and efficacy. Indwelling sin is a law even *in* believers, though not *to* them. Paul said, "I *find*, then . . . a law of sin." It was a discovery which he had made as a regenerate man. From painful experience he found there was that in him which hindered his communion with God, which thwarted his deepest longings to live a sinless life. The operations of divine grace preserve in believers a constant and ordinarily prevailing will to do good, notwithstanding the power and efficacy of indwelling sin to the contrary. But the will in unbelievers is completely under the power of sin—their *will* of sinning is never taken away. Education, religion and convictions of conscience may restrain unbelievers, but they have *no* spiritual inclinations of will to do that which is pleasing to God.

That the very nature of man is corrupt, that it defiles everything which issues from him, is apparent not only by his sinning from earliest youth. Second, it is apparent by his sinning *constantly*. Not only is his first act sinful; all his subsequent actions are such. "And GOD saw that the wickedness of man was great in the earth, and that every imagination of the thoughts of his heart was only evil continually" (Gen. 6:5)—nor has man improved the slightest since then. Not that everything done by the natural man is *in its own nature* sinful; but as the acts are those of a sinner, they cannot be anything else than sinful. The act itself may be the performance of duty; yet if there is no respect for the commandment of God, it is sinful. To provide food and raiment is a duty, but if this duty is done from no spiritual motive (out of subjection to God's authority or the desire to please Him) or end (that God may be glorified), it is sinful. "The plowing of the wicked is sin" (Prov. 21:4); plowing is a duty in itself; nevertheless it is sinful as being the action of a sinner.

Third, it is not thus with a few, but with *every* member of Adam's fallen race. This further demonstrates that all evil proceeds from the very nature of man. "All flesh had corrupted his way upon the earth" (Gen. 6:12). "There is none righteous, no, not one. . . . They are all gone out of the way, they are together become unprofitable; there is *none* that doeth good" (Rom. 3:10-12). All members of the human race sin thus of their own accord. "A child left to himself bringeth his mother to shame" (Prov. 29:15). A child does not have to be taught to sin; he has only to be left to himself, and he will soon bring his parents to shame. Things which are not natural have to be taught us and diligently practiced before we learn them. Throw a child into the water, and it is helpless; throw an animal in, and it will at once begin to swim, for its nature teaches it to do so. "Train up a child in the way he should go" (Prov. 22:6). Much diligence and patience are required in those who would thus train the child; but no instructors are needed to inform him of the way in which he should *not* go. His depraved nature urges him into forbidden paths; indeed, it makes him delight in them.

Chapter 19

EXTENT

WHEN SEEKING TO UNFOLD some other great truths of Scripture by means of contemplating separately their component parts, we reminded the reader how very difficult it was to avoid some overlapping. The same thing needs to be pointed out here in connection with the subject we are now considering. A river has many tributaries and a surveyor must necessarily trace out each one separately, yet he does so with the knowledge that they all run out of or into the same main stream. A tree has many boughs which, though distinct members of it, often interweave. So it is with our present theme, and as we endeavor to trace its various branches there is of necessity a certain measure of repetition. Though in one way this is to be regretted, being apt to weary the impatient, yet it has its advantages, for it better fixes in our minds some of the principal features.

We began by showing the solemn *reality* of man's spiritual impotence, furnishing clear proofs from Holy Writ. Next, we endeavored to delineate in detail the precise *nature* of man's inability: that it is penal, moral, voluntary and criminal. Then we considered the *root* of the awful malady, evidencing that it lies in the corruption of our very nature. We now examine the *extent* of the spiritual paralysis which has attacked fallen man's being. Let us state it concisely before elaborating and offering confirmation. The spiritual impotence of the natural man is total and entire, irreparable and irremediable as far as all human efforts are concerned. Fallen man is utterly indisposed and disabled, thoroughly opposed to God and His law, wholly inclined to evil. Sooner would thistles yield grapes than fallen man originate a spiritual volition.

Reign of Sin in Unregenerate

We have supplied a number of proofs that man's nature is now thoroughly corrupt. This is seen in the fact that he is sinful from his earliest years; the first dawnings of reason in a child are fouled by sin. It appears too in that men sin continually. As Jeremiah 13:23 expresses it, they are "accustomed to do evil." It is also evidenced by the universal prevalence of this disease; not only some, nor even the great majority, but all without exception are depraved. It is demonstrated by their freedom in this state. All sin continually of their own accord. A child has only to be left to himself and he will quickly put his mother to shame. Moreover, men cannot be restrained from their sin. Neither education nor religious instruction, neither expostulation nor threatening (human or divine) will deter them; that which is bred in the bone comes out in the flesh. Corruption can neither be eradicated nor moderated. The tongue is a little member, yet God Himself declares it is one which no man can tame (James 3:8).

"The *law of sin* which is in my members" (Rom. 7:23). The first thing which attends every law as such is its rule or *sway*: "The law hath dominion over [literally 'lords it over'] a man as long as he liveth" (Rom. 7:1). The giving of law is the act of a superior, and in its very nature it exacts obedience by way of dominion. The law of sin possesses no moral authority over its subjects, but because it exerts a powerful and effectual dominion over its slaves it is rightly termed a law. Though it has no rightful government over men, yet it has the equivalent, for it dominates as a king: "Sin hath reigned unto death" (Rom. 5:21). Because believers have been delivered from the complete dominion of this evil monarch, they are exhorted, "Let not sin therefore *reign* in your mortal body, that ye should obey it in the lusts thereof" (Rom. 6:12). Here we learn the precise case with the unregenerate: Sin reigns undisputedly within them, and they yield ready and full obedience to it.

The second thing which attends all law as such is its *sanctions*, which have efficacy to move those who are under the law to do the things it requires. In other words, a law has rewards and penalties accompanying it, and these serve as inducements to obedience even though the things commanded are unpleasant. Speaking generally, all laws owe their efficacy to the rewards and punishments annexed to them. Nor is the "law of sin"—indwelling corruption—any exception. The pleasures and profits which sin promises its subjects are rewards which the vast majority of men lose their souls to obtain. A striking biblical illustration of this is the occasion when the law of sin contended against the law of grace in Moses, who chose "rather to suffer affliction with the people of God, than to enjoy the pleasures of sin for a season; esteeming the reproach of Christ greater riches than the treasures in Egypt: for he had respect unto the recompense of the reward" (Heb. 11:25-26).

In the above example we see the conflict in the mind of Moses between the law of sin and the law of grace. The motive on the part of the law of sin, by which it sought to influence him and with which it prevails over the majority, was the temporary reward which it set before him, namely, the present enjoyment of the pleasures of sin. By that it contended with the eternal reward annexed to the law of grace, called here "the recompense of the reward." By this wretched reward the law of sin keeps the whole world in obedience to its commands. Scripture, observation and personal experience teach us how powerful and potent this influence is. This was what induced our first parents to taste the forbidden fruit, Esau to sell his birthright, Balaam to hire himself to Balak, Judas to betray the Saviour. This is what now moves the vast majority of our fellowmen to prefer Mammon to God, Belial to Christ, the things of time and sense to spiritual and eternal realities.

The law of sin also has *penalties* with which it threatens any who are urged to cast off its yoke. These are the sneers, the ostracism, the persecutions of their peers. The law of sin announces to its votaries that nothing but unhappiness and suffering is the portion of those who would be in subjection to God, that His service is oppressive and joyless. It represents the yoke of Christ as a grievous burden, His gospel as quite unsuited to those who are young and healthy, the Christian life as a gloomy and miserable thing. Whatever troubles and tribulations come on the people of God because of their fidelity to Him, whatever hardships and self-denial the duties of mortification require, are represented by the law of sin as so many penalties following the neglect of its commands. By these it prevails over the "fearful, and unbelieving," who have no share in the life eternal (Rev. 21:8). It is hard to say where its greater strength lies: in its pretended rewards or in its pretended punishments.

The power and effect of this law of sin appears from its very *nature*. It is not an outward, inoperative, directing law, but an inbred, working, effectual law. A law which is proposed to us cannot be compared for efficacy with a law bred in us. God wrote the moral law on tables of stone, and now it is found in the Scriptures. But what is its efficacy? As it is external to men and proposed to them, does it enable them to perform the things which it requires? No indeed. The moral law is rendered "weak through the flesh" (Rom. 8:3). Indwelling corruption makes it impossible for man to meet its demands. And how does God deliver from this awful bondage? In this present life by making His law *internal* for His elect, for at their regeneration He makes good that promise "I will put my law in their inward parts, and write it in their hearts" (Jer. 31:33). Thus His law becomes an internal, living, operative and effectual principle within them.

Now the law of sin is an *indwelling* law. It is "sin that dwelleth in me"; it is "in my members." It is so deep in man that in one sense it is said to be the man himself: "I know that in me (that is, in my flesh,) there dwelleth no good thing" (Rom. 7:18; cf. vv. 20, 23). From this reasoning we may perceive the full dominion it has over the natural man. It always abides in the soul, and is never absent. It "dwelleth," has its constant residence, in us. It does not come upon the soul only at certain times; if that were so, much might be accomplished during its absence, and the soul might fortify itself against it. No, it never leaves. Wherever we are, whatever we are engaged in, this law of sin is present. Whether we are alone or in company, by night or by day, it is our constant companion. A ruthless enemy indwells our soul. How little this is considered by men! O the woeful security of the unregenerate: a fire is in their bones, fast consuming them. The watchfulness of most professing Christians corresponds little to the danger of their state.

Being an indwelling law, sin applies itself to its work with great facility and ease. It needs not force open any door nor use any stress whatever. The soul cannot apply itself to any duty except by those very faculties in which this law has its residence. Let the mind or understanding be directed to anything, and there are ignorance, darkness, madness to contend with. As for the will, in it are spiritual deadness, mulish stubbornness, devilish obstinacy. Shall the affections of the heart be set on divine objects? How can they be, when they are wholly inclined toward the world and present things and are prone to every vanity and defilement? Water never rises above its own level. How easy it is, then, for indwelling sin to inject itself into all we do, hindering whatever is good and furthering whatever is evil. Does conscience seek to assert itself? Then our corruptions soon teach us to turn a deaf ear to its voice.

The Scripture everywhere declares the seat of this law of sin to be *the heart.* "Out of the heart are the issues of life" (Prov. 4:23). It is there that indwelling corruption keeps its special residence; it is there this evil monarch holds court. It has invaded and possessed the throne of God within us. "The heart of the sons of men is full of evil, and *madness* is in their heart while they live" (Eccles. 9:3). Here is the source of all the madness which appears in men's lives. "All these evil things [mentioned in vv. 21-22] come from *within,* and defile the man" (Mark 7:23). There are many outward temptations and provocations which befall man, which excite and stir him up to many evils; yet they merely open the vessel and let out what is stored within it. "An evil man out of the evil treasure of his heart bringeth forth that which is evil: for of the abundance of the heart his mouth speaketh" (Luke 6:45). This "evil treasure" or store is the principle of all moral action on the part of the natural man. Temptations and occasions put nothing into men; they only draw out what was in them before. The root or spring of all wickedness lies in the center of our corrupt being.

Enmity of Carnal Mind Against God

Let us next consider the outstanding property of indwelling sin. "The carnal mind is enmity against God: for it is not subject to the law of God, neither indeed can be" (Rom. 8:7). That which is here called the carnal mind is the same as the law of sin. It is to be solemnly noted that the carnal mind is not only an enemy, for as such there would be a possibility of some reconciliation with God; it is enmity itself, thus not disposed to accept any terms of peace. Enemies may be reconciled, but enmity cannot. The only way to reconcile enemies is to destroy their enmity. So the apostle tells us, "When we were enemies, we were reconciled to God by the death of his Son" (Rom. 5:10)); that is, a supernatural work has been accomplished in the elect on the ground of the merits of Christ's sacrifice, which results in the reconciliation of those who were enemies. But when the apostle came to speak of enmity there was no other way but for it to be destroyed: "Having *abolished* in his flesh the enmity" (Eph. 2:15).

Let it also be duly considered that the apostle used a noun and not an adjective: "The carnal mind is enmity against God" (Rom. 8:7). He did not say that it merely is opposed to God, but that it is positive opposition itself. It is not black but blackness; it is not an enemy but enmity; it is not corrupt but corruption itself; not rebellious but rebellion. As C. H. Spurgeon so succinctly expressed it, "The heart, though it be deceitful, is positively deceitful: it is evil in the concrete, sin in the essence: it is the distillation, the quintessence of all things that are vile; it is not envious against God, it is enmity itself—not at enmity, it is actual enmity." This is unspeakably dreadful. To the same effect are those fearful words of the psalmist: "Their inward part is very wickedness" (5:9). Beyond *that* human language cannot go.

This carnal mind is in every fallen creature, not even excluding the newborn infant. Many who have had the best of parents have turned out the worst of sons and daughters. This carnal mind is in each of us every moment of our lives. It is there just as truly when we are unconscious of its presence as when we are aware of the rising of opposition in us to God. The wolf may sleep, but it is a wolf still. The snake may rest among the flowers, and a boy may stroke its back, but it is a snake still. The sea is the house of storms even when it is placid as a lake. And the heart, when we do not see its seethings, when it does not spew out the hot lava of its corruption, is still the same dread volcano.

The extent of this fearful enmity appears in the fact that *the whole* of the carnal mind is opposed to God: every part, every power, every passion of it. Every faculty of man's being has been affected by the fall. Take the memory. Is it not a solemn fact that we retain evil things far more easily than those which are good? We can recollect a foolish song much more readily than we can a passage of Scripture. We grasp with an iron hand things which concern our temporal interests, but hold with feeble fingers those which respect our eternal welfare. Take the imagination. Why is it that when a man is given that which intoxicates him, or when he is drugged with opium, his imagination soars as on eagles' wings? Why does not the imagination work thus when the body is in a normal condition? Simply because it is depraved; and unless our body enters a sordid environment the fancy will not hold high carnival. Take the judgment. How vain—often mad—are its reasonings even in the wisest of men.

This fearful enmity is irremediable. "It is not subject to the law of God, neither indeed can be" (Rom. 8:7). Even though divine grace intervenes and subdues its force, yet it does not effect the slightest change in its nature. It may not be so powerful and effectual in operation as when it had more life and freedom, yet it is enmity still. As every drop of poison is poison and will infect, as every spark of fire is fire and will burn, so is every part and degree of the law of sin *enmity*—it will poison, it will burn. The Apostle Paul can surely be regarded as having made as much progress in the subduing of this enmity as any man on earth, yet he exclaimed, "O wretched man that I am!" (Rom. 7:24) and cried for deliverance from this irreconcilable enmity. Mortification abates its awful force, but it does not effect any reformation in it. Whatever effect divine grace may work *upon* it, no change is made in it; it is enmity still.

Not only is this awful enmity inbred in every one of Adam's fallen race, not only has it captured and dominated every faculty of our beings, not only is it present within us every moment of our lives, not only is it incapable of reconciliation. Most frightful of all, this indwelling sin is "enmity *against*

God." In other passages it is exhibited as our own enemy: "Abstain from fleshly lusts, which war against the soul" (I Peter 2:11): those indwelling corruptions are constantly seeking to destroy us. This deadly poison of sin, this ruinous law of indwelling evil, consistently opposes the new nature or law of grace and holiness in the believer: "The flesh lusteth against the Spirit" (Gal. 5:17); that is, the principle of sin fights against and seeks to vanquish the principle of spirituality. It is dreadful to relate that its proper formal object is God Himself. It is "enmity against God."

This frightful enmity has, as it were, received from Satan the same command which the Assyrians had from their monarch: "Fight neither with small nor great, save only with the king" (I Kings 22:31). Sin sets itself not against men but against the King of heaven. This appears in the judgments which men form of God. What is the natural man's estimate of the Creator and Ruler of this world? For answer let us turn to the regions of heathendom. Consider the horrible superstitions, the disgusting rites, the hideous symbols of Deity, the cruel penances and gross immoralities which everywhere prevail in lands without the gospel. Consider the appalling abominations which for so long passed, and which in numerous instances still pass, under the sacred name of divine worship. These are not merely the products of ignorance of God; they are the immediate fruits of positive enmity against Him.

But we need not go so far afield as heathendom. The same terrible feature confronts us in so-called Christendom. Witness the multitudinous and horrible errors which prevail on every side in the religious realm today, the degrading and insulting views of the Most High held by the great majority of church members. And what of the vast multitudes who make no profession at all? Some think of and act toward the great Jehovah as One who is to be little regarded and respected. They consider Him as One entitled to very little esteem, scarcely worthy of any notice at all. "Therefore they say unto God, Depart from us, for we desire not the knowledge of thy ways. What is the Almighty, that we should serve him? And what profit should we have, if we pray unto him?" (Job 21:14-15). Such is the language of their hearts and lives, if not of their lips. Countless others flatly deny the existence of God.

The most solemn and dreadful aspect of the subject we are here contemplating is that the outstanding property of the "flesh" or indwelling sin consists of enmity against God Himself, such enmity that "is not subject to the law of God, neither indeed can be" (Rom. 8:7). This frightful and implacable enmity is entire and universal, being opposed to all of God. If there were anything of God—His nature, His character or His works—that indwelling corruption was not enmity against, then the soul might have a retreat within itself where it could shelter and apply itself to that which is of God. Unfortunately, such is the enmity of fallen man that it hates *all* that is of God, everything wherein or whereby we have to do with Him.

Sin is enmity against God, and therefore against all of God. It is enmity against His law and against His gospel alike, against every duty to Him, against any communion with Him. It is not only against His sovereignty, His holiness, His power, His grace, that sin rears its horrible head; it abhors everything of or pertaining to God. His commandments and His threatenings, His promises and His warnings, are equally disliked. His providences are reviled and His dealings with the world blasphemed. And the nearer anything approaches to God, the greater is man's enmity against it. The more of spirituality and holiness manifested in anything, the more the flesh rises up against it. That which is most of God meets with most opposition. "Ye have set at naught *all* my counsel and would *none* of my reproof" (Prov. 1:25) is the divine indictment. The wicked heart of man is opposed to not merely some parts of God's counsel but the whole of it.

Not only is this fearful enmity opposed to everything of God, but it is all-inclusive in the soul. Had indwelling sin been content with partial dominion, had it subjugated only a part of the soul, it might have been more easily and successfully opposed. But this enmity against God has invaded and captured the entire territory of man's being; it has not left a single faculty of the soul free from its tyrannical yoke; it has not exempted a single member from its cruel bondage. When the Spirit of God comes with His gracious power to conquer the soul, He finds nothing whatever in the sinner's soul which is in sympathy with His operations, nothing that will cooperate with Him. All within us alike opposes and strives against His working. There is not the faintest desire for deliverance within the unregenerate: "The *whole* head is sick, and the *whole* heart faint" (Isa. 1:5). Even when grace has made its entrance, sin still dwells in all its coasts.

Distasteful and humiliating as this truth may be, we must dwell further on it and amplify what has been merely affirmed. We showed how this fearful enmity is evidenced by the *judgments* or concepts which men form of God. Sin has so perverted the human mind that distorted views and horrible ideas are entertained of the Deity. Nor is this all. Sin has so inflated the creature that he considers himself competent to comprehend the incomprehensible. Filled with pride, he refuses to acknowledge his limitations and dependence; and in his flight after things which are far beyond his reach, he indulges in the most impious speculations. When he cannot stretch himself to the infinite dimensions of truth, he deliberately contracts the truth to his own little measure. This is what the apostle meant by fallen man's "vanity of mind."

The natural man's enmity against God appears in his *affections*. As the superlatively excellent One, God has paramount claims on man's heart. He should be the supreme object of his delight. But is He? Far from it. The smallest trifles are held in greater esteem than is God, the fountain of all true joy. The unregenerate see in Him no beauty that they should desire Him. When they hear of His sublime attributes they dislike them. When they hear His Word quoted it is repugnant to them. When invited to draw near to His throne of grace they have no inclination to do so. They have no desire for fellowship with God; they would rather think and talk about anything other than the Lord and His government. They secretly hate His people, and will only tolerate their presence so long as they conform to their wishes. The pleasures and baubles of this world entirely fill their hearts. Corrupted nature can never give birth to a single affection which is really spiritual.

The natural man's enmity appears in his *will*. Inevitably so, for God's will directly crosses His. God is infinitely holy; man is thoroughly evil; therefore God commands the things which man hates and forbids the things man likes. Hence man despises His authority, refuses His yoke, rebels against His government and goes his own way. Men have no concern for God's glory and no respect for His will. They will not listen to His reproofs nor be checked in their defiant course by His most solemn threatenings. They are as intractable as a wild ass' colt. They are like a bullock unaccustomed to the yoke. They prate of the freedom of their wills, but their wills are active *against* God and never toward Him. They are determined to have their own way no matter what the cost. When Christ is presented to them they will not come to Him that they might have life. Sooner will water flow uphill of its own accord than the will of man incline itself to God.

The enmity of the natural man against God appears in his *conscience*. Because he is anxious to be at peace with himself in the reflections which he makes upon his own life and character, it is obvious that his conscience must be a perpetual source of false representations of God. When guilt rankles in his breast, man will blaspheme the justice of his Judge. And self-love prompts him to denounce the punishment of himself as remorseless cruelty. A guilty conscience, unwilling to relinquish its iniquities and yet desirous of being delivered from fears of punishment, prompts men to represent Deity as subject to the weaknesses and follies of humanity. God is to be flattered and bribed with external marks of submission and esteem, or else insulted when the worshiper regards Him as cruel. Conscience fills the mind with prejudices against the nature and character of God, just as a human insult fills our heart with prejudice against the one who mortifies our self-respect. Conscience cannot judge rightly of one whom it hates and dreads.

The enmity of the natural man against God evidences itself in his *practice*. This dreadful hatred of God is not a passive thing, but an active principle. Sinners are involved in actual warfare against their Maker. They have enlisted under the banner of Satan and they deliberately oppose and defy the Lord. They scoff at His Word, disregard His precepts, flout His providences, resist His Spirit, and turn a deaf ear to the pleas of His servants. Their hearts are fully set to do wickedness. "Their throat is an open sepulchre; with their tongues they have used deceit: the poison of asps is under their lips: Whose mouth is full of cursing and bitterness: Their feet are swift to shed blood: destruction and misery are in their ways: and the way of peace have they not known: there is no fear of God before their eyes" (Rom. 3:13-18). There is in every sinner a deeply rooted aversion for God, a seed of malice. While God leaves sinners alone, their malice may not be clearly revealed; but let them feel a little of His wrath upon them, and their hatred is swiftly manifest.

The sinner's enmity against God is unmixed with *any* love at all. The natural man is utterly devoid of the principle of love for God. As Jonathan Edwards solemnly expressed it, "The heart of the sinner is as devoid of love for God as a corpse is of vital heat." As the Lord Jesus expressly declared, "I know you, that ye have not the love of God in you" (John 5:42). And remember, that fearful indictment was made by One who could infallibly read the human heart. Moreover that indictment was passed on not the openly vicious and profane but on the strictest religionists of His day. Reader, you may have a mild temper, an amiable disposition, a reputation for kindness and generosity; but if you have never been born again you have no more real love in your heart for God than Judas had for the Saviour. What a frightful character—the unmitigated enemy of God!

The power of man's enmity against God is so great that *nothing finite* can break it. The sinner cannot break it himself. Should an unregenerate person read this and be horrified at the hideous picture which it presents of himself, and should he earnestly resolve to cease his vile enmity against God, he cannot do so. He can no more change his nature than the Ethiopian can change the color of his skin. No preacher can persuade him to throw down the weapons of his rebellion and become a friend of God. One may set before him the excellence of the divine character and plead with him to be reconciled to God, but his heart will remain as steeled against Him as ever. Even though God Himself works miracles in the sight of sinners, no change is effected in their hearts. Pharaoh's enmity was not overcome by the most astonishing displays of divine power, nor was that of the religionists of Palestine in Christ's day.

Indwelling sin may be likened to a powerful and swiftly flowing river. So long as its tributaries are open and waters are continually supplied to its streams, though a dam is set up, its waters rise and swell until it bears down on all and overflows the banks about it. Thus it is with the enmity of the carnal mind against God. While its springs and fountains remain open, it is utterly vain for man to set up a dam of his convictions and resolutions, promises and penances, vows and self-efforts. They may check it for a while, but it will rise up and rage until sooner or later it breaks down all those convictions and resolutions or makes itself an underground passage by some secret lust which will give full vent to it. The springs of that enmity must be subdued by regenerating grace, the streams abated by holiness, or the soul will be drowned and destroyed. Even after regeneration, indwelling sin gives the soul no rest, but constantly wages war upon it.

The Christian is, in fact, the only one who is conscious of the awful power and ragings of this principle of enmity. How often he is made aware that when he would do good, evil is present with him, opposing every effort he makes Godward. How often, when his soul is doing quite another thing, engaged in a totally different design, sin starts something in his heart or imagination which carries it away to that which is evil. Yes, the soul may be seriously engaged in the mortification of sin, when indwelling corruption will by some means or other lead the soul into trifling with the very sin which it is endeavoring to conquer. Such surprisals as these are proofs of the habitual propensity to evil of that principle of enmity against God from which they proceed. The ever abiding presence and continual operation of this principle prevent much communion with God, disturb holy meditations and defile the conscience.

But let us return to our consideration of the enmity of the unregenerate. This enmity in the heart of the sinner is so great that he is God's *mortal* enemy. Now a man may feel unfriendly toward another, or he may cherish ill will against him, yet not be his mortal enemy. That is, his enmity against the one he hates is not so great that nothing will satisfy him but his death. But it is far otherwise with sinners and God. They are His *mortal* enemies. True, it does not lie in their power to kill Him, yet the desire is there in the heart. There is a principle of enmity within fallen man which would rejoice if Deity could be annihilated. "The fool hath said in his heart, There is no God" (Ps. 14:1). In the Bible the words "there is" are in italics—supplied by the translators for clarity. But the original has it, "The fool hath said in his heart, *No God.*" It is not the denial of God's existence, but the affirmation that he desires no contact with Him: "I desire no God; I would that He did not exist."

Here is the frightful climax: The carnal mind is enmity with the very being of God. Sin is destructive of all being. Man is suicidal—he has destroyed himself. He is homicidal—his evil influence destroys his fellowmen. He is guilty of deicide—he wishes he could annihilate the very being of God. But the sinner does not regard himself as being so vile. He does not consider himself to be the implacable and inveterate enemy of God. He has a far better opinion of himself than that. Consequently, if he hears or reads anything like this, he is filled with objections: "I do not believe I am such a dreadful creature as to hate God. I do not feel such enmity in my heart. I am not conscious that I harbor any ill will against Him. Who should know better than myself? If I hate a fellowman I am aware of it; how could I be totally unconscious of it if there is in my soul such enmity against God?"

Several answers may be given to these questions. First, if the objector would seriously examine his heart and contemplate himself, unless he were strangely blinded, he would certainly discover in himself those very elements in which enmity essentially consists. He loves and respects his friends, he is fond of their company, he is anxious to please them and promote their good. Is this his attitude toward God? If he is honest with himself, he knows it is not. He has no respect for His authority, no concern for His glory, no desire for fellowship with Him. He gives God none of his time, despises His Word, breaks His commandments, rejects His Son. He has been opposed to God all his life. These things are the very essence of enmity.

Second, the sinner's ignorance and unconsciousness of his enmity against God are due to the false conceptions which he entertains of His nature and character. If he were better acquainted with the God of Holy Writ, he would be more aware of his hatred of Him. But the God he believes in is merely a creation of his own fancy. The true God is ineffably holy, inflexibly just. His wrath burns against sin and He will by no means clear the guilty. If mankind likes the true God, why is it that they have set up so many false gods? If they admire the truth, why have they invented so many false systems of religion? The contrariety between the carnal mind and God is the contrariety between sin and holiness. The divine law requires man to love God supremely; instead, he loves himself supremely. It requires him to delight in God superlatively; instead, he wholly delights in all that is not of God. It requires him to love his neighbor as himself; instead, his heart is inordinately selfish.

Third, we have said that the enmity of the natural man against God is a mortal one. This the sinner will not admit. But indubitable proof of the assertion is found in man's treatment of God when, in the person of His Son, He became incarnate. When God brought Himself as near to man as Infinity could approach, man saw in Him "no beauty" that he should desire Him; rather was He despised and rejected by him. Not only did man dislike Him (Isa. 53:2-3), but he *hated* Him "without a cause" (John 15:25). So bitter and relentless was that hatred that man exclaimed, "This is the heir: come, let us kill him" (Luke 20:14). And what form of death did man select for Him? The most painful and shameful his malignity could devise. And the Son of God is still despised and rejected. Remember His words "He that hateth me hateth my Father also" (John 15:23). Our proof is complete.

What bearing on our subject has this lengthy discourse on man's enmity? Why take up the total depravity of fallen man when we are supposed to be considering his spiritual impotence? We have not wandered from our theme at all. Instead, while dealing with the root and extent of man's impotence, we have followed strictly the order of Scripture. What is the very next word of the apostle's after Romans 8:7? This: "So then they that are in the flesh *cannot* please God" (v. 8). It is just because man is corrupt at the very center of his being, because indwelling sin is a law over him, because his mind (the noblest part of his being) is enmity against God, that he is completely incapable of doing anything to meet with the divine approbation.

Here is inevitable inference, the inescapable conclusion: *"So then"*—because fallen man's mind is enmity with God and incapable of subordination to His law—"they that are in the flesh cannot please God" (Rom. 8:8). To be "in the flesh" is not necessarily to live immorally, for there is the religiousness as well as the irreligiousness of the flesh. So great, so entire, so irremediable is this impotence of fallen man that he is unable to effect any change in his nature, acquire any strength by his own efforts, prepare himself to receive divine grace, until the Spirit renews him and works in him both to will and to do of God's good pleasure. He is unable to discern spiritual things (I Cor. 2:14), incapable of believing (John 8:47), powerless to obey (Rom. 8:7). He cannot think a good thought of himself (II Cor. 3:5), he cannot speak a good word; indeed, without Christ he "can do *nothing*" (John 15:5). Thus, the sinner is "without strength," wholly impotent and unable to turn himself to God.

Chapter 20

PROBLEM

WE HAVE NOW ARRIVED at the most difficult part of our subject, and much wisdom from above is needed if we are to be preserved from error. It has been well said that truth is like a narrow path running between two precipices. The figure is an apt one, for fatal consequences await those who depart from the teaching of God's Word, no matter which direction that departure may take. It is so with the doctrine of man's impotence. It matters little whether the total bondage of the fallen creature and his utter inability to perform that which is good in the sight of God are repudiated and the freedom of the natural man is insisted on, or whether his complete spiritual impotence is affirmed and at the same time his responsibility to perform that which is pleasing to God is denied. In either case the effect is equally disastrous. In the former, the sinner is given a false confidence; in the latter, he is reduced to fatalistic inertia. In either case the *real* state of man is grossly misrepresented.

Man's Inability and God's Demands

The careful reader must have felt the force of the difficulties which we shall now examine. May God's Spirit enable us to throw some light on them. If the carnal mind is such fearful enmity against God that it is not subject to His law, "neither indeed can be," then why does He continue to press its demands on us and insist that we meet its requirements under pain of eternal death? If the fall has left man morally helpless and reduced him to the point where he is "without strength," then with what propriety can he be called on to obey the divine precepts? If man is so thoroughly depraved that he is the slave of sin, wherein lies his accountability to live for the glory of God? If man is born under "the bondage of corruption," how can he possibly be "without excuse" in connection with the sins he commits?

In seeking to answer these and similar questions we must of necessity confine ourselves to what is clearly revealed on them in Holy Writ. We say "of necessity," for unless we forsake our own thoughts (Isa. 55:7) and completely submit our minds to God's, we are certain to err. In theory this is granted by most professing Christians, yet in practice it is too often set aside. In general it is conceded, but in particular it is ignored. A highly trained intellect may draw what appear to be incontestable conclusions from a scriptural premise; yet, though logic cannot refute them, the practices of Christ and His apostles prove them to be false. On the one hand we may take the fact that the Lord has given orders for His gospel to be preached to every creature. Then must we not infer that the sinner has it in his own power to either accept or reject that gospel? Such an inference certainly appears reasonable, yet it is erroneous. On the other hand take the fact that the sinner is spiritually impotent. Then is it not a mockery to ask him to come to Christ? Such an inference certainly appears reasonable; yet it is false.

It is at this very point that most of Christendom has been deluged with a flood of errors. Most of the leading denominations began by taking the Word of God as the foundation and substance of their creed. But almost at once that foundation was turned into a platform on which the proud intellect of man was exercised, and in a very short time human reason—logical and plausible—supplanted divine revelation. Men attempted to work out theological systems and articles of faith that were thoroughly "consistent," theories which—unlike the workings of both nature and providence—contained in them no seeming "contradictions" or "absurdities," but which commended themselves to their fellowmen. But this was nothing less than a presumptuous attempt to compress the truth of God into man-made molds, to reduce that which issued from the Infinite to terms comprehensible to finite minds. It is another sad example of that egotism which refuses to receive what it cannot understand.

Biblical Harmony

It is true that there is perfect harmony in all parts of divine truth. How can it be otherwise, since *God* is its Author? Yet men are so blind that they cannot perceive this perfect harmony. Some cannot discern the consistency between the infinite love and grace of God and His requiring His own Son to pay such a costly satisfaction to His broken law. Some cannot see the consistency between the everlasting mercy of God and the eternal punishment of the wicked, insisting that if the former be true the latter is impossible. Some cannot see the congruity of Christ satisfying every requirement of God on behalf of His people and the imperative necessity of holiness and obedience in them if they are to benefit thereby; or between their divine preservation and the certainty of destruction were they to finally apostatize. Some cannot see the accord between the divine foreordination of our actions and our freedom in them. Some cannot see the agreement between efficacious grace in the conversion of sinners and the need for the exercise of their faculties by way of duty. Some cannot see the concurrence of the total depravity or spiritual impotence of man and his responsibility to be completely subject to God's will.

As a sample of what we have referred to in the last two paragraphs, note the following quotation:

> We deny duty-faith, and duty-repentance—these terms signifying that it is every man's duty to spiritually and savingly repent and believe (Gen.

6:5; 8:21; Matt. 15:19; Jer. 17:9; John 6:44, 65). We deny also that there is any capability in man by nature to any spiritual good whatever. So that we reject the doctrine that men in a state of nature should be exhorted to believe in or turn to God (John 12:39, 40; Eph. 2:8; Rom. 8:7, 8; I Cor. 4:7). We believe that it would be unsafe, from the brief records we have of the way in which the apostles, under the immediate direction of the Lord, addressed their hearers in certain special cases and circumstances, to derive absolute and universal rules for ministerial addresses in the present day under widely-different circumstances. And we further believe that an assumption that others have been inspired as the apostles were has led to the grossest errors amongst both Románists and professed Protestants. Therefore, that for ministers in the present day to address unconverted persons, or indiscriminately all in a mixed congregation, calling upon them to savingly repent, believe, and receive Christ, or perform any other acts dependent upon the new creative power of the Holy Ghost, is, on the one hand, to imply creature power and on the other, to deny the doctrine of special redemption.

It may come as a surprise to many of our readers to learn that the above is a verbatim quotation from the Articles of Faith of a Baptist group in England with a considerable membership, which will permit no man to enter their pulpits who does not solemnly subscribe to and sign his name to the same. Yet this is the case. These Articles of Faith accurately express the belief of the great majority of certain Baptist groups in the United States on this subject. In consequence, the gospel of Christ is deliberately withheld from the unsaved, and no appeals are addressed to them to accept the gospel offer and receive Christ as their personal Lord and Saviour. Need we wonder that fewer and fewer in their midst are testifying to a divine work of grace in their hearts, and that many of their churches have ceased to be.

It is a good thing that many of the Lord's people are sounder of heart than the creeds held in their heads, yet that does not excuse them for subscribing to what is definitely unscriptural. It is far from a pleasant task to expose the fallacy of these Articles of Faith, for we have some friends who are committed to them; yet we would fail in our duty to them if we made no effort to convince them of their errors. Let us briefly examine these Articles. First, they deny that it is the duty of every man who hears the gospel to spiritually and savingly repent and believe, notwithstanding the fact that practically all the true servants of Christ in every generation (including the Reformers and nine-tenths of the Puritans) have preached that duty. It is the plain teaching of Holy Writ. We will not quote from the writings of those used of the Spirit in the past, but confine ourselves to God's Word.

God Himself "now commandeth all men everywhere to repent" (Acts 17:30). What could possibly be plainer than that? There is no room for any quibbling, misunderstanding or evasion. It means just what it says, and says just what it means. The framers of those Articles, then, are taking direct issue with the Most High. It is because of his "hardness and impenitence of heart" that the sinner treasures up to himself "wrath against the day of wrath" (Rom. 2:5). "He that believeth on him is not condemned: but he that believeth not is condemned already, *because* he hath not believed in the name of the only begotten Son of God. And this is the condemnation, that light is come into the world, and men loved darkness rather than light, because their deeds were evil" (John 3:18-19). Here too it is impossible to fairly evade the force of our Lord's language. He taught that it is the duty of all who hear the gospel to savingly believe on Him, and declared that rejecters are condemned because they do not believe. When He returns it will be "in flaming fire taking vengeance on them that know not God, and that *obey not* the gospel" (II Thess. 1:8).

Next, note that the framers of these Articles follow their denial by referring to six verses of Scripture, the first four of which deal with the desperate wickedness of the natural man's heart and the last two with his complete inability to turn to Christ until divinely enabled. These passages are manifestly alluded to in support of the contention made. Each reader must decide their pertinence for himself. The only relevance they can possess is on the supposition that they establish a premise which requires us to draw the conclusion so dogmatically expressed. We are asked to believe that since fallen man is totally depraved we must necessarily infer that he is not a fit subject to be exhorted to perform spiritual acts. Thus, when analyzed, this Article is seen to consist of nothing more than an expression of human *reasoning*.

Not only does the substance of this Article of Faith consist of nothing more substantial and reliable than a mental inference, but when weighed in the balances of the sanctuary it is found to clash with the Scriptures, that is, with the practice of God's own servants recorded in them. For example, we do not find the psalmist accommodating his exhortations to the sinful inability of the natural man. Far from it. David called on the ungodly thus: "Be wise now therefore, O ye kings: be instructed, ye judges of the earth. Serve the LORD with fear, and rejoice with trembling. Kiss the Son, lest he be angry, and ye perish from the way, when his wrath is kindled but a little. Blessed are all they that put their trust in him" (Ps. 2:10-12). David did not withhold these warnings because the people were such rebels that they would not and could not give their hearts' allegiance to the King of kings. He uncompromisingly and bluntly commanded them to do so whether they could or not.

It was the same with the prophets. If ever a man addressed an unregenerate congregation it was when Elijah the Tishbite spoke to the idolatrous Israelites: "Elijah came unto all the people, and said, How long halt ye between two opinions? If the LORD be God, follow him: but if Baal, then follow him" (I Kings 18:21). That exhortation was not restricted to the remnant of renewed souls, but was addressed to the nation indiscriminately. It was a plain call for them to perform a spiritual duty, for them to exercise their will and choose between God and the devil. In like manner Isaiah called on the debased generation of his day: "Wash ye, make you clean; put away the evil of your doings from before mine eyes; cease to do evil; learn to do well" (1:16-17). One prophet went so far as to say to his hearers, "Make you a new heart and a new spirit" (Ezek. 18:31), yet he was in perfect accord with his fellow prophet Jeremiah who taught the helplessness of man in those memorable questions "Can the Ethiopian change his skin? Or the leopard his spots?" These men, then, did not decide they must preach only that which lay in the power of their hearers to comply with.

The words "We deny also that there is any capability in man by nature to any spiritual good whatever" will strike the vast majority of God's people as far too sweeping. They will readily agree that fallen man possesses no *power* at all to perform any spiritual acts; yet they will insist that nothing prevents the spiritual obedience of any sinner except his own unwillingness. Man by nature—that is, as he originally left the hands of his Creator—was endowed with full capability to meet his Maker's requirements. The fall did not rob him of a single faculty, and it is his retention of all his faculties which constitutes him still a responsible creature. Of the last four passages referred to in the Article (John 12:39, 40, etc.) two of them relate to the spiritual impotence of fallen man and the other two to divine enablement imparted to those who are saved.

With regard to the other Articles affirming that it "would be unsafe" for us now to derive rules for ministerial address from the way in which the apostles spoke to their hearers, this is their summary method of disposing of all those passages in the Old and New Testaments alike which are directly opposed to their theory. Since the Lord Jesus Himself did not hesitate to say to the people, "Repent ye, and believe the gospel" (Mark 1:15), surely His servants today need not have the slightest hesitation in following His example. If ministers of the Word are not to find their guidance and rules from the practice of their Master and His apostles, then *where* shall they look for them? Must each one be a rule unto himself? Or must they necessarily place themselves under the domination of self-made popes? These very men who are such sticklers for "consistency" are not consistent with themselves, for when it comes to matters of church polity they take the practice of the apostles for their guidance! Lack of space prevents further comment on this.

To human reason there appears to be a definite conflict between two distinct lines of divine truth. On the one hand, Scripture plainly affirms that fallen man is totally depraved, enslaved by sin, entirely destitute of spiritual strength, so that he is unable of himself to either truly repent or savingly believe in Christ. On the other hand, Scripture uniformly addresses fallen man as a being who is accountable to God, responsible to forsake his wickedness and serve and glorify his Maker. He is called on to lay down the weapons of his warfare and be reconciled to God. The Ruler of heaven and earth has not lowered the standard of holiness under which He placed man. He declares that notwithstanding man's ruined condition, he is "without excuse" for all his iniquities. The gospel depicts man in a lost state, "dead in trespasses and sins"; nevertheless it exhorts all who come under its sound to accept Christ as their Lord and Saviour.

Such in brief is the problem presented by the doctrine we are here considering. The unregenerate are morally impotent, yet are they fully accountable beings. They are sold under sin, yet are they justly required to be holy as God is holy. They are unable to comply with the righteous requirements of their Sovereign, yet they are exhorted to do so under pain of eternal death. What, then, should be our attitude to this problem? First, we should carefully *test* it and thoroughly satisfy ourselves that both of these facts are plainly set forth in Holy Writ. Second, having done so, we must *accept* them both at their face value, assured that however contrary they may seem to us, yet there is perfect harmony between all parts of God's Word. Third, we must hold *firmly* to *both* these lines of truth, steadfastly refusing to relinquish either of them at the dictates of any theological party or denominational leader. Fourth, we should humbly *wait* on God for fuller light on the subject.

But such a course is just what the proud heart of man is disinclined to follow. Instead, he desires to reduce everything to a simple, consistent and coherent system, one which falls within the compass of his finite understanding. Notwithstanding the fact that he is surrounded by mystery on every side in the natural realm, notwithstanding the fact that so very much of God's providential dealings both with the world in general and with himself in particular are "past finding out," he is determined to philosophize and manipulate God's truth until it is compressed into a series of logical propositions which appear reasonable to him. He is like the disciples whom our Lord called "fools" because they were "slow of heart to believe *all* that the prophets have spoken" (Luke 24:25). Those disciples were guilty of picking and choosing, believing what appealed to their inclination and rejecting that which was distasteful and which appeared to them to clash with what they had been taught.

Antinomian-Pelagian Debate

The testimony of the prophets did not seem to the disciples to be harmonious; one part appeared to conflict with another. In fact, there were two distinct lines of Messianic prediction which looked as though they flatly contradicted each other. The one spoke of a suffering, humiliated and crucified Messiah; the other of an all-powerful, glorious and triumphant Messiah. And because the disciples could not see how *both* could be true, they held to the one and rejected the other. Precisely the same capricious course has been followed by theologians in Christendom. Conflicting schools or parties among them have, as it were, divided the truth among themselves, one party retaining this portion and jettisoning that, and another party rejecting this and maintaining that. They have ranged themselves into opposing groups, each holding some facets of the truth, each rejecting what the opponents contend for. Party spirit has been as rife and as ruinous in the religious world as in the political.

On the one side Arminians have maintained that men are responsible creatures, that the claims of God are to be pressed upon them, that they must be called on to discharge their duty, that they are fit subjects for exhortation.

Yet while steadfastly adhering to this side of the truth, they have been guilty of repudiating other aspects which are equally necessary and important. They have denied—in effect if not in words—the total depravity of man, his complete spiritual helplessness, the bondage of his will under sin, and his utter inability to cooperate with the Holy Spirit in the work of his salvation. On the other side Antinomians, while affirming all that the Arminians deny, are themselves guilty of repudiating what their opponents contend for, insisting that since the unregenerate have no power to perform spiritual acts it is useless and absurd to call on them to do so. Thus they aver that gospel offers should not be made unto the unregenerate.

These Antinomians consider themselves to be towers of orthodoxy, valiant defenders of the truth, sounder in the faith than any other section of Christendom. Many of them wish to be regarded as strict Calvinists; but whatever else they may be, they certainly are not *that*, for Calvin himself taught and practiced directly the contrary. In his work *The Eternal Predestination of God* the great Reformer wrote:

> It is quite manifest that all men without difference or distinction are outwardly called or invited to repentance and faith; . . . the mercy of God is offered to those who believe and to those who believe not, so that those who are not Divinely taught within are only rendered inexcusable, not saved.

In his *Secret Providence of God* he asked:

> And what if God invites the whole mass of mankind to come unto Him, and yet knowingly and of His own will denies His Spirit to the greater part, "drawing" a few only unto obedience unto Himself by His Spirit's secret inspiration and operation—is the adorable God to be charged, on that account, with inconsistency?

In the same work Calvin stated:

> Nor is there any want of harmony or oneness of truth when the same Saviour, who invites all men unto Him without exception by His external voice, yet declares that "A man can receive nothing except it be given him from above:" John 19:11.

Many regarding themselves as Calvinists have departed far from the teaching and practice of that eminent servant of God.

There is no difference in principle between the unregenerate being called on to obey the gospel and accept its gracious overtures, and the whole heathen world being required to respond to the call of God *through nature* before His Son became incarnate. In his address to the Athenians the apostle declared on Mars Hill, "God that made the world and all things therein, seeing that he is Lord of heaven and earth, dwelleth not in temples made with hands; neither is worshipped with men's hands, as though he needed any thing, seeing he giveth to all life, and breath, and all things; and hath made of one blood all nations of men for to dwell on all the face of the earth, and hath determined the times before appointed, and the bounds of their habitation; that they should seek the Lord, if haply they might feel after him, and find him" (Acts 17:24-27). The force of that statement is this: Seeing God is the Creator, the Governor of all, He cannot be supposed to inhabit temples made by men, nor can He be worshiped with the products of their hands; and seeing that He is the universal Benefactor and Source of life and all things to His creatures, He is on that account required to be adored and obeyed; and since He is sovereign Lord appointing the different ages of the world and allotting to the nations their territories, His favor is to be *sought after* and His will submitted to.

The voice of nature is clear and loud. It testifies to the being of God and tells of His wisdom, goodness and power. It addresses all alike, bidding men to believe in God, turn to Him and serve Him. "The heavens declare the glory of God; and the firmament sheweth his handywork" (Ps. 19:1). These are the preachers of nature to all nations alike. They are not silent, but vocal, speaking to those in every land: "Day unto day uttereth speech, and night unto night sheweth knowledge. There is no speech nor language, where their voice is not heard. Their line is gone out through all the earth, and their words to the end of the world" (vv. 2-4). In view of these and similar phenomena the apostle declares, "That which may be known of God is manifest in them; for God hath shewed it unto them. For the invisible things of him from the creation of the world are clearly seen, being understood by the things that are made, even his eternal power and Godhead; so that they are without excuse" (Rom. 1:19-20).

Now why do not Antinomians object to nature addressing men indiscriminately? Why do not these hyper-Calvinists protest against what we may designate the theology of the sun and the moon? Why do they not exclaim that there is no proper basis for such a call as nature makes? This view not only mocks the unregenerate, but belittles God, seeing that it is certain to prove fruitless, for He has not purposed that either savage or sage should respond to nature's call. But with the sober and the spiritual this branch of the divine government needs no apology. It is in all respects worthy of Him who is wonderful in counsel and excellent in working. Those groups of mankind who do not have the sacred Scriptures are as truly rational and accountable beings as those who are reared with God's written Word. Their having lost the power to read God's character in His works, as well as the inclination to seek after and find Him, does not in the least divest the Lord of His right to require of them both that inclination and power, and to deal with them by various methods of providence according to their several advantages.

It is altogether reasonable that intelligent creatures who, by falling into apostasy, have become blind to God's excellences and enemies to Him in their minds, should yet be commanded to yield Him the homage which is His due and should be urged and exhorted by a thousand tongues, speaking from every quarter of the heaven and the earth, to turn to Him as their supreme good, although it is absolutely certain that without gifts they do not possess, without a supernatural work of grace being wrought in their hearts, not one of them will ever incline his ear. Who does not perceive that this is an unimpeachable arrangement of things, in every respect worthy of the character of Him who is "righteous in all his ways, and holy in all his works" (Ps. 145:17)? The light of nature leaves all men without excuse, and God has a perfect right to require them to seek Him without vouchsafing the power of doing so, which power He is under no obligation to grant.

Exactly analogous to this is the case of those who come under the sound of the gospel, yet without being chosen to salvation or redemption by the precious blood of the Lamb. The love of God in Christ to sinners is proclaimed to them, and they are exhorted and entreated by all sorts of arguments to believe in Christ and be saved. Let it be clearly pointed out that no obstacle lies in the way of the reprobates' believing but what exists in their own evil hearts. Their minds are free to think and their wills to act. They do just as they please, unforced by anyone. They choose and refuse as seems good to themselves. The secret purpose of God in not appointing them to everlasting life or in withholding from them the renewing operations of His Spirit has no causal influence on the decision to which they come. Their advantages are vastly superior to the opportunities of those who enjoy only the light of nature.

The manifestation of the divine character granted to those living in Christendom is incomparably brighter and more impressive than that given to those born in heathendom, and consequently their responsibility is proportionately greater. Much more is given the former, and, on the ground of equity, much more will certainly be required of them (Luke 12:48). What, then, shall we say of the conduct of the Most High in His dealings with such persons? Shall we presumptuously question His sincerity in exhorting them by His Word or His sincerity in urging them by the general operations of His Spirit (Gen. 6:3; Acts 7:51)? With equal propriety we might question the sincerity of nature, when it bears witness to God's power in the shaking of the earth and the kindling of the volcano; or we might doubt God's goodness in clothing the valleys with corn and filling the pastures with flocks, leaving Himself "not . . . without witness" (Acts 14:17), in order that men "should *seek* the Lord, if haply they might feel after him, and find him" (Acts 17:27).

We by no means affirm that what we have pointed out entirely removes the difficulty felt by those who do not perceive the justice in exhorting sinners to perform acts altogether beyond their power. But we do insist that, in the light of God's method of dealing with the vast majority of men in the past, withholding the gospel effectually blunts its point. Ministers err grievously if they allow their hands to be tied or their mouths muzzled, thus disobeying Christ. The only difference between those living under the gospel and those who have only the light of nature seems to be that the grace of the one allotment is far greater than that of the other, that the responsibility is higher in proportion, and that the condemnation which results from disobedience must therefore be more severe in the one case than in the other in the great day of accounts. To those divinely called to preach the gospel the course is clear.

They are to go forth in obedience to their commission, appealing to "every creature," urging their hearers to be reconciled to God.

Speaking for himself, the writer (who for more than twenty years was active in oral ministry) never found any other consideration to deter him from sounding forth the universal call of the gospel. He knew there might well be some in his congregation who had sinned that sin for which there is no forgiveness (Matt. 12:31-32), others who had probably sinned away their day of grace, having quenched the Spirit (I Thess. 5:19) till it was no longer possible to renew them again to repentance (Luke 13:24-25; 19:48). Yet since this was mercifully concealed from him, he sought to cry aloud and spare not. He knew that the gospel was to be the savor of death unto death to some, and that God sometimes sends His servants forth with a commission similar to that of Isaiah's (6:9-10). Still that furnished no more reason why he should be silent than that the sun and moon should cease proclaiming their Creator's glory merely because the world is blind and deaf.

In this same connection it is pertinent to consider the striking and solemn case of Pharaoh. It indeed presents an awe-inspiring spectacle, yet that must not hinder us from looking at it and ascertaining what light it throws on the character and ways of the Most High. It is the case not merely of an isolated individual, but of a fearfully numerous class—the vessels of wrath fitted to destruction. It is true that Pharaoh was not called on to believe and be saved, he was not exhorted to yield himself to the constraining love of God as manifested in the gift of His Son; but he *was* required to submit himself to the authority of God and to accede to His revealed will. He was ordered to let Jehovah's people go that they might serve Him in the wilderness, and he was required to comply with the divine command not sullenly or reluctantly, not as a matter of necessity, but with his whole heart.

A Promise for Every Command of God

Let it not be overlooked that every divine command virtually implies a promise, for our duty and our welfare are in every instance inseparably joined (Deut. 10:12-13). If God is truly obeyed He will be truly glorified, and if He is truly glorified He will be truly enjoyed. Had the king of Egypt obeyed, certainly his fate would have been different. He would have been regarded not with disapproval but with favor; he would have been the object not of punishment but rather of reward. Nevertheless, it was not intended that he should obey. The Most High had decreed otherwise. Before Moses entered the presence of Pharaoh and made known Jehovah's command, the Lord informed His servant, "I will harden his heart that he shall *not* let the people go" (Exodus 4:21). This is unspeakably awful, yet it need not surprise us. The same sun whose rays melt the wax hardens the clay—an example in the visible realm of what takes place in the hearts of the renewed and of the unregenerate.

Not only was it God's intention to harden Pharaoh's heart so that he should not obey His command, but He plainly declared, "In very deed for this cause have I raised thee up; for to show in thee my power; and that my name may be declared throughout all the earth" (Exodus 9:16). The connection in which that solemn verse is quoted in Romans 9:17 makes it unmistakably plain that God ordained that this haughty monarch should be an everlasting monument to His severity. Here we witness the Ruler of this world dealing with men—for Pharaoh was representative of a large class—dealing with them about what concerns their highest interests, their happiness or their woe throughout eternity, not intending their happiness, not determining to confer the grace which would enable them to comply with His will, yet issuing *commands* to them, denouncing their threatenings, working signs and wonders before them, enduring them with much long-suffering while they add sin to sin and ripen for destruction. Yet let it be remembered that there was nothing which hindered Pharaoh from obeying except his own depravity. Whatever objection may be brought against the Word calling on the nonelect to repent and believe may with equal propriety be brought against the whole procedure of God with Pharaoh.

In their Articles of Faith the hyper-Calvinists declare, "We deny duty-faith and duty-repentance—these terms signifying that it is every man's duty to spiritually and savingly repent and believe." Those who belong to this school of theology insist that it would be just as sensible to visit our cemeteries and call on the occupants of the graves to come forth as to exhort those who are dead in trespasses and sins to throw down the weapons of their warfare and be reconciled to God. Such reasoning is unsound, for there is a vast and vital difference between a spiritually dead soul and a lifeless body. The soul of Adam became the subject of penal and spiritual death; nevertheless it retained all its natural powers. Adam did not lose all knowledge nor become incapable of volition; nor did the operations of conscience cease within him. He was still a rational being, a moral agent, a responsible creature, though he could no longer think or will, love or hate, in conformity to the law of righteousness.

It is far otherwise with physical dissolution. When the body dies it becomes as inactive, unintelligent and unfeeling as a piece of unorganized matter. A lifeless body has no responsibility, but a spiritually dead soul is accountable to God. A corpse in the cemetery will not "despise and reject" Christ (Isa. 53:3), will not "resist the Holy Ghost" (Acts 7:51), will not disobey the gospel (II Thess. 1:8); but the sinner can and *does* do these very things, and is justly condemned for them. Are we, then, suggesting that fallen man is *not* "dead in trespasses and sins"? No indeed, but we do insist that those solemn words be rightly interpreted and that no false conclusions be drawn from them. Because the soul has been deranged by sin, because all its operations are unholy, it is correctly said to be in a state of spiritual death, for it no more fulfills the purpose of its being than does a dead body.

The fall of man, with its resultant spiritual death, did not dissolve our relation to God as the Creator, nor did it exempt us from His authority. But it forfeited His favor and suspended that communion with Him by which alone could be preserved that moral excellence with which the soul was orig-inally endowed. Instead of attempting to draw analogies between spiritual and physical death and deriving inferences from them, we must stick very closely to the Scriptures and regulate all our thoughts by them. God's Word says, "You hath he quickened, who were dead in trespasses and sins: *wherein in times past ye walked*" (Eph. 2:1-2). Thus the spiritual death of the sinner is a state of *active* opposition against God—a state for which he is responsible, the guilt and enormity of which the preacher should constantly press upon him. Why do we speak of active opposition against God as being *dead* in sins? Because in Scripture "death" does not mean cessation of being, but a condi-tion of separation and alienation from God (Eph. 4:18).

The solemn and humbling fact that fallen man is fully incapable of any-thing spiritually good or of turning to God is clearly revealed and insisted on in His Word (John 6:44; II Cor. 3:5, etc.), yet the majority of professing Christians have rejected that fact. It is important to note that the grounds and reasons for which it has been opposed by some *are not scriptural.* They do not allege that there is any specific statement of Holy Writ which directly contradicts it. They do not affirm that any passage can be produced from the Word which expressly tells us that fallen man *has* the power of will to do anything spiritually good, or that he is able by his own strength to turn to God, or even prepare himself to do so. Instead, they are obliged to fall back on a *process of reasoning*, making inferences and deductions from certain general principles which the Scriptures sanction. It is at once apparent that there is a vast difference in point of certainty between these two things.

Principle of Exhortation in Scripture

The principal objection made against the doctrine of fallen man's inability is drawn from the supposed inconsistency between it and the principle of exhortation which runs all through Scripture. It is pointed out that commands and exhortations are addressed to the descendants of Adam, that they are manifestly responsible to comply with them, that they incur guilt by failure to obey. Then the conclusion is drawn that, therefore, these commandments would never have been given, that such responsibility could not belong to man, and such guilt could not be incurred, unless they were *able to will* and to do the things commanded. Thus their whole argument rests not on anything actually stated in Scripture, but on certain notions respecting the reasons why God issued these commands and exhortations, and respecting the ground upon which moral responsibility rests.

In like manner we find the hyper-Calvinists pursuing an identical course in their rejection of the exhortation principle. Though at the opposite pole in doctrine—for they contend for the spiritual impotence of fallen man—yet they concur with others in resorting to *a process of reasoning.* They cannot pro-duce a single passage *from God's Word* which declares that the unregenerate must not be urged to perform spiritual duties. They cannot point to any oc-casion on which the Saviour Himself warned His apostles against such a procedure, not even when He commissioned them to go and preach His gospel. They cannot even discover a word from Paul cautioning either Timothy or Titus to be extremely careful when addressing the unsaved lest they leave their hearers with the impression that their case was far from being desperate.

Not only are the hyper-Calvinists unable to produce one verse of Scripture containing such prohibitions or warnings as we have mentioned above, but they are faced with scores of passages both in the Old and the New Testaments which show unmistakably that the servants of God in biblical times followed the very opposite course to that advocated by these twentieth century theorists. Neither the prophets, the Saviour, nor His apostles shaped their policy by the state of their hearers. They did not accommodate their message according to the spiritual impotence of sinners, but plainly enforced the just requirements of a holy God. How, then, do these men dispose of all those passages which speak directly against their theories? By what is called (in some lawcourts) a process of "special pleading." We quote again from their Articles of Faith:

> We believe that it would be unsafe, from the brief records we have of the way in which the apostles, under the immediate direction of the Lord, addressed their hearers in certain special cases and circumstances, to derive absolute and universal rules for ministerial addresses in the present day under widely-different circumstances.

Thus they naïvely attempt to neutralize and set aside the practice of our Lord and of His apostles. It is very much like the course followed by the Pharisees, who drew up their own rules and regulations, binding them upon the people, against whom Christ preferred the solemn charge of "making the word of God of none effect through your tradition" (Mark 7:13). The statement "We believe it would be unsafe" is lighter than chaff when weighed against the authority of Holy Writ. If God's servants today are not to be regulated by the recorded examples of their Master and His apostles, where shall they turn for guidance?

And why do the framers of these Articles of Faith consider it "unsafe" to follow the precedents furnished by the Gospels and the Acts? Their next Article supplies the answer:

> Therefore, that for ministers in the present day to address unconverted persons, or indiscriminately all in a mixed congregation, calling upon them to savingly repent, believe, and receive Christ, or perform any other acts dependent upon the new-creative power of the Holy Ghost, is, on the one hand, to imply creature power, and, on the other, to deny the doctrine of special redemption.

Here they come out into the open and show their true colors, as mere rationalizers. They object to indiscriminate exhortations because *they* cannot see the consistency of such a policy with other doctrines. Just as extreme Arminians reject the truth of fallen man's moral impotence because they are unable to reconcile it with the exhortation principle, so Antinomians throw overboard human responsibility because they consider it out of harmony with the spiritual helplessness of the sinner.

Witness the consistency of man. As God Himself tells us, "Verily, every man at his best estate is altogether vanity" (Ps. 39:5). No wonder, then, that He bids us *"Cease ye from man, whose breath is in his nostrils: for wherein is he to be accounted of?"* (Isa. 2:22). Yes, "Cease ye from man"—religious man as much as irreligious man; cease placing any confidence in or dependence on him, especially in connection with spiritual and divine matters, for we cannot afford to be misdirected in these. Then what should the bewildered reader do? He must weigh everything he hears or reads in the balances of the Lord, testing it diligently by Holy Writ: "Prove all things; hold fast that which is good" (I Thess. 5:21). And what is the servant of Christ to do? He must execute the commission his Master has given him, declare all the counsel of God (not mangled bits of it), and leave the Lord to harmonize what may seem contradictory to him—just as Abraham proceeded to obediently sacrifice Isaac, even though he was quite incapable of harmonizing God's command with His promise "In Isaac shall thy seed be called" (Gen. 21:12).

It will be no surprise to most of our readers that those ministers who are restricted from calling on the unsaved to repent and believe the gospel are also very slack in exhorting professing Christians. The divine commandments are almost entirely absent from their ministry. They preach a lot on doctrine, often on experience, but life conduct receives the scantiest notice. It is not too much to say that they seem to be afraid of the very word "duty." They preach soundly and beneficially on the obedience which Christ gave to God on behalf of His people, but they say next to nothing of that obedience which the Lord requires from those He has redeemed. They give many comforting addresses from God's promises, but they are woefully remiss in delivering searching messages on His *precepts.* If anyone thinks this charge is unfair, let him pick up a volume of sermons by any of these men and see if he can find a single sermon on one of the precepts.

As an example of what we have just mentioned we quote at some length from a series of "Meditations on the Preceptive part of the Word of God" by J. C. Philpot. Note that these were not the casual and careless utterances of the pulpit, but the deliberate and studied products of his pen. In his first article on the precepts of the Word of God, Mr. Philpot said:

> It is a branch of Divine revelation which, without wishing to speak harshly or censoriously, has in our judgment been sadly perverted by many on the one hand, and we must say almost as sadly neglected, if not altogether ignored and passed by, by many on the other. . . . It is almost become a tradition in some churches professing the doctrines of grace to disregard the precepts and pass them by in a kind of general silence.

This declaration was sadly true, for the charge preferred characterized the greater part *of his own ministry* and applied to the preachers in his own denomination. That Mr. Philpot was fully aware of this sad state of affairs is clear from the following:

Consider this point, ye ministers, who Lord's day after Lord's day preach nothing but doctrine, doctrine, doctrine; and ask yourselves whether the same Holy Spirit who revealed the first three chapters of the epistle to the Ephesians did not also reveal the last three? Is not the whole epistle equally inspired, a part of that Scripture of which we read, "All Scripture is given by inspiration of God and is profitable for doctrine, for reproof, for correction, for instruction in righteousness, that the man of God may be perfect, thoroughly furnished unto all good works" (II Tim. 3:16, 17)? How, then, can you be "a man of God perfect" (that is, complete as a minister) and "thoroughly furnished unto all good works," if you wilfully neglect any part of that Scripture which God has given to be profitable to you, and to others by you? . . . Can it be right, can it be safe, can it be Scriptural, to treat all this fulness and weight of precept with no more attention than an obsolete Act of Parliament?

To the same effect, he declared:

To despise, then, the precept, to call it legal and burdensome, is to despise not man, but God, who hath given unto us His Holy Spirit in the inspired Scriptures for our faith and obedience. . . . Nothing more detects hypocrites, purges out loose professors, and fans away that chaff and dust which now so thickly covers our barn floors than an experimental handling of the precept. A dry doctrinal ministry disturbs no consciences. The loosest professors may sit under it, nay, be highly delighted with it, for it gives them a hope, if not a dead confidence, that salvation being wholly of grace they shall be saved whatever be their walk of life. But the experimental handling of the precept cuts down all this and exposes their hypocrisy and deception.

In developing his theme Mr. Philpot rightly began by discussing its importance, and this at considerable length. First, he called attention to its "bulk," or the large place given to precepts in the Word:

The amount of precept in the epistles, measured only by the test of *quantity* would surprise a person whose attention had not been directed to that point, if he would but carefully examine it. But it is sad to see how little the Scriptures are read amongst us with that intelligent attention, that careful and prayerful studiousness, that earnest desire to understand, believe, and experimentally realise their Divine meaning, which they demand and deserve, and which the Word of God compares to seeking as for silver, and searching "as for hid treasure" (Prov. 2:4).

How much less are the Scriptures read today than they were in Mr. Philpot's time!

Next, he pointed out the following:

Were there no precepts in the New Testament we should be without *an inspired rule of life*, without an authoritative guide for our walk and conduct before the Church and the world. . . . But mark what would be the consequence if the preceptive part of the New Testament were taken out of its pages as so much useless matter. It would be like going on board of a ship bound on a long and perilous voyage, and taking out of her just before she sailed, all her charts, her compass, her sextants, her sounding line, her chronometer; in a word, all the instruments of navigation needful for her safely crossing the sea, or even leaving her port.

He disposed of the quibble that if there were no precepts, the church would still have the Holy Ghost to guide her by saying, "If God has mercifully and graciously given us rules and directions whereby to walk, let us thankfully accept them, not question and cavil how far we could have done without them."

Under his third reason for showing the *importance* of the precepts are some weighty remarks from which we select the following:

> Without a special revelation of the precepts in the word of truth we should not know what was the will of God as regards all spiritual and practical obedience, so, without it as our guide and rule, we *should not be able to live to His glory.* . . . Be it, then, observed, and ever borne in mind that, as the glory of God is the end of all our obedience, it must be an obedience according to His own prescribed rule and pattern. In this point lies all the distinction between the obedience of a Christian to the glory of God and the self-imposed obedience of a Pharisee to the glory of self. . . . Thus we see that if there were no precepts as our guiding rule, we could not live to the glory of God, or yield to Him an acceptable obedience; and for this simple reason, that we should not know how to do so. We might wish to do so; we might attempt to do so; but we should and must fail.

This section on the importance of the precepts was denied by pointing out: "On its fulfillment turns *the main test of distinction* between the believer and the unbeliever, between the manifested vessel of mercy and the vessel of wrath fitted to destruction." At the close of this division he said, "Take one more test from the Lord's own lips. Read the solemn conclusion of the Sermon on the Mount—that grand code of Christian precepts."

After quoting Matthew 7:24-27 Mr. Philpot asks:

> What is the Lord's own test of distinction between the wise man who builds on the rock, and the foolish man who builds on the sand? The rock, of course, is Christ, as the sand is self. But the test, the mark, the evidence, the proof of the two builders and the two buildings is the hearing of Christ's sayings and *doing* them, or the hearing of Christ's sayings and *doing them not*. We may twist and wriggle under such a text, and try all manner of explanations to parry off its keen, cutting edge; we may fly to arguments and deductions drawn from the doctrine of grace to shelter ourselves from its heavy stroke, and seek to prove that the Lord was there preaching the law and not the gospel, and that as we are saved by Christ's blood and righteousness, and not by our own obedience or our good works, either before or after calling, all such tests and all such texts are inapplicable to our state as believers. But after all our questionings and cavillings, our nice and subtle arguments, to quiet conscience and patch up a false peace, there the word of the Lord stands.

It is disastrous that such cogent arguments have carried little weight and that the precepts are still sadly neglected by many of the Lord's servants.

Chapter 21

COMPLEMENT

LET US BEGIN by defining our term. The "complement" of a thing is that which gives it completeness. In contemplating the natural condition of Adam's children we obtain a one-sided and misleading view if we confine our attention to their spiritual helplessness. That they *are* morally impotent, that they are totally depraved, that they are thoroughly under the bondage of sin, has been amply demonstrated. But that does not supply us with a complete diagnosis of their present state before God. Though fallen man is a wrecked and ruined creature, nevertheless he is still accountable to his Maker and Ruler. Though sin has darkened his understanding and blinded his judgment, he is still a rational being. Though his very nature is corrupt at its root, this does not exempt him from loving God with all his heart. Though he is "without strength," yet he is not "without excuse." And why not? Because side by side with fallen man's inability is *his moral responsibility.*

Moral Responsibility of Man

It is at this very point that the people of God, and especially His ministers, need to be much on their guard. If they appropriate one of the essential parts of the doctrine of Scripture but fail to lay hold of the equally essential supplementary part, then they will necessarily obtain a distorted view of the doctrine. "The word of God is quick, and powerful, and sharper than any *two-edged* sword" (Heb. 4:12). The word emphasized in the above quotation is of paramount importance, though its significance seems to be discerned by few today. *Truth is twofold.* Every aspect of truth presented in the Word is balanced by a counterpart aspect; every element of doctrine has its corresponding obligation. These two sides of the truth do not cross each other, but run parallel. They are not contradictory but complementary. The one aspect is just as essential as the other, and *both* must be retained if we are to be preserved from dangerous error. It is only as we hold firmly to "*all* the counsel of God" that we are delivered from the fatal pitfalls of false theology.

God Himself has illustrated this duality of truth by communicating the same concept to us in the form of the *two* Testaments, the Old and the New, the contents of which, broadly speaking, exemplify those two summarizations of His nature and character: "God is light" (I John 1:5); "God is love" (I John 4:8). This same fundamental feature is seen again in the two principal communications which God has made, namely, His law and His gospel. That which characterizes the divine revelation in its broad outlines also holds equally good in connection with its details. Promises are balanced by precepts, the gifts of grace with the requirements of righteousness, the bestowments of abounding mercy with the exactions of inflexible justice. Correspondingly, the duties placed upon us answer to this twofold revelation of the divine character and will; as light and the Giver of the law, God requires the sinner to repent and the saint to fear Him; as love and the Giver of the gospel, the one is called upon to believe and the other to rejoice.

The doctrine of man's accountability and responsibility to God is set forth so plainly, so fully and so constantly throughout the Scriptures that he who runs may read it, and only those who deliberately close their eyes to it can fail to perceive its verity and force. The entire volume of God's Word testifies to the fact that He requires from man right affections and right actions, and that He judges and treats him according to these. "So then every one of us shall give account of himself to God" (Rom. 14:12) that the rights of God may be enforced upon moral agents. In the day of the revelation of His righteous judgment, God "will render to every man according to his deeds" (Rom. 2:5-6). Then will be fulfilled that word of Christ's "He that rejecteth me, and receiveth not my words, hath one that judgeth him: the word that I have spoken, the same shall judge him in the last day" (John 12:48). Men are responsible to employ in God's service the faculties He has given them (Matt. 25:14-30; Luke 12:48). They are responsible to improve the opportunities God has afforded them (Matt. 11:20-24; Luke 19:41-42).

Thus it is clear that—in keeping with the Word of God as a whole and with all His ways both in creation and providence—the doctrine of man's inability has a complementary and balancing doctrine, namely, his responsibility; and it is only by maintaining both in their due proportions that we shall be preserved from distorting the truth. But man is a creature of extremes, and his tendency to lopsidedness is tragically evidenced all through Christendom. The religious world is divided into opposing parties which contend for bits of the truth and reject others. Where can be found a denomination which preserves a due balance in its proclamation of God's law and God's gospel? In the presentation of God as light and God as love? In an equal emphasis on His precepts and His promises? And where shall we find a group of churches, or even a single church, which is preserving a due proportion in its preaching on man's inability and man's responsibility?

On every side today men in the pulpits pit one part of the truth against another, overstressing one doctrine and omitting its complement, setting those things against each other which God has joined together, confounding what He has separated. So important is it that God's servants should preserve the balance of truth, so disastrous are the consequences of a one-sided ministry, that we feel impressed to point out some of the more essential balancing doctrines which must be preserved if God is to be duly honored and His people rightly edified. We shall later resume the subject of human responsibility in order to throw light on the problem raised by the doctrine of man's impotence.

Means of Salvation

First, let us consider *the causes and the means of salvation*. There are no less than seven things which do concur in this great work, for all of them are said, in one passage or another, to "save" us. Salvation is ascribed to the love of God, to the atonement of Christ, to the mighty operations of the Spirit, to the instrumentality of the Word, to the labors of the preacher, to the conversion of a sinner, to the ordinances, or sacraments. The view of salvation entertained today by the majority of professing Christians is so superficial, so cramped, so inadequate. Indeed, so great is the ignorance which now prevails that we had better furnish proof texts for each of these seven concurring causes lest we be charged with error on so vital a subject.

Salvation is ascribed to God the Father "Who hath saved us, and called us with an holy calling" (II Tim. 1:9)—because of His electing love in Christ. To the Lord Jesus: "He shall save his people from their sins" (Matt. 1:21)—because of His merits and satisfaction. To the Holy Spirit: "He hath saved us, by the renewing of the Holy Spirit" (Titus 3:5)—because of His almighty efficacy and operations. To the instrumentality of the Word, "the engrafted word, which is able to save your souls" (James 1:21)—because it discovers to us the grace whereby we may be saved. To the labors of the preacher: "In doing this thou shalt both save thyself, and them that hear thee" (I Tim. 4:16)—because of their subordination to God's work. To the conversion of a sinner in which repentance and faith are exercised by us: "Save yourselves from this untoward generation"—by the repentance spoken of in verse 38 (Acts 2:40); "By grace are ye saved through faith" (Eph. 2:8). To the ordinances, or sacraments: "Baptism doth also now save us" (I Peter 3:21)—because it seals the grace of God to the believing heart.

Now these seven things must be considered in their *order* and kept in their place, otherwise incalculable harm will be done. For instance, if we elevate a subsidiary cause above a primary one, all sense of real proportion is lost. The love and wisdom of God comprise the prime cause, the first mover of all the rest of the causes which contribute to our salvation. Next are the merit and satisfaction of Christ, which are the result of the eternal wisdom and love of God and also the foundation of all that follows. The omnipotent operations of the Holy Spirit work in the elect those things which are necessary for their participation in and application of the benefits purposed by God and purchased by Christ. The Word is the chief means employed in conversion, for faith comes by hearing (Rom. 10:17). As the result of the Spirit's operations and His application of the Word, we are brought to repent and believe. In this it is the Spirit's general custom to employ the ministers of Christ as His subordinate agents. Baptism and the Lord's Supper are to confirm repentance and faith in us.

Not only must these seven concurring causes of salvation be considered in their proper order and kept in their due place, but they must not be confounded with one another so that we attribute to a later one what belongs to a primary one. We must not attribute to the ordinances that which belongs to the Word; the Word is appointed for conversion, the ordinances for confirmation. A legal contract is first offered and then sealed (ratified) when the parties are agreed: "Then they that [1] gladly received his word were [2] baptized" (Acts 2:41). Nor must we ascribe to the ordinances that which belongs to conversion. Many depend on their outward hearing of the Word as ground for partaking of the Lord's Supper: "We have eaten and drunk in thy presence, and thou hast taught in our streets" (Luke 13:26). But sound conversion, not frequenting the means of grace, is our title to pardon and life: "Be ye doers of the word, and not hearers only" (James 1:22).

Again, we must not ascribe to conversion what belongs to the Spirit. Our repentance and faith are indispensable for the enjoyment of the privileges of Christianity, yet these graces do not spring from mere nature but are wrought in us by the Holy Spirit. Nor must we ascribe to the Spirit that honor which belongs to Christ, as if our conversion were meritorious, or that the repentance and faith worked in us deserved the benefits we have come to possess. No, that honor pertains to the Lamb alone, who merited and purchased all for us. Neither must we ascribe to Christ that which belongs to the Father, for the Mediator came not to take us away from God, but to bring us to Him: "Thou . . . hast redeemed us to God" (Rev. 5:9). Thus all things pertaining to our salvation must be ranged in their proper place, and we must consider what is peculiar to the love of God, the merit of Christ, the operations of the Spirit, the instrumentality of the Word, the labors of the preacher, the conversion of a sinner, the ordinances.

Unless we observe the true order of these causes and rightly predicate what pertains to each, we fall into disastrous mistakes and fatal errors. If we ascribe all to the mercy of God so as to shut out the merit of Christ, we exclude God's great design in the cross—to demonstrate His righteousness (Rom. 3:24-26). On the other hand, if we proclaim the atonement of Christ in a manner that lessens esteem of God's love, we are apt to form the false idea that He is all wrath and needed blood to appease Him; whereas Christ came to demonstrate His goodness (II Cor. 5:19). If we ascribe to the merits of Christ that which is proper to the work of the Spirit, we confound things that are to be distinguished, as if Christ's blood could take us to heaven without a new nature being wrought in us. If we ascribe our conversion to the exercise of our own strength, we wrong the Holy Spirit. If, upon pretended conversion, we neglect the means and produce no good works, we err fatally.

Not only must these seven things not be confounded, but they must not be separated from one another. We cannot rest on the grace of God without the atonement and merits of Christ, for God does not exercise His mercy to the detriment of His justice. Nor can we rightly take comfort in the sacrifice of Christ without regeneration and true conversion wrought in us by the Spirit, for we must be vitally united to Christ before we can receive His benefits. Nor must we expect the operations of the Spirit without the instrumentality of the Word, for of the church it is said that Christ (by the Spirit) would "sanctify and cleanse it with the washing of water by the word" (Eph. 5:26). Nor must we conclude that we are regenerated by the Spirit without repentance and faith, for these graces are evidences of the new birth. Nor must the ordinances of baptism and the Lord's Supper be slighted; otherwise we dislocate the method by which God dispenses His grace.

Second, *Christ must not be divided,* either in His natures or His offices. There may be an abuse of the orthodox assertion of His deity, for if we reflect exclusively on that and neglect His great condescension in becoming flesh, we miss the chief intent of His incarnation—to bring God near to us in our nature. On the other hand, if we altogether consider Christ's humanity and overlook His Godhead, we are in danger of denying His supereminent dignity, power and merit. Man is always disturbing the harmony of the gospel and setting one part against another. Unitarians deny that Christ is God and so impeach His atonement, pressing only His doctrine and example. Carnal men reflect only on Christ's redemption as the means of our atonement with God, and so overlook the necessary doctrine of His example, of Christ's appearing in order to be a pattern of obedience in our nature—so often pressed in Scripture (John 13:15; I Peter 2:21; I John 2:6). Let us not put asunder what God has joined together.

So with Christ's offices. His general office is but one, to be Mediator, or Redeemer, but the functions which belong to it are three: prophetic, priestly and royal, one of which concerns His mediation with God, the other His dealings with us. We are to reflect on Him in both parts: "Consider the Apostle *and* High Priest of our profession, Christ Jesus" (Heb. 3:1). The work of an apostle has to do with men, that of a high priest with God. But some are so occupied with Christ's mediation with God that they give little thought to His dealings with men; others so consider His relation to men that they overlook His mediation with God. Regarding His very priesthood, some are so concerned with His sacrifice that they ignore His continual intercession and thus fail to appreciate what a comfort it is to present our requests by such a worthy hand to God; yet both are acts of the same office.

Great harm has been done by so preaching the sacrifice and intercession of Christ that His doctrine and government have been made light of. This is one of the most serious defects today in a considerable section of Christendom which prides itself on its orthodoxy. They look so much to the Saviour that they have scarcely any eyes for the Teacher and Master. The whole religion of many professing Christians consists in depending on Christ's merits and trusting in His blood, *without* any real concern for His laws, by believing and obeying of which we are interested in the fruits of His righteousness and sacrifice. But the Word of God sets before us an entirely different sort of religion and does not make one office of the Redeemer disturb another. None find true rest for their souls until they take Christ's yoke upon them. He is the Saviour of none unless He is first their Lord.

The Scriptures of truth set forth Christ under such terms as not only intimate privilege to us, but speak of duty and obedience as well. "God hath made that same Jesus . . . both Lord and Christ" (Acts 2:36). He is Lord, or supreme Governor, as well as Christ the anointed Saviour; not only a Saviour to redeem and bless, but a Lord to rule and command. "Him hath God exalted . . . to be a Prince and a Saviour, for to give repentance to Israel, and forgiveness of sins" (Acts 5:31). Here again the compound terms occur because of His double work—to require and to give. Christ is such a Prince that He is also a Saviour, and such a Saviour that He is also a Prince; and as such He must be apprehended by our souls. Woe be to those who divide what God has joined. Also, "Christ is the head of the church: and he is the saviour of the body" (Eph. 5:23). On the one side, as Christ saves His people from their sins, so He also governs them; on the other side, His dominion over the church is exercised in bringing about its salvation.

The carnal segment of the religious world snatches greedily at comforts but has no heart for duties; it is all for privileges but wants nothing of obligations. This libertine spirit is very natural to all of us: "Let us break their bands asunder, and cast away their cords from us" (Ps. 2:3). It was thus with men when Christ was in their midst: "We will not have this man *to reign over us*" (Luke 19:14). Had He presented Himself to them simply as Redeemer He would have been welcome, but they had no desire for a Sovereign over them. Christ is wanted for His benefits, such as pardon, eternal life and everlasting glory; but the unregenerate cannot endure His strict doctrine and righteous laws—submission to His scepter is foreign to their nature.

On the other hand there are some who so extol the mediation of Christ with men that they ignore His mediation with God. Some are so absorbed with the letter of His doctrine that they overlook the necessity of the Holy Spirit to interpret it for them and apply it to their hearts. Men are such extremists that they cannot magnify one thing without deprecating another. They rejoice in the Spirit's communicating the Scriptures, but they deprecate His equally important work of opening hearts to receive them (Acts 16:14). Others so urge Christ as Lawgiver that they neglect Him as the fountain of grace. They are all for His doctrine and example, but despise His atonement and continued intercession. It is this taking of the gospel piecemeal instead of whole which has wrought such damage and corrupted the truth. Oh, for heavenly wisdom and grace to preserve the balance and to preach a full gospel.

We have pointed out that side by side with the fact of fallen man's spiritual impotence must be considered the complementary truth of his moral responsibility. We have sought to show the vital importance of holding fast to *both* and presenting them in their due proportions, thereby preserving *the balance* between them. In order to make this the more obvious and impressive, and at the same time to demonstrate the disastrous consequences of failing to do this, we have enlarged on the general principle of maintaining the gospel in its fullness instead of taking it piecemeal. We have endeavored to enforce the necessity for adhering to what God has joined together and of not confounding what He has separated, illustrating the point by a presentation of the seven concurring causes of salvation and of the natures and offices of Christ. We now resume that line of thought.

Third, *the order of the covenant must not be disturbed.* Said David of the Lord, "He hath made with me an everlasting covenant, ordered in all things, and sure" (II Sam. 23:5). Certain writers have expressed themselves quite freely on the everlastingness of this covenant, and also on its sureness; but they have said very little on the *ordering* of it, and still less on the necessity of our abiding by its arrangements. No one will have any part in this covenant unless he is prepared to take the whole compact. Within the contract God has so arranged things that they may not and do not hinder one another. This order of the covenant appears chiefly in the right statement of privileges and conditions, means and ends, duties and comforts.

1. *Privileges and conditions.* "Through this man is preached unto you the forgiveness of sins: and by him all that believe are justified from all things" (Acts 13:38-39). Do not those words state a condition which excludes the infidel and includes the penitent believer? "If I wash thee not, thou hast no part with me," declared the holy Saviour (John 13:8). Unless we are cleansed by Him we can have no part with Him in His benefits. "He became the author of the eternal salvation unto all them that *obey* him" (Heb. 5:9). Christ would act contrary to His divine commission, contrary to the covenant agreed upon by Him, were He to dispense His grace upon any other terms. Some men trust in their own external and imperfect righteousness, as if that were the only plea to make before God; whereas others look at nothing in themselves—either as conditions, evidence or means—and think their only plea is Christ's merits.

But neither those who trust in their own works nor those who think that no consideration is to be had for repentance, faith and new obedience adhere to the covenant of grace. Those who preach such a course offer men a covenant of their own modeling, not the covenant of God which is the sole charter and sure ground of the Christian's hope. The blood of Christ accomplishes its work, but repentance and faith must also do theirs. True, they have not the least degree of that honor which belongs to the love of God, the sacrifice of Christ or the operations of the Spirit; nevertheless repentance, faith and new obedience must be kept in view in their place. Is it not self-evident that none of the privileges of the covenant belong to the impenitent and unbelieving? It is the Father's work to love us, Christ's to redeem, and the Spirit's to regenerate; but *we* must accept the grace offered—that is, repent, believe and live in obedience to God.

2. *Means and ends.* There is a right order of means and ends, that by the former we may come to the latter. The greater end of Christianity is our coming to God, and the prime and general means are the office and work of Christ: "For Christ hath also once suffered for sins, the just for the unjust, that he might bring us to God" (I Peter 3:18). The subordinate means are

the fruits of Christ's grace in sanctifying us and enabling us to overcome temptations—more expressly by patient suffering and active obedience. By patient suffering: "If so be that we suffer with him, that we may be also glorified together" (Rom. 8:17). "Wherefore let them that suffer according to the will of God commit the keeping of their souls to him in well doing, as unto a faithful Creator" (I Peter 4:19). By obedience: "Know ye not, that to whom ye yield yourselves servants to obey, his servants ye are to whom ye obey; whether of sin unto death, or of obedience unto righteousness?" (Rom. 6:16). "He that saith, I know him, and keepeth not his conmmandments, is a liar, and the truth is not in him" (I John 2:4).

Now the great difficulty in connection with our salvation (I Peter 4:18) lies not in a respect to the end but the means. There is some difficulty about the end, namely, to convince men of an unseen bliss and glory; but there is far more about the means. There is not only greater difficulty in convincing their minds, but in gaining their hearts and bringing them to submit to that patient, holy, self-denying course whereby they may obtain eternal life. Men wish the end, but refuse the means. Like Balaam (Num. 23:10) they want to die the death of the righteous, but are unwilling to live the life of the righteous. When the Israelites despised the land of Canaan (Ps. 106:24-25) it was because of the difficulty of getting to it. They were assured that Canaan was a land flowing with milk and honey, but when they learned there were giants to be overcome first, walled towns to be scaled and numerous inhabitants to be vanquished, they demurred. Heaven is a glorious place, but it can only be reached by the way of denying self; and this few are willing to do. But the covenant expressly urges this upon us (Matt. 16:24; Luke 14:26).

3. *Duties and comforts.* Also there is a right order of duties and comforts. "Come unto me, all ye that labour and are heavy laden, and I will give you rest. Take my yoke upon you, and learn of me; for I am meek and lowly in heart: and ye shall find rest unto your souls" (Matt. 11:28-29). Observe carefully how commands and comforts, precepts and promises are here interwoven, and let us not separate what God has joined together. We must diligently attend to both in our desires and practices alike. We must not pick and choose what suits us best and pass by the rest, but earnestly seek after God and diligently use all His appointed means that He may "fulfil *all* the good pleasure of his goodness, and the work of faith with power" (II Thess. 1:11). But of how many must God say, as He did of old, "Ephraim is as a heifer that is taught and loveth to tread out the corn, but will not break the clods" (Hosea 10:11, an ancient translation). People desire privileges but neglect duties; they are all for wages but reluctant to work for them.

So it is even in the performance of duties: some are welcomed and done, others are disliked and shirked. But every duty must be observed in its place and season, and one must never be set against another. In resisting sin some avoid sensuality but yield to worldliness, deny fleshly lusts but fall into deadly errors. So with graces: Christians look so much to one that they forget the others. We are told to take unto ourselves "the *whole* armour of God" (Eph. 6:11), not simply a breastplate without a helmet. We must not play up knowledge so as to neglect practice, nor fervor of devotion so as to mislead us into ignorance and blind superstition. Some set their whole hearts to mourn for sin and think little of striving after a sense of their Saviour's love; others prattle of free grace but are not watchful against sin nor diligent in being fruitful.

Lest some imagine that we have departed from the landmarks of our fathers and have inculcated a spirit of legality, we propose to supply a number of quotations from the writings of some of the most eminent of God's servants in the past, men who in their day lifted up their voices in protest against the lopsided ministry which we are decrying, and who stressed the vital importance of preserving the balance of truth and of according to each segment its due place and emphasis. For the evil we are resisting is no new thing, but one that has wrought much havoc in every generation. The pendulum has ever swung from one extreme to the other, and few have been the men who preserved the happy mean or who faithfully declared all the counsel of God.

We begin with a portion of Bishop J. C. Ryle's *Estimate of Manton*, the Puritan:

> Manton held strongly the need of preventing and calling grace; but that did not hinder him from inviting all men to repent, believe, and be saved. Manton held strongly that faith alone lays hold on Christ and appropriates justification; but that did not prevent him urging upon all the absolute necessity of repentance and turning from sin. Manton held strongly to the perseverance of God's elect; but that did not hinder him from teaching that holiness is the grand distinguishing mark of God's people, and that he who talks of "never perishing" while he continues in wilful sin, is a hypocrite and a self-deceiver. In all this I frankly confess I see much to admire. I admire the Scriptural wisdom of a man who, in a day of hard and fast systems, could dare to be apparently inconsistent in order to "declare all the counsel of God." I firmly believe that this is the test of theology which does good in the church of Christ. The man who is not tied hand and foot by systems, and does not pretend to reconcile what our imperfect eyesight cannot reconcile in this dispensation, he is the man whom God will bless.

If Manton were on earth today we do not know where he would be able to obtain a hearing. One class would denounce him as a Calvinist, while another would shun him as an Arminian. One would accuse him of turning the grace of God into lasciviousness, while another would charge him with gross legality. All would say he was not consistent with himself, that one of his sermons contradicted another; that he was a "yea and nay preacher," one day building up and the next day tearing down what he had previously erected. So long as he confined himself to what *their* Articles of Faith expressed, Calvinists would allow him to address them; but as soon as he began to press duties upon them and exhort to performance of those duties, he would be banished from their pulpits. Arminians would tolerate him just so long as he kept to the human responsibility side of the truth, but the moment he mentioned unconditional election or particular redemption they would close their doors against him.

That prince of theologians, John Owen, in his work "The Causes, Ways, and Means of Understanding the Mind of God," after fully establishing "the necessity of an especial work of the Holy Spirit in the illumination of our minds to make us understand the mind of God as revealed in the Scriptures," and before treating of the means which must be used and the diligent labors put forth by us, began his fourth chapter by anticipating and disposing of an objection. A certain class of extremists (termed enthusiasts in those days) argued that, if our understanding of the Scriptures was dependent upon the illuminating operations of the Holy Spirit, then there was *no need* for earnest effort and laborious study on our part. After affirming that the gracious operations of the Spirit "do render all our use of proper means for the right interpretation of the Scripture, in a way of duty, indispensably necessary," Mr. Owen went on to point out:

> But thus it hath fallen out in other things. Those who have declared any thing either of doctrine or of the power of the grace of the Gospel, have been traduced as opposing the principles of morality and reason, whereas on their grounds alone, their true value can be discovered and their proper use directed. So the apostle preaching faith in Christ with righteousness and justification thereby, was accused to have made void the law, whereas without his doctrine the law would have been void, or of no use to the souls of men. So he pleads "Do we then make void the law through faith? God forbid: yea, we establish the law" (Rom. 3:31). So to this day, justification by the imputation of the righteousness of Christ and *the necessity of our own obedience*, the efficacy of Divine grace in conversion and the liberty of our wills, the stability of God's promises and our diligent *use of means*, are supposed inconsistent.

It will be seen from the closing sentences of the above quotation that there were some in the days of the Puritans who made a god of consistency, or rather of what they *considered* to be consistent, and that they pitted parts of the truth against their own favorite doctrines, rejecting anything which they considered to be inharmonious or incongruous. But Owen refused to accede to them and preferred to be regarded as inconsistent with himself rather than withhold those aspects of the gospel which he well knew were equally glorifying to God and profitable for His people. It is striking to note that the particular things singled out by him for mention are the very ones objected to by the hyper-Calvinists today, which shows how far astray they are from what Owen taught. We continue to quote from him:

> So it is here also. The necessity of the communication of spiritual light unto our minds to enable us to understand the Scriptures, and the exercise of our own reason in the use of external means, are looked on as irreconcilable. But as the apostle saith, "Do we make void the law by faith? yea, we establish it;" though he did it not in that place, nor unto those

ends that the Jews would have had and used it. So we may say, do we by asserting the righteousness of Christ make void our own obedience, by the efficacy of grace destroy the liberty of our wills, by the necessity of spiritual illumination take away the use of reason? yea, we establish them. We do it not, it may be, in such a way or in such a manner as some would fancy and which would render them all on our part really useless, but in a clear consistency with and proper subserviency unto the work of God's Spirit and grace.

"The people answered him, We have heard out of the law that Christ abideth for ever: and how sayest thou, The Son of man must be lifted up?" (John 12:34). In his comments upon this verse, that grand old commentator Matthew Henry said:

> They alleged those scriptures of the O.T. which speak of the perpetuity of the Messiah, that He should be so far from being cut off in the midst of His days, that He should be a "Priest forever" (Psa. 110:4) and a King "forever" (Psa. 89:29, etc.). That He should have length of days forever and ever, and His years "as many generations" (Psa. 61:6); from all this they inferred the Messiah should *not* die. Thus great knowledge in the letter of the Scripture, if the heart be unsanctified, is capable of being abused to serve the cause of infidelity and to fight Christianity with its own weapons. Their perverseness will appear if we consider that when they vouched the Scripture to prove that the Messiah "abideth forever," they took no notice of those texts which speak of the Messiah's death and sufferings: they had heard out of the law that He "abideth forever," but had they never heard out of the law that Messiah "shall be cut off" (Dan. 9:26), that He shall "pour out His soul unto death" (Isa. 53:12), and particularly that His "hands and feet" should be pierced? Why then do they make so strange of His being "lifted up?"

The folly of these skeptical Jews was not one whit greater than that of rationalistic Calvinists. The one group refused to believe one part of Messianic prophecy because they were unable to harmonize it with another; the latter reject the truth of human responsibility because they cannot perceive its consistency with the doctrine of fallen man's spiritual impotence. Aptly did Matthew Henry follow up the above remarks by immediately adding:

> We often run into great mistakes, and then defend them with Scripture arguments, by putting those things asunder which God in His Word has put together, and opposing one truth under the pretence of supporting another. We have heard out of the Gospel that which exalts free grace, we have heard also that which enjoins duty, and we must cordially embrace both, and not separate them, or set them at variance.

Divine grace is not bestowed with the object of freeing men from their obligations but rather with that of supplying them with a powerful motive for more readily and gratefully discharging those obligations. To make God's favor a ground of exemption from the performance of duty comes perilously near to turning His grace into lasciviousness.

In his "Precious Remedies Against Satan's Devices," Thomas Brooks wrote:

The fourth device Satan hath to keep souls off from holy exercises, is by working them to make false inferences on those blessed and glorious things that Christ hath done. As that Jesus Christ hath done all for us, therefore there is nothing for us to do but to joy and rejoice. He hath perfectly justified us, fulfilled the law, statisfied Divine justice, pacified His Father's wrath, and is gone to Heaven to prepare a place for us, and in the meantime to intercede for us; and therefore away with praying, mourning, hearing, etc. Ah! what a world of professors hath Satan drawn in these days from religious services by working them to make such sad, wild and strange inferences from the excellent things the Lord Jesus hath done for His beloved ones.

The Puritan named one remedy for this:

> To dwell as much on those scriptures that show you the duties and services that Christ requires of you, as upon those scriptures that declare to you the precious and glorious things Christ hath done for you. It is a sad and dangerous thing to have two eyes to behold our dignity and privileges, and not one to see our duties and services. I should look with one eye upon the choice things Christ hath done for me to raise up my heart to love Christ with the purest love and to joy in Him with the strongest joy, and to lift up Christ above all who hath made Himself to be my all; and I should look with the other eye upon those services and duties that the scriptures require of those for whom Christ hath done such blessed things, as I Cor. 6:19, 20; 15:58; Gal. 6:9; I Thess. 5:16, 17; Phil. 2:12; Heb. 10:24, 25. Now a soul that would not be drawn away by this device of Satan must not look with a squint eye upon these blessed scriptures, and many more of like import, but he must *dwell upon* them, make them to be his chiefest and choicest companions, and this will be a happy means to keep him close to Christ.

Our principal design in writing further on the fact that man's spiritual impotence is his moral responsibility is to make plainly manifest the tremendous importance of preserving the balance of truth, which is mainly a matter of setting forth each element of it in its scriptural proportions. Almost all theological and religious error consists of truth perverted, truth wrongly divided, truth misapplied, truth overemphasized, truth viewed in a wrong perspective. The fairest face on earth, possessed of the most comely features, would soon become ugly and unsightly if one feature continued growing while the others remained undeveloped. Physical beauty is mainly a thing of due proportion. And thus it is with the Word of God: Its beauty and blessedness are best perceived when it is presented in its true proportions. Here is where so many have failed in the past; some favorite doctrine has been concentrated on, and others of equal importance neglected.

Need for Balanced Teaching

It is freely granted that in these degenerate days the servant of God is often called upon to give special emphasis to those verities of Holy Writ which are now so generally ignored and denied. Yet even here much wisdom is needed lest our zeal run away with us. The requirements of that phrase "meat in due season" must ever be borne in mind. When working among

Arminians we should not altogether omit the human responsibility side of the truth, yet the main emphasis ought to be placed on the divine sovereignty and its corollaries, which are so sadly perverted, if not blankly denied, by free-willers. Contrariwise, when ministering to Calvinists our chief aim should be to bring before them not those things they most *like* to hear, but those which they most *need*—those aspects of truth they are least familiar with. Only thus can we be of the greatest service to either group.

To illustrate what we have just said, take the subject of prayer. In preaching on it to Arminians, it would be well to define very clearly what this holy exercise is not designed to accomplish and what is its spiritual aim, showing that our prayers are not intended for the overcoming of any reluctance in God to grant the mercies we need, still less our supplications meant to effect any change in the divine purpose. "The counsel of the LORD standeth for ever, the thoughts of his heart to all generations" (Ps. 33:11). Rather the purpose of prayer is the subjecting of ourselves to God in asking for those things which are according to His will. In preaching to Calvinists we should warn against that fatalistic attitude which assumes that it will make no difference to the event whether we petition God or not, reminding them that "the effectual fervent prayer of a righteous man availeth much" (James 5:16). Some Arminians need rebuking for irreverence and unholy familiarity in addressing the Most High, while some Calvinists should be encouraged to approach the throne of grace with holy boldness, with the liberty of children petitioning their father.

The same course needs to be followed when expounding the great subject of salvation. Discrimination must be used as to *which* aspects most need to be set before any particular congregation. The manner in which this most blessed theme should be presented calls for much understanding, not only of the subject itself but also of the truth. Some doctrines are more difficult to apprehend than others (II Peter 3:16), and they need to be approached gradually and given out "here a little, there a little." We are well aware that in offering such counsel we lay ourselves open to the charge of acting craftily; in reality we are simply advocating the very policy pursued by Christ and His apostles. Of the Saviour it is recorded that "with many such parables spake he the word unto them, *as they were able to hear it*" (Mark 4:33); and addressing His apostles He said, "I have yet many things to say unto you, but ye cannot bear them now" (John 16:12; cf. I Cor. 3:1-2; 9:19-22).

What we have advocated above is simply adopting our presentation of the truth according to the state of our congregation. There is a vast difference between presenting the *way* of salvation to the unconverted and expounding the *doctrine* of salvation to those who are converted, though too many preachers make little distinction here. Great care needs to be exercised when preaching from one of the Epistles to a general congregation, lest on the one hand the children's bread be cast to the dogs or, on the other, seekers after the Lord be stumbled. While it is true that, in the absolute sense, no sinner can save himself or even contribute anything toward his salvation by any physical or mental act of his own, yet he must be constantly reminded that the gospel sets before him an external Saviour (rather than One who is working secretly and invincibly in him) whom he is responsible to promptly receive on the terms by which He is offered. to him.

It is most important that pulpit and pew alike should have a right conception of the relation of faith to salvation—a full-orbed conception and not a restricted and one-sided view. Believing is not only an evidence of salvation and a mark of regeneration, but it is also necessary *in order to* obtain salvation. True, the sinner is not saved for his faith; yet it is equally true that he cannot be saved without it. That believing is in one sense a saving act is clearly affirmed: "But we are not of them who draw back unto perdition; but of them that believe to the saving of the soul" (Heb. 10:39). Take the case of Cornelius. It is plain from Acts 10:2, 4 that a work of grace had been wrought in his heart before Peter was sent to him; yet Acts 11:14 makes it equally clear that it was necessary for the apostles to go and speak words "whereby he and his house should be saved." One of those "words" was "To him give all the prophets witness, that through his name whosoever *believeth in him* shall receive remission of sins" (10:43). Let it not be objected that we are hereby making a saviour of faith, for Christ did not hesitate to say "Thy faith hath saved thee" (Luke 7:50).

As an example of how well Calvin himself preserved the balance of truth we quote the following from his *Institutes*:

> Yet at the same time a pious man will not overlook inferior causes. Nor, because he accounts those from whom he has received any benefit, the ministers of the Divine goodness, will he therefore cast them by unnoticed, as though they deserved no thanks for their kindness; but will feel and readily acknowledge his obligation to them, and study to return it as ability and opportunity may permit. Finally, he will reverence and praise God as the principal Author of benefits received, will honour men as His ministers; and will understand, what, indeed, is the fact, that the will of God has laid him under obligations to those persons by whose means the Lord has been pleased to communicate His benefits.

While ascribing supreme honor and glory to the Author of every blessing, we must not despise the instruments He may design to employ in the imparting of them.

The great Reformer went on:

> If He suffer any loss either through negligence or through imprudence, he will conclude that it happened according to the Divine will, but *will also* impute the blame of it to himself. If any one be removed by disease, whom, while it was his duty to take care of him, he has treated with neglect,—though he cannot be ignorant that that person had reached those limits which it was impossible for him to pass, yet he will not make this a plea to extenuate his guilt; but, because he has not faithfully performed his duty towards him, will consider him as having perished through *his* criminal negligence. Much less, when fraud and preconceived malice

appear in the perpetration either of murder or of theft, will he excuse those enormities under the pretext of the Divine Providence: in the *same* crime he will distinctly contemplate the righteousness of God *and* the iniquity of man, as they respectively discover themselves.

How far was Calvin from the squint-eyed vision of many who claim to be his admirers! Writing on "the conducting of prayer in a right and proper manner," he stated:

> The fourth and last rule is, That thus prostrate with true humility, we should nevertheless be animated to pray by the certain hope of obtaining our requests. It is indeed an apparent contradiction to connect a certain confidence of God's favour with a sense of His righteous vengeance, though these two things are perfectly consistent if persons oppressed by their own guilt be encouraged solely by the Divine goodness. For as we have before stated that repentance and faith, of which one terrifies and the other exhilarates, are inseparably connected, so their union is necessary in prayer. And this agreement is briefly expressed by David: "I will come into Thy house in the multitude of Thy mercy: and in Thy fear will I worship toward Thy holy temple" (Psa. 5:7). Under the goodness of God he comprehends faith, though not to the exclusion of fear, for His majesty not only commands our reverence, but our own unworthiness makes us forget all pride and security and fills us with fear. I do not mean a confidence which delivers the mind from all sense of anxiety, and soothes it into pleasant and perfect tranquility, for such a placid satisfaction belongs to those whose prosperity is equal to their wishes, who are affected by no care, corroded by no anxiety and alarmed by no fear. And the saints have an excellent stimulus to calling upon God when their needs and perplexities harass and disquiet them and they are almost despairing in themselves, till faith opportunity relieves them; because amid such troubles the goodness of God is so glorious in their view, that though they groan under the pressure of present calamities and are likewise tormented with the fear of greater in future, yet a reliance on it alleviates the difficulty of bearing them and encourages a hope of deliverance.

Here we have brought together two radically different exercises of the mind, which are totally diverse in their springs, their nature and their tendency—fear and confidence, perturbation and tranquillity: two spiritual graces which some imagine neutralize each other—humility and assurance. A sight of God's ineffable holiness fills a renewed heart with awe; and when it is coupled with a sense of His high majesty and inflexible righteousness, the soul—conscious of its excuseless sins, its defilement and its guilt—is made to fear and tremble, feeling utterly unfit and unworthy to address the Most High. Yes, but if the humbled saint is able to also contemplate the goodness of God, view Him as the Father of mercies and consider some of His exceeding great and precious promises which are exactly suited to his dire needs, he is encouraged to hope. And while his humility does not then degenerate into presumption, yet is he constrained to come boldly to the throne of grace and present his petitions.

Calvin spoke clearly on this point:

The prayers of a pious man, therefore, must proceed from *both* these dispositions, and must also contain and discover them both: though he must groan under present evils and is anxiously afraid of new ones, yet at the same time he must resort for refuge to God, not doubting His readiness to extend the assistance of His hand. For God is highly displeased by our distrust, if we supplicate Him for blessings which we have no expectation of receiving. There is nothing, therefore, more suitable to the nature of prayers, than that they be conformed to this rule:—not to rush forward with temerity, but to follow the steps of faith. "If any of you lack wisdom, let him ask of God, that giveth to all men liberally, and upbraideth not. But let him ask in faith, nothing wavering" (James 1:5, 6). Where, by opposing "faith" to "wavering" he very aptly expresses its nature. And equally worthy of attention is what he adds, that they avail nothing who call upon God in unbelief and doubt, and are uncertain in their minds whether they shall be heard or not.

The charge preferred by God against Israel's priests of old—"Ye have not kept my ways, but have been *partial* in the law" (Mal. 2:9)—applies to many preachers today. Some have gone to such extremes that they have denied there is any such thing as God chastising His own dear children. They argue that since "he hath not beheld iniquity in Jacob, neither hath he seen perverseness in Israel" (Num. 23:21), and since He has declared of His bride, "Thou art all fair, my love; there is no spot in thee" (Song of Sol. 4:7), there remains no occasion for the rod. It is this dwelling on favorite portions of truth to the exclusion of others which has led many into grievous errors. The nonimputation of sin *to* believers and the chastising of sin *in* believers are both plainly taught in the Scriptures (e.g., II Sam. 12:13-14 where both facts are mentioned side by side). Whether or not they can be reconciled to mere human reason, both must be firmly held by us.

As Matthew Henry tersely expressed it, "In the doctrine of Christ there are paradoxes which to men of corrupt mind are stumblingstones." It is the twofoldness of truth which has (in part) furnished occasion for infidels to declare that the Bible is full of contradictions; being blind spiritually, they are unable to perceive the perfect harmony of the whole. To what a sorry pass have things come, then, when some who wish to be regarded as the very champions of orthodoxy make the same charge against those who contend for the *entire* faith once delivered to the saints. The truth, the whole truth, and nothing but the truth, is the standard which must be applied to the pulpit as well as the lawcourt. One element of truth must not be pressed to such an extreme that another is denied; each must be given its due and distinctive place.

It is a favorite device of Satan's to drive us from one extreme to another. This may be seen by observing the order of the temptations which he set before the Saviour. First he sought to overthrow Christ's faith, to bring Him to doubt the Word of God and His goodness to Him. He said something like this: "God has proclaimed from heaven that Thou art His beloved Son, yet He is allowing Thee to starve to death here in the wilderness," as is clear from his "If thou be the Son of God, command that these stones be made bread." Failing to prevail by such an assault, Satan then took a contrary course in his next attack, seeking to bring the Lord Jesus to act presumptuously: "If thou be the Son of God, cast thyself down: for it is written, He shall give his angels charge concerning thee: and in their hands they shall bear thee up, lest at any time thou dash thy foot against a stone." The force of this was: "Since Thou art so fully assured of the Father's loving care, demonstrate Thy confidence in His protection; since Thy faith in His Word is so unshakable, count upon His promise that no harm shall befall Thee even though Thou castest Thyself from the pinnacle of the temple."

The above has been recorded for our learning, for it shows us the guile of the devil and the cunning tactics which he employs, especially that of swinging from one extreme to another. Let it be borne in mind that as he dealt there with Christ the Head, so Satan continues to act with all Christ's members. If he cannot bring them to one extreme, he will endeavor to drive them to another. If he cannot bring a man to covetousness and miserliness, he will attempt to drive him to prodigality and thriftlessness. If a man is of the sober and somber type, let him beware lest the devil, in condemning him for this, lead him into levity and irreverence. The devil cannot endure one who turns neither to the right hand nor to the left; nevertheless, we must seek to keep the golden mean, neither doubting on the one hand nor presuming on the other, giving way neither to despair nor to recklessness.

Let us not forget that truth itself may be misused (II Peter 3:16), and the very grace of God may be turned into lasciviousness (Jude 4). Solemn warnings are these. "Commit thy way unto the LORD; trust also in him; and he shall bring it to pass" (Ps. 37:5). That is a blessed promise, yet I altogether pervert it if I use it to the neglect of duty and sit down and do nothing. "Stand fast therefore in the liberty wherewith Christ hath made us free" (Gal. 5:1). That is an important precept, yet I put it to wrong use if I so stand up for my own rights that I exercise no love for my brothers in Christ. "Who are kept by the power of God through faith unto salvation ready to be revealed in the last time" (I Peter 1:5). That too is a blessed promise, yet it does not exempt me from using all proper means for my preservation. The Christian farmer knows that unless God is pleased to bless his labors he will reap no harvest, but that does not hinder him from plowing and harrowing.

Let us close these remarks by a helpful quotation from one who showed the perfect consistency between Romans 8:38-39 and I Corinthians 9:27: "But I keep under my body, and bring it into subjection: lest that by any means, when I have preached to others, I myself should be a castaway." Charles Hodge stated:

> The reckless and listless Corinthians thought they could safely indulge themselves to the very verge of sin; while this devoted apostle considered himself as engaged in a life-struggle for his salvation. The same apostle, however, who evidently acted on the principle that the righteous scarcely are saved and that the kingdom of heaven suffereth violence, at other

times breaks out in the most joyous assurance of salvation, and says that he was persuaded that nothing in heaven, earth or hell could ever separate him from the love of God. The one state of mind is the necessary condition of the other. It is only those who are conscious of this constant and deadly struggle with sin, to whom this assurance is given. In the very same breath Paul says, "O wretched man that I am" and "thanks be to God who giveth us the victory" (Rom. 7:24, 25). It is the indolent and self-empty professor who is filled with a carnal confidence.

Chapter 22

ELUCIDATION

HAD WE FOLLOWED a strictly logical order, this branch of our subject would have immediately followed our discussion of the problem which is raised by this doctrine. But we considered it better to first build a broader foundation for our present remarks by considering its "complement." We showed (1) that there is a twofoldness of truth which characterizes the whole of divine revelation; (2) that parallel with the fact of man's spiritual impotence runs his full responsibility; (3) that the acid test of sound theology consists in preserving the balance of truth or presenting its component parts in their proper perspective; (4) that the servant of God must always strive to set forth each aspect of the gospel in its fair proportions, being impervious to the charge of inconsistency which is sure to be hurled at him by extremists.

God's Requirements Versus Man's Impotence

Let us now restate the problem to which this and the following chapters endeavor to present a solution. How can fallen man be held responsible to glorify God when he is incapable of doing so? How can it conform with the mercy of God for Him to require the debt of obedience when we are unable to pay it? How can it consist with the justice of God to punish with eternal suffering for the neglect of what lies altogether beyond the sinner's power? If fallen man be bound fast with the cords of sin, with what propriety can God demand of him the performance of a perfect holiness? Since the sinner is the slave of sin, how can he be a free agent? Can he really be held accountable for not doing what it is impossible for him to do? If the fall has not annulled human responsibility, must it not to a considerable extent have modified it?

It is not for the benefit of the carping critic or the objecting infidel that we take up such questions as these, but with the desire to help our fellow Christians. Though such problems do not to the least degree shake their confidence in the character of the Lord or the integrity of His Word, some believers are at a loss to see how His ways can be equal. On the one hand Scripture declares, "The carnal mind is enmity against God: for it is not subject to the law of God, neither indeed can be." Therefore it is incapable of doing anything else but sin: "So then they that are in the flesh *cannot* please God" (Rom. 8:7-8). Yet on the other we are informed that "the wrath of God is revealed from heaven against all ungodliness and unrighteousness of men"

(Rom. 1:18) and that "every transgression and disobedience" shall receive "a just recompense of reward" (Heb. 2:2). Nor is any deliverance from God's wrath obtainable through the gospel except on such conditions as no natural man can comply with; nevertheless, noncompliance with those conditions brings additional condemnation.

To those who give serious thought to this subject it almost seems to make out the Most High to be what the slothful servant said: "Reaping where thou hast not sown, and gathering where thou hast not strawed" (Matt. 25:24). That this is far from being the case every regenerate heart is fully assured, yet the removal of this God-dishonoring suspicion is earnestly desired by those who are perplexed by it. These points have engaged our mind for many years, and it is our desire to pass on to other members of the household of faith what has been a help to us. How fallen man can be morally impotent yet morally responsible is the matter we shall try to elucidate.

In seeking the solution to our problem we shall first aim to cast upon it the light furnished by *the relationship* which exists between the Creator and the creature, between God and fallen man. When facing the difficulties raised by the truth of the moral impotence of fallen man, it is of vast importance that we clearly recognize and tenaciously hold the fact that God has not forfeited His right over the creature even though the creature has lost his power to meet God's requirements. At this point, especially, much of the difficulty is removed. Further light is thrown upon the nature of human responsibility when we obtain a right view of man's moral agency. By far the greater part of the difficulty vanishes when we correctly define and state the nature of man's impotence: what it is not, and what it does consist of. Finally, it will be found that man's own conscience and consciousness bear witness to the fact of his accountability.

In seeking to show the relationship which exists between the Creator and the creature, between God and the fallen man, let us inquire, What is the foundation of moral obligation? What is the rule of human duty? It should be evident to any anointed eye that there can be only one answer to these questions: The will of God, the will of God as revealed to us. God is our Maker and as such He has the right to unlimited control over the creatures of His hands. That right of God is absolute, uncontrolled and without any limitation. It is the right of the potter over the clay. Moreover, the creature is entirely dependent upon the Creator: "In him we live, and move, and have our being" (Acts 17:28). He that "formeth the spirit of man within him" sustains that spirit and the body which it inhabits. In reference to our bodies we have no self-sustaining power; let God's hand be withdrawn, and we return to the dust. The soul of man is equally dependent upon the sustaining power of God.

Man's Obligation

Because God is who He is and because man is the work of His hands, the will of God must be the foundation of moral obligation. "All things were

created by him, and for him" (Col. 1:16). "Thou hast created all things, and
for thy pleasure they are and were created" (Rev. 4:11). But God is not only
our Creator. He is also our Ruler and Governor, and His rights over us are
made known by His will, by His expressed will. Man is bound to do what
God commands and to abstain from what He forbids, simply *because* He
commands and forbids. Beyond that there is no reason. Direct reference to
the divine will is essential to any moral virtue. When an action is done
regardless of God's will, no honor is shown Him and no virtue pertains to it.
Such is the clear and definite teaching of Holy Writ; it knows no foundation
of right or wrong, no obligation, except *the will* of the Most High.

It therefore follows that the will of God revealed is the rule of duty. It
is self-evident that the will of God cannot direct and govern us except as it
is made known to us, and in His Word *it is* made known. God's *own* rule of
action is His will, for there can be no higher or holier rule. "He doeth according to his will in the army of heaven, and among the inhabitants of the
earth" (Dan. 4:35); "He saith to Moses, I will have mercy on whom I will
have mercy, and I will have compassion on whom I will have compassion"
(Rom. 9:15). To the will of God our blessed Redeemer uniformly referred
as both the obligation and rule of *His own* action. "I delight to do thy will,
O my God: yea, thy law is within my heart" (Ps. 40:8); "I seek not mine
own will, but the will of the Father which hath sent me" (John 5:30). Even
when the desire of His sinless humanity was for an escape from the awful
cup, His holy soul felt the binding obligation of the divine will: "Not as I
will, but as thou wilt." Does not that settle the question once for all? If
the incarnate Son looked no higher, no lower, no farther, why should we?
Compliance with the will of God *because* it is the will of God is the perfection
of moral virtue.

It is a striking fact that whenever the heart of man is pierced by the
arrows of the Almighty and his soul is bowed down before the Majesty of
heaven, whenever he begins to feel the awful burden of his guilt and his
conscience is agitated over his fearful accountabilities and how they are to
be met, his inquiry always is "Lord, what *wilt* Thou have me to do?" Everyone who has been taught of God knows this to be true. There is therefore
a revealed testimony in every renewed heart to the righteousness of God's
rule and the reality of its obligation. This is the basic principle of Christian
fidelity and fortitude. Under its influence the regenerate soul has only one
inquiry in reference to any proposed enterprise: *Is it the will of God?* Satisfied with this, his heart tells him it *must* be done. Difficulties, hardships, dangers, death present no obstacle; onward he presses in the path marked out
for him by the will of his Father. Obedience to *that* is his only responsibility.

The whole question of man's responsibility is resolved thus: Has God
revealed, has God commanded? It must be grounded on the simple authority
of the Most High. God neither reveals what is untrue nor commands what
is unjust; therefore the first principle of our moral duty is to know, acknowledge and perform the divine will as the ultimate fact in the government of

God over us. This question must be resolved altogether irrespective of the
state into which the fall has brought man; otherwise God must cease to be
God and the creature must sit in judgment on his Creator. But men in the
enmity of their carnal mind and the pride of their heart dare to sit in judgment upon the rule God has given them, measuring it by how far they
consider it suitable to their condition, how far it complies with their ability,
how far it commends itself to their reason—which is the very essence of unbelief and rebellion, the opposite of faith and obedience. Responsibility rests
not upon anything in the creature, but on the authority of God who has
made known His will to us. Responsibility is our obligation to respond to
God's will.

We turn next to consider the moral agency of man. Since God supplied
all other creatures with faculties suited to them and abilities to fill their
several purposes and to attain their different ends (as fish to swim in water,
and birds to fly in the air), so He was no less gracious to man. He who did
not deny capacity to His lower creatures did not withhold it from the noblest
of His earthly works. How could God have pronounced him "very good"
(Gen. 1:31) if he lacked the natural capacity to fulfill the end of his creation? As he was to be subject to moral government, man was endowed with
moral agency. Man then has been fitted to serve his Maker, because he has
been invested with faculties suited to the substance of the divine commands;
therefore it is our certain duty to obey whatever laws God gives us.

In amplifying what has just been said, we must consider the question
What is the essence of moral agency? The answer is rational intelligence.
If man was incapable of comparing ideas, of marking their agreement or
difference to draw conclusions and infer results of conduct, he would not be
a moral agent. That is to say, he would not be under a law or revealed will
and liable to punishment for its violation or reward for its obedience. We do
not treat infants or idiots as subjects of moral government, nor do we regard
brute beasts as responsible moral agents. The unhappy maniac is pitied, not
blamed. But something more than a capacity to reason is included in the
idea of moral agency; there are processes of reason, such as a mathematical
demonstration, which contain no moral character.

Man's Power of Choice

To will is an act of the mind directing its thoughts to the production of an
action and thereby exerting its power to produce it. The faculty of the will
is that power or principle of the mind by which it is capable of choosing.
An act of the will is simply a choice. When the herdsmen of Abraham and
his nephew quarreled, the patriarch proposed a separation and graciously
offered the young man his choice of the whole land. "Then Lot *chose him*
all the plain of Sodom." What does that choice signify? He took a view
of the different localities, observed their relative features, balanced in his
mind their respective advantages and disadvantages; and that which pleased
him best offered the most powerful motive or incentive, and so was his

choice. Such power of choice is necessary to constitute moral agency. Anyone who is physically forced to perform an act contrary to his desires, be it good or bad, is not accountable for it.

Conscience is a moral sense which discerns between moral good and evil, perceiving the difference between worthiness and blamableness, reward and punishment. A moral agent is one who has a capacity for being influenced in his actions by moral inducements or motives exhibited to the understanding or reason, so as to engage to a conduct agreeable to the moral faculties. That such a faculty exists within us is witnessed to by the consciousness of men the world over. There is an inward monitor from whose authority there is no escape, ever accusing or excusing. When its authority is defied, sooner or later conscience smites the transgressor with deep remorse and causes him to shrink from the anticipation of a reckoning to come. In a healthy state man recognizes the claims made by his moral faculty to supreme dominion over him. Thus the Creator has placed within our own beings His vice-regent, ever testifying to our responsibility to render obedience to Him.

Man's responsibility does not rest on anything within himself, but is based solely upon God's rights over him—His right to command, His right to be obeyed. The faculties of intelligence, volition and conscience merely *qualify* man to discharge his responsibility. In addition to these faculties of his soul, man has also been given *strength* or power to meet the requirements of his Maker. God originally made him "upright" (Eccles. 7:29) and placed within him holy tendencies which perceived the glory of God, a heart which responded to His excellence. Man was made in the image of God, after His likeness (Gen. 1:27); in other words, he was "created in righteousness and true holiness" (Eph. 4:24). Man's understanding was spiritually enlightened, his will rightly inclined; therefore he was capacitated to love the Lord his God with all his faculties and to render Him sinless obedience. Thus was he fitted to discharge his responsibility.

How was it possible for such a creature—so richly endowed by his Creator, so "very good" in his being, so capacitated to love and serve his Maker—to fall? It was possible because he was not constituted immutable, that is, incapable of any change. Creaturehood and mutability (liability to change) are correlated terms. Having been given everything necessary to constitute him a moral agent, everything which fitted him to meet the divine requirements, man was made the subject of moral government. A rule of action was set before him, a rule which was vested with sanctions: reward for obedience, punishment for disobedience. Man then was put on probation under a covenant of works. He was duly tried, his fealty to God being tested by Satan. Man deliberately cast off his allegiance to God, rejected His authority, preferred the creature to his Creator and thereby fell from his original estate.

It needs to be pointed out—for in some circles of professing Christians it is quite unknown—that when God placed Adam under the covenant of works and put him on probation, he acted not simply as a private individual but as a public person, as the federal head, as the legal representative and father of all his posterity. Such was the constitution which it pleased the Lord to appoint to the human race at the beginning of its history; and whether we can or cannot perceive the propriety and righteousness of such an arrangement, no spiritual mind will doubt its wisdom or justice once he is satisfied it is definitely revealed in Holy Writ. Had Adam survived his testing and remained loyal to his Ruler, the whole of his posterity would have shared his reward. Instead, he rebelled and sinned; in consequence, "by the offence of one judgment came upon all men to condemnation; . . . by one man's disobedience many were made sinners" (Rom. 5:18-19); "in Adam all die" (I Cor. 15:22).

As the result of our federal head's transgression, we are born into this world depraved creatures, unable to render acceptable obedience to the divine law. But the fall has neither changed man's *relationship* to God nor canceled his responsibility. He is still a subject of the divine government, still a moral agent, still accountable for his actions, still required to love and serve the Lord his God. God has not lost His right to enforce His just demands, though man has lost his power to meet them; depravity does not annul obligation. A human creditor may without the slightest injustice sue a prodigal debtor who has squandered his substance in riotous living. How much more so the divine Creditor! The entrance of sin has neither weakened God's right to demand subjection from His creatures nor invalidated their obligation to discharge their duty.

In seeking to supply solution to the problem of how one who is morally impotent can be justly held to be fully accountable to God, before we endeavor to point out more clearly the exact nature of that impotence (what it does not and what it does consist of), we feel it necessary to further amplify the fact that we must first throw upon this problem the light which is furnished by the relationship which exists between the Creator and the creature, between God and fallen man. Unless we follow *this* order we are certain to go wrong. It is only in God's light we can ever "see light." God inhabits eternity; man is but a thing of time. Since God is both before and above man, we must start with God in our thoughts and descend to man, and not start with the present condition of fallen man and then seek to think backward to God.

Rights of God over Man

That upon which we must first concentrate is not the rights of man but the rights of God, the rights of God over man. The relation in which the Creator stands to His creatures makes them, in the strictest sense, His property. The Almighty has an absolute right to appropriate and control the products of His own omnipotence and will. Observe how the psalmist ascribes the supremacy of God to the dependence of all things upon Him for their original existence. "For the Lord is a great God, and a great King above all gods. In his hand are the deep places of the earth: the strength of the hills is his also. The sea is his, and he made it: and his hands formed the dry land. O come, let us worship and bow down: let us kneel before the LORD our maker. *For* he is our God; and we are the people of his pasture, and the sheep of his hand" (Ps. 95:3-7).

Since creation itself gives the Most High an absolute right to the disposal of His creatures, His constant preservation of them continually augments His title. To keep in being calls for the exercise of power no less than to create out of nothing. To God as Creator we owe our original existence; to God as Preserver we are indebted for our continued existence. Upon this sure foundation of creation and preservation God possesses an unquestionable and inalienable propriety in all His creatures, and consequently they are under a corresponding obligation to acknowledge His dominion. Their dependence upon Him for past, present and continued existence makes it a matter of imperative duty to submit to His authority. From the fact that we are His property it follows that His will is our law. "Shall the thing formed say to him that formed it, Why hast thou made me thus?" (Rom. 9:20). God's right to govern us is the necessary consequence of the mutual relations existing between Creator and creatures.

The dominion of God was not adjusted with reference to man, but man was constituted with reference to it. That is to say, it pleased the Lord to appoint and institute a system of moral government, and accordingly He constituted man a moral agent, fitted to His requirements. Man was endowed with understanding, conscience, affections and will, capable of bearing the image of his Maker's holiness, of appreciating the distinctions between right and wrong, of feeling the supremacy of moral law. To such beings God sustains the relation of Ruler, for a moral creature is necessarily the subject of obligation. It must seek the law of its being beyond itself; the ultimate standard of its conduct must be found in a superior will to which it is responsible. To all created intelligences the authority of their Creator is absolute, complete and final. Thus the will of God, now expressed, is to them the sole standard of moral obligation. To deny this would be to make the creature independent.

The essential elements which constitute all true government were present when God placed man in Eden: there was competent authority, a rule of action proclaimed, and a suitable sanction to enforce that rule. As we have pointed out, the relationship obtaining between God and His creatures is such as to invest Him with an absolute right to exact obedience from them. As dependence is the very condition of his being, man possesses no authority to move, to exert a single faculty or to lose a single quality without evoking the divine displeasure. So absolutely is the creature the property of its Maker that it has no right to think its own thoughts or indulge its own inclinations. Moral agents must act, but their actions must be determined and regulated by the will of their Maker. "And the LORD God commanded the man, saying, Of every tree of the garden thou mayest freely eat" (Gen.

2:16); without the grant, it would have been an act of theft for Adam to partake of any of them!

J. H. Thornwell stated:

> A creature has no more right to act than it has power to be, without the consent of the Almighty. Dependence, absolute, complete, inalienable is the law of its existence. Whatever it performs must be in the way of obedience; there can be no obedience without an indication of the will of a ruler, and no such indication without a government. It is, therefore, undeniably necessary that to justify a creature in acting at all there must be some expression, more or less distinct, direct or indirect of the will of its Creator. As, then, the Almighty, from the very necessity of the case, must will to establish some rule, we are prepared to inquire what kind of government He was pleased to institute.

As we mentioned previously, it was a moral government, of moral creatures, who were placed under revealed law. It was law to which was attached penal sanction, and this in the very nature of the case. In order to enforce His authority as Ruler, in order to make manifest the estimate He places upon His law, God determined that disobedience to that law must be visited with summary punishment. How else could God's hatred of sin be known? Since the moral conduct of a creature is to be regulated with a specific reference to God's authority, unless He allowed it to be a god—uncontrolled, independent—there must be a recognition of His right to command. The actions of a moral creature must proceed from a sense of obligation corresponding to the rights of the Ruler. But there could be no such sense of obligation unless the law was enforced by a penal sanction; for without such, the obedience of the creature would be merely the result of persuasion rather than authority.

Precept without penalty is simply advice, or at most a request; and rewards without punishment are nothing but inducements. Had Adam and Eve been placed under *such* principles, the result would evidently have been but a system of persuasion and not of authoritative rule (which is precisely what most human government, in the home, the church and the state, has now degenerated into). In such a case their obedience would have been nothing more than pleasing themselves, following the impulse of their own desires, and not submitting to the rightful demands of their Creator; they would have been acting out their own wills and not the will of the Most High. It should be quite plain to the reader that such an (inconceivable) arrangement would have vested the creature with absolute sovereignty, making it a law unto itself, entirely independent of its Maker. The essence of all morality is compliance with the will of God, not because it commends itself to our reason or is agreeable to our disposition, but simply because it *is* His will.

In order that the will of God may be felt as law and may produce in the creature a corresponding sense of obligation, it must be enforced by a penal sanction. Declared penalty for disobedience upholds the authority of the Creator and keeps prominently in view the responsibility of the creature. It makes clear the just supremacy of the One and the due subordination of the other. The moral sense in man, even in fallen man, bears witness to the rightness of this basic fact. Conscience is a prospective principle; its decisions are by no means final, but are only the prelude of a higher sentence to be pronounced in a higher court. Conscience derives its power from anticipations of the future. It brings before its possessor the dread tribunal of eternal justice and almighty power; it summons us into the awful presence of a right-loving and sin-hating God. It testifies to an ultimate reward for right doing and an ultimate punishment for wrongdoing.

We again quote Thornwell:

> When a man of principle braves calumny, reproach and persecution, when he stands unshaken in the discharge of duty and public opposition and private treachery, when no machinations of malice or seductions of flattery can cause him to bend from the path of integrity,—that must be a powerful support through which he can bid defiance to the "storms of fate." He must feel that a strong arm is underneath him; and though the eye of sense can perceive nothing in his circumstances but terror, confusion, and dismay, he sees his mountain surrounded by "chariots of fire and horses of fire," which sustain his soul in unbroken tranquility. In the approbation of his conscience there is lifted up the light of the Divine countenance upon him, and he feels the strongest assurance that all things shall work together for his ultimate good. Conscience anticipates the rewards of the just, and in the conviction which it inspires of Divine protection lays the foundation of heroic fortitude.
>
> When, on the contrary, the remembrance of some fatal crime rankles in the breast, the sinner's dreams are disturbed by invisible ministers of vengeance and the fall of a leaf can strike him with horror; in every shadow he sees a ghost; in every tread he hears an avenger of blood; and in every sound the trump of doom. What is it that invests his conscience with such terrible power to torment? Is there nothing here but the natural operation of a simple and original instinct? Who does not see that the alarm and agitation and fearful forebodings of the sinner arise from the terrors of an offended Judge and insulted Lawgiver. An approving conscience is the consciousness of right, of having done what has been commanded, and of being now entitled to the favour of the Judge. Remorse is the sense of ill-desert. The criminal does not feel that his present pangs are his punishment; it is the future, the unknown and portentous future, that fills him with consternation. He deserves ill, and the dread of receiving it makes him tremble.

Let there be no uncertainty on this point. Were it possible to remove the penalty from the divine law, we should be wresting the scepter from the hands of Deity, divesting Him of power to enforce His just demands, denuding Him of the essential dignity of His character, reducing Him to a mere suppliant at the feet of His creatures. Modern theology (if it deserves to be called theology) presents to men a parody of God, who commands the respect of none, who is disrobed of His august and glorious majesty, who, far from doing His will in the army of heaven and among the inhabitants of the earth, is pictured as a kindly petitioner seeking favors at the hands of worms of the dust. Such a "god" has no powerful voice which shakes the earth and makes guilty rebels quail, but only offers entreaties which may be despised with impunity. Unless God is able to enforce His will He ceases to be God. If He speaks with authority, resistless power stands ready to support His command.

"And the Lᴏʀᴅ God commanded the man, saying, Of every tree of the garden thou mayest freely eat: but of the tree of the knowledge of good and evil thou shalt not eat of it" (Gen. 2:16-17). *There* was the original command given to man at the dawn of human history. It surely was uttered in a tone which carried the conviction that it *must* be obeyed. "For in the day that thou eatest thereof thou shalt surely die." *There* was the penal sanction enforcing the authority of the Lawgiver, the plainly announced penalty for transgression. Man was not left in ignorance or uncertainty of what would follow the forbidden act. The loss of God's favor, the incurring of His sore displeasure, certain and inescapable destruction would be the portion of the disobedient. And that awful threat was no isolated and exceptional one, but the enunciation of an abiding principle which God has constantly pressed upon men all through His Word: "The soul that sinneth, it shall die"; "The wages of sin is death." Even when the Saviour commissioned His servants to go forth and preach the gospel to every creature, He expressly told them to make known that "he that believeth not shall be damned." Such a God is not to be trifled with!

Let us digress for a moment. In view of what has been said above, the discerning reader will hardly need for us to point out to him the unspeakable solemnity, the immeasurable awfulness, the consummate folly of the course followed in the vast majority of the pulpits for many years. Even where the requirements of the moral law have been insisted on, its fearful penal sanction scarcely ever has been pressed. It has either been flatly denied that God will consign to everlasting woe all who have trampled on His commandments and died impenitent of their rebellion, or else a guilty silence has been maintained and in its stead a one-sided portrayal of the divine character presented, all the emphasis being placed on His love and mercy. Disastrous indeed must be the consequence of such a course, and disastrous indeed has it proved. An insulted Deity is now allowing us to reap what we have sown.

Problem of Lawlessness

A law which is not enforced by penalties will not be obeyed. True alike of God's law or man's, God's law will exert very little restraining influence upon the unregenerate if fear of the wrath to come is not definitely before their minds; and the multitude will have little respect for the statutes of the realm once they cease to regard the magistrate with "terror" (Rom. 13:2-4). For generations past there has been scarcely anything from the pulpit to inspire fear of God, and now there is practically no fear of magistracy left. Respect for the divine authority has not been faithfully proclaimed and enforced, and now there is only a mere pretense of respect for human authority. The terrible penalty for disobeying God's law—endless suffering in the lake of fire—has not been plainly and frequently held before those in the pew, and now we are witnessing a miserable parody, a mere formal pretense of enforcing the prescribed penalties for violations of human laws.

During the course of the last century, churchgoers grew less and less afraid of the consequences of breaking God's precepts; now the masses, even children, are less and less afraid of transgressing the laws of our country. Witness not merely the leniency but the utter laxity of most of our magistrates in dismissing offenders either with a warning or a trifling fine; witness the many murderers sentenced to death "with strong recommendation for mercy" and the increasing number of those whose capital punishment is remitted; witness the pathetic spectacle of governments afraid to act firmly, making "appeals" and "requests," instead of using their authority. And what we are now seeing in the civil realm is the inevitable repercussion of what took place in the religious. We sowed the wind; a righteous God is now allowing us to reap the whirlwind. Nor can there be any hope of a return to law and order, either between the nations or in our civil life, until the law of God is again given its proper place in our homes and churches, until the authority of the Lawgiver is respected, until the penalty for breaking His law is proclaimed.

Returning to our more immediate discussion, it should be pointed out that the fall did not to the slightest degree cancel man's responsibility. How could it? Man is just as much under the authority of God now as he was in Eden. He is still as truly the subject of divine command as he ever was, and therefore as much responsible to render perfect and ceaseless obedience to the divine law. The responsibility of man, be he unfallen or fallen, is that of a subject to his sovereign. They who imagine that man's own willful sin has canceled his obligation show how completely darkened is their judgment. Since God continues to be man's rightful Lord and man is His lawful subject, since He still possesses the right to command and we are still under obligation to obey, it should not be thought strange that God deals with man according to this relationship, and actually requires obedience to His law though man is no longer able to give it.

No, the fall of man most certainly has neither annulled nor impaired man's responsibility. Why should it? It was not God who took from man his spiritual strength and deprived him of his ability. Man was originally endowed with power to meet the righteous requirements of his Maker; it was by his own madness and wickedness that he threw away that power. Does a human monarch forfeit his right to demand allegiance from his subjects as soon as they turn rebels? Certainly not. It is his prerogative to demand that they throw down the weapons of their warfare and return to their original loyalty. Has then the King of kings no such right to require that lawless rebels become loyal subjects? We repeat, it was not God who stripped man of original righteousness, for he had lost it before God passed sentence upon him, as his "I was naked" (Gen. 3:10) acknowledged. If inability canceled man's obligation, there would be no sin in the world, and consequently no judgment here or hereafter. For God to allow that fallen creatures be absolved from loving Him with all their hearts would be to abrogate His government.

God's sovereignty and man's responsibility are never confounded in the Scriptures but, from the two trees in the midst of Eden's garden (the "tree of life" and "the tree of knowledge of good and evil" [Gen. 2:9]) onward, are placed in juxtaposition. Human responsibility is the necessary corollary of divine sovereignty. Since God is the Creator, since He is sovereign Ruler over all, and since man is simply a creature and a subject, there is no escape from his accountability to his Maker. For what is man responsible? Man is obligated to answer to the relationship which exists between him and his Creator. He occupies the place of creaturehood, subordination, complete dependence; therefore he must acknowledge God's dominion, submit to His authority, and love Him with all his heart and strength. The discharge of human responsibility is simply to recognize God's rights and act accordingly, rendering His unquestionable due.

Man's Accountability to God

Responsibility is entirely a matter of relationship and the discharge of those obligations which that relationship entails. When a man takes a wife he enters into a new relationship and incurs new obligations, and his marital responsibility lies in the fulfillment of those obligations. If a child is given to him a further relationship is involved with added obligations (to both his wife and child), and his parental responsibility consists of the faithful meeting of those obligations. Once it is known who God is and what is man's relationship to Him, the question of his responsibility is settled once for all. God is our Owner and Governor, possessed of absolute authority over us, and this must be acknowledged by us in deed as well as word. Thus we are responsible to be in complete subjection to the will of our Maker and Lord, to employ in His service the faculties He has given us, to use the means He has appointed, and to improve the opportunities and advantages He had provided us. Our whole duty is to glorify God.

From the above definition it should be crystal clear that the fall did not and could not to the slightest degree cancel or impair human responsibility. The fall has not altered the fundamental relationship subsisting between Creator and creature. God is the Owner of sinful man as truly and as fully as He was of sinless man. God is still our Sovereign and we are still His subjects. God's absolute dominion over us pertains as strictly now as it did in Eden. Though man has lost his power to obey, God has not lost His right to demand. To argue that inability cancels responsibility is the height of absurdity. Because an intoxicated employee is incapable of performing his duties, is his master deprived of the right to demand their accomplishment? Man cannot blame God for the wretched condition in which he now finds himself. The entire onus rests on the creature, for his moral impotence is the immediate effect of his own wrongdoing.

God's right to command and man's obligation to give perfect and perpetual obedience remain unshaken. God gave man his "substance" (Luke 15), but he spent it in riotous living; nevertheless God may justly challenge His own. If an earthly master gives a servant money and sends him to purchase supplies, may he not lawfully demand those supplies even if that servant spends the money in debauchery and gambling? God supplied Adam with a suitable stock, but he trifled it away. Surely then God is not to suffer because of the creature's folly; He should not be deprived of His right because of man's crime. The fact that man is a spiritual embezzler cannot destroy God's authority to require what the creature cannot be excused from. A debtor who cannot pay the debts which he has incurred remains under the obligation of paying. God not only possesses the right to demand from man the debt of obedience; from Genesis 3 to the last chapter of the New Testament He exercises and enforces that right and will yet make it publicly manifest before the assembled universe.

Though it be true that man himself is entirely to blame for the wretched spiritual condition in which he now finds himself, that the guilt of his depravity and powerlessness lies at his own door, yet we must not lose sight of the fact that his very impotence is a penal infliction, a divine judgment upon his original rebellion. Moral inability is the necessary effect of disobedience, for sin is essentially destructive, being opposed to all that is holy. God has so ordered it that the effects which sin has produced in man furnish a powerful witness to and an unmistakable demonstration of the exceeding sinfulness of sin and the dreadfulness of the malady which it produces. Sin not only defiles but enervates. It not only makes man obnoxious in the pure eyes of his Maker, but it saps man of his original strength to use his faculties right; and the more he now indulges in sin the more he increases his inability to walk uprightly.

Further light is cast on the problem of fallen man's responsibility by obtaining a right view of the precise *nature of his inability.* Let us begin by pointing out what it does not consist of. First, the moral inability of fallen man does not lie in the absence of any of those faculties which are necessary to constitute him a moral agent. By his transgression man lost both his spiritual purity and power, but he lost none of his original faculties. Fallen man possesses every faculty with which unfallen man was endowed. He is still a rational creature. He has an understanding to think with, affections capable of being exercised, a conscience to discern between right and wrong, a will to make choice with. Because man is in possession of such capacities he has faculties suited to the substance of the divine commands. Because he is a moral agent he is under moral government, and must yet render an account to the supreme Governor.

At this point notice must be taken of an error which obtains in the minds of some, tending to obscure and undermine the truth of fallen man's unimpaired responsibility. God declared that in the day Adam ate of the forbidden fruit he should "surely die," which has been wrongly understood to mean that his spirit would be extinguished and that, consequently, while the natural man possesses a soul he has no spirit, and cannot have one until he is born again. This is quite wrong. In Scripture "death" signifies separation and never annihilation. At physical death the soul is not exterminated but separated from the body. The spiritual death of Adam was not the extinction of any part of his being, but the severance of his fellowship with a holy God. In consequence Adam's descendants are born into this world "dead in trespasses and sins," which is defined as "being alienated from the life of God through the ignorance that is in them, because of the blindness of their heart" (Eph. 4:18).

When the prodigal's father said, "This my son was dead, and is alive again" (Luke 15:24), he most certainly did not mean that the son had ceased to exist, but simply that the prodigal had been "in the far country" and had now returned. The lake of fire into which the wicked are cast is termed the second death (Rev. 20:14) because they are "punished with everlasting destruction from the presence of the Lord, and from the glory of his power" (II Thess. 1:9). That the natural man *is* possessed of a spirit is clear from "the LORD which . . . formeth the spirit of man within him" (Zech. 12:1); "What man knoweth the things of a man, save the spirit of man which is in him?" (I Cor. 2:11); "The spirit shall return unto God who gave it" (Eccles. 12:7). It is a serious mistake to say that when Adam died in Eden any portion of his tripartite nature ceased to exist. Fallen man, we repeat, possesses all the faculties which unfallen man had.

When the Scriptures affirm "They that are in the flesh cannot please God" (Rom. 8:8) it is not because these lack the necessary faculties. That "cannot" must be understood in a way which comports fully with fallen man's responsibility, otherwise we should be guilty of making one verse contradict another. The "cannot" of Romans 8:8 (and similar passages) is in no way analogous to the "cannot walk" of a man who has lost his legs, or the "cannot see" of one who is deprived of his eyes. In such cases the individuals "cannot" because they do not have the requisite faculties or organs. A person who was devoid of such members at his birth could not possibly be held accountable for the non-exercise of them. But the moral impotence of the sinner is far otherwise. He *does* possess moral faculties, and the reason he fails to use them for the glory of God is solely because of his hatred of Him, because of the corruption of his nature, the enmity of his mind, the perversity of his will; and for these he is responsible.

For a man to be so enslaved by strong drink that he cannot help getting inebriated, far from excusing him, adds to his condemnation. For a man to give way to speaking what is untrue, forming the habit of telling falsehoods until he becomes such a confirmed liar that he is incapable of uttering the truth, only evidences the awful depths of his depravity. But ponder carefully the nature of his incapability. It is not because he has lost any faculty, for he still possesses the organs of speech, but because he has sunk so low that he can no longer use those organs to good purpose. Thus it is with the natural man and his incapability of pleasing his Maker. Man is endowed with moral faculties but he perverts them, puts them to wrong use. He has the same heart for loving God as for hating Him, the same members for serving Him as for disobeying Him.

Stephen Charnock said:

> It is strange if God should invite the trees or beasts to repent, because they have no foundation in their nature to entertain commandments and invitations to obedience and repentance; for trees have no sense and beasts have no reason to discern the difference between good and evil. But God addresseth Himself to men that have senses open to objects, understanding to know, wills to move, affections to embrace objects. These understandings are open to anything but that which God doth command, their wills can will anything but that which God doth propose. The commandment is proportioned to their rational faculty and the faculty is proportioned to the excellency of the command.
>
> We have affections, as love and desire. In the commands of loving God and loving our neighbour there is only a change of the object of our affections required; the faculties are not weakly but by viciousness of nature, which is of our own introduction. It is strange, therefore, that we should excuse ourselves and pretend we are not to be blamed because God's command is impossible to be observed, when the defect lies not in the want of a rational foundation, but in our own giving up ourselves to the flesh and the love of it, and in wilful refusal of applying our faculties to their proper objects, when we can employ those faculties with all vehemence about those things which have no commerce with the Gospel.

This is a suitable place for us to mention and correct a mistake which occurs in some of our earlier writings. Lacking the light which God has now vouchsafed us, we then taught (1) that fallen man still possessed a natural ability to render to God the obedience which He requires, though he lacks the necessary moral ability; and (2) that because man is possessed of such natural ability he is a responsible creature. The first mistake was really more a matter of terms than anything else, for all that we meant to signify by "natural ability" was the possession of faculties which capacitated man to act as a moral agent; nevertheless, as wrong terms conduce to wrong ideas we must correct them. The second was an error in doctrine, due to our ignorance. In this present work we have shown that the basis of human responsibility consists not in anything in man, but rather in his relationship to God, and that the faculties which make him a moral agent merely equip him to discharge his responsibility.

Chapter 23

AFFIRMATION

MANY ABLE WRITERS, in their efforts to solve the problem presented by the moral impotence and yet the moral responsibility of fallen man, have stressed the distinction between natural and moral ability and inability. They have not seen how a man could be held accountable for his actions unless he was, in some sense, capable of performing his duty. That capability they have ascribed to his being in possession of all the faculties requisite for the performance of obedience to the divine law. But it is now clear to us that these men employed the wrong term when they designated this possession of faculties a "natural ability," for the simple but sufficient reason that fallen man has lost the power or strength to *use* those faculties right; it is surely a misuse of terms to predicate "ability" in one who is *without strength*. To affirm that the natural man possesses ability of any sort is really a denial of his total depravity.

In the second place, it should be pointed out that the moral inability of the natural man is not brought about by any *external compulsion*. It is an utterly erroneous idea to suppose that the natural man possesses or may possess a genuine desire and determination to do that which is pleasing to God and to abstain from what is displeasing to Him, but that a power outside himself thwarts him and obliges him to act contrary to his inclinations. Were such the case, man would be neither a moral agent nor a responsible creature. If some physical law operated upon man (like that which regulates the planets), if some external violence (like the wind) carried men forward where they did not desire to go, they would be exempted from guilt. Those who are compelled to do what they are decidedly averse to cannot be justly held accountable for such actions.

Influence of Motives on the Will

One of the essential elements of moral agency is that the agent acts without external compulsion, in accord with his own desires. The mind must be capable of considering the motives to action which are placed before it and of choosing its own course—by "motives" we mean those reasons or inducements which influence to choice and action. Thus that which would be a powerful motive in the view of one mind would be no motive at all in the view of another. The offer of a bribe would be sufficient inducement to move one judge to decide a case contrary to evidence and law; to another such an offer, far from being a motive for wrongdoing, would be highly repellent. The temptation presented by Potiphar's wife, which was firmly resisted by Joseph, would have been an inducement sufficiently powerful to ruin many a youth of less purity of heart.

It should be quite evident that no external motive (inducement or consideration) can have any influence over our choices and actions except so far as they make an appeal to inclinations already existing within us. The affections of the heart act freely and spontaneously: in the very nature of the case we cannot be compelled either to love or to hate any object. Neither an infant nor an idiot is capable of weighing motives or of discerning moral values; therefore they are not accountable creatures, amenable to law. But because man, though fallen and under the dominion of sin, is still a rational being, possessed of the power to ponder the motives set before his mind and to decide good and evil, he is fully accountable, for he freely chooses that which, on the whole, he most prefers. Moral agency can only be destroyed by a force from without obliging man to act contrary to his nature and inclinations.

There is nothing outside of man which imposes on him any necessity of sinning or which prevents his turning from sin to holiness. There is no force brought to bear immediately on man's power of volition, or even on the connection between his volitions and his actions, which obliges him to follow the course he does. No, what man does ordinarily he does voluntarily or spontaneously in the uncontrolled exercise of his own faculties. No compulsion whatever is imposed on him. He does evil, nothing but evil, simply because he chooses to do so; the only immediate and direct cause of his doing evil is that he so wills it. Therefore since man is a responsible creature who, without any external power forcing him to act contrary to his desires, freely rejects the good and chooses the evil, he must be held accountable for his criminal conduct.

What has been pointed out considerably relieves the difficulty presented by the impotence of fallen man to meet the just requirements of God. If the reader will carefully ponder the case it should be apparent to him that the problem of human inability and accountability is by no means so formidable as it appears at first sight. The case of the fallen creature is vastly altered once it is clear what his impotence does not consist of. It makes a tremendous difference that his inability to obey his Maker does not lie in the absence of those faculties by which obedience is performed. So too the complexion of the case is radically changed when we perceive that man is not the victim of a hostile power outside himself which forces him to act contrary to his own desires and inclinations.

Grounds for Man's Blame

It will thus be evident that far from fallen man being an object of pity because of his moral impotence, he is justly to be blamed for the course which he pursues. We do not condemn a legless man because he is unable to walk, but rightly commiserate with him. We do not censure a sightless man for not admiring the beauties of nature; rather our compassion goes out to him. But how different is the case of the natural man in connection with his firm obligations to serve and glorify his rightful Lord! He is in possession of all the requisite faculties, but he voluntarily misuses them, deliberately following a course of madness and wickedness; for that he is most certainly culpable. His guiltiness will appear yet more plainly in what follows, when we understand what his moral impotence *does* consist of, when we consider the several elements which comprise it.

A further word needs to be added on the error of affirming that fallen man possesses a natural "ability" to obey God. Most of the writers who affirm this (Calvinists) take the ground that all the natural man lacks in order to perform that which is pleasing to God is a *willingness* to do so; that since his mental and moral endowments are admirably suited to the substance of the divine commandments, and since he is still possessed of every faculty which is required for the discharge of his duty, he *could* obey God if he *would*. But this is far from being the case. The condition of fallen man is much worse than that. He not only will not, but he cannot please God. Such is the emphatic and unequivocal teaching of Holy Writ, and it must be held fast by us at all costs, no matter what difficulties it may seem to involve. Yet we are fully convinced that this cannot, does not in the least, annul man's responsibility or make him any less blameworthy than was sinless Adam in committing his first offense.

"Unto them that are defiled and unbelieving is nothing pure; but even their mind and conscience is defiled" (Titus 1:15). In the unregenerate the mind and conscience are under an inherent and universal incapacity to form a right judgment or come to a right decision in regard to things pertaining to God, and as pertaining to Him. It is not merely that they are in the condition of one with a thick veil before his eyes, while the eyes themselves are sound and whole; rather they are like one whose eyes are *diseased*—weakened, decayed in their very internal organism. A diseased physical eye may be incapable of giving safe direction. But the eyes of fallen man's heart and understanding are so seriously affected that they cannot receive or even tolerate any spiritual light at all, until the great Physician heals them.

The solemn and terrible fact is that the brighter and more glorious is the divine light shed on the unregenerate, the more offensive and unbearable it is to them. The eyes of our understanding are radically diseased, and it is the understanding—under false views and erroneous estimates of things— which misleads the affections and the will. How, then, can we with the slightest propriety affirm that man still possesses a "natural ability" to receive God's truth to the saving of his soul? In man as created there *was* a perfect adaptation of faculties and a capability of receiving the divine testimony. But in fallen man, though there is a suitableness in the essential nature of his faculties to receive the testimony of God—so that his case is far superior to that of the brute beast—yet his ability to use those faculties and actually to receive God's testimony for suitable ends is completely deranged and destroyed.

Disorganization of Man's Being

The entrance of sin into man has done far more than upset his poise and disorder his affections. It has corrupted and disorganized his whole being. His intellectual faculties are so impaired and debased that his understanding is quite incapable of discerning spiritual things in a spiritual manner. His heart (including the will), which is the practical principle of operation, is "desperately wicked" and in a state of "blindness" (Eph. 4:18). The mind of fallen man is not only negatively ignorant, but positively *opposed* to light and convictions. To say that the natural man could please God if he would is false. His impotence is insurmountable, for he lacks the nature or disposition to will good. Therefore many men have greatly erred in supposing that the faculties of man are as capable now of receiving the testimony of God as they were before the fall.

Unwillingness is not all that the Scriptures predicate of fallen man. They declare sin has so corrupted his being that he is completely incapable of holy perceptions; it has utterly disabled him to perform spiritual acts. Moses told the people of Israel, "Ye have seen all that the LORD did before your eyes in the land of Egypt unto Pharaoh, and unto all his servants, and unto all his land; the great temptations which thine eyes have seen, the signs, and those great miracles: yet the LORD hath not given you *a heart to perceive,* and eyes to see, and ears to hear, unto this day" (Deut. 29:2-4). The faculties were there, but the people had not obtained power from God to perceive. Earlier Moses had said, "And the LORD heard the voice of your words, when ye spake unto me; and the LORD said unto me, I have heard the voice of the words of this people, which they have spoken unto thee: they have well said all that they have spoken. O that there were such an *heart* in them, that they *would* fear me, and keep all my commandments always, that it might be well with them, and with their children for ever" (Deut. 5:28-29). The faculties were there, but they lacked the spiritual power to use them. The unregenerate man is utterly disabled by indwelling sin in all the faculties of his spirit and soul and body from thinking, feeling or doing any spiritual good toward God.

Yet these facts do not to the slightest degree destroy or even lessen man's responsibility to glorify his Maker. This will more fully appear as we now consider what man's inability actually consists of. First, it is a *voluntary* inability. It was so originally. Adam acted freely when he ate of the forbidden fruit, and in consequence he lost his native holiness and became in bondage to evil. Nor can his descendants justly murmur at their inheriting the depravity of their first parents and being made answerable for their inability to will or to do good, as part of the forfeiture penalty due the first transgression; their moral impotence consists of their own voluntary continuation of Adam's offense. The entire history of sin lies in inclination and self-determination. It must not be supposed for a moment that after the first sin of Adam all self-determination ceased.

W. G. Shedd stated:

> Original sin, as corruption of nature in each individual, is only the *continuation* of the first inclining away from God. The self-determination of the human will from God the creature, as an ultimate end, did not stop short with the act in Eden, but goes right onward to every individual of Adam's posterity, until regeneration reverses it. As progressive sanctification is the continuation of that holy self-determination of the human will which begins in its regeneration by the Holy Spirit, so the progressive depravation of the natural man is the continuation of that sinful self-determination of the human will which began in Adam's transgression.

The very origin and nature of man's inability for good demonstrates that it cannot annul his responsibility; it was *self-induced* and is now *self-perpetuated*. Far from human depravity being a calamity for which we are to be pitied, it is a crime for which we are rightly to be blamed. Far from sin being a weakness or innocent infirmity rising from some defect of creation, it is a hostile power, a vicious enmity against God. The endowments of the creature placed him under lasting obligation to his Creator, and that obligation cannot be canceled by any subsequent action of the creature. If man has deliberately destroyed his power, he has not destroyed his obligation. God does no man wrong in requiring from him what he cannot now perform, for by his own deliberate act of disobedience man deprived himself and his posterity of that power; and his posterity consent to Adam's act of disobedience by deliberately choosing and following a similar course of wickedness.

But how can man be said to act voluntarily when he is *impelled* to do evil by his own lusts? Because he *freely chooses* the evil. This calls for a closer definition of freedom or voluntariness of action. A free agent is one who is at liberty to act according to his own choice, without compulsion or restraint. Has not fallen man this liberty? Does he, in any instance, break God's law by compulsion, against his inclinations? If it were true that the effect of human depravity is to destroy free agency and accountability, it would necessarily follow that the more depraved or vicious a man becomes the less capable he is of sinning, and that the most depraved of all commit the least sin of any. This is too absurd to need refutation.

Though on the one hand it is a fact that fallen man is the slave of sin and the captive of the devil, yet on the other it is equally true that he is still a voluntary and accountable agent. Man has not lost the essential power of choice, or he would cease to be man. Though in one sense he is impelled hellward by the downward trend of his depravity, yet he elects to sin, consenting to it. Though the rectitude of our will is lost, nevertheless we still act spontaneously. "The soul of the wicked desireth evil" (Prov. 21:10), and for that he is to be blamed. If a man picked your pocket and, when arrested, said, "I could not help myself; I have a thieving disposition, and I am obliged to act according to my nature," his judge would reply, "All the more reason why you should be in prison."

Because fallen man possesses the power of choice and is a rational creature, he is obligated to make a wise and good choice. The fault lies entirely at his own door that he does not do so, for he deliberately chooses the evil. "They have chosen their own ways, and their soul delighteth in their abominations. I also will choose their delusions, and will bring their fears upon them; because when I called, none did answer; when I spake, they did not hear: but they did evil before mine eyes, and *chose* that in which I delighted not" (Isa. 66:3-4). The bondage of the will to sinful inclinations neither destroys voluntariness nor responsibility, for the enslaved will is still a self-determining faculty and, therefore, under inescapable obligations to choose what man knows to be right. That very bondage is culpable, for it proceeds from self and not from God. Though man is the slave of sin it is a voluntary servitude, and therefore it is inexcusable.

The will is biased by the disposition of the heart: as the heart is, so the will acts. A holy will has a holy bias and therefore is under a moral necessity of exerting holy volitions: "A good tree cannot bring forth evil fruit." But a sinful will has a sinful bias because it has an evil disposition and therefore is under a moral necessity of exerting sinful volitions. But let it be pointed out once more that the evil disposition of man's will is not the effect of some original defect in the creature, for God made man "upright." No, his sinful disposition is the abiding self-determination of the human will. Its origin is due to the misuse Adam made of his freedom, and its continuation results from the unceasing self-determination of every one of his posterity. Each man perpetuates and prolongs the evil started by his first parents.

Because man *must* act according to the state of his heart, does this destroy his freedom? Certainly not, for acting according to his heart simply means doing as he pleases. And doing as we please is the very thing in which all free agency consists. The pulse can beat and the limbs can act in bodily disorders, whether we will or no. We would, with good reason, consider ourselves unfairly dealt with if we were blamed for such actions; nor does God hold us accountable for them. A good man's pulse may beat as irregularly in sickness as the worst villain's in the world; his hands may strike convulsively those who seek to hold him still. For such actions as these we are not accountable because they have no moral value. No evil inclination of ours nor the lack of a good one is *necessary* in order to do them; they are independent of *us*.

If all our actions were involuntary and out of our power, in no way necessarily connected with our disposition, our temper of mind, our choice, then we should not be accountable creatures or the subjects of moral government. If a good tree could bring forth evil fruit and a corrupt tree good fruit, if a good man out of the good treasure of his heart could bring forth evil things, and an evil man out of his evil treasure good things, the tree could never be known by its fruit. In such a case, all moral distinctions would be at an end and moral government would cease to be, for men could no longer be dealt with according to their works—rewarded for the good and punished for the evil. The only man who is justly held accountable, rewardable or punishable is one whose actions are properly his own, dictated by himself and impossible without his consent.

Here, then, is the answer to the objection that if fallen man is *obliged* to act according to the evil bias of his heart, he cannot rightly be termed a free agent. Necessity and choice are incompatible. Any inability to act otherwise than agreeably to our own minds would be an inability to act other than as free agents. But that necessity which arises from, or rather consists in, the temper and choice of the agent himself is the very opposite of acting against his nature and freedom. The sinner acts freely because he consents, even when irresistibly influenced by his evil lusts. Of Christ we read, "The spirit *driveth* him into the wilderness" (Mark 1:12), which indicates a forcible motion and powerful influence; yet of this same action we are also told, "Then was Jesus *led* up of the spirit into the wilderness" (Matt. 4:1), which plainly signifies His freedom of action. So too the Christian is both drawn and taught of God (John 6:44-45). Liberty of will and the victorious efficacy of divine grace are united together.

Second, fallen man's inability is *moral,* not physical or constitutional. Unless this is clearly perceived we shall be inclined to turn our impotence into an excuse or ground of self-extenuation. Man will be ready to say, "Even though I possess the requisite faculties for the discharge of my duty, if I am *powerless* I cannot be blamed for not doing it." A person who is paralyzed possesses all the members of his body, but he lacks the physical power to use them; and no one condemns him for his helplessness. It needs to be made plain that when the sinner is said to be morally and spiritually "without strength," his case is entirely different from that of one who is paralyzed physically. The normal or ordinary natural man is not without either mental or physical strength to use his talents. What he lacks is *a good heart,* a disposition to love and serve God, a desire to please Him; and for *that* lack he is justly blamable.

The mental and moral faculties with which man is endowed, despite their impaired condition, place him under moral obligation to love and serve his Creator. The illustrious character and perfections of God make it unmistakably clear that He is infinitely worthy of being loved and served; therefore we are bound to love Him, which is what a good heart essentially does. There is no way of evading the plain teaching of Christ on this subject in the parable of the talents: "Thou *oughtest* therefore to have put my money to the exchangers, and then at my coming I should have received mine own with úsury" (Matt. 25:27). In the light of the immediate context, this clearly means that man *ought* to have had a heart to invest to the best advantage (use right) the talents which were committed to him.

The inability of the natural man to meet the holy and just requirements of God consists in the opposition of his heart to Him because of the presence and prevalence of a vicious and corrupt disposition. Men know that God does not desire from them a selfish and wicked heart, and they also know that He has the right to require from them a good and obedient heart. To deny that God has the right to require a holy and good heart from fallen man would be tantamount to saying He had no right to require anything from them; then it would follow that they were incapable of sinning against Him. For if God had no right to require anything from man, he would not be guilty of disobedience against Him. If God has no right to require a good heart from man, then He has no right to require him to do anything which he is *unwilling* to do, which would render him completely innocent.

A child has no right to complain against a parent for requiring him to do that which he has faculties to perform, but for which he has no heart. A servant has no right to murmur against a master for reasonably requiring him to do that which his endowments fit him to perform, but for which he is unwilling. A subject has no right to find fault with a ruler for requiring him to perform that which the good of his country demands, and which he is capacitated to render, merely because he lacks the disposition to do it. All human authority presupposes a right to require that of men which they are qualified to perform, even though they may have no heart for it. How much less reason, then, have those who are the subjects of divine authority to complain of being required to do that which their faculties fit them for but which their hearts hate. God has the same supreme right to command cordial and universal obedience from Adam's posterity as He has from the holy angels in heaven.

For the sake of those who desire additional insight on the relation of man's inability to his responsibility, we feel we must further consider this difficult but important (perhaps to some, abstruse and dry) aspect of our subject. Light on it has come to us "here a little, there a little"; but it is our duty to share with others the measure of understanding vouchsafed us. We have sought to show that the problem we are wrestling with appears much less formidable when once the precise nature of man's impotence is properly defined. It is due neither to the absence of requisite faculties for the performance of duty nor to any force from without which compels him to act contrary to his nature and inclinations. Instead, his bondage to sin is *voluntary;* he freely chooses the evil. Second, it is a *moral* inability, and not physical or constitutional.

In saying that the spiritual impotence of fallen man is a moral one, we mean that it consists of an evil heart, of enmity against God. The man has no affection for his Maker, no will to please Him, but instead an inveterate desire and determination to please himself and have his own way, at all costs. It is therefore a complete misrepresentation of the facts to picture fallen man as a being who *wishes* to serve God but who is *prevented* from doing so by his depraved nature; to infer that he genuinely endeavors to keep His law but is hindered by indwelling sin. The fact is that he always acts *from* his evil heart and not *against* it. Man is not well disposed toward his Creator, but ill disposed. No matter what change occurs in his circumstances, be it from poverty to wealth, sickness to health, or vice versa, man remains a *rebel*—perverse, stubborn, wicked—with no desire to be any better, hating the light and loving the darkness.

It therefore follows that man's voluntary and moral inability to serve and glorify God is, third, a *criminal* one. As we have pointed out, a wicked heart is a thing of an entirely different order from weak eyesight, a bad memory or paralyzed limbs. No man is to blame for physical infirmities, providing they have not been self-induced by sinful conduct. But a wicked heart is a moral evil, indeed the sum of all evil, for it hates God and is opposed to our neighbors, instead of loving them as we are required. To say that a sinner cannot change or improve his heart is only to say he cannot help being a most vile and inexcusable wretch. To be unalterably in love with sin, far from rendering it less sinful, makes it more so. Surely it is self-evident that the more wicked a man's heart is, the more evil and blameworthy he is. The only other possible alternative would be to affirm that sin itself is not sinful.

It is because the natural man loves sin and hates God that he has no inclination and will to keep His law. But far from excusing him, that constitutes the very essence of his guilt. We are told that Joseph's brothers "hated him, and *could not* speak peaceably unto him" (Gen. 37:4). Why was it that they were unable to speak peaceably to him? Not because they lacked vocal organs, but because they hated him so much. Was such inability excusable? No, in that consisted the greatness of their guilt. An apostle makes mention of men "having eyes full of adultery, and that *cannot* cease from sin" (II Peter 2:14). But was not their impotence culpable? Surely it was; the reason they could not cease from sin was that their eyes were "full of adultery." Far from such an inability being an innocent one, it constituted the enormity of their crime; far from excusing them, it made their sin greater. Men must indeed be blind when they fail to see it is their moral impotence, their voluntary slavery to sin, which makes them obnoxious in the sight of the holy One.

A man's heart being fully set in him to do evil does not render his sinful actions the less criminal, but the more so. Consider the opposite: Does the strength of a virtuous disposition render a good action less or more praiseworthy? God is no less glorious because He is so infinitely and unchangeably holy in His nature that He "*cannot* be tempted with evil" (James 1:13) nor act otherwise than in the most righteous and perfect manner. Holiness constitutes the very excellence of the divine character. Is Satan any less sinful and criminal because he is of such a devilish disposition, so full of unreasonable malice against God and men, as to be incapable of anything but the most horrible wickedness? So of humanity. No one supposes that the want of a will to work excuses a man from work, as physical incapacity does. No one imagines that the covetous miser, with his useless hoard of gold, with no heart to give a penny to the poor, is for that reason excused from deeds of charity as though he had nothing *to* give.

God's Just Rights

How justly, then, may God still enforce His rights and demand loyal allegiance from men. God will not relinquish His claims because the creature has sinned nor lower His requirements because he has ruined himself. Were God to command that which we ardently desired and truly endeavored to do, but for which we lacked the requisite faculties, we should not be to blame. But when He commands us to love Him with all our hearts and we refuse to do so, we are most certainly to blame, notwithstanding our moral impotence, because we still possess the necessary faculties for the exercise of such love. This is precisely what sin consists of: the want of affection for God with its suitable expression in obedient acts, the presence of an inveterate enmity against Him with its works of disobedience. Were God to grant rebels against His government the license to freely indulge their evil proclivities, that would be to abandon the platform of His holiness and to condone if not endorse their wickedness.

William Cunningham said:

> There is no difficulty in seeing the reasons why God might address such commands to fallen and depraved men. The moral law is a transcript of God's moral perfections, and must ever continue unchangeable. It must always be binding, in all its extent, upon all rational and responsible creatures, from the very condition of their existence, from their necessary relation to God. It constitutes the only accurate representation of the duty universally and at all times incumbent upon rational beings,—the duty which God must of necessity impose upon and require of them. Man was able to obey this law, to discharge this whole duty, in the condition in which he was created. If he is now in a different condition—one in which he is no longer able to discharge this duty—this does not remove or invalidate his obligation to perform it; it does not affect the reasonableness and propriety of God, on the ground of His own perfections, and of the relation in which He stands to His creatures, proclaiming and imposing this obligation—requiring of men to do what is still as much as ever incumbent upon them.

It has generally been lost sight of that the moral law is not only the rule of our *works* but also of our *strength*. Inasmuch as well-being is the ground of welldoing—the tree must be good before the fruit can be—we are obliged to conclude that the law is the rule of our *nature* as truly as it is of our deeds. "Thou shalt love the LORD thy God with all thine heart, and with all thy soul, and with all thy *might*" (Deut. 6:5). That was said not only to unfallen Adam but also to his fallen descendants. The Saviour repeated it: "Thou shalt love the Lord thy God with all thy heart, and with all thy soul, and with all thy strength" (Luke 10:27). The law not only requires us to love, but to have minds equipped with all strength to love God, so that there may be life and vigor in our love and obedience to Him. The law requires no more love than it does strength; if it did not require strength to love, it would require no love either. Thus it is plain that God not only enforces His rightful demands upon fallen man, but also has not abated one iota of His requirements because of the fall.

If the divine law said nothing more to the natural man today than "Thou shalt love the Lord thy God with what strength thou now hast"—rather than with the strength He requires him to have and which He first gave to him, so that both strength and faculty, love and its manifestation, came under the command—it would amount to "Thou needest not love the Lord thy God at all, for thou art now without strength and therefore incapable of loving and serving Him, and art not to be blamed for having none." But as we have shown, man is *culpable* for his impotence. The only reason why he does not love God is because his heart holds enmity against Him. Did a murderer ever plead at the bar of justice that he hated his victim so intensely that he could not go near him without killing him? If such were his acknowledgment, it would only aggravate his crime; he would stand condemned by his own word. Hell, then, *must be* the only final place for inalienable rebels against God.

We should also call attention to the propriety of the divine law being pressed upon fallen man, in all the length and breadth of its requirements, both as a means of knowledge and a means of conviction, even though no longer available as a standard which he is able to measure up to. In spite of man's inability to obey it, the law serves to *inform* him of the holy character of God, the relation in which he stands to Him, and the duty which He still requires of him. Also it serves as an essential means of *convicting* men of their depravity. Since they are sinners, it is most important that they should be made aware of the fact. If their duty is made clear, if they are told to do that which is incumbent upon them, they are more likely to perceive how far short they come. If they are stirred up to compliance with God's requirements, to a discharge of their obligations, they will discover their moral helplessness in a way more forcible than any sermons can convey.

In the next place let us point out that fallen man is responsible *to use means* both for the avoidance of sin and the performance of holiness. Though the unregenerate are destitute of spiritual life, they are not therefore mere machines. The natural man has a rational faculty and a moral sense which distinguish between right and wrong, and he is called upon to exert those faculties. Far from being under an inevitable necessity of living in known and gross sins, it is only because of deliberate perversity that any do so. The most profane swearer is able to refrain from his oaths when in the presence of someone whom he fears and to whom he knows it would be displeasing. Let a drunkard see poison put into his liquor, and it would stand by him untasted from morning until night. Criminals are deterred from many offenses by the sight of a policeman, though they have no fear of God in their hearts. Thus self-control is not utterly outside man's power.

"Enter not into the path of the wicked, and go not in the way of evil men. Avoid it, pass not by it, turn from it, and pass away" (Prov. 4:14-15). Is not the natural man capable of heeding such warnings? It is the duty of the sinner to shun everything which has a tendency to lead to wrongdoing, to turn his back on every approach to evil and every custom which leads to wickedness. If we deliberately play with fire and are burned, the blame rests wholly on ourselves. There is still in the nature of fallen man some power to resist temptation, and the more it is asserted the stronger it becomes; otherwise there would be no more sin in yielding to an evil solicitation than there is sin in a tree being blown down by a hurricane. Moreover, God does not deny grace to those who humbly and earnestly seek it from Him in His appointed ways. When men are influenced to passion, to allurements, to vice, they are blamable and must justly give account to God.

No rational creature acts without some motive. The planets move as they are driven, and if a counterinfluence supervenes, they have no choice but to leave their course and follow it. But man has a power of resistance which they do not have, and he may strengthen by indulgence or weaken by resistance the motives which induce him to commit wrong. How often we hear of athletes voluntarily submitting to the most rigorous discipline and self-denial; does not that evince that the natural man has power to refrain from self-indulgence when he is pleased to use it. Highly paid vocalists, abstaining from all forms of intemperance in order to keep themselves physically fit, illustrate the same principle. Abimelech, a heathen king, took Sarah for himself; but when God warned him that she was another man's wife, he did not touch her. Observe carefully what the Lord said to him: "I know that thou didst this in the integrity of thine heart; for I also withheld thee from sinning against me: therefore suffered I thee not to touch her" (Gen. 20:6). Abimelech had a natural "integrity" which God acknowledged to be in him, though He also affirmed His own power in restraining him. If men would nourish their integrity, God would concur with them to preserve them from many sins.

Not only is man responsible to use means for the avoidance of evil, but he is under binding obligation to employ the appointed means for the furtherance of good. It is true that the efficacy of means lies in the sovereign power of God and not in the industry of man; nevertheless He has established a definite connection between the means and the end desired. God has appointed that bodily life shall be sustained by bodily food, and if a man deliberately starves himself to death he is guilty of self-destruction. Men still have power to utilize the outward means, the principal ones of which are hearing the Word and practicing prayer. They have the same feet to take them to church as conduct them to the theater, the same ability to pray to God as the heathen have to cry to idols. Slothfulness will be reproved in the day of judgment (Matt. 25:26). The sinner's plea that he had no heart for these duties will mean nothing. He will have to answer for his contempt of God.

Because he is a rational creature, man has the power to exercise consideration. He does so about many things; why not about his soul? God Himself testifies to this power even in a sinful nation. To His prophet He said, "Thou shalt remove from thy place to another place in their sight: it may be they will *consider*, though they be a rebellious house" (Ezek. 12:3). Christ condemned men for their failure at this very point: "Ye hypocrites, ye can discern the face of the sky and of the earth; but how is it that ye do not discern this time? Yea, and why even of yourselves *judge ye not what is right?*" (Luke 12:56-57). If men have the ability to take an inventory of their business, why not of their eternal concerns? Refusal to do so is criminal negligence. "All the ends of the world shall *remember and* turn unto the LORD" (Ps. 22:27). The natural man possesses the faculty of memory and is obligated to put it to the best use. "Let us search and try our ways, and turn again to the LORD" (Lam. 3:40). Failure to do so is willful negligence.

Man has not only physical organs but affections, or passions. If Esau could weep for the loss of his blessing, why not for his sins? Observe the charge which God brought against Ephraim: "They will not frame their doings *to* turn unto their God" (Hosea 5:4). They would entertain no thoughts nor perform any actions that had the least prospect toward reformation. The unregenerate are capable of considering their ways. They know they shall not continue in this life forever, and most of them are persuaded in their conscience that after death there is an appointed judgment. True, the sinner cannot save himself, but he can obstruct his own mercies. Not only do men refuse to employ the means which God has appointed but they scorn His help by fighting against illumination and conviction. Remember Joseph's brothers: "We are verily guilty concerning our brother, in that we saw the anguish of his soul, when he besought us, and we *would not hear*" (Gen. 42:21). "Ye do always resist the Holy Ghost" (Acts 7:51).

Summary of Man's Liability to God

How can the natural man be held responsible to glorify God when he is incapable of doing so? Let us summarize our answers. First, sin has not produced any change in the essential relation between the creature and the Creator; nothing can alter God's right to command and to be obeyed. Second, sin has not taken away the moral agency of man, consequently he is as much a subject of God's moral government as he ever was. Third, since man still possesses faculties which are suited to the substance of God's commands, he is under binding obligations to serve his Maker. Fourth, the moral inability of man is not brought about by any external compulsion, for nothing outside of man can impose upon him any necessity of sinning; because all sin issues out of his own heart, he must be held accountable for it. Fifth, man's servitude to sin was self-induced and is self-perpetuated, and since he freely chooses to do evil he is inexcusable. Sixth, man's inability is moral and not constitutional, consisting of enmity against and opposition to God; therefore it is punishable. Seventh, because man refuses to use those means which are suited to lead to his recovery and scorns the help which is proffered him, he deliberately destroys himself.

It should be pointed out that, in spite of all the excuses offered by the sinner in defense of his moral impotence, in spite of the outcries he makes against the justice of being required to render to God that which lies altogether beyond his power, the sentence of his condemnation is articulated *within his own being.* Man's very consciousness testifies to his responsibility, and his conscience witnesses to the criminality of his wrongdoing. The common language of man under the lashings of conscience is "I might have done otherwise; O what a fool I have been! I was faithfully warned by those who sought my good, but I was self-willed. I had convictions against wrongdoing, but I stifled them. My present wretchedness is the result of my own madness. No one is to blame but myself." The very fact that men universally blame themselves for their folly establishes their accountability and evinces their guilt.

If we are to attain anything approaching completeness of this aspect of our subject it is necessary to consider the particular and special case of the *Christian's inability.* This is a real yet distinct branch of our theme, though all the writers we have consulted appear to have studiously avoided it. This is in some respects admittedly the most difficult part of our problem, yet that is no reason why it should be evaded. If Holy Writ has nothing to say on the subject, then we must be silent too; but if it makes pronouncement, it is our duty to believe and try to understand what that pronouncement signifies. As we have seen, the Word of God plainly and positively affirms the moral impotence of the natural man to do good, yet at the same time teaches throughout that his depravity does not supply the slightest extenuation for his transgression against the divine law. But the question we now desire to look squarely in the face is How is it with the one who has been born again? Wherein does his case and condition differ from what it was previously, both with respect to his ability to do those things which are pleasing to God and with respect to the extent of his responsibility?

Are we justified in employing the expression "the Christian's spiritual impotence?" Is it not a contradiction in terms? Scripture *does* warrant the use of it. "Without me ye can do nothing" (John 15:5) connotes that the believer has no power of his own to bring forth any fruit to the glory of God. "For to will is present with me; but how to perform that which is good I find not" (Rom. 7:18). Such an acknowledgment from the most eminent of the apostles makes it plain that no saint has strength of his own to meet the divine requirements. "Not that we are sufficient of ourselves to *think* any thing as of ourselves" (II Cor. 3:5). If insufficient of ourselves to even think a good thought, how much less can we perform a good deed. "For the flesh lusteth against the Spirit, and the Spirit against the flesh: and these are contrary the one to the other: so that ye *cannot* do the things that ye would" (Gal. 5:17). That "cannot" clearly authorizes us to speak of the Christian's inability. Every prayer for divine succor and strength is a tacit confirmation of the same truth.

Then if such be the case of the Christian, is he in this regard any better off than the non-Christian? Does not this evacuate regeneration of its miraculous and most blessed element? We must indeed be careful not to disparage the gracious work of the Spirit in the new birth, nevertheless we must not lose sight of the fact that regeneration is only the *beginning* of His good work in the elect (Phil. 1:6), the best of whom are but imperfectly sanctified in this life (Phil. 3:12). That there is a real, radical difference between the unregenerate and the regenerate is gloriously true. The former are dead in trespasses and sins; the latter have passed from death to life. The former are the subjects and slaves of the devil; the latter have been delivered from the power of darkness and translated into the kingdom of God's dear Son (Col. 1:13). The former are completely and helplessly under the dominion of sin; the latter have been made free from sin's dominion and have become the servants of righteousness (Rom. 6:14, 18). The former despise and reject Christ; the latter love and desire to serve Him.

In seeking to grapple with the problem of the Christian's spiritual inability and the nature and extent of his responsibility, there are two dangers to be avoided, two extremes to guard against: (1) practically reducing the Christian to the level of the unregenerate, which is virtually a denial of the reality and blessedness of regeneration; (2) making out the Christian to be very nearly independent and self-sufficient. We must aim at preserving the balance between "Without me ye can do nothing" (John 15:5) and "I can do all things through Christ which strengtheneth me" (Phil. 4:13). What we are now discussing is part of the Christian paradox, for the believer is often a mystery to himself and a puzzle to others because of the strange and perplexing contrarieties meeting in him. He is the Lord's free man, yet declares, "I am carnal, sold under sin" (Rom. 7:14). He rejoices in the law of the Lord, yet cries, "O wretched man that I am!" (Rom. 7:24). He acknowledges to the Lord "I believe," yet in the same breath prays, "Help Thou my unbelief." He declares, "When I am weak then am I strong." One moment he is praising his Saviour and the next groaning before Him.

Wherein does the regenerate differ from the unregenerate? First, the regenerate has been given an understanding that he may know Him who is true (I John 5:20). His mind has been supernaturally illumined; the spiritual light which shines in his heart (II Cor. 4:6) capacitates him to discern spiritual things in a spiritual and transforming manner (II Cor. 3:18); nevertheless its development may be hindered by neglect and sloth. Second, the regenerate has a liberated will, so that he is capacitated to consent to and embrace spiritual things. His will has been freed from that total bondage and dominion of sin under which he lay by nature; nevertheless he is still dependent upon God's working in him both to will and to do of His good pleasure. Third, his affections are changed so that he is capacitated to relish and delight in the things of God; therefore he exclaims, "O how love I Thy law." Before, he saw no beauty in Christ, but now He is "altogether lovely." Sin which was formerly a spring of pleasure is now a fountain of sorrow. Fourth, his conscience is renewed, so that it reproves him for sins of which he was not previously aware and discloses corruptions which he never suspected.

But if on the one hand there is a radical difference between the regenerate and the unregenerate, it is equally true that there is a vast difference between the Christian in this life and the Christian in the life to come. While we must be careful not to belittle the Spirit's work in regeneration, we must be equally on our guard lest we lose sight of the believer's entire dependence on God. Although a new nature is imparted at regeneration, the believer is still a creature (II Cor. 5:17); the new nature is not to be looked to, rested in or made an idol. Though the believer has had the principle of grace communicated to him, yet he has no store of grace within himself from which he may now draw. He is but a "babe" (I Peter 2:2), completely dependent on Another for everything. The new nature does not of itself empower or enable the soul for a life of obedience and the performance of duty; it simply fits and makes it compatible to these. The principle of spiritual life requires its Bestower to call it into operation. The believer is, in that respect, like a becalmed ship—waiting for a heavenly breeze to set it in motion.

Yet in another sense the believer resembles the crew of the ship rather than the vessel itself, and in this he differs from those who are unrenewed. Before regeneration we are wholly passive, incapable of any cooperation; but after regeneration we have a renewed mind to judge aright and a will to choose the things of God when moved by Him; nevertheless we are dependent on His moving us. We are daily dependent on God's strengthening, exciting and directing the new nature, so that we need to pray "Incline my heart unto thy testimonies . . . and quicken thou me in thy way" (Ps. 119:36-37). The new birth is a vastly different thing from the winding of a clock so that it will run of itself; rather the strongest believer is like a glass without a base, which cannot stand one moment longer than it is held. The believer has to wait upon the Lord for his strength to be renewed (Isa. 40:31). The Christian's strength is sustained solely by the constant operations and communications of the Holy Spirit, and he lives spiritually only as he clings close to Christ and draws virtue from Him.

There is a suitableness or answerableness between the new nature and the requirements of God so that His commands "are not grievous" to it (I John 5:3), so that Wisdom's ways are found to be "pleasant" and all her paths "peace" (Prov. 3:17). Nevertheless the believer stands in constant need of the help of the Spirit, working in him both to will and to do, granting fresh supplies of grace to enable him to perform his spiritual desires. A simple delight in the divine law is not of itself sufficient to produce obedience. We have to pray, "Make me to go in the path of thy commandments" (Ps. 119:35). Regeneration conveys to us an inclination and tendency for that which is good, thereby fitting us for the Master's use; nevertheless we have to look outside ourselves for enabling grace: "Be strong in the grace that is in Christ Jesus" (II Tim. 2:1). Thereby God removes all ground for boasting. He would have all the glory given to His grace: "By the grace of God I am what I am" (I Cor. 15:10).

If enough rain fell in one day to suffice for several years we would not so clearly discern the mercies of God in His providence nor be kept looking to Him for continued supplies. So it is in connection with our spiritual lives: we are daily made to feel that "our sufficiency is of God." The believer is entirely dependent on God for the exercise of his faith and for the right use of his knowledge. Said the apostle: "I live; yet not I, but Christ liveth in me" (Gal. 2:20), which gives the true emphasis and places the glory where it belongs. But he at once added, "And the life which I now live in the flesh I live by the faith of the Son of God [by the faith of which He is its Object], who loved me, and gave himself for me." *That* preserves the true balance. Though it was Christ who lived in and empowered him, yet he was not passive and idle. He put forth acts of faith in Him and thereby drew virtue from Him; thus he could do all things through Christ strengthening him.

Responsibility of the Christian

It is at that very point the responsibility of the Christian appears. As a creature his responsibility is the same as pertains to the unregenerate, but as a new creature in Christ Jesus (II Cor. 5:17) he has incurred increased obligations: "Unto whomsoever much is given, of him shall be much required" (Luke 12:48). The Christian is responsible to walk in newness of life, to bring forth fruit for God as one who is alive from the dead, to grow in grace and in the knowledge of the Lord, to use his spiritual endowments and to improve or employ his talents. The call comes to him *"Stir up* the gift of God, which is in thee" (II Tim. 1:6). Isaiah the prophet complained of God's people, "There is none that stirreth up himself *to* lay hold of thee" (64:7), which condemns slothfulness and spiritual lethargy. The Christian is responsible to use all the means of grace which God has provided for his well-being, looking to Him for His blessing upon them. When the Scripture says, "The Spirit also helpeth our infirmities" (Rom. 8:26), the Greek verb is "helpeth together"—He cooperates with our diligence not our idleness.

The Christian has received spiritual life, and all life is a power to act by. Inasmuch as that spiritual life is a principle of grace animating all the faculties of the soul, he is capacitated to use all means of grace which God has provided for his growth and to avoid everything which would hinder or retard his growth. He is required to keep the heart with all diligence (Prov. 4:23), for if the fountain is kept clean, the springs which issue from it will be pure. He is required to "make not provision for the flesh, to fulfil the lusts thereof" (Rom. 13:14), not allowing his mind and affections to fix themselves on sinful or unlawful objects. He is required to deny himself, take up his cross and follow the example which Christ has left him. He is commanded to "love not the world, neither the things that are in the world" (I John 2:15), and therefore he must conduct himself as a stranger and pilgrim in this scene of action, abstaining from fleshly lusts which war against the soul (I Peter 2:11) if he would not lose the heavenly inheritance (I Cor. 9:27). And for the performance of these difficult duties he must diligently and earnestly seek supplies of grace counting on God to bless the means to him.

No small part of the Christian's burden and grief is the inward opposition he meets, thwarting his aspirations and bringing him into captivity to that which he hates. The believer's "life" is a *hidden* one (Col. 3:3), and so also is his conflict. He longs to love and serve God with all his heart and to be holy in every detail of his life, but the flesh resists the spirit. Worldliness, unbelief, coldness, slothfulness exert their power. The believer struggles against their influence and groans under their bondage. He desires to be clothed with humility, but pride is constantly breaking forth in some form or other. He finds that he cannot attain to that which he desires and approves. He discovers a wide disparity between what he knows and does, between what he believes and practices, between his aims and realizations. Truly he is "an unprofitable servant." He is so often defeated in the conflict that he is frequently faint and weary in the use of means and in performance of duty; he may question the genuineness of his profession and be tempted to give up the fight.

In seeking to help distressed saints concerning this acute problem, the servant of God needs to be very careful lest he foster a false peace in those who have a historical faith in the gospel but are total strangers to its saving power. God's servant must be especially watchful not to bolster the false hopes of those who delight in the mercy of God but hate His holiness, who misappropriate the doctrine of His grace and make it subservient to their lusts. He must therefore call upon his hearers to honestly and diligently examine themselves before God, that they may discover *whence* the inward oppositions arise and *what are* their reactions to them. They must determine whether these inconsistencies spring from an unwillingness to wear the yoke of Christ, their whole hearts accompanying and consenting to such resistances to God's righteous requirements, or whether these oppositions to God's laws have their rise in corruptions which they sincerely endeavor to oppose, which they hate, which they mourn over, which they confess to God and long to be released from.

When describing the conflict in himself between the flesh and the spirit—between indwelling sin and the principle of grace he had received at the new birth—the Apostle Paul declared, "For that which I do [which is contrary to the holy requirements of God] I allow not [I do not approve of it; it is foreign to my real inclinations and purpose of heart]: but what I hate, that do I" (Rom. 7:15). Paul detested and yearned to be delivered from the evil which rose up within him. Far from affording him any satisfaction, it was his great burden and grief. And thus it is with every truly regenerated soul when he is in his right mind. He may be, yes is, frequently overcome by his carnal and worldly lusts; but instead of being pleased at such experience and contentedly lying down in his sins, as a sow delights to wallow in the mire, he cries in distress, confesses such failures as grievous sins, and prays to be cleansed from them.

"If I were truly regenerate, how could sin rage so fiercely within and so often obtain the mastery over me?" This question deeply exercises many of

God's people. Yet the Scripture declares, "A just man falleth seven times" (Prov. 24:16); but it at once adds "and riseth up again." Did not David lament, "Iniquities prevail against me" (Ps. 65:3)? Yet if you are striving to mortify your lusts, looking daily to the blood of Christ to pardon, and begging the Spirit to more perfectly sanctify you, you may add with the psalmist, "As for our transgressions, thou shalt purge them away." Indeed, did not the highly favored apostle declare, "For we know that the law is spiritual: but I am carnal, sold [not 'unto' but] under sin" (Rom. 7:14). There is a vast difference between Paul and Ahab, of whom we read that he "did sell himself to work wickedness in the sight of the LORD" (I Kings 21:25). It is the difference between one who is taken captive in war, becoming a slave unwillingly and longing for deliverance, and one who voluntarily abandons himself to a course of open defiance of the Almighty and who so loves evil that he would refuse release.

We must distinguish between sin's dominion over the unregenerate and sin's tyranny and usurpation over the regenerate. Dominion follows upon *right* of conquest or subjection. Sin's great design in all of us is to obtain undisputed dominion; it has it in unbelievers and contends for it in believers. But every evidence the Christian has that he is under the rule of grace is that much evidence he is not under the dominion of sin. "For I delight in the law of God after the inward man: But I see another law in my members, warring against the law of my mind, and bringing me into captivity to the law of sin which is in my members" (Rom. 7:22-23). That does not mean that sin always triumphs in the act, but that it is a hostile power which the renewed soul cannot evict. It wars against us in spite of all we can do. The general makeup of believers is that, notwithstanding sin being a "law" (governing force) not "to" but "in" them, they "would [desire and resolve to] do good," but "evil is present" with them. Their habitual inclination is to good, and they are brought into captivity against their will. It is the "flesh" which prevents the full realization of their holy aspirations in this life.

But if the Son has "made us free" (John 8:36), how can Christians be in bondage? The answer is that Christ has already freed them from the guilt and penalty, love and dominion of sin, but not yet from its presence. As the believer hungers and thirsts after righteousness, pants for communion with the living God, and yearns to be perfectly conformed to the image of Christ, he is "free from sin"; but as such longings are more or less thwarted by indwelling corruptions, he is still "sold under sin." Then let prevailing lusts humble you, cause you to be more watchful and to look more diligently to Christ for deliverance; then those very exercises will evidence a principle of grace in you which desires and seeks after the destruction of inborn sin. Those who have hearts set on pleasing God are earnest in seeking enabling grace from Him, yet they must remember He works in them both to will and to do of *His* good pleasure, maintaining His sovereignty in this as in everything else. Bear in mind that it is *allowed* sin which paralyzes the new nature.

Thus God has not yet uprooted sin from the soul of the believer, but allows him to groan under its uprisings, that his pride may be stained and his heart made to constantly feel he is not worthy of the least of God's mercies. To produce in him that feeling of dependence on divine power and grace. To exalt the infinite condescension and patience of God in the apprehension of the humbled saint. To place the crown of glory on the only head worthy to wear it: "Not unto us, O LORD, not unto us, but unto *thy name* give glory, for thy mercy, and for thy truth's sake" (Ps. 115:1).

Chapter 24

OPPOSITION

In bringing this study to a close it seems desirable that we should consider the opposition made against this truth before giving an exposition of it. This subject of the moral inability of fallen man for good is peculiarly repugnant to his pride, and therefore it is not surprising that his outcry against it is so loud and prolonged. The exposure of human depravity, the disclosure of the fearful ruin which sin has wrought in our constitution, cannot be a pleasant thing to contemplate and still less to acknowledge as a fact. To heartily own that by nature I am devoid of love for God, that I am full of inveterate enmity against Him, is diametrically opposed to my whole makeup. It is only natural to form a high estimate of ourselves and to entertain exalted views of both our capabilities and our good intentions. To be assured on divine authority that our hearts are incurably wicked, that we love darkness rather than light, that we hate alike the law and the gospel, is revolting to our whole being. Every possible effort is put forth by the carnal mind to repudiate such a flesh-withering and humiliating description of human nature. If it cannot be refuted by an appeal to facts, then it must be held up to ridicule.

Man's Refusal to Accept the Doctrine

Such opposition to the truth should neither surprise nor discourage us, for it has been plainly announced to us: "The natural man receiveth not the things of the Spirit of God: for they are foolishness unto him" (I Cor. 2:14). The very fact that they are foolishness to him should lead us to expect he will laugh at and scorn them. Nor must we be alarmed when we find this mocking of the truth is far from being confined to avowed infidels and open enemies of God; this same antagonism appears in the great majority of religious persons and those who pose as the champions of Christianity. Passing through a seminary and putting on the ministerial garb does not transform the unregenerate into regenerate men. When our Lord announced, "The truth shall make you free," it was the religious leaders of the Jews who declared they were never in bondage; and when He affirmed, "Ye are of your father the devil, and the lusts of your father ye will do," they replied, "Say we not well that thou art a Samaritan, and hast a devil?" (John 8).

Principal Objections

It is just because the fiercest opposition to this truth comes from those inside Christendom, not from those outside, that we consider it wise to face the principal objections. We do so to place the Lord's people on their guard and to let them see there is no weight in such criticism. We would not waste time in seeking to close the mouths of those whom God Himself will deal with in due time, but we desire to expose their sophistries so that those with spiritual discernment may perceive that their faith rests on a foundation which no outbursts of unbelief can shake. Every objection against the doctrine of man's spiritual impotence has been overthrown by God's servants in the past, yet each fresh generation repeats the arrogance of its forebears. We have already refuted most of these objections in the course of this study, yet by now assembling them together and showing their pointlessness we may render a service which will not be entirely useless.

1. If fallen man is unable to keep God's law, he cannot be obligated to keep it. Impotence obviously cancels responsibility. A child three or four years of age ought not to be whipped because it does not read and write. A legless man should not be sent to prison because he does not walk. Surely a just and holy God does not require sinful creatures to render perfect obedience to a divine and spiritual law.

How is this objection to be met? First, by pointing out that it is not based upon Holy Writ but is merely human reasoning. Scripture affirms again and again that fallen man *is* spiritually impotent, "without strength," and that he "cannot please God"; from that nothing must move us. Scripture nowhere states that spiritual helplessness releases man from God's claims upon him; therefore no human reasoning to the contrary, however plausible or pleasing, is entitled to any consideration from those who tremble at God's Word. Scripture reveals that God does hold fallen man responsible to keep His law, for He gave it to Israel at Sinai and pronounced His curse upon all transgressors of it.

What has been pointed out should be sufficient for any simple soul who fears the Lord. But lest it be thought that this is all which can be said by way of refutation, lest it be supposed that this objection is so forceful that it cannot be met in a more direct rebuttal, we add the following: To declare that man cannot be obligated to keep the law if he is unable to do so demands an inquiry into both the *nature* and the *cause* of his inability. Once that investigation is entered into, the sophistry of the objection will quickly appear. Wherein lies man's inability to keep God's law? Is it the absence of the requisite faculties or his unwillingness to use aright the faculties with which he is endowed? Were fallen man devoid of reason, conscience, will, there would be some force in this objection; but since he is possessed of all those faculties which constitute a moral being, it is quite inane and invalid. There is no analogy whatever between the sinner's inability to travel the highway of holiness and the inability of a legless man to walk.

The worthlessness of this objection is made evident not only when we examine the nature of man's spiritual impotence; it equally appears void when we diagnose its cause. *Why* is fallen man unable to keep God's law? Is it because he is worked upon by some almighty being who prevents him from rendering obedience? Were fallen man truly desirous of serving and pleasing God, were it a case of his ardently longing to do so but being thwarted because another more powerful than himself hindered him, there would be some force to this objection. But God, far from placing any obstacle in our way, sets before us every conceivable inducement to comply with His precepts. If it be argued that the devil is more powerful than man and that he is continually seeking to turn him from the path of rectitude, the answer is that Satan can do nothing without our own consent. All he can do is to tempt to wrongdoing; it is man's own will which either yields or refuses.

In reply to what has last been pointed out, someone may say, "But fallen man has no sufficient power of his own with which to successfully resist Satan's evil solicitations." Suppose that be so, then what? Does that oblige us to take sides with the enemies of the truth and affirm that therefore man is to be excused for his sinful deeds, that he is *not* obligated to render perfect obedience to the law merely because he does not have the power to cope with his adversary? Not at all. Once more we must inquire as to the cause. Why is it that man cannot put the devil to flight? Is it because he was originally vested with less moral strength than his foe possesses? No indeed, for he was made in the image and likeness of God. Man's present inability has been brought about by an act of his own and not by any stinginess or oversight of his Creator. "Thou hast destroyed thyself" (Hosea 13:9) is the divine verdict. Though man is unable to recover what he lost, he has none but himself to blame for his willful and wicked destruction of his original strength.

It is at this very point man twists and wriggles most, seeking to get from under the onus which righteously rests on him. When Adam offended against the divine law he sought to throw the blame upon his wife, and she in turn upon the devil; ever since then the great majority have attempted to cast it on God Himself, on the pretext that He is the One who gave them being and sent them into the world in their present handicapped condition. It must be kept steadily in mind that original ability destroyed by self-determination does not and cannot destroy the original obligation any more than weakened moral strength by self-indulgence and the formation of evil habits destroys or diminishes obligation. To say otherwise would be to declare that the result of sin excuses sin itself, which is a manifest absurdity. Man's wrongdoing certainly does not annul God's rights. God is no Egyptian taskmaster requiring men to make bricks without straw. He endowed man with everything requisite for the discharge of his duty, and though man has squandered his substance in riotous living, that does not free him from God's just claims upon him.

The drunkard is certainly less able to obey the law of temperance than the sober man is, yet that law has precisely the same claims upon the former as it has upon the latter. In commercial life the loss of ability to pay does not release from obligation; the loss of property does not free man from his indebtedness. A man is as much a debtor to his creditors after his bankruptcy as he was previously. It is a legal maxim that bankruptcy does not invalidate contracts. Someone may point out that an insolvent debtor cannot be sued in the courts. Nevertheless, even if human law declares it equitable to free an insolvent debtor, the law of God does not. And that verdict is righteous, for the sinner's inability to give God His due is *voluntary*—he does not wish to pay because he hates Him. Thus both the nature and the cause of man's inability demonstrate that he is "without excuse."

2. When inquiry is made as to the cause of man's spiritual impotence and when it has been shown that this lies not in the Creator but in man's own original rebellion, the objector, far from being silenced, will demur against his being penalized for what his first parents did. He may ask, "Is it just that I should be sent into this world in a state of spiritual helplessness because of *their* offense? I did not make myself; if I was created with a corrupt nature, why should I be held to blame for its inevitable fruits?" First, let it be pointed out that it is not essential in order for a fallen creature to be blamable for his evil dispositions and acts that he must first be inherently holy. A person who is depraved, who from his heart hates God and despises His law, is nonetheless a sinner because he has been depraved from his birth. His having sinned from the beginning and throughout his existence is surely no valid excuse for his sinning now. Nor is his guilt any the less because his depravity is so deeply rooted in his nature. The stronger his enmity against God the greater its heinousness.

But how can man be condemned for his evil heart when Adam corrupted human nature? Fallen man is voluntarily an enemy to the infinitely glorious God and nothing can extenuate such vile hostility. The very fact that in the day of judgment "every mouth will be stopped" (Rom. 3:19) demonstrates there can be no force in this objection. It is the free and self-determined *acting out* of his nature for which the sinner will be held accountable. The fact that we are born traitors to God cannot cancel our obligation to give Him allegiance. None can escape the righteous requirements of the law by deliberate opposition to it. That man's nature is the direct consequence of Adam's transgression does not to the slightest degree mitigate his own sins. Is it not a solemn fact that each of us has *approved* Adam's transgression by following his example and joining with him in rebellion against God? That we go on to break the divine law demonstrates that we are justly condemned with Adam. If we resent our being corrupted through Adam, why not repudiate him and refuse to sin, stand out in opposition to him and be holy?

Yet still the carnal mind will ask, "Since I lost all power to love and serve God even before I was born, how can I be held accountable to do what I cannot? Wherein is the justice in requiring from me what it is impossible to render?" Exactly what was it that man lost by the fall? It was *a heart that loved God*. And it is the possessing of a heart which has no love for God that is the very essence of human depravity. It is this in which the vileness of fallen man consists: no heart for God. But does a loveless heart for God excuse fallen man? No indeed, for that is the very core of his wickedness and guilt. Men never complain of their lack of power for loving the world. And why are they so thoroughly in love with the world? Is it because the world is more excellent and glorious than God is? Certainly not. It is only because fallen man has a heart which naturally loves the world, but he has no heart with which to love God. The world suits and delights him, but God does not; rather, His very perfections repel him.

Now let us put it plainly and honestly: Can our being devoid of any true love for God free us from our obligation *to* love Him? Can it to the slightest degree lessen our blame for *not* loving Him? Is He not infinitely worthy of our affections, our homage, our allegiance? None would argue in any other connection as does the objector here. If a king rules wisely and well, is he not entitled to the honor and loyalty of his subjects? If an employer is merciful and considerate, has he not the right to expect his employees to further his interests and carry out his orders? If I am a kind and dutiful parent, shall I not require the esteem and obedience of my children? If my servant or child has no heart to give what is due, shall I not justly consider him blamable and deserving of punishment? Or shall we reason so insanely that the worse man grows the less he is to blame? "A son honoureth his father, and a servant his master: if then I be a father, where is mine honour? And if I be a master, where is my fear? saith the LORD of hosts" (Mal. 1:6).

3. It is objected that if the sinner is so enslaved by sin that he is impotent to do good, his free agency is denied and he is reduced to a mere machine. This is more a metaphysical question than a practical one, being largely a matter of terms. There is a real sense in which the natural man is in bondage; nevertheless within certain limits he is a free agent, for he acts according to his own inclinations without compulsion. There is much confusion on this subject. Freedom of will is not freedom from action; inaction of the will is no more possible than is inaction of the understanding. Nor is freedom of will a freedom from the internal consequences of voluntary action; the formation of a habit is voluntary, but when formed it cannot be eradicated by volition. Nor is freedom of will a freedom from the restraint and regulation of law; the glorified saints will be completely delivered from sin yet regulated by the divine will. Nor is freedom of will a freedom from bias; Christ acted freely, yet being the holy One He could not sin. The unregenerate act freely, that is, spontaneously, agreeably to their desires; yet being depraved, they can neither will nor do anything which is spiritual.

4. If man is spiritually impotent, all exhortations to the performance of spiritual duties are needless and useless. This objection assumes that God would not address His commands to men unless they were able to obey them. This idea is most presumptuous, for in it man pretends to be capable of judging the reasons which regulate the divine procedure. Has God no right to press His claims because man has wickedly squandered his power to meet

them? The divine commands cover not what we can do, but what we should do; not what we are *able* to do, but what we *ought* to do. The divine law is set before us, in all the length and breadth of its holy requirements, as a means of knowledge, revealing to us God's character, the relation in which we stand to Him, and the duty which He justly requires of us. It is also a means of conviction, both of our sin and inability. If men are sinners it is important that they should be made aware of the fact—by setting before them a perfect standard that they may see how far short they come of it. If men are unable to discharge the duties incumbent upon them, it is necessary that they should be made aware of their woeful condition—that they should be made to realize their need of salvation.

5. To teach men they are spiritually impotent is to cut the nerve of all religious endeavor. If man is helpless, what is the use of urging him to strive? Necessity is a sufficient reason to act without further encouragement. A man in the water who is ready to drown will try to save his life, even though he cannot swim and some on the banks tell him it is impossible. Again we would press the divine side. There is a necessity on us whenever there is a command from God. If He requires, it behooves man to use the means and leave the issue with Him. Again, spiritual inability is no excuse for negligence and inertia, because God does not refuse strength to perform His bidding if it is humbly, contritely and trustfully sought. When did He ever deny grace to the sinner who waited upon Him in earnest supplication and in consistent use of the means for procuring it? Is not His Word full of promises to seeking souls? If a man has hands and food is set before him, is it not an idle excuse for him to say he cannot eat because he is not moved from above?

6. If the sinner is spiritually powerless, it is only mocking him to tell him to repent of his sins and believe the gospel. To call on the unregenerate to savingly receive Christ as his Lord and Saviour is far from mocking him. Did the Son of God mock the rich young ruler when He told him to sell all that he had and follow Him and then he should have treasure in heaven? Certainly not. Had the ruler no power to sell his possessions? Was it not rather lack of inclination, and for such lack was he not justly blamable? Such a demand served to expose the state of his heart. He loved money more than Christ, earthly things above heavenly. The exhortations, warnings and promises set down in the Word are to be pressed on the ungodly so as to make them more inexcusable, so that they may not say in the day to come that, had they been invited to receive such good things, they would have embraced them; that, had they been admonished for their sins, they would have forsaken them. Their own conscience will convict them, and they will know a prophet of God spoke to them.

7. Finally, it is objected that the doctrine of man's spiritual impotence stifles all hope. To tell a man his condition is irremediable, that he can do nothing whatever to better himself, will drive him to despair. This is precisely what is desired. One principal end which must be kept before the preacher is to shatter the self-sufficiency of his hearer. His business is to

undermine the spirit of self-righteousness, to break down self-satisfaction, to sweep away those refuges of lies in which men shelter, to convince them of the utter futility of seeking to win heaven by their own endeavors. His business is to bring before them the exalted claims of God's law and to show how far short we come of it, to expose the wickedness of the human heart, to reveal the ruin which sin has wrought, to bring the sinner face to face with the thrice holy God and to make him realize he is utterly unfit to stand before Him. In a word, the business of God's servant is to make his hearer conscious that unless a miracle of grace is performed in him he is lost forever. Not until the sinner feels that he is helpless and hopeless in himself is he prepared to look outside of himself. Despair opens the door of hope! "Thou hast destroyed thyself, but *in me* is thine help" (Hosea 13:9).

Chapter 25

EXPOSITION

(Intended chiefly for preachers)

THE PRECEDING CHAPTERS should have made it clear that the subject of the sinner's moral impotence is far more than an academic one, more than a flight into theological metaphysics. Rather is it a truth of divine revelation —a unique one—for it will not be found enunciated in any of the leading religions of antiquity, like Zoroastrianism, Buddhism or Confucianism. Nor do we remember finding any trace of it in the poets and philosophers of early Greece. It is truth which is made prominent in the Scriptures, and therefore must be given a place in the pulpit if it is to declare "all the counsel of God." It is closely bound up with the law and the gospel, the great end of the former being to demonstrate its reality, of the latter to make known the remedy. It is one of the chief battering rams which the Spirit directs against the insensate pride of the human heart, for belief in his own capabilities is the foundation on which man's self-righteousness rests. It is the one doctrine which above all others reveals the catastrophic effects of the fall and shuts up the sinner to the sovereign mercy of God as his only hope.

Generalization Not Sufficient

It is not sufficient for the preacher to generalize and speak of "the ruin which sin has wrought" and affirm that man is "totally depraved"; such expressions convey no adequate concept to the modern mind. It is necessary that he should particularize and show from Holy Writ that "they that are in the flesh cannot please God." His task is to paint fallen human nature in its true colors and not deceive by flattery. The state of the natural man is far, far worse than he has any consciousness of. Though he knows he is not perfect, though in serious moments he is aware that all is not well with him, yet he has no realization whatever that his condition is desperate and irremediable so far as all self-help is concerned. A great many people regard religion as a medicine for the soul, and suppose that if it is taken regularly it will ensure their salvation; that if they do this and that and avoid the other, all will be well in the end. They are totally oblivious to the fact that they are "without strength" and can no more perform spiritual duties than the Ethiopian can change his skin or the leopard his spots.

It is a matter of first importance that the moral inability of fallen man should be understood by all. It concerns both young and old, illiterate and educated; therefore each should have right views on the issue. It is most essential that the unsaved should be made aware not only that they are unable to do what God requires of them, but also *why* they are unable. They should be told the fact that it is impossible for them to "fulfill all righteousness," but also the cause of this impossibility. Their self-sufficiency cannot be undermined while they believe they have it in their own power to perform God's commands and to comply with the terms of His gospel. Nevertheless they must not be left with the impression that their impotence is a calamity for which they are not to blame, a deprivation for which they are to be pitied; for they are endowed with faculties suited to respond to law and gospel alike. A mistake concerning either of these truths—man's impotence and man's responsibility—is likely to have a fatal consequence.

On the other hand, as long as men imagine they have it in their own power to perform their whole duty or do all that God requires of them in order for them to obtain pardon and eternal life, they feel at ease and are apt to neglect to diligently apply themselves to the performance of that duty. They are not at all likely to pray in earnest or to watch against sin with any anxiety. They neither see the need of God's working in them "both to will and to do of his good pleasure" nor the necessity of their "working out their own salvation with fear and trembling." To wake men out of this dream of self-sufficiency the Saviour has given such alarming declarations as these: "Except a man be born again, he cannot see the kingdom of God" (John 3:3); "No man can come to me, except the Father which hath sent me draw him" (John 6:44). And to cut off effectually from the unregenerate all hope of obtaining mercy on the ground of the supposed acceptableness of anything *they* have done or can do until created in Christ Jesus unto good works, His apostle declared, "They that are in the flesh *cannot* please God" (Rom. 8:8).

On the other hand, should the unregenerate be allowed to suppose they are devoid of those faculties which are necessary for knowing God's will and doing those things which are pleasing in His sight, such a delusion is likely to prove equally fatal to them. For in that case how could they ever be convinced of either sin or righteousness: of sin in themselves and of righteousness in God? How could they ever perceive that the ways of the Lord are just and their own unjust? If in fact the natural man had no kind of capacity any more than has the horse or mule to love and serve God, to repent and believe the gospel, then the pressing of such duties upon him would be most unreasonable, nor could their noncompliance be at all criminal. Accordingly we find that after our Lord informed Nicodemus of the necessity of man's being born again before he could "see" or believe to the saving of his soul, He declared that he was "condemned already" for not believing (John 3:18). Then He cleared up the whole matter by saying, "This is the condemnation, that light is come into the world, and men loved darkness rather than light, because their deeds were evil. For every one that doeth evil hateth the light, neither cometh to the light, lest his deeds should be reproved" (vv. 19-20).

Clear Distinctions Necessary

From these and similar verses well-instructed scholars of the Word of God have been led to draw a sharp distinction between the absence of natural faculties and the lack of moral ability, the latter being the essence of moral depravity. The absence of natural faculties clears one from blame, for one who is physically blind is not blameworthy because he cannot see, nor is an idiot to be condemned because he is devoid of rationality. Moral inability is of a totally different species, for it proceeds from an evil heart, consisting of a culpable failure to use in the right way those talents with which God has endowed us. The unregenerate man who refuses to obtain *any* knowledge of God through reading His Word is justly chargeable with such neglect; but the saint is not guilty because he fails to arrive at a *perfect* knowledge of God, for such an attainment lies beyond the reach of his faculties.

Some may object to what has just been pointed out and say that this is a distinction of no consequence; inability *is* inability; what a man cannot do he *cannot* do; whether it be owing to a lack of faculties or the absence of a good heart, it comes to the same thing. All this is true so far as the *end* is concerned, but not so far as the *criminality*. If an evil disposition were a valid excuse, then all the evil in the world would be excusable. Because sin cannot be holiness, is it the less evil? Because the sinner cannot, at the same time, be a saint, is he no more a sinner? Because an evil-minded man cannot get rid of his evil mind while he has no inclination to do so, is he only to be pitied like one who labors under a misconception? True also, this distinction affords no relief to one who is dead in sin, nor does it inform him how he can by his own effort become alive to God; nevertheless, it adds to his condemnation and makes him aware of his awful state.

For vindicating the justice of God, for magnifying His grace, for laying low the haughtiness of man, moral inability is a distinction of vital consequence, however hateful it may be to the ungodly. Unless the line is drawn between excusing a wicked heart and pitying a palsied hand, between moral depravity and the lack of moral faculties, the whole Word of God and all His ways with man must appear invalid, shrouded in midnight darkness. Deny this distinction, and God's requiring perfect obedience from such imperfect creatures must seem altogether unreasonable, His condemning to everlasting misery every one who does evil (when doing evil is what no man can avoid) excessively harsh. But let men be made aware of the horrible plague of their hearts, let the distinct difference between the absence of moral faculties and the sinful misuse of them be seen and felt, and every mouth will be stopped and all the world become guilty before God.

Though at first it may seem to the preacher that the proclamation of human impotence defeats his ends and works against the highest interest of his hearers, yet if God is pleased to bless his fidelity to the truth (and faith may always count upon such blessing), it will do the hearer good in his latter end, for it will drive him out from the hiding place of falsehood, it will bring him to realize his need of fleeing for refuge to the glorious hope set before him in the gospel. By pulling down strongholds, casting down imaginations and every high thing that exalts itself against God, the way is paved for bringing into captivity every thought to the obedience of Christ. To see oneself "without strength" and at the same time "without excuse" is indeed humiliating, yet this must be seen by the sinner—before either the justice of the divine law or one's utter helplessness and conviction of guilt—as the chief prerequisite for embracing Christ as one's all-sufficient Saviour.

It will thus be seen that there are two chief dangers concerning which the preacher must be on his guard while endeavoring to expound this doctrine. First, while pressing the utter inability of the natural man to meet the just claims of God or even so much as perform a single spiritual duty, he must not overthrow or even weaken the equally evident fact of man's moral responsibility. Second, in his zeal to leave unimpaired the moral agency and personal accountability of the sinner, he must not repudiate his total depravity and death in trespasses and sins. This is no easy task, and here as everywhere the minister is made to feel his need of seeking wisdom from above. Yet let it be pointed out that prayer is not designed as a substitute for hard work and study, but rather as a preparative for the same. Difficulties are not to be shunned, but overcome by diligent effort; but diligent effort can only be rightly directed and effectually employed as divine grace enables, and that grace is to be expectantly sought.

Probably it is best to begin by considering *the fact* of man's impotence. At first this may be presented in general terms and in its broad outlines by showing that the thrice holy God can require nothing less than holiness from His creatures, that He can by no means tolerate any sin in them. The standard which God has set before men is the moral law which demands perfect and perpetual obedience; being spiritual it enjoins holiness of character as well as conduct, purity of heart as well as acts. Such a standard fallen man cannot reach, such demands he cannot meet, as is demonstrated from the entire history of the Jews under that law.

Next it should be pointed out that the Lord Jesus did not lower that standard or modify God's commands, but uniformly and insistently upheld the one and pressed the other, as is unmistakably clear in Matthew 5:17-48; nevertheless He repeatedly affirmed the moral impotence of fallen man (John 5:44; 6:44; 8:43). This same twofold teaching is repeated by the apostles, especially in the epistles to the Romans and Corinthians.

From the general we may descend to the particular and show *the extent* of man's impotence and depravity. Sin has so ruined the whole of his being that the understanding is darkened, the heart corrupted, the will perverted, each detail being proved and illustrated from Scripture. Then in summing up this solemn aspect, appeal may be made to that word of Christ's where He declared not merely that there were many things (or even some things) man could not do without His enablement, but that without Him man could do *nothing*" (John 15:5)—nothing good, nothing acceptable to God. If man could prepare himself to turn to God, or turn of himself after the Holy Spirit has prepared him, he could do much. But since it is God who works in us "both to will and to do of his good pleasure" (Phil. 2:13), He is the One who first implants the desire and then gives the power to fulfill it. Not only must the understanding be so enlightened as to discern the good from the evil, but the heart has to be changed so as to prefer the good before the evil.

Next it is well to show clearly *the nature* of man's inability: what it does not consist of (the lack of faculties suited to the performance of duty) and what it does consist of. Care needs to be taken and arguments given to show that man's inability is moral rather than physical, voluntary rather than compulsory, criminal rather than innocent. After this has been done at some length, confirmation may be obtained by an appeal to the hearer's own experience. If honest he must acknowledge that his own consciousness testifies to the fact that he sins willingly and therefore wilfully, and that his conscience registers condemnation upon him. The very facts that we sin freely and that conscience accuses us show we ought to have avoided it. Whatever line a man takes in attempting to justify his own wrongdoing, he promptly forsakes it whenever his fellowmen wrong him. He never argues that *they* were unable to do otherwise, nor does he excuse them on the ground of their inheriting a corrupt nature from Adam! Moreover, in the hour of remorse, the man who has squandered his substance and wrecked his health does not even excuse himself, but freely owns "What a fool I have been! There is no one to blame but myself."

The impotence of the natural man to choose God for his portion is greater than that of an ape to reason like an Isaac Newton, yet there is this vital difference between the two: the inability of the former is a criminal one, that of the latter is not so because of its native and original incapacity. Man's moral inability lies not in the lack of capacity but in lack of desire. One incurs no guilt when there is a willingness of mind and a desire of heart to do the thing commanded but no capacity to carry it out. But where there is capacity (competent faculties) but unwillingness, there is guilt—wherever disaffection for God exists so does sin. Man's moral inability consists of an inveterate aversion for God, and it is this corruption of heart which alone has influence to prevent the proper use of the faculties with which he is endowed, and issues in acts of sin and rebellion against God. Even the bare knowledge of duty in all cases renders moral agents under obligation to do it: "To him that knoweth to do good, and doeth it not, to him it is sin" (James 4:17).

It is very necessary that the preacher should be perfectly clear in his own mind that the moral impotence of the natural man is *not* of such a nature as to exempt him from God's claims or excuse him from the discharge of his duties. Some have drawn the erroneous conclusion that it is incongruous to call upon the unregenerate to perform spiritual duties. They say that only exhortations suited to the state of the unregenerate, such as the performance of civil righteousness, should be addressed to them. The truth is that a perfect heart and a perfect life are as much required as if men were not fallen creatures, and required of the greatest sinner as much as of the best saint. The righteous demands of the Most High must not be whittled down because of human depravity. David did not trim his exhortations to meet the inability of man: "Kiss the Son, lest he be angry, and ye perish from the way" (Ps. 2:12). Isaiah did not keep back the command "Wash you, make you clean; put away the evil of your doings from before mine eyes" (1:16) though he knew the people were so corrupt they would not and could not comply.

Urgent Invitation Obligatory

Nor should the preacher have the slightest hesitation in urging the unregenerate to use the means of grace and in declaring it is men's certain duty *to* employ them. The divine ordinances of hearing and reading the Word, of praying and conversing with God's people, are thereby made a real test of men's hearts—as to whether they really desire salvation or despise it. Though God does renew men by His Spirit, yet He appoints the means by which sinners are to be subservient to such a work of grace. If they scorn and neglect the means, the blame is in themselves and not in God. If we are not willing to seek salvation, it proves we have no desire to find it; then in the day to come we shall be reproved as wicked and slothful servants (Matt. 25:26). The plea that man has no power will then mean nothing, for then the fact that his lack of power consists only in a lack of heart will appear with sunlight clearness, and he will be justly condemned for contempt of God's Word; his blood will be upon his own head for disregarding the warnings of God's servants.

Yet so perverse is fallen human nature that men will argue, "What is the good of using the means when it does not lie in our power to give effect to them?" Even if there were no hope of success, God's command for us to use the means is sufficient to demand our compliance: "Master, we have toiled all the night, and have taken nothing: nevertheless at thy word I will let down the net" (Luke 5:5). I cannot infallibly promise a farmer who plows and sows that he will have a good crop, yet I may assure him that it is God's general way to bless the prudent and diligent. I cannot say to everyone who desires posterity, "Marry and you shall have children." But I may point out that if people refuse the ordinance of marriage they will never have any lawful children. The preacher needs to point out the grave peril incurred by those who spurn the help God proffers. Felix "trembled" (Acts 24:25), but he failed to act on his convictions. Unless the Lord is sought while He is "near" us (Isa. 55:6), He may finally abandon us. Every resistance to the impressions of the Spirit leaves the heart harder than it was before.

After all that has been said it is scarcely necessary for us to press upon the preacher the tremendous importance of this doctrine. It displays as no other the perfect consistency of divine justice and grace. It reveals to the believer that his infirmities and imperfections are not the comforting cover-up of guilt that he would like to think they are. All moral infirmity, all lack of perfect holiness, is entirely his own fault, for which he should be deeply humbled. It shows sinners that their perdition is really altogether of themselves, for they are unwilling to be made clean. The kindest thing we can do for them is to shatter their self-righteous hopes, to make them realize both their utter helplessness and their entire inexcusableness. The high demands of God are to be pressed upon them with the design of bringing them to cry to Him to graciously work in them that which He requires. Genuine conviction of sin consists in a thorough realization of responsibility and guilt, of our inability and dependence upon divine grace. Nothing is so well calculated to produce that conviction, under the Spirit's blessing, as the faithful preaching of this unpalatable truth.

Moody Press, a ministry of the Moody Bible Institute, is designed for education, evangelization and edification. If we may assist you in knowing more about Christ and the Christian life, please write us without obligation to: Moody Press, c/o MLM, Chicago, Illinois 60610.

SCRIPTURE INDEX